TOURISM POLICY AND INTERNATIONAL TOURISM

IN OECD MEMBER COUNTRIES

EVOLUTION OF TOURISM IN OECD MEMBER COUNTRIES IN 1986

**REPORT ADOPTED IN JULY 1987
BY THE OECD TOURISM COMMITEE
DERESTRICTED BY THE OECD
COUNCIL IN SEPTEMBER 1987**

ORGANISATION FOR ECONOMIC CO-OPERATION AND DEVELOPMENT

Pursuant to article 1 of the Convention signed in Paris on 14th December, 1960, and which came into force on 30th September, 1961, the Organisation for Economic Co-operation and Development (OECD) shall promote policies designed:

- to achieve the highest sustainable economic growth and employment and a rising standard of living in Member countries, while maintaining financial stability, and thus to contribute to the development of the world economy;
- to contribute to sound economic expansion in Member as well as non-member countries in the process of economic development; and
- to contribute to the expansion of world trade on a multilateral, non-discriminatory basis in accordance with international obligations.

The original Member countries of the OECD are Austria, Belgium, Canada, Denmark, France, the Federal Republic of Germany, Greece, Iceland, Ireland, Italy, Luxembourg, the Netherlands, Norway, Portugal, Spain, Sweden, Switzerland, Turkey, the United Kingdom and the United States. The following countries became Members subsequently through accession at the dates indicated hereafter: Japan (28th April, 1964), Finland (28th January, 1969), Australia (7th June, 1971) and New Zealand (29th May, 1973).

The Socialist Federal Republic of Yugoslavia takes part in some of the work of the OECD (agreement of 28th October, 1961).

Publié en français sous le titre :

**POLITIQUE DU TOURISME
ET TOURISME INTERNATIONAL
DANS LES PAYS MEMBRES DE L'OCDE**

TABLE OF CONTENTS

INTRODUCTION

MIXED RESULTS IN 1986

At the beginning of the 1980s, international tourism proved its ability to stand up fairly well to the unfavourable economic situation by maintaining the levels achieved after two decades of virtually uninterrupted growth. By the end of 1983, there were signs of an upswing that did, in fact, take place the following year. In spite of the many disturbances that have beset international tourism since mid-1985, almost all the indicators still show an upward trend, as can be seen from the final figures for 1986 (see also the table below):

- Arrivals at frontiers: + 3 per cent (against + 5 per cent in 1985);
- Nights spent in the various means of accommodation: + 2 per cent (against + 2 per cent);
- Receipts in real terms: no change (against + 5 per cent);
- Receipts in dollars: $92.2 billion.

However, while the overall figures are still reasonable, three factors adversely affected international tourism in the OECD area, especially in the European Member countries, although it is impossible to assess their individual impact. These factors were the fears for personal safety aroused by terrorism, the consequences of the Chernobyl accident, and the continuing fall of the dollar against European currencies.

In Europe, then, no growth was recorded in the volume of nights spent and receipts in real terms were down by 4 per cent against the previous year. This downturn, due in part to the fall-off in North American and Japanese tourists, might have been even more marked had it not been for the increase in intra-regional tourism, which benefited the Mediterranean countries in particular, at the expense of Scandinavia. By the same token, the pattern of the United States market shifted to the advantage of Canada (+ 18 per cent), Australia (+ 25 per cent) and New Zealand (+ 27 per cent).

Faced with the size of the difficulties encountered in 1986, European national tourist authorities joined forces to counter the potentially disastrous consequences of a year which could have had very serious effects on the

businesses that depend, directly or indirectly, on tourism. Because of this action, backed up by the international co-operation encouraged by the OECD Tourism Committee, first figures for 1987 indicate a turn for the better.

International tourism, expressed in terms of *the number of tourist arrivals at frontiers* (for 14 countries), has continued to grow since 1984. Total volume in 1986 was up by 13 per cent compared with 1983. This continuing expansion was largely due to higher figures in North America and Spain (+ 10 per cent in both cases), which offset the downturn in France (– 2 per cent) and in Italy (– 1 per cent).

In the absence of comparable data for all countries, the table at the end of this section sets out as much information as possible on *nights spent* by foreign tourists. The figures are derived from data on nights spent in hotels and similar establishments (see Chapter II, Table 2) and in all means of accommodation (see Chapter II, Table 3), the latter category serving as highest common denominator wherever possible. Overall, the volume of nights spent (19 countries) increased slightly (by 2 per cent) in 1986, a growth due solely to expansion in Canada (+ 14.4 million nights) and Spain (+ 8.8 million) where it was the biggest customers who made the difference; in Canada, tourists from the United States (69 per cent of the total, + 18 per cent), and in Spain, British visitors (39 per cent of the total, + 35 per cent). These increases sufficed to offset the downturn in more than half of the countries, where the sharpest falls took place in the Nordic countries which in total lost 5 per cent and more than a million nights and, above all, in the United Kingdom (– 7 per cent, i.e. 12 million fewer nights).

Broadly speaking, it was in the Mediterranean countries that the volume of nights spent increased (+ 22 per cent in Turkey, 12 per cent in Portugal, 11 per cent in Spain and 4 per cent in Italy). In the Nordic countries the downturn of the previous year continued in Denmark (– 5 per cent, against – 2 per cent), Finland (– 4 per cent, against – 1 per cent) and Sweden (– 4 per cent, against – 1 per cent), and in Norway the upward trend

	Arrivals at frontiers[1]		Nights spent in means of accommodation[2]		Receipts in national currency		Receipts in real terms[3]	
	% 85/84	% 86/85	% 85/84	% 86/85	% 85/84	% 86/85	% 85/84	% 86/85
Austria			-1.9	0.4	4.1	0.6	0.7	-1.0
Belgium[4]			5.3	-0.2	2.7	2.7	-2.0	1.3
Denmark			-1.5	-5.1	5.0	1.3	0.1	-2.2
Finland			-0.7	-3.6	5.7	-2.6	-0.3	-6.0
France	3.9	-1.8	3.1	0.7	7.3	-6.8	1.7	-8.8
Germany			7.4	-1.0	12.7	-2.0	10.4	-1.5
Greece	19.0	6.9	8.1	-0.5	33.4	30.1	12.4	6.5
Iceland	14.4	16.5			61.0		21.6	
Ireland		-5.1	-2.2	0.8	17.4	-5.2	12.7	-8.6
Italy	9.1	-0.6	1.0	4.1	10.8	-12.1	1.2	-17.2
Luxembourg[4]			-10.5	7.4	2.7	2.7	-2.0	1.3
Netherlands			3.2	-2.3	1.3	-6.2	-1.3	-6.2
Norway			1.9	-4.1	20.5	12.9	13.9	5.2
Portugal	21.1	8.4	17.1	12.4	36.5	22.3	14.4	9.4
Spain	0.7	9.6	-11.4	11.1	10.2	21.6	1.7	11.7
Sweden			-0.7	-4.2	9.1	7.9	1.7	3.1
Switzerland	0.4	-3.4	0.6	-0.7	4.4	-1.9	0.7	-2.3
Turkey	23.8	-8.4	31.0	21.8	145.0	6.9	70.5	-20.2
United Kingdom	6.1	-4.9	8.5	-7.1	18.1	-0.9	12.1	-4.4
EUROPE[5]	5.8	1.6	2.2	0.5			5.1	-3.5
Canada	1.5	18.6	0.3	18.6	14.3	26.4	9.8	21.4
United States	1.0	4.7			2.8	10.6	-0.6	8.3
NORTH AMERICA[5]	1.2	10.1	0.3	18.6			1.5	11.2
Australia	12.6	25.1	6.7		26.0	31.5	17.4	20.2
New Zealand	24.3	17.6			2.9		-10.7	
Japan	10.3	-11.4			16.8	-9.9	14.3	-10.4
AUSTRALASIA-JAPAN[5]	12.5	2.7					12.4	3.9
OECD[5]	5.1	3.0	2.1	1.9			4.6	-0.4
Yugoslavia	18.5	5.9	20.2	1.1	48.3	49.9	-14.5	-20.5

1. Arrivals of tourists except in Australia, Ireland, Italy, Japan, Spain, Turkey and the United kingdom where arrivals concern visitors.
2. Nights spent in all means of accommodation except in Finland, the Netherlands and Spain where nights spent concern hotels and similar establishments.
3. After correcting for the effects of inflation in each country. For the regional and OECD totals, the receipts of the individual countries are weighted in proportion to their share in the total expressed in dollars.
4. Receipts apply to both Belgium and Luxembourg.
5. Overall trends for countries with data available from 1984 to 1986.

of the previous year was reversed (– 4 per cent). The situation in Austria and Switzerland continued to give cause for concern, as a new upturn from the plateau reached some years back would appear to be difficult.

The *volume of nights* spent by foreign tourists in hotels and similar establishments increased (+ 3 per cent), whereas for all means of accommodation it remained about the same (+ 1 per cent). In spite of appearances, it cannot be deduced from this that international demand for supplementary accommodation is declining, since in many cases countries provide one or the other figure. Indeed, for the countries for which both types of information are available, higher demand for supplementary accommodation as compared with hotels and similar establishments was recorded in Belgium, Italy, Luxembourg, Norway, Sweden, Switzerland and Turkey.

The four *main generating countries* accounted for 46 per cent of arrivals at frontiers and 56 per cent of nights spent in the OECD area. Because of the size of these markets, any change in the destination of tourists from those countries will affect the general trends. So

the decline in the number of American tourists coming to Europe, which began towards the end of 1985 and continued throughout 1986, resulted in a fall of 30 per cent in both arrivals and nights. However, since the relative share of the United States market is smaller in Europe (6 per cent of arrivals and 10 per cent of nights spent) than that of the other three main generating countries, the increase in the number of nights spent by tourists from Germany (+ 3 per cent) and the United Kingdom (+ 15 per cent) offset this decline; between them the two latter countries accounted for almost 40 per cent of the European market in terms of nights spent. The only exceptions to the general trend were the Scandinavian countries, Belgium and the Netherlands. A downturn for the French market affected some traditional favourite countries of destination, notably the United Kingdom (– 5 per cent) and Ireland (– 4 per cent).

In nine Member countries the volume of *receipts in national currencies* was lower in 1986 than in 1985. However, expressed in *current dollars* (the common unit of account used in assessment of world trade perfor-

Trend of international tourism in the OECD area
(Indices : 1980 = 100)

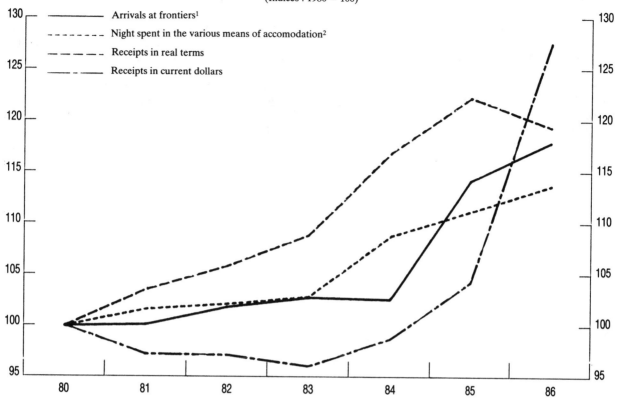

———————— Arrivals at frontiers[1]

– – – – – – – – Night spent in the various means of accomodation[2]

– – – – – Receipts in real terms

——— – ——— Receipts in current dollars

1. Derived from data provided by 13 countries.
2. Derived from data provided by 16 countries.

mances), total volume increased by 24 per cent to $92.2 billion; this was partly due to the fact that, throughout the period, the appreciation of national currencies against the dollar was on such a scale that it more than compensated for the fall recorded in certain countries in terms of national currencies. The same applied to expenditure, which in current dollar terms was up 31 per cent to a total of $96.1 billion. As a result, the tourism balance of the OECD as a whole, which had been in equilibrium since 1982, showed a $3.9 billion deficit. The surplus of receipts over expenditure in the European Member countries as a whole partly offset the negative balances recorded in the other regions. Europe contributes 79 per cent to total receipts, and 68 per cent to total expenditure, and since these were up by 27 per cent and 41 per cent respectively, Europe was in surplus by $7.5 billion. However, contrary to the situation between 1982 and 1985, this sum was not large enough to offset the deficits recorded in the other regions, which include three of the six biggest generating countries in dollar terms (the United States, Japan and Canada).

In real terms, after allowing for the impact of inflation and the movement of the dollar exchange rate against other currencies, total receipts for the OECD as a whole remained at the 1985 level, in which year there had been a rise of 5 per cent. Europe and Japan recorded substantial falls with the most precipitous declines in Turkey (– 20 per cent), Italy (– 17 per cent) and Japan (– 10 per cent). On the other hand, Canada, Australia and Spain experienced the most vigorous expansions of 21 per cent, 20 per cent and 12 per cent respectively.

In spite of a decline during the first half of the year, the number of passengers carried by international air transport increased in 1986, thanks to a revival which took place during the autumn months. The question of deregulation still looms large for air transport services – whose satisfactory evolution is essential to the development of international tourism. It led to continued consultations between the industry, governments and consumer organisations but the main event of the year was the action by the Commission of the European Communities which, following the Decision of the European Court of Justice, upheld efforts to enforce the application to the air transport industry of the rules of competition stipulated in the Treaty of Rome. In that context the way is still open for a pragmatic approach to a "European deregulation" which would create the right conditions for the expansion of certain forms of international tourism and benefit both the industry and the consumer.

The OECD Tourism Committee continued its efforts to ensure that the right conditions prevail for the liberalisation of international tourism. Among other items, the joint work of the Committee on Capital Movements and Invisible Transactions and the Tourism Committee on Member countries' position was completed with regard to the extended obligations concerning "travel and tourism" in the Code of Liberalisation of Current Invisible Operations which were adopted by the OECD Council in 1985 (see Chapter V of the 1986 edition). In most Member countries, the sector has now been fully liberalised in the sense of the enlarged obligations, and good progress has been achieved in Greece, Portugal and Turkey. With the same aim in mind, the Tourism Committee is continuing its review of obstacles to international tourism and is in the process of updating the inventory it first established in 1983, the main results of which were set out in the 1985 edition. Two of the other subjects considered by the Committee in 1986 were employment in the hotel industry and its role in reducing unemployment, and the improvement of the instruments used to measure the impact of tourism on national economies (see Chapter V).

I

GOVERNMENT POLICY AND ACTION

Chapter I of the 1987 edition has been modified from that of earlier editions and its contents are now arranged by country. This development is in response to the request by the Tourism Committee that the publication should set out the policies for tourism in a clearer manner, with the aim of making analysis of the information easier in the sector and to assist the decision-making process.

The information on governmental policy and activities in OECD Member countries, assembled by means of an annual questionnaire prepared by the Tourism Committee for this purpose, is therefore set out as follows:

– An introductory section covering the importance of tourism as an economic activity in the country and the prospects for its developments; followed by
– Government policy: objectives, priorities, plans and programmes together with the institutional framework; and
– Actions and measures undertaken during 1986 in implementation of the tourism policies, including the development of supply, marketing, the protection of the tourist as a consumer, the staggering of holidays and international co-operation.

However, the reader who is looking for more detailed information on the government policy of a particular country should consult the 1983 and 1985 editions (covering the years 1982 and 1985) in which consolidated summaries are set out.

It seems, however, desirable to bring out in a succinct form a number of common threads which appear to emerge from the individual national contributions. In a difficult year for a large number of OECD countries, particularly in Europe, the importance of tourism as a source of inward income and one of the few sectors where there is a substantial scope for increasing employment opportunities has become more apparent to governments and a series of new initiatives have been taken in various countries.

One theme has been the importance of the effective use of the central administrative structures. In Yugoslavia, as part of its new development policy, a Federal Commission on Tourism has been established to find out why Yugoslavia was lagging behind the other Mediterranean tourist countries; in Australia, an enquiry was instituted to review the effectiveness of Commonwealth tourism promotion, and in Germany the Bundestag invited the Federal Government to undertake a number of projects to improve co-operation and efficiency.

A coherent marketing approach is one way to assist these aims and Canada has made a major investment in a training "Marketing Management Program" for improving the effectiveness of business performance. This direct co-operation with industry has been more pronounced with budgetary restriction and in the United Sates, co-financing of long-term co-operation between central and local government and the industry is now regarded as almost the norm. At the same time, centralised marketing of the national product abroad has been improved in several countries. It seems clear that domestic and foreign promotion need to be kept separate and both Finland and Sweden have reviewed the strategies of their national tourist boards, Ireland has set up a Tourism Development Team to this end, while in the Netherlands there has been a major programme to make more use of Dutch embassies abroad in promoting tourism.

The importance of tourism as an activity in its own right was emphasised in a major report to the Norwegian Parliament, which treats travel and tourism on a par with other industries, and in Sweden tourism acquired its first minister, responsible also for sport and leisure. A substantial increase in the promotional budgets in Spain and Australia, in a time of general restriction, seems to endorse the importance of tourism against other industries.

A recurrent issue in tourism is the relationship between the central administration and the regions, particularly in countries with a federal structure. This was particularly acute in Italy in 1986 with the entry into force of the 1983 Tourism Act, since so far only nine of the 21 regions have brought their organisation in line with the provisions of the Act. Spain and Portugal, on the other hand, have been successful in establishing an effective balance between central and regional administrations, with Portugal having completed its tourism regional structure in 1986. The Netherlands has followed a different route, with a coherent series of tourism-recreational development plans for the 12 provinces in which particular schemes are proposed and, if approved by the central government, receive subsidies for their implementation. A similar policy for the development of special regions has been followed by Japan in their programme for "New Sites of Discovery" which is designed to bring foreign visitors to areas not previously on foreign itineraries, either because of lack of publicity or because of insufficient facilities geared towards catering for non-Japanese tourists.

Associated with the growing awareness of the importance of tourism has been an increased perception of the need to protect the tourist against unpleasant surprises. In Portugal, Japan and Canada, the system of protection and compensation against defaulting travel agents has been reinforced and in Australia, a National Compensation Fund has been established. The systematised classification of hotels in the United Kingdom and the elaboration of criteria for rating hotels, restaurants and camp sites in Greece, Turkey and Yugoslavia have a similar purpose, as do the new controls in Britain of bureaux de change and the increased importance placed on detailed price information in Switzerland. The traveller's way has also been smoothed in the United States by the visa waiver legislation which comes into force in 1987 and by expanding the immigration pre-inspection system; in Australia customs procedures have been streamlined and inbound duty free shopping has been introduced, which will be a major contribution to passenger safety and comfort.

The protection of the tourist is closely associated with the need for improvement of the information that can be provided to him. The explosion of information technology over recent years has been particularly noticeable in the elaboration of booking and reservation systems. More and more national systems are being linked with those of their neighbours, and within the next two years almost the whole of North Europe and Scandinavia will be interlinked. The Italian authorities have put particular emphasis on the development of information and booking systems. A major problem, however, is the control of such systems by a small number of commercial organisations which may discriminate in favour of their subsidiaries or associates in the provision of information and both the United States Department of Transportation and IATA have been actively seeking ways to ensure fair access by any user.

Central government itself also requires a better idea of internal developments to assist in policy decisions, and

in Australia, Canada, Germany, Sweden, and Yugoslavia new programmes have been introduced to improve the quality and speed of statistical information to be made available to the central tourism authorities. This is complementary to the ongoing market research which is carried out by all Member countries, details of which are set out in a number of the national reports. A particularly interesting development has been the programme in Japan to find out how to encourage Japanese tourists to travel abroad and the problems they face, as part of the effort to increase the tourism outflow of expenditure and thereby reduce the overall balance of payments surplus.

Tourism and national conservation have always had a difficult interrelationship and many countries appear determined to avoid some of the earlier disasters in the impact of tourism on the environment. In Australia, the protection and management of the Great Barrier Reef and the Western Tasmania Wilderness has been fully organised and a new programme covering the National Rain Forests is under way. Canada too has given particular attention to its national heritage with the establishment of several new National Parks and a reinforced Public Safety Directive, while in the United Kingdom the first marine nature reserve was established around Lundy Island. In Turkey, comprehensive plans to maintain the balance between resource utilisation and preservation have led to an extensive programme of archaeological and cultural improvement, including the restoration and adaptation of historic buildings to serve as tourist centres. The Mediterranean is particularly vulnerable to the pollution resulting from tourist activities and during 1986, Greece, Turkey and Italy all introduced new measures to combat water pollution and improve the standards of health protection in coastal resorts, beaches and marinas.

A major problem which faces the tourism industry of most OECD countries is that of seasonality. The concentration of holidays into peak periods leads to inefficient use of facilities and to a reduction in the pleasure that the tourist gains from his vacation. Three main directions are being pursued to ease this congestion. Firstly, to stagger the dates of holidays in schools by areas of the country, a policy which has had some success in the Netherlands, although in Australia several states have moved towards a more concentrated pattern. Secondly, to encourage the provision of facilities for all-weather holidays, as in Ireland and the United Kingdom, and the financing of heated swimming pools in Greece, or by encouraging festivals and out-of-season events, particularly slanted to the conference trade, as in Italy, Portugal and the United States. Finally, to develop social tourism, by providing for the use of facilities which would otherwise be under-used, through subsidising holidays for the elderly, for the underpriviliged and for young people. Programmes to this effect are particularly developed in France, Greece, Switzerland and Turkey.

Tourism is a multifaceted industry. Each country has its particular problems and strong points. The national reports which follow reflect the extremely varied nature of tourism within the OECD area, but they also bring out very strongly the opportunities that exist for co-operation between Member countries, and the need to avoid a situation in which protectionist actions in one's own domestic market are matched by cut-throat subsidised competition for the markets in other countries. The maintenance of such a balance and the provision of a forum where problems and policies can be put forward to other countries, constitutes the principal *raison d'être* of the OECD Tourism Committee.

AUSTRALIA

Australian tourism is an expanding industry which contributes around 6 per cent to GDP. In 1986/87 it is estimated that expenditure derived from tourism will total over A$22 billion, creating, directly or indirectly, employment for around 405 000 people, i.e. 6 per cent of the total workforce.

Receipts from international tourism are an increasingly important source of foreign currency. It is of interest that tourism (including relevant airline revenue), in being valued at A$3.4 billion in 1986/87, has for the first time matched our single largest rural industry, wool, as a foreign exchange earner.

It is estimated that in 1986/87 tourism (international and domestic) will generate around A$2 300 million in indirect taxes.

Prospects for international tourism: Imbalances in international trade and uncertainties in the international economy as major trading nations initiate or carry through adjustment processes is a concern to Australian tourism authorities. However the implications for inbound tourism to Australia in 1987 would be difficult to quantify and indeed in 1986 we have experienced strong growth from several major markets despite discouraging economic indicators in those countries.

Despite a 15 per cent increase in the Australian Tourist Commission's (ATC) budget over the last two years, promotional activities overseas have been curtailed by the devaluation of the Australian dollar. Vis-à-vis the currencies of our two main target markets, the United States and Japan, the Australian dollar has depreciated by 26 per cent and 53 per cent respectively since late 1984. Nevertheless it may be sufficient at this stage to merely maintain the momentum of the very successful promotional campaigns initiated in 1984. The ATC expects a 17 per cent increase (to 1.7 million) in visitor arrivals from all countries in 1987, including a 32 per cent increase (to 330 000) in arrivals from the US and a 44 per cent increase (to 230 000) in arrivals from Japan.

After an average devaluation, in trade-weighted terms, of 24 per cent in 1985, a further devaluation of around 12 per cent occurred through 1986. Sufficient data is available to suggest that some markets responded to this situation in 1986 and set a base for expectations in 1987. For example, devaluation is believed to be the main factor underlying an estimated 40 per cent increase in visitor arrivals from Australia's largest market, New Zealand, in 1986. However, with very little change in relativities between the respective currencies in 1986, a modest increase of 3 per cent (to 350 000) in New Zealand arrivals is anticipated in 1987.

New international airline services and/or airfare initiatives played a part in 1986 in the expansion of, in particular, the New Zealand and Japanese markets. Further additions to international air services into Australia are anticipated in 1987.

A high awareness of Australia in several major markets, stemming from a number of international sporting events held here in 1986, and the success overseas of Australian products such as films, has enhanced Australia's image as a tourist destination. Continued high promotional commitment and a competitive product are expected to ensure that Australia's position as an exciting new destination for international travellers will be sustained throughout 1987. In 1988 Australia will celebrate its bicentenary. This will encompass a number of major events of international tourism appeal (eg. Expo '88) and it is expected that overseas visitor arrivals will exceed 2 million for the first time.

Prospects for domestic tourism: Domestic indicators of tourism growth are also favourable. Traditionally, tourism has kept ahead of retail sales which are a good indicator of consumer confidence and spending. Available data suggests a 1 per cent increase in retail sales in real terms in 1986 over 1985 and a 2.5 per cent increase in tourism has been estimated for 1986. A 3 per cent growth is expected in 1987.

Government policy

In the Commonwealth sphere the functions of tourism policy formulation and tourism promotion remain separate, with the Department of Sport, Recreation and Tourism having responsibility for the former and the ATC the latter.

The Australian Government has maintained its strong commitment to the development of the tourism industry in line with general policy objectives adopted when it came to office in March 1983. The Government has initiated a number of programmes to give effect to this policy. A major one has been the increase in the budget of the ATC, the national tourism promotional authority, by 190 per cent from A$10 million in 1982/83, to A$29 million in 1986/87. With this increased funding, the ATC hopes to realise its target of doubling the 1983/84 level of overseas visitors to Australia to two million in 1988 (Australia's bicentenary year).

In recognition of the rapid expansion of tourism in the last three years, and its increasing importance to the Australian economy, an inquiry was initiated in early 1986 to review the effectiveness of Commonwealth administration of its tourism promotion functions and related issues. The Report of the inquiry was released in December 1986 and its principal recommendations have been accepted by the Government. The report, which follows close consultation with industry and State governments, is in two parts; the development of a strategic framework for the Australian tourism industry; and a review of the ATC's operations.

The Commonwealth will take the lead in identifying the problems and accepting the major responsibility to develop, in co-operation with all interested parties, a definitive blueprint for the future planned growth of tourism in Australia.

A restructuring of the ATC has commenced, in line with recommendations designed to make it a leaner and more results-oriented organisation with greater emphasis on planning and evaluation. The ATC will use the trading name "Tourism Australia". It will withdraw from domestic tourism marketing and concentrate on promoting Australia internationally.

Actions and measures taken in 1986

From 1st May 1986, inwards duty-free shopping has been available to international passengers arriving at Australian international airports. Goods available for purchase are restricted to tobacco, alcohol and perfumes. Inwards duty-free shopping was introduced to enhance aircraft safety, through reducing the amount of flammable liquid and glass on board, to improve passenger comfort by reducing the quantities of hand luggage, and to save the airlines fuel through reduced weight carried. Revenues collected by the Government from inwards duty free business concessions at airports will be credited for cost recovery purposes.

Transport: Information on the development of transport policy in the air, road and rail sectors is presented in Chapter IV.

Facilitation: In response to worsening congestion at major international airports, the Government provided an increase in Customs staffing for passenger processing and announced a review of processing procedures and resource requirements. The aim of the review is to further streamline Customs and Immigration procedures and to improve service to the public. It will also examine aspects of airline operations to avoid unnecessary peaks in aircraft arrivals.

Conservation measures: Zoning and management plans for the Great Barrier Reef are continuing to be developed by the Great Barrier Reef Marine Park Authority and all sections of the Park have now been declared protected areas. The Federal and Tasmanian governments have established joint management arrangements for the Western Tasmania Wilderness National Parks World Heritage area and the Federal Government is providing A$4 million over the two fiscal years to 1986/87 and 1987/88 for this purpose.

The Federal Government has agreed to provide A$22.5 million over the two fiscal years to 1986/87 and 1987/88 for a national rain forest conservation programme which will include, inter alia, studies of the tourism potential of certain rain forests and funding for interpretative and visitor facilities.

Vocational training: 1986 saw greater priority being given to the issue of training within the tourism and hospitality industry. The Federal Government established a Committee to discuss ways of implementing the recommendation made by the Tourism Training Review Group in its 1985 report on tourism training in Australia. The Committee has provided a strategic framework for training in all sectors of the tourism industry and detailed immediate and longer-term needs and action required to meet them.

A national tourism awareness campaign aims, inter alia, to encourage greater involvement in training programmes directed towards increasing the level and quality of service.

The Federal Government-sponsored youth traineeship scheme, aimed at stimulating youth employment and improving the life-time employment prospects of young people, became firmly established during 1986. With the tourism and hospitality sector targeted as one of four major industries involved in the programme, positions within the industry have been committed to the training of young Australians seeking careers in tourism and hospitality.

Employment: Full and part-time employment in the tourism industry is estimated at 405 000 in 1986/87, 6 per cent of the Australian workforce. Unofficial data suggests expansion may have been particularly rapid in the accommodation sector, with a 16 per cent increase in total employment to 78 500 in the year to June 1986.

Aids and incentives: A 150 per cent taxation deduction is available to companies which undertake eligible basic research, applied research and experimental development to create new or improved materials, devices, products, processes or services. Innovative tourism developments breaking new ground in construction technology or computer-based management systems, for example, may therefore be eligible for assistance to undertake necessary research and development.

A$2 million was allocated in 1986/87 to support the growth of tourism in the economically depressed Hunter and Illawarra steel regions of New South Wales. This is part of an on-going programme for Federally funded infrastructure projects in the regions which will provide up to A$18 million to 1987/88 for tourism projects.

Marketing: In 1986/87 the ATC has been allocated A$29 million for promotion of Australia. The ATC budget increase has enabled a continuation of the highly successful television and radio campaign in the United States, which is now firmly established as Australia's second-largest visitor market.

The National Tourism Campaign is aimed at improving public awareness (especially within the industry) of the importance of tourism to the Australian economy and the importance of making tourists feel welcome. In 1986/87, A$1 million has been allocated for this purpose, with A$0.5 million from the ATC and the balance from States and Territories. An additional contribution is expected to be received from the industry.

Marketing research: Conducted on the present and potential demand for tourism on a national and international level, this includes five major surveys and reports described below.

A regular survey of domestic tourism on a nationwide basis, the results of which are published annually in the Domestic Tourism Monitor: these market surveys aim to provide an accurate estimate of the volume of overnight domestic travel in Australia and within each state and territory in Australia and information regarding the characteristics of domestic travellers such as age, sex, occupation and income.

A survey of international visitors based on interviews at major Australian international airports: the survey, commissioned by the ATC, aims to provide information about the travel behaviour, expenditure patterns and attitudes of visitors to Australia. The International Visitor Survey (IVS) was previously conducted during the period April 1979 to March 1980, calendar years 1981, 1983, 1984, 1985 and 1986. In 1987 a number of smaller surveys will be undertaken to monitor tourist satisfaction and the IVS will be resumed in 1988.

A survey of visitors attending the World Cup of Athletics held in Canberra in October 1985 and of local accommodation establishments to estimate the income and employment impact of the event at a regional level: the survey involved interviews of interstate and international visitors in which questions were asked about the duration and region of their stay (pre and post event), means of transport, accommodation, age and sex characteristics. In addition, pre and post surveys were conducted of hotels/motels, caravan parks and transport sectors regarding booking arrangements, capacity and expectations regarding demand.

Development of a methodology to rank prospective international sporting events according to their likely impact on the economy: the methodology outlines five measures against which different events can be compared – impact on GDP, export earnings, returns on costs, government assistance as a proportion of total costs and location of the event. Testing of this model has not yet been undertaken.

A review of tourism statistics collected by the Australian Bureau of Statistics (ABS) was carried out to identify gaps or deficiencies in existing collections. As a result, collection of accommodation statistics has been expanded to include arrivals of visitors at hotels and motels, classification by star grading and separation of short-term and long-term caravan park statistics. Data on holiday flats and apartments will be included commencing September 1987. The ABS has also undertaken to include tourist accommodation, travel agents, motor vehicle hire and tourist attractions in the 1987/88 Selected Services Industries Survey.

Formulation of methodology which will be used to develop a forecasting model for estimating the future demand for tourism goods and services in Australia. In short, the methodology involves time series analysis of various economic, social and demographic variables which affect demand for and supply of tourism goods and services on a global scale (thereby taking into account the effect of substitute goods and services, i.e. alternative destinations).

Protection of the tourist as a consumer: Overseas and domestic tourists are now being given greater consumer protection when dealing with travel agents, following the introduction by several State and Territory Governments of a licensing system for all travel agents, and the establishment of a National Compensation Fund. Under these arrangements compensation is to be available to consumers in participating States/Territories through the Fund, which has been established with contributions from travel agents. Licensing criteria cover financial performance, minimum experience/qualifications for managers and defined standards for premises.

Staggering of holidays: Several States/Territories previously operating a three-term year have opted for a four-term year in 1987, resulting in an increased alignment of school holiday periods. As this is perceived to be detrimental to the tourism industry, the matter has recently been discussed by the Australian Standing Committee on Tourism (comprising senior officials of State/Territory tourism authorities) and will shortly be discussed by the Tourist Ministers' Council with a view to seeking consideration by education authorities of the possibility of increasing the limited staggering that now exists between States operating the four-term system. In the meantime, the Queensland Government has announced that a new four-semester year will operate in that State in 1988. The change is expected to alleviate the problem.

International co-operation: During 1985/86 significant bilateral contacts occurred with a number of visiting ministers and officials from China, Japan, Jamaica, the Netherlands, Seychelles and Thailand.

In February 1986, a high-level Japanese Tourism Mission authorised by the Japanese Government visited Australia with a brief to investigate ways of increasing Japanese tourism to Australia. The mission focused on several key areas of the tourism exchange between Australia and Japan, notably visas, air transport, language and investment matters. It also served as a catalyst for closer consultation between senior industry leaders of both countries on tourism issues of mutual interest.

AUSTRIA

Tourism is an important economic activity in Austria. Receipts from tourism provided 7.6 per cent of Austrian GNP in 1985 and around a quarter of a million people are directly employed in the industry, some 7.5 per cent of the total work force. International tourism to Austria has been on a plateau since the beginning of the eighties and its contribution to total export receipts has fallen from 37 per cent in 1980 to 29 per cent in 1985. The industry is excessively dependent upon a single market, the Federal Republic of Germany, which accounted for two-thirds of nights spent by foreign tourists in 1986, but considerable efforts have been made to widen the field, with recent growth being particularly notable from France and Italy; non-German visitors have been most attracted to the cultural capacities of Vienna and Salzburg.

Government policy

The objectives and priorities of Austrian tourism policy are set out:

– The government declarations of 31st May 1983 and 28th January 1987;
– The Tourism Promotion Programme 1980-1989;
– The Austrian Regional Policy Law; and
– The resolution adopted on the "1984 Day of Austrian Tourism".

The main objectives of Austrian tourism policy are:

– To strengthen the love for Austria, civic ideals, environmental awareness and a proper attitude towards tourism;

– To increase the emotional well-being of its guests, taking into account the increased stress of everyday life in industrialised countries;
– To make tourism independent of the weather, above all during summer, by developing special attractions to prolong the season;
– To make use of existing and emerging gaps in the market with regard to international tourism;
– To strengthen the commercial potential of tourism in Austria abroad as well as to improve marketing;
– To reduce the cost increase in tourism enterprises;
– To further improve the quality of the hotel industry and gastronomy;
– To offer more leisure facilities;
– To make investments more flexible;
– To maintain and, where possible, increase the advertising potential of the Austrian National Tourist Office; and
– To maintain and expand traditional markets at close range as well as to open up new markets in more remote regions.

Tourism has been contributing towards achieving the economic goals of Austrian policy with respect to employment, regional affairs, and foreign trade for a long time. Every effort is made therefore to attain further improvements in tourism in both quality and modernisation. Special opportunities are seen in cultural and conference tourism. All the considerations and activities need to bear in mind, however, that human performance capabilities, exploitability of the environment and regional economic viability have their limits. Tourism development is tailored to the variety of leisure and recreation needs – with due involvement of the local population – in order to achieve best possible results.

The financial support given to the encouragement of tourism is organised on the following lines. In line with fiscal equalisation, communities receive ear-marked contributions to a total amount of Sch 70 million per annum for the promotion of tourism. Allocation of this money is effected on the basis of population figures; if required, this allocation criterium may be waived. The respective contributions are the only legally stipulated and guaranteed federal support given to tourism communities. Financial support is allocated according to guidelines issued by the Federal Ministry for Economic Affairs (formerly, for Commerce, Trade and Industry) with the agreement of the Federal Ministry of Finance. They are similar to the instructions governing the granting of tourism promotion funds. Essential promotion criteria are investment for the improvement of tourism infrastructure and for the creation of facilities of superior tourism quality.

Tourism policy and measures adopted by the Federal Ministry for Economic Affairs are as follows:

- *Investment promotion*: On the grounds of budget consolidation, the 1987 budget proposal shows a reduction of promotional expenditure for investment, sales and co-operation. Sch 70 million were available in 1986 for the promotion of communities by means of fiscal equalisation funds with a view to tourism. Another Sch 70 million are ear-marked for 1987.
- *Marketing promotion*: An increase in the contribution of the Federal Government of about 5 per cent is envisaged, i.e. from Sch 224.2 million in 1986 to Sch 235.9 million in 1987. Austrian tourism advertising receives financial support on a basis of 60 per cent from the federal government, 20 per cent from the Federal Chamber for Economy, and 20 per cent from the federal provinces.

Actions and measures taken in 1986

Development of supply: Special attention is being paid to regional concerns in accordance with the means available. Youth employment programmes of the individual provinces are being encouraged via tourism associations and enterprises in addition to the agreements which already exist between the federal government and the federal provinces.

A special kind of secondary training focussing on "calculation" and "written reports" is offered to rural families taking in guests on a non-licensed basis. A seminar for consultants in the field of rural husbandry was organised under the title "Holidays on a farm – written reports". With a view to receiving guests from abroad, farmers also attended language classes to be able to converse with their guests.

Tourism and environmental protection are very often in contrast to each other. A closer co-operation between tourism experts and ecologists is being aimed at.

National parks have been created in a number of federal provinces, consisting, to a considerable extent, of entirely unspoilt territory offering exquisite natural beauties. "Nature instruction paths" are being laid out in all Austrian provinces, to bring those walking along the paths closer to nature and to offer them pertinent instruction. A book on Austrian nature instruction paths is being prepared.

Marketing research: During the year, Austrian market research was particularly directed towards:

- Participation in the annual German travel analysis which provides valuable material on the vacational behaviour of guests from Germany;
- An investigation giving detailed results on travel habits of Belgians;
- Interviews with guests from Belgium, France, Germany, Italy, the Netherlands, Sweden, Switzerland, the United Kingdom and the United States in connection with a study project "Austria's Image Abroad";
- A survey, in which 3 000 Austrians participated, on "alternative styles of living and consumer goods", which examined, among others, the attitudes adopted towards mass tourism and living without a car;
- A study on "export advertising of Austrian entrepreneurs" which provided an analysis of the current situation as regards means of advertising specially relating to Austria;
- The economic repercussions of tourism in a study entitled "the importance of tourism in Austria";
- A basic investigation on progressive marketing measures in the Italian market.

Marketing publicity abroad: International advertising for Austrian tourism is decidedly offer-oriented and has been intensified by image-related statements. An "ad-and-insert" campaign has been developed, aimed at increasing awareness and improvement of the Austrian image with opinion leaders, especially those on an advanced social level. Austria presents a genuine alternative to the often drab reality of everyday life and Austria's landscape and style of living are vital motives for a holiday in this country. Investigations and studies provide information on aspirations and expectations of guests vis-à-vis Austria as a holiday country. In an extensive study on information needs of tourists coming to Austria, the overriding importance of the individual tailor-made prospectus (describing the particular offer of a given community) have become evident. Advertising for inland tourism has been aimed at increasing the awareness and importance of touring in one's own country. Secondary training seminars for staff of tourism organisations have been initiated on a local basis.

International co-operation: Within the framework of "trilateral market research" among Austria, Switzerland and Germany, a project covering "Near and Middle East" was concluded.

BELGIUM

Government policy

Tourism policy and promotion fall under the responsibility of the Flemish, French and German communities as a whole. However, at the national level, coordination is ensured by the *Service central du tourisme* in the Ministry of Communications.

Actions and measures taken in 1986

Belgium concentrates in particular on developing packages in both Flanders and Wallonia with the aim of providing comprehensive arrangements as regards accommodation, cultural activities, relaxation and gastronomy for both foreign and Belgian tourists.

The staggering of holidays continues to be a prime concern and it is planned to hold discussions on this subject with representatives of the employers, white and blue-collar workers and teachers,as well as with the entire tourism sector.

Efforts are being made to improve tourist facilities so as to provide products of a high standard that are available throughout the season.

Market research: The *West-Vlaams Economisch Studiebureau* has carried out a survey of the holiday habits of Belgians; the survey was financed by the private sector and the findings will be published in 1988.

Marketing: There has been a change in the policy as regards representation abroad, the aim now being to concentrate promotional resources on the more profitable markets. There is close collaboration with the radio and television stations, which means that publicity can be given to a particular tourist event or to the attractions of a particular region.

International co-operation: Foreign students are accepted under certain conditions for training courses in tourism.

There is active co-operation with the European Group for the Ardennes and the Eifel with a view to opening to hikers the ski terrain and trails along the borders between Belgium, Germany and the Grand Duchy of Luxembourg.

CANADA

With annual total revenues estimated at C$19.9 billion in 1985, tourism represents approximately 4.4 per cent of GNP, tourism is the fifth most important earner of foreign exchange for Canada. Travellers from other countries accounted for C$5.0 billion, or 25 per cent of the total, while Canadian travellers accounted for the other C$14.9 billion, or 75 per cent.

Direct employment in the Canadian tourism industry totalled 590 000, an increase of 3 per cent over 1984. About C$4.6 billion in federal government revenues were generated by 1985 receipts, as well as C$4.4 billion in provincial and municipal government revenues. The 1985 receipts generated about C$13.4 billion in direct income for Canadians, up 7 per cent from the previous year.

The tremendous growth Canadian tourism experienced in 1986 was largely due to Expo '86, but even without Expo there would have been an increase of about 5 per cent in foreign visitors to Canada because of favourable exchange rates, lower energy prices and healthy economic growth in most western economies. In 1987, there will not be a high-profile event such as Expo to attract extraordinary numbers of tourists to Canada, but the other factors just mentioned will continue to encourage travel to Canada. Travel to Canada in 1987 is therefore expected to decrease somewhat with respect to 1986, but to remain well above pre-1986 levels. In 1987, total long-term visitors to Canada are expected to number 14.3 million, and travel receipts could reach C$5.9 billion. The travel account deficit is forecast to be about C$1.9 billion in 1987, up from the 1986 level of C$1.1 billion, but well below the levels recorded for 1983, 1984 and 1985.

Government policy

Tourism Canada is an integral part of the Department of Regional Industrial Expansion (DRIE) established in 1983 following a government reorganisation bill. Its daily administration is carried out by the Assistant Deputy Minister for Tourism, supported by officials in charge of Product Development, Market Development, Management Services and Liaison, and Research.

Tourism policy in 1986 continued with the same aims, objectives and priorities set after the consultation process in 1985. These include co-operative ventures in a number of areas such as marketing, e.g. the establishment of the Tourism Marketing Council; research, e.g. the establishment of the Canadian Tourism Research Institute, and product development, e.g. a series of cultural tourism pilot projects with a variety of partners. There has also been continued co-operation with provincial governments on projects covered under the tourism sub-agreements. (See details in Section on "Actions and measures" presented below).

In line with the increased emphasis on basing decisions for marketing and development on research and statistical data, a US/Canada joint market research agreement was initiated for foreign markets. The Tourism Canada survey on the US pleasure travel market conducted in 1985 has provided the basis for many marketing and development initiatives.

The National Task Force on Tourism Data presented its final report and recommendations to Ministers at the Federal/Provincial/Territorial Tourism Ministers' meeting in November 1986. The recommendation for the formation of a Canadian Tourism Research Institute has already been acted upon and the new Institute is housed within the Conference Board of Canada. One of the first projects will be to identify the impact of Canadian tax reform proposals on the tourism industry. Another important outcome from this Task Force has been the decision to produce a tourism satellite account within the framework of the National Accounts. This will highlight the importance of tourism within the Canadian economy.

Actions and measures taken in 1986

Accommodation: Tourism Canada recently introduced "A Marketing Management Program for Canada's Tourism Industry", its second in the "Tourism is Your Business" series. The programme demonstrates how professional management can lead to improved business performance and productivity through well-planned and executed marketing strategies and techniques. It is directed to owners and operators of small and medium-sized businesses representing all supply elements of the tourism industry. The programme has two principle elements – a written one and a video. The written includes a working manual, a companion study guide and a leader's guide. The ten chapters each deal with a different aspect of marketing management. The video component consists of thirteen segments (each 24 minutes) produced to broadcast standards that com-

plement the chapters of the publications. There is also a 15-minute introductory overview which serves to introduce the viewer to the programme structure, the topics discussed and its utilisation and availability.

A similar programme on "Financial Management for Canada's Lodging Industry" has been extremely well received by both educators and industry members and is presently being adapted for international markets. Information on both programmes can be obtained from AV Resources and Distribution Centre, DRIE, 235 Queen Street, 2nd Floor West, Ottawa, Ontario K1A OH5.

Transport: Tourism Canada represents the Department of Regional Industrial Expansion in interdepartmental working groups developing the Canadian position in international air bilateral agreement negotiations. Tourism Canada's objective in participating is to ensure that recommended actions or positions take into consideration the implications for Canada's ability to attract international tourism business.

Pending the outcome of ongoing US-Canada air bilateral negotiations, Tourism Canada commenced discussions with Transport Canada on a joint initiative to assess the market potential and the short-term feasibility of improving transborder air access to Vancouver and Quebec from the USA.

More information on the development of transport policy in the air, rail, and cruise sectors is presented in Chapter IV.

Environment: Because of its crucial importance in keeping these assets intact, numerous measures taken in order to protect environment are presented hereafter. A policy for national marine parks was approved by the Minister of the Environment and given wide public distribution. Negotiations were launched with the provincial government of British Columbia toward the establishment of a national park in the South Moresby area of the Queen Charlotte Islands. An agreement was signed with the Government of the Northwest Territories setting out the terms and conditions for the establishment of Ellesmere Island National Park Reserve. Agreement-in-principle was reached by the federal and provincial Ministers for the establishment of a new national park on the Bruce Peninsula of Ontario. The first three rivers were formally designated as part of the Canadian Heritage Rivers System, the Alsek River in Kluane National Park Reserve in the Yukon Territory, the French River in Ontario and the Clearwater River in Saskatchewan; eight additional rivers are now nominated.

National Parks have been studying and managing their natural resources through the application of the Natural Resource Management Process. A national study team has evaluated the Process and recommendations for its modification better to serve the Parks preservation mandate are presently being incorporated.

The major recommendation is the extension of the Process to those natural resource components in National Historic Parks and Sites and Heritage Canals.

The adoption of a new Public Safety Directive for National Parks will lead to greater rigour in carrying out hazard assessments and subsequent planning to ensure visitor safety.

There have been continuing efforts to resolve and finalise native claims agreement essential to park establishment (Northern Yukon), to finalise gazetting of park reserves as National Parks (Kluane), and Parks have continued with the overall commitment to employment and business development opportunities for native people in northen parks.

Important actions for national historic parks and sites included: Stabilisation work on the Gulf of Georgia Cannery at Steveston, British Columbia; the development of Fort Rodd Hill; the acquisition of the Journey's End property from the Department of National Defence; the stabilisation of Dawson City National Historic Site; the stabilisation of structures on Heritage Canals; major restoration and stabilisation work for the Fortifications of Quebec; the stabilisation of Grande Greve, Forillon National Park; the reconstruction of the Queen's Battery building, Signal Hill; and the erection of thirty Historic Sites and Monuments Board plaques.

Vocational training: The provision of institutional vocational training is the primary responsibility of provincial governments in Canada.

The activities of provincial governments are supported and supplemented by programmes of Employment and Immigration Canada (EIC), the federal department with responsibility for employment. Through a series of training assistance programmes, EIC provides funds for the training of disadvantaged persons (e.g. minority groups, long-term unemployed and persons entering or re-entering the workforce). The tourism industry was one of four industries receiving priority under these programmes.

In response to industry requests for government action to assist it to improve training, Tourism Canada is working with five sector associations in a pilot project to develop job standards and design and implement certification programmes for tourism occupations. It is expected that job standards and certification programmes in six occupations (executive housekeeper, front office manager, restaurant/food and beverage manager, executive chef, senior travel counsellor and travel agency manager) will be established (or existing programmes adapted) and in place by the end of 1988. The objective is to provide guidance to educators, increase career prestige and awareness and improve career progression opportunities.

Employment: Unemployment rates are high in the tourism industry in Canada but tourism is also a growth industry which is expected to continue to grow in the future. High turnover rates and the seasonal nature of a large proportion of the jobs partially explain the high unemployment.

Employment and Immigration Canada has designated the tourism industry as a priority industry for training programmes designed to alleviate labour market imbalances and ease unemployment.

Aids and incentives: Overall, Canada has a modern tourism plant offering good quality accommodation, good transportation access, attractive cities, sophisticated dining, shopping, world-class events and convention centres. It is felt, however, that it still has a largely untapped development potential. Government aid and incentive programmes are important considerations in encouraging the establishment of new and upgrading existing tourism product lines.

The major instrument of public financial incentives is the current second generation Tourism Development Subsidiary Agreements signed by the federal Department of Regional Industrial Expansion with the ten provinces and two territories. These pacts will provide a total of C$387 million during their five-year terms, expiring in 1990. Federal contribution will be C$206 million, or 54 per cent and that of the provinces/territories C$176 million. Under the agreements, direct financial assistance is available through repayable and non-repayable contributions to applicants from the private and public sector as well as non-profit organisations. The prime emphasis of these incentives is on tourism product development which is earmarked for 73 per cent of the funds, followed by 14 per cent for market development, 4.4 per cent for industry organisations, 4.3 per cent for research, planning and feasibility studies, and the rest for miscellaneous activities. By the end of 1986, 1 396 projects with a total investment of C$617 million were submitted for consideration of assistance under the sub-agreements. Of these, 491 projects proposing a total of C$235 million in investment were approved to receive C$140 million in incentive aid. An additional 264 projects were under active consideration. Others were ineligible or withdrawn.

Tourism firms under C$2 million in annual revenue continue to benefit from loan guarantees under the Small Businesses Loans Act designed to foster development of small businesses. There are also tax incentives (e.g. preferential tax rates, small business deductions and deferred income plans) targetted at small businesses.

Firms in the tourism sector are also entitled to a range of services available from the Federal Business Development Bank (FBDB). It offers three principal services to the Canadian business community: financial services (loans, loan guarantees and financial planning), investment banking and management services such as counselling, training and information. In 1986, the FBDB made 1 189 loans to firms in the tourism sector for a total of C$ 235.9 million, accounting for close to 30 per cent of the bank's total lending in the year.

The past year also saw Tourism Canada explore with Canadian provincial/territorial tourism officials the ways and means of improved access to traditional financing, for increased equity investment, and for a more effective role for government in stimulating tourism development in Canada. The purpose of this effort is to assist in the development of a domestic investment strategy for the public and private sectors.

Marketing research: The National Task Force on Tourism Data reported in November 1986 to the federal, provincial and territorial ministers responsible for tourism. Major recommendations of the Task Force included the establishment of a separately funded Tourism Research Institute at the Conference Board of Canada, revision of several demand surveys, and the creation of a Satellite Account for Tourism in the system of National Accounts at Statistics Canada.

Results from the United States Pleasure Travel Market Study conducted in 1985 formed the basis for a new Tourism Canada advertising campaign in the United States. Results have been made available to a wide variety of public and private sector tourism agencies.

An agreement to conduct a five-year joint market research programme in the overseas market was signed by Canada and the United States in May 1986. Studies have been carried out in France, Federal Republic of Germany, Japan and the United Kingdom. Results will be available by mid-1987.

The Canadian Travel Survey was conducted in 1986 with a larger sample than in previous years, thanks to provincial participation.

Marketing strategies and measures: Tourism Canada's marketing priority for 1986/87 continued to be the development of international markets.

The Tourism Marketing Council was created by Canada's ministers of tourism to address issues affecting Canada's international marketing efforts. The Council has 14 public sector members representing each of the federal, provincial and territorial tourism ministries, and 14 private sector members representing the Tourism Industry Association of Canada as well as tourism-related industries that operate nationally and spend a minimum of C$500 000 annually on international tourism marketing. Objectives of the Council are:

- To provide a forum for public and private sector tourism partners to regularly discuss their own marketing plans and to comment on the plans of others; and
- To achieve the co-ordination of Canadian tourism marketing efforts, by both public and private sector partners, in international markets.

The Council is not a decision-making body and members do not give up any authority and/or responsibility for their marketing efforts.

Marketing activity emphasis continued to be placed on Canada's primary international market, the United States. Based on the results of the major 1985 US Pleasure Travel Market Study, marketing efforts positioned Canada as an appealing and accessible destination which is foreign yet friendly. The touring potential, cultural diversity and favourable exchange rates were promoted in campaigns designed to generate awareness of Canada during the key vacation planning period. Advertising in the United States highlighted travel experiences through its theme "Canada, the World Next Door", and three sub-themes, which were most clearly demonstrated in the television advertisements – the "Wild World", "Old World" and "New World". These sub-themes correspond to Americans' main areas of interest: outdoor recreation, multi-cultural diversity and the excitement of Canada's cities – all supporting the strong touring segment identified in the 1985 research. Television, magazine and newspaper advertising were employed to present a multi-faceted, highly accessible and above all engaging image of Canada, and were concentrated in the four US census regions with the greatest potential – New England, Mid-Atlantic, East, North Central and Pacific. An increased number of joint advertising campaigns were carried out in the United States with public and private sector partners.

Overseas market development activities were primarily concentrated in Japan, the United Kingdom, the Federal Republic of Germany and France. Advertising efforts in all overseas markets were almost totally carried out in co-operation with travel industry public and private sector partners. Apart from television advertising in the United Kingdom and a television event in France, all campaigns utilised print advertising vehicles. Tourism Canada and the United States Travel and Tourism Administration signed a multi-year agreement to jointly survey potential international travellers in 18 overseas countries. Surveys were carried out in Japan, France, the United Kingdom and the Federal Republic of Germany in 1986.

Joint marketing agreements were established with major partners, such as Air Canada, the Canadian Ski Council and the National Tour Association, to jointly promote and stimulate travel to Canada. As part of an assessment of alternative tourism programme delivery mechanisms, contracts were signed with Canadian Pacific Air Lines to deliver Canadian tourism market development activities in Italy and New Zealand.

Protection of the tourist as a consumer: In British Columbia, following a change in the Minister responsible for the administration of the Travel Agents Registration Act, delays were encountered in implementing the changes summarised in 1986. However, the Advisory Board of Industry personnel is about to be instituted.

In Quebec, minor regulatory changes are in the process of being implemented. They relate to the staggering of renewal dates and a new deadline for the submission of financial statements.

In Ontario, the most recent set of changes to the Travel Industry Act and regulations have been implemented. The next set of changes is being considered, with the kick-off coming in the form of a White Paper from ACTA-Ontario, the trade association in the province. They relate to the contributions to the Compensation Fund and an increase in the maximum claim from the Fund per client from C$3.5 to C$5 million. The proposal will also see the size of the Fund increase from C$3 million to C$5 million, if the proposal is put forward and accepted.

The Alliance of Canadian Travel Associations (ACTA) remains committed to the ultimate implementation of its Performance Plan; however, it now enjoys a lower priority ranking in its list of objectives than was once the case. The reason for this is outlined below and concerns the implementation of the Wylie-Crump Default Protection Plan.

Wylie-Crump Limited, a private insurance broker from Vancouver, approached various ACTA provincial associations with a proposal that included the offering of Default Protection to consumers. Wylie-Crump offers a combined package which includes the traditional types of travellers' insurance (cancellation, baggage loss, hospital and medical, etc.) with a protection against the default of a supplier of services after the passenger's money has been paid for them. The programme has been endorsed by ACTA associations in Atlantic Canada, Manitoba, Saskatchewan, Alberta and (excluding the Default Protection aspect) British Columbia. Saskatchewan had earlier entered into an agreement with Wylie-Crump which was in effect a trial run for the nation-wide programme. ACTA nationally has endorsed the spirit of the programme. With its longer history of involvement, ACTA-Saskatchewan reports that it is satisfied with the product and encouraging reports are also being received from the recently added provincial associations.

International co-operation: The Canadian International Development Agency (CIDA) reported technical assistance projects related to tourism which amounted to C$8.9 million in 1986. These covered a project on the protection of the environment as support to tourism in St. Kitts, a tourism sector study and an airport sector evaluation in Leeward and Windward, and a maritime training programme in the Caribbean region.

DENMARK

In Denmark, the tourism industry is today the fourth largest export industry with foreign-exchange earnings of just over Dkr 14 billion. According to national and international forecasts, tourism will be one of the most important sectors by the year 2000. Realising this, a number of countries have implemented initiatives with a view to strengthening their tourism sector. This means that the Danish tourism industry will probably be facing increased competition from abroad in the coming years. Against this background, the government is definitely of the opinion that a special effort should be made to enable this sector to utilise its potentials.

In recent years, tourism has become increasingly important to the economy, and it has therefore been relevant to take up tourism policy for renewed discussion. As a result of this recognition of the growing importance of the tourism sector, the Minister of Industry presented a "Statement on Tourism Policy" to the Danish Parliament, in November 1986. This Statement builds on the assumption that there has never before been such a broad and growing appreciation of the potential of tourism among the population, industrialists and political parties. The government's statement on tourism policy is therefore intended to encourage a debate on how tourism should be developed in the next decades. This should include an evaluation of the framework to be provided by the public authorities for the most effective operation of the tourism industry, both in the home market and in the export markets. The intention is not to guide tourism in a certain direction, but rather to remove some barriers in order to establish the most favourable conditions for the industry. To facilitate the development of the industry, it is stated that higher priority should be given to co-ordination of the authorities' activities with the tourism industry and co-operation between the Ministry of Industry and the Danish Tourist Board.

Government policy

The government department with overall responsibility for tourism is the Ministry of Industry. It provides almost 100 per cent of the funding for the Danish Tourist Board, a public body not regulated by legislation, but managed through regulations which give authority to the Board in directing its current affairs through its administrative body. Its access to the central administration and government goes through the Ministry of Industry, which includes tourism, from which its financial resources derive.

To date, tourism policy in Denmark has generally concentrated, through the activities of the Danish Tourist Board, on higher foreign-exchange earnings from tourism, while maintaining due consideration for natural and environmental assets. This is an important and desirable aim, but is insufficient to constitute a complete and foresighted tourism policy which takes account of the many different interests concerned with tourism.

Actions and measures taken in 1986

The "Statement on Tourism Policy" includes an action plan dealing with what measures can be taken in order to improve the conditions of the industry on a long-term basis.

Among other items, the Government has proposed that measures be taken in the following fields:

- The promotion of domestic tourism by the Danish Tourist Board;
- Product development and research through the establishment of local innovation and experimental centres for implementation of pilot projects concerning tourism in the future;
- Distribution of tourism partly through product development, partly through more varied seasonal patterns;
- Greater importance to be attached to tourism policy in national and regional planning and in environmental and conservation work;
- Development of a coherent training system specially aimed at covering the needs of the tourism industry for employees trained to serve the tourists of the future;
- Studies to identify ways in which information technology can be used in the industry, and existing electronic information systems should be expanded;

- The statistical material to be extended and the degree of detail improved;
- Market surveys and analyses to be undertaken to improve the decision-making basis of the industry.

The time-limit for the implementation of the action plan, which to a certain extent is being financed by public funds, will initially be three years.

New procedures: Within the physical planning system, procedures have been established to ensure that tourism aspects are taken into account when planning on a regional basis. To do this, the Ministry of Industry and the Ministry of the Environment have stressed the importance of integrating the needs of the sector in local communities through regional planning at an early stage. Statistical material as an instrument for directing the development of the industry is also taken up in the Statement, which states that studies must be undertaken to find out how this material can be improved to optimise the value of information as a measuring instrument. An interdepartmental working group has been set up in order to investigate and establish a formal education system to meet the needs of the tourism sector.

Finally, a contact committee, with broad participation from the appropriate branches of the industry, has been set up. The objective of this committee, which is chaired by the Minister of Industry, is to keep the Minister informed on recent developments in the industry and it is to serve as a general forum for discussion and debate between the public sector and the industry.

Marketing research: The Danish Tourist Board conducted a market analysis of the Dutch market. The following subjects were studied:

- The holiday patterns over recent years;
- The general opinion on holidays;
- The general opinion on holidays in Denmark compared to holidays in competing countries;
- Profile of the Dutch holiday-maker in Denmark;
- Future holiday planning.

The Board also conducted a border analysis with the intention of estimating the length of stay of foreign visitors, the size of travel groups, the types of accommodation used and level of expenditure. A random sample of 1 000 outgoing tourists was chosen for this purpose.

Marketing strategies: A collective plan for the marketing of the Board is drawn up with aims, strategies and activities for each specific foreign country. From 1988, this will also take account of the Danish market. The long-term objectives are to optimise and stabilise the foreign currency income and to aim at those segments of the tourist market which can be most profitable. One way of increasing stability is to widen the gathering ground for tourists to Denmark and so disperse the risk.

In order to attain the long-term targets, the following strategies are used:

i)   Denmark is to be marketed as a quality product, with emphasis on a favourable price/quality relationship, rather than on the price alone;

ii) Denmark is to be marketed as a land with abundant attractions and activities;

iii) The tourist products are to be developed with a view to facilitating the tourist's insight into the lifestyle and the everyday life of the Danes;

iv) Denmark is to be marketed to different segments in the respective markets. The products should be developed in order to meet the requirements of children, young people and senior citizens, as well as the business traveller's market (congresses, incentives and the company meeting market);

v)   The marketing plan has to increase the spread with regard to season, geography and nationality. Emphasis should particularly be placed on the marketing of Denmark as an all-year-round holiday destination.

Depending on the market, the main target groups will be:

i)   Families with children;

ii) The 45-year old and over, including senior citizens;

iii) Single-parent families;

iv) Tourists seeking a relaxed lifestyle.

The Danish Tourist Board has prepared a three-year plan which focused on the analysis of diverse markets, as follows:

– In 1987: The Nordic, Swiss, Austrian and North Italian markets;

– In 1988: The Swedish and Finnish markets;

– In 1989: One or more segments of the German market and an emerging new market for Denmark, i.e. Spain.

These market analyses, which will be predominantly consumer surveys, will have the following objectives: to determine product preferences; ways to reach the target groups; and attitudes towards Denmark as a holiday destination.

FINLAND

International tourism is not a major contributor to the Finnish economy, with the "travel" account making up only one per cent of the gross domestic product, the lowest of the Scandinavian countries. There is a substantial negative balance of expenditure abroad, with receipts amounting to only two-thirds of expenditure. Domestic tourism predominates with foreign tourism contributing only a quarter of the total nights spent in all means of accommodation. It is estimated that in 1986, the receipts from foreign tourism, including international fare payments, made up approximately 4.4 per cent of the value of exports of goods and services. As an employer of labour, the hotel and catering trade employed on average during 1986 some 67 000 staff, of whom the average unemployment rate was 7.5 per cent.

Government policy

The main body responsible for tourism in Finland is the Finnish Tourist Board, established on 1st March 1973 as a state office under the Ministry of Trade and Industries by Decree 187/73. The organisation of the Board has undergone some alterations in 1986 (Decree 800/86, 7th November 1986). The main change was the division of promotion of tourism between two departments of the Board. The Marketing Department is now in charge of international promotion which entails closer links with the Board's offices abroad. The Development Department is responsible for promotion of domestic tourism in addition to its former duties (research and development). However, the objectives of the Board and the overall policy of the Finnish Government towards the development of tourism remain those set out at length in last year's Annual Report.

Actions and measures taken in 1986

The most important seminar prepared by the Finnish Tourist Board at the national level was the sixth "Symposium on Tourism" which was held during May 1986. Development of tourist attractions and activities continued in association with the tourist industry. Grants and loans were distributed for marketing and information and for the development of tourist services.

Research: Research centred on market surveys and surveys on the supply and demand of travel services. Market surveys were started in Canada and Spain. A report on domestic holidays was published in 1986, entitled "How the Finns spent their holidays in 1985".

Similar investigations were carried out in other Nordic countries and a joint Nordic report is to be issued.

Marketing: From 1st October 1986 the Board has had a marketing representative in Madrid. The most important sales event organised in Finland by the Board, in co-operation with Finnair and the tourist industry, was the third Finland Purpuri Travel Mart, held in May 1986. The retailer training programme continued in Sweden and the Federal Republic of Germany. Consumer-oriented operations include general-interest marketing and limited joint campaigns and direct sales work. The last year of the 3-year general-interest campaign continued in the main marketing areas. Sales operations directed at particular target groups continued in the Netherlands and were started in other areas. Marketing was supplemented by publications produced by the Finnish Tourist Board. In 1986, 2.5 million copies of various printed material were published and distributed in Finland and abroad.

International co-operation: Collaboration with other countries included some on the basis of intergovernmental agreements. In addition, Finland hosted in May 1986 the World Tourism Organisation Commission for Europe in Helsinki. Baltic collaboration continued, with several Finnish coastal cities participating along with the Board itself.

FRANCE

With an export/import ratio of some 150 per cent and a surplus twice that of the motor industry, international tourism continues to be one of France's main export sectors, after agro-food and land transport equipment. In 1985 the sector included over 806 000 directly-employed permanent workers, i.e. 3.7 per cent of the total workforce, or 9.9 per cent of all tertiary employment.

Government policy

When the new Government was formed in March 1986, tourism was assigned to the Ministry of Industry.

The departmental reorganisation decided at that time, and promulgated in the ministerial order of 20th October 1986, included the abolition of the sub-directorate for promotion (since it was intended to set up a body covering all promotion and information activities, whether national or regional, public or private), and the establishment of a department, headed by a special counsellor (appointed in July), which is responsible for institutional communications strategy and public relations campaigns both in France and on the main foreign markets. These campaigns are carried out by the *Direction de l'industrie touristique, département "Image de la France"*.

The plan for a new promotion body, called *Maison de la France*, was the result of a redefinition of central government, local government and professional responsibilities and resources.

The *Maison de la France* became operational at the beginning of 1987, in the provisional form of an "economic interest group" focusing on the following activities:

– Market research (permanent monitoring of foreign markets and the execution of special studies when requested);
– Tourist information (carrying on work done by the former sub-directorate for promotion and taking over the activities previously performed by the National Agency for Tourist Information, an administrative public agency which was wound up on the launching of the new body);
– Promotion of tourism in France, mainly focusing on foriegn countries;
– Directing a network of representatives abroad;
– Innovation and prospective analysis.

The operating resources of the new body included an initial contribution from the government and the secondment of staff from the Ministry and from French tourism offices abroad managed by the Directorate for the Tourist Industry, together with contributions expected from new members and income from special services commissioned by local authorities or the travel industry.

The *Image de la France* department in the Ministry was further intended to take over the work previously done by the *Mission Accueil*, and exploit the findings of a major study on marketing and France's image abroad.

On 10th December the Secretary of State for Tourism formally presented proposals for a major drive on tourist reception to the Council of Ministers, focusing on three main aspects:

– Better information for foreign tourists;
– Greater attention to tourist reception by the industry;
– Increasing general awareness of the importance of tourist reception.

Actions and measures taken in 1986

The regional aspect of tourism had already been emphasised in the Goverment/Region plan-contract policy, to which the Government is devoting FF 966 million over the duration of the 1984-88 plan (the Secretariat of State for Tourism providing FF 165 million, the remainder coming mainly from interministerial resources). It was further developed in 1986, with the tabling of legislation concerning the regional organisation of tourism. Under this Act, which entered into force on 3rd January 1987, a Regional Committee for Tourism will be set up in each programme region, its legal status and organisational principles being decided by the regional council concerned, to draw up a regional development scheme for tourism and leisure-time activities.

According to the survey of tourism budgets in the regions and *départements* carried out by the Secretariat of State for Tourism in the summer of 1986, after initial extrapolation, total capital and operating expenditure in continental France amounted to FF 1 184 million. This is made up of FF 351 million for the regions (3.1 per cent of their total budget) and FF 833 million for the *départements* (0.75 per cent of their total budget), and is four times the budget of the Ministry responsible for tourism (FF 282 million in 1986, i.e. 0.03 per cent of the central government budget) and roughly the same as the total amount of public money devoted to tourism.

Accommodation: After over two years' discussion with all the national hotel organisations, the ministerial order of 14th February 1986, fixing the standards and procedures for ranking hotels and other tourist accommodation, replaced the revised order of 16th December 1964. The new text provides for:

– Better adjustment to more diversified demand (new accommodation for families, with rooms for 3 or 4 people, and kitchenettes in many cases);
– Stronger guarantees with regard to amenities (sanitary equipment and telephones).

The new order also helps hotels to meet these new requirements (they have five years to comply; there are broader offset arrangements for some types of equipment; and an unstarred category of tourist hotel has been recognised, in order to promote establishments guaranteeing good quality services at very low prices).

After partial decontrol of hotel prices, applying to 3 and 4 star establishments only (May 1986), the prices of all services provided by the whole range of hotels and catering establishments (including bars and restaurants) were completely freed on 2nd December 1986.

Development of tourism: Three important measures were taken in this respect in 1986.

The first was the decision in November to set up a *Fonds d'aide au conseil et à l'innovation touristique* (tourism counselling and innovation fund) focusing on the development of new products, market research and expert analysis of projects. This fund is intended to help the promoters of local schemes and assist the provision of very varied types of accommodation in rural areas. Geographically the focus is on vulnerable sectors, largely in mountain areas. Regions or groups of communes that have a contract with the government are eligible.

The second concerns the definition, by the Interministerial Committee for Rural Planning and Development, of the four cases having priority for FIDAR loans, tourism in rural areas being one of these. Development of tourism potential has to include:

– Better economic organisation of the sector (feasibility studies, associations of producers);
– Improved quality of services and reception (modernisation, creation of up-market facilities, occupational training);
– Creation of "development and tourism growth centres", to align reception and marketing to the standards required by the international leisure market;
– Redeployment of the products provided by small resorts;
– Development of major sites of international interest that have not yet been properly exploited.

The third measure is the inclusion of research on major focal points of tourist activity or attraction among the activities of the Directorate for the Tourism Industry. The analysis and inventory of these special areas, using the available econometric instruments, should facilitate inter-ministerial co-ordination in the period after the 1984-1988 Plan, as well as providing a promotional tool.

Social and family tourism: In this field, and in liaison with the major associations, priority has been given to the renovation and enhancement of existing facilities rather than to new constructions. France has a considerable capacity in this respect, particularly with regard to "holiday villages", but the facilities have to be adapted to the new requirements of both French and foreign visitors.

GERMANY

Within the framework of its replies to a parliamentary enquiry on "tourism policy", the Federal Government commented at length on the economic importance of tourism. In this context, it also drew attention to the difficulties which still exist in measuring the economic importance of tourism in a plausible manner. Improvements are not to be expected before it is possible to incorporate tourism into the System of National Accounts. However, it may be regarded as quite apparent that the total turnover in the tourism industry is larger than that of the steel industry, the chemical industry or even agriculture.

It has often been publicly stated that the number of jobs in tourism is larger than that of the whole German automobile industry (excluding sub-contractors). The latest 1985 sample survey shows that about 840 000 people work in the hotel and catering trades: this represents two-thirds of the employment in the tourist industry.

Government policy

The Government Department with overall responsibility for tourism is the Federal Ministry of Economics. It provides around 90 per cent of the funding for the *Deutsche Zentrale für Tourismus e.V.* (DZT) – the national organisation for tourism promotion. The remaining 10 per cent is from the DZT's own resources including income from members, which accounts for about 5 per cent of the total. Membership of the DZT includes the transport sector, hotels and restaurants, trade and city associations, tour operators, communities, etc.

In October 1986, the *Deutsche Bundestag* discussed again tourism policy and adopted a resolution inviting the Federal government to:

- Eliminate the impediments still existing in Europe;
- Replace public-sector activities in tourism by private activities wherever this is possible;
- Intensify the activities of the DZT abroad both financially and staffwise;
- Support an investigation of the reasons why the demand for domestic tourism services has been stagnant and to work toward the preparation of statistics that are more strongly tailored to the needs of the tourism industry and better integrated into the overall system of economic and social statistics (improved data provision);

- Work toward a further improvement of the infrastructure taking into account ecological requirements;
- Improve co-operation between public and private institutions in tourism and set up a co-ordinating body for that purpose; and
- Report to the *Deutsche Bundestag* regularly on the execution of such measures.

After a break-down in the period 1983/85, the Advisory Council on Tourism attached to the Federal Minister of Economics had two extensive consultations with the Minister. The main aim of these consultations was to improve co-operation in marketing the range of German tourism services and to co-ordinate even more effectively the main efforts in tourism with private sector marketing activities. These consultations are to continue at six-monthly intervals.

Actions and measures taken in 1986

Marketing: The Federal Government does not conduct any marketing-oriented analyses, but supports financially the studies of the *Deutscher Fremdenverkehrsverband e.V.* and the *Deutsche Zentrale für Tourismus e.V.*

International co-operation: Within the framework of technical co-operation, DM 2.5 million were spent on the implementation of the following measures:

- The funding of the costs of experts at catering trade schools;
- The establishment and extension of a catering trade school; and
- The provision of an adviser to a tourism organisation.

A further DM 688 000 was also devoted to the training of 74 students (of which 20 participated in a brief seminar in Germany).

Grants to 47 developing countries' participation in the International Tourism Exchange in 1986 amounted to some DM 257 000.

The German Finance Company for Investments in Developing Countries (DEG) authorized the outlay of DM 3.4 million for three projects to be co-financed, as follows:

- Equity participation: DM 0.8 million; and
- Quasi-equity participation loans: DM 2.6 million.

GREECE

The Greek tourism industry is a very major contributor to the Greek economy and has now passed shipping as the largest single generator of inward invisible income. Originally, Greece was a centre for cultural tourism but from the late seventies it directed its attentions to the general market for the typical Mediterranean package of sea and sun at an affordable price. The charter sector from European markets predominates but with a substantial element of short-stay "shopping" visits from Yugoslavia, which was particularly notable in 1986 as a result of the devaluation of the drachma. The latter more than made up for the decline in United States tourists during the year.

The upgrading of tourist services and a resurgence of visitors from the United States are expected to lead to a growth during 1987 of between 6 and 7 per cent in the number of arrivals. Foreign exchange earnings from tourism are expected to increase by some 12 per cent.

Government policy

The national body for the implementation of Greek national tourism policy is the National Tourism Organisation of Greece (NTOG). This organisation, which was established in 1951, is an autonomous legal entity, directly supervised by the Ministry of National Economy and is the designated state organisation for the development and promotion of Greek tourism. Its current objectives are set out in the 1983/87 programme of economic and social development for Greece as a whole, which for tourism has three main aims:

- To increase the international competitiveness of Greek tourism by improvement of the quality of the services offered;
- To make the best use of idle or under-utilised capacity; and
- To implement a balanced pattern of supply.

These objectives are elaborated upon in the first section of last year's Annual Report and no substantial changes took place in the objectives or organisational structure during 1986.

Actions and measures taken in 1986

Accommodation and restaurants: The process of drafting a plan for a system of criteria to classify Greek hotels by number of stars was completed. At the same time, a committee has been examining the reform of hotel and camping site specifications. The assessment of

Greek tourist potential has continued, which has required the mandatory registration of accommodation which complied with NTOG specifications but which had not previously been declared. A Bill modifying and supplementing provisions contained in Law 392/76 concerning camping grounds is still under development and the drafting of a Presidential Decree concerning fire protection of tourist installations has continued.

The procedure of redrafting specifications for the classification of refreshment centres and premises serving meals, which was started on the initiative of the NTOG and of the Ministry of Trade, has continued. The Joint Committees of Inspection of centres for refreshments and meals, which consist of NTOG inspectors and competent representatives of several ministries (Trade, Public Order, Health and Welfare) have been in full operation. Their brief is to inspect such centres throughout the country, and it is envisaged that these joint Committees will continue their work for a number of years. NTOG employees have participated in primary and secondary scale committees for classifying centres of refreshment and restaurants in all Prefectures in Greece.

Environmental protection: The NTOG has continued to finance restoration work on ancient as well as more modern monuments, in co-operation with the Archaeological Society, and is pursuing a programme for restoring and converting traditional habitations into hostels. The eligibility of houses for such conversion under Law 1262/82 is determined by a committee of the ministers jointly responsible.

In co-operation with the Ministry of Agriculture and the Ministry of Area Planning and the Environment, legislation was adopted during the year for specifications concerning conversion of the use of wooded areas to cater for tourists, with extremely strict measures for protecting the environment. A long-term contract is still in progress for protection of the flora and fauna of the Amvrakikos Gulf area, associated with modest tourist development.

A new Law, 1650/86, concerning the protection of the environment, has been passed and work is continuing on legislation concerning procedure to be followed in area planning for tourist installations including blending the buildings in with the landscape, and for declaring areas as saturated in cases where there are environmental problems. Agencies which are authorised to impose sanctions on those who pollute the environment, including the Ministry of Mercantile Marine (which is responsible for penalties relating to the pollution of the sea from various sources) have pursued their activities and more surveys for biological purification of sewage have been undertaken. New legislation for the use of the seashore by private individuals was prompted by the Ministry of Finance, and a study was completed concerning the installation by Prefectures of sanitary facilities for bathers from prefabricated elements.

The NTOG participated in the National Committee for environmental protection as part of the European Year of Environment and has maintained its financing of local authorities and private agencies involved in cave exploration and exploitation. It has encouraged the mass media to continue to impress upon the public the importance of environmental protection.

Vocational training and employment: The School of Tourist Professions operates seven basic training centres, all of whose programmes have been upgraded. The courses were extended from one to two years. An additional school was installed in a new privately-owned hotel at Iraklion (Crete). A statistical enquiry has been carried out in the industry and among graduates of the School, in order to determine market requirements so as to establish its needs for staff and the standards of specialisation which should be demanded. A programme of professional retraining began in October 1986 and ended in March 1987. Preparations are continuing to start a three-year training course in the Rhodes Senior College, with the introduction of new subjects such as computers, architecture, the equipping of establishments, etc.

At five different technical training centres, three-year practical tuition has continued in hotel management, restaurant catering, receptionist duties and handling of travel agency work. 850 people participated in these courses, and during the winter months, seminars for vocational postgraduate training took place in seven Greek towns, for a total of 800 employees.

The Organisation for Employment of the Labour Potential (OAED) carried out a programme of professional training in co-operation with the Council for Equality between the Sexes, for the personnel who would be working at the women's co-operatives during the summer at Petra in Mitilini, at Mesta in Chios, at Litohoro in Katerini and at Ampelakia in Larissa. Forty to fifty people will work in each location. The OAED, in co-operation with the School for Tourist Professions, has also operated a special patisserie section for women who intend to set up women's co-operatives.

Aid and incentives: The policy of incentives in the form of credit facilities and fiscal exemption for tourist enterprises has been maintained. These include granting of loans for improvements and modernisation of premises to hotel enterprises, other tourist accommodation and camping grounds, the granting of medium-term loans for the construction of heated swimming-pools, credit incentives to local authority agencies and individuals engaged in traditional arts and crafts and recreational centres, a one per cent tax deduction on gross receipts of hotel enterprises and general tourism agencies for advertising expenses abroad, the removal of entertainment tax on centres which function within tourist premises and the collection of a percentage by hotel enterprises on foreign currency converted into drachmae and on telephone calls. The government has continued to finance and subsidise the creation of new units catering for tourists, mainly in parts of the country in need of tourist development and forming part of the overall plan for regional development, and the conversion of traditional habitations into tourist accommodation.

Development of new forms of tourism: The introduction of a programme for health tourism is under study. During its experimental stage, it is envisaged that at least 10 000 people could participate. The programme is intended for under-privileged Greeks with health problems. Participants would stay for 10 days at one of five spas during the off-peak period, being subsidised at a rate of Dr 800 per day. During this stage, the NTOG would allocate about Dr 100 million to the project. Other new developments being promoted include maritime tourism, athletic meetings, international conferences and winter sports, and to cover these, a sizeable information brochure is being produced. A new Law 1652/86 provides for the operation of time-sharing schemes by hotel enterprises.

Social tourism activities during 1986 included the regular programme which gave 25 000 people a seven-day vacation at little cost to the participants; this was a substantial drop on previous years. The Secretariat-General for Youth has also organised summer and winter holiday programmes jointly with the NTOG, covering some 20 000 people. This involved a joint subsidy by the two organisations of around Dr 100 million. Hospitality was provided for 344 political refugees for a fortnight in a number of hotels; their travelling expenses in Greece and to and from their countries of residence was also provided for. The programme for encouraging internal tourism, which covers persons over 60, young people under 25, members of recognised excursion associations, or other groups of more than four people, both Greek residents and Greeks resident abroad, entitles beneficiaries to 20 per cent rebates on all accommodation outside the peak season, for minimum periods of two nights. This programme is sponsored by local NTOG units, the state hotel chain "Xenia", the Tourist Trades Training Centre and units of the Women's Agricultural Tourist Co-operatives, as well as such private enterprises as care to join the programme.

Credits provided under the 1986 Public Works Programme were utilised mainly for tourist infrastructure projects, notably:

– For promotion of three main systems aiming at developing new forms of tourism (health tourist centres, winter sports centres and marinas);

- For the completion of projects included in the special programmes (exploitation of traditional settlements, frontier entry stations, highway stations, recreation spaces, golf courses, etc.); and
- For execution of special European Communities programmes.

Marketing research: The results of the research collected during 1984/85 at the main entry and exit points for visitors to Greece were issued in a special leaflet under the title "Special research regarding the characteristics of foreign tourist demand in Greece during the period 1984/85". The results of work undertaken during July 1982 on the islands of Paros, Santorini and Kithira were published under the title "Research on social approval of tourism – Paros, Santorini, Kithira". A critical review of tourist traffic 1983/85 was also published.

To help in establishing the appropriate policy to cope with the increase in arrivals of foreign tourists and shaping forecasts for 1987, an evaluation was made of

data collected for 1985-86, a questionnaire was completed by NTOG branches abroad and views were exchanged with private tourist agencies by means of a conference in Athens, organised during 1986 by the NTOG.

Staggering of holidays: To extend the season, more loans have been given for the construction of heated swimming-pools at a number of main tourist establishments. The projects for social tourism and other new forms of tourism have been concentrated on off-peak periods and, associated with the plans for regional development, programmes have been implemented which give subsidies to a number of shipping lines to less popular destinations and provides free travel to a number of the smaller islands in the Dodecanese, Cyclades and Chios outside the main tourist season.

International co-operation: During 1986, new agreements were signed with Italy and Albania, as well as "Agreed Minutes" with Israel. These will enter into force after ratification by Parliament.

IRELAND

Tourism makes a significant contribution to the quality of life in Ireland through the provision of economic and social benefits. In 1985, for instance, the Irish tourism industry earned an estimated Ir£900.2 million (an increase of 14 per cent over 1984), including carrier receipts of Ir£173 million and Ir£269.2 million from domestic tourism. This accounted for approximately 5.1 per cent of GNP. The indirect effects of further spending, through the multiplier effect of tourism spending in the economy, increase this percentage to 8 per cent. This outstanding performance of the tourism industry was due in particular to the United States, which became the most important revenue generating market.

The rather exceptional events in Europe during 1986 caused a drop in the number of arrivals from the United States to Ireland of 17 per cent, which had an overall negative effect on the results of the tourism industry. Total earnings thus amounted to Ir£843.3 million, a decrease of 12 per cent, of which Ir£626.8 million came from international visitors. And while tourism revenue has accounted for 6.5 per cent of the country's exports of goods and services in 1985, it only accounted for 5.9 per cent in 1986. Still, as such, it represents a major contribution to the balance of payments account, particularly since tourism has a low import content (less than 8 per cent).

A significant proportion of foreign tourism spending in Ireland accrues to the Exchequer: every pound spent by a visitor within Ireland yields 49.9 pence to which 25.6 pence must be added for fares to Irish transport companies. Home holidays produce a net additional tax yield of 17.0 pence. For example, in 1985, the Exchequer earned Ir£333 million in additional tax revenue through tourism, a 25 per cent increase over 1984.

The stimulus provided by tourism also has a ripple effect on incomes and employment in all sectors of the economy. It is estimated that as many as 91 000 jobs (compared to 90 000 in 1982) throughout the economy are dependant on tourism, directly and indirectly; this represents 7 per cent of the active civilian population. At a time when unemployment is worsening in Ireland, touching 250 000 persons or 19.3 per cent of the active population in 1986, tourism is one of the rare industries showing a small but steady growth in employment.

Economic, market and marketing research allows Bord Failte to forecast revenue. These forecasts are based on individual markets development projections, current trends as well as various factors likely to affect tourism in the coming years. Thus, for instance, the American market is anticipated to remain depressed due to the fall in the value of the dollar. Forecasts also take into account the contraction in the Tourist Board's budget for 1987 and unchanged (compared with 1986) tourism promotional budgets for the following three years.

IRELAND. **Forecast for the development of international tourism**

In 1985 Ir£ (millions)

	1987	1988	1989	1990
Britain	185	189	192	196
North America	153	157	162	172
Continental Europe	85	88	91	94
Northern Ireland	34	35	36	37
Other areas	22	23	24	25
Total	479	492	505	524
Excursionists	20	20	21	21
Carrier receipts	147	151	155	161
TOTAL	646	663	681	706

Government policy

The Government Department with overall responsibility for tourism was the Department of Tourism, Fisheries and Forestry. It is now the Department of Tourism and Transport which has taken up that responsibility until the beginning of 1987. It provides most of the budget for *Bord Failte*, the national tourist organisation, set up in 1955 and responsible for the promotion and development of tourism. The Board consists of a Chairman and eight members appointed by the Minister. The formulation of the national policy for tourism is the responsibility of the Department in consultation with *Bord Failte* which then devises the policies and strategic plans for achieving national objectives. *Bord Failte* is responsible for a wide range of tourism-related activities, of which promotion is the most significant in terms of budgetary allocation. Following the publication of the tourism policy document in 1984, all Government Departments with functions relating to tourism are to take full cognizance of the needs of the industry and consult with the Department responsible for tourism when proposals impinging upon tourism are being considered.

Although the national objective of Government policy on tourism is "to optimise the economic and social benefits to Ireland by the promotion and development of tourism both to and within the country", it is accepted that the balance between the two aspects will remain strongly in favour of the economic one over the next five years. Against this background attention will be focused on maximising foreign tourist revenue over the planning period, and, as presented above, a specific target of Ir£706 million (in 1985 prices) has been set for international tourist revenue by 1990.

In fact, given the overall economic situation and the likelihood of little growth in *Bord Failte*'s budget, only modest growth (2 to 4 per cent per year) is expected in international tourism revenue in real terms over the next few years. Even in order to achieve this growth rate, access services by air and sea are crucial, as recognised by Government in the White Paper on Tourism Policy published in 1985. Thus *Bord Failte* is involved in the question of fares, routes, capacities, standards and regulatory matters with the carriers and Government. For instance, 1986 saw new scheduled services to Shannon by both Pan American and Delta Air Lines, which should in the long term have a particularly favourable impact on generating new traffic from the southern and western States.

Since it is recognised worldwide that tourism is one of the industries offering the best opportunity for international growth over the next decade, the Government in its White Paper also gave priority to this industry in its efforts to tackle unemployment. In spite of this, no funds were specifically allocated to job creation in the tourism sector in 1986. However, the Government had established a special Tourism Development Team within *Bord Failte* in 1985 to act as a catalyst identifying tourism opportunities and matching suitable developers and investors to appropriate projects. The National Development Corporation has also been empowered to make investments in suitable tourism projects. Thus, the driving force for achieving the employment related goals will be the private entrepreneur.

Actions and measures taken in 1986

Aids and incentives: The Government announced a new grant scheme for hotels and guest houses in the latter part of 1985. The Reconstruction and Development Scheme, administered by the *Bord Failte*, provided Ir£2 million in 1986 to stimulate employment intensive capital investment in export tourism hotels and guest houses, to improve overall standards and to encourage the provision of all-weather facilities in order to assist the extension of the tourist season. Total investment by the private sector resulting from the availability of this grant scheme is estimated at Ir£20 million – giving a significant boost to the building and allied trades and to employment.

Other funds were made available to the tourism sector by Government. The Tourist Traffic Act, 1975 and the Special Border Areas Programme Fund have made grant assistance possible to stimulate investment in tourism activities, facilities and amenities which are in short supply, below standard or where the return on investment is unacceptable without financial assistance. The judgements as to what development and investments are required come from market research, carried out each year, on visitor needs and preferences, their likes and dislikes and their opinions about activities, facilities and services.

In 1986, grants totalled Ir£430 000 for accommodation; caravan and camping parks, hostels, farmhouses, town and country homes) and Ir£722 000 for the development of amenities (angling, waterways, marine development, historical and cultural attractions, access, signposting and village improvement schemes, national and forest park development, recreational facilities and resorts, regional development).

The accommodation sector also benefits from a Consultancy Service introduced by *Bord Failte* in 1984 and which continues to provide advisory and evaluation services to hoteliers to assist them in exploiting the full tourism potential of their premises. The Board also established a Consultative Advisory Group, which is working on developing grading criteria to cover both the physical and personal standards for hotels, with a report due by early 1987.

Ever conscious of keeping prices at a competitive level while ensuring value for money, *Bord Failte* makes representations to Government to reduce taxation, particularly in relation to VAT. In 1985 it had seen a first reduction in VAT from 18 per cent to 10 per cent on hotel accommodation and the hire of cars, caravans, mobile homes, tents, boats and bicycles. In 1986, VAT was also reduced from 25 per cent to 10 per cent on meals and some services, such as hairdressing.

Catering: A decision by Government to liberalise the opening hours of public houses satisfied a long-standing request by the tourism industry and organisations.

Staggering of holidays: Another major concern of *Bord Failte* is seasonality, which is a particular problem in Ireland with about three quarters of all tourists arriving in the six months from May to October. In order to alleviate this problem, actions are undertaken along two axes: on the supply side, grant assistance is given with an eye to all-weather facilities as a means to extending the season, and on the demand side, special marketing campaigns promote the off-peak periods to the export and domestic tourism markets. The Departments of Education and Labour are also examining the feasibility of rescheduling school and work holidays.

Environment: The White Paper on Tourism Policy devoted much attention to the physical environment recognising how important it is to the industry. The establishment of an Inter-Departmental Policy Co-ordination Committee on Tourism complements and gives greater impetus to the efforts and initiatives of *Bord Failte* in resolving environmental problems which threaten tourism. Furthermore, the Board makes the needs of tourism in relation to environmental conservation clear to planning authorities through inputs to development plans and by making use of their role as a legally prescribed body under the Planning Acts. In addition, it commissions special studies, ensures that any grand aided projects meet environmental standards, and organises competitions such as Tidy Towns, National Gardens, etc.

Marketing: The extent to which a tourist board should foster domestic tourism is difficult to determine. Since the emphasis in Ireland is at present on achieving economic benefits, and these being much higher from overseas tourists, *Bord Failte* has adopted a policy whereby domestic tourism is promoted as a support for facilities and accommodation required for export tourism. Two surveys help achieve this objective: the detailed survey of departing visitors to determine trip and personal profiles, and the national holiday survey which measures home holiday volumes and profile information on such holidaymakers.

The selection of target segments within the international tourism market is based on research (overseas travellers by area of residence) to determine the potential return from each one. The marketing strategy for 1986 thus focused on attracting first time holidaymakers without Irish ties from North America, Britain, Continental Europe and Australia/New Zealand.

ITALY

1986 was marked by a series of unforeseen events that caused sharp reversals of the trends in tourism demand. Following the Chernobyl disaster, the Achille Lauro hijacking and terrorist activities in the Mediterranean area, the authorities were obliged to take preventive measures in order to protect foreign and Italian travellers.

In addition, promotional programmes were revised and directed primarily to regaining the 1985 levels of tourism from the United States. Greater efforts were made to limit as far as possible the adverse effects on employment within the industry and on its profitability through a co-ordinated approach on the part of the various government agencies, tourism businesses and airlines to improve Italy's brand image, which has sometimes suffered from a lack of proper public relations work vis-à-vis the mass media.

However, the rapid response of the industry to these changes in demand has helped to limit the damage: the drop in the number of United States tourists, which has mainly affected the luxury and top-category hotels, was offset by the continued large influx of tourists from Germany, Austria, France and Belgium. Domestic tourists seem to have preferred the mountain regions, held to be less polluted, and this has helped to take some of the pressure off the coastal areas, which are showing signs of serious overcrowding.

The studies carried out by the national and regional authorities responsible for the planning and co-ordination of tourism activities to examine possible ways of developing international tourism have revealed the importance of psychological factors (e.g. motivations, emotional reactions prompted by the fear of terrorism or pollution, etc.).

In view of the recent trends in the value of the United States and Canadian dollars, the mark and the yen, there is likely to be an increase in the number of tourists from Japan and Germany, and a continued fall in the number from the United States and Canada. However, the policy of deregulating air fares ought to give a boost to long-distance travel, even if the price of oil does not fall.

As regards the psychological factors, the surveys carried out recently in Italy by CENSIS and FIAVET reveal that the main reasons why foreigners want to visit Italy are for its artistic and historical heritage, and for its environment, and this is particularly true in the case of non-European tourism and for short visits, which have shown a proportionately greater increase than visits of an average or longer duration. The main drawbacks would seem to be traffic congestion, the lack of basic services and pollution.

The value-for-money factor will have an effect on the demand for top-quality hotels, whose clientele is more exacting and traditionally North American in origin. Demand might be influenced in the short term by promotional campaigns in the United States, but more time is required for the effects to be felt of schemes to promote the attractions of the environment or the country's cultural riches.

However, there is expected to be a substantial increase in 1987 in the number of tourists from northern and central Europe and Japan, as well as a slight upturn in the numbers from the United States as the result of promotional campaigns.

In addition, the ongoing process of European integration, where some particularly positive progress was made in 1986 from both political and economic standpoints, should encourage continued expansion of tourism within the Community. In this connection, mention should be made of the launch of Community-wide schemes in the area of tourism, which are designed to encourage the adoption of joint strategies to attract more non-European tourists to Europe. It is generally felt that, despite the sharp increases in competition between the European countries in the Mediterranean area, the best results are likely to be obtained by promoting a community spirit that would highlight Europe's common historical and cultural heritage whilst at the same time emphasizing the specific characteristics of each country.

Government policy

The Government's responsibility as regards tourism is vested in the Ministry of Tourism and Entertainment (*Ministero del Turismo et dello Spettacolo*). The Italian State Tourist Agency (*Ente Nazionale Italiano per il Turismo*), which was set up in 1919, is a semi-public body 90 per cent of whose funds are provided by central government; it is responsible for promoting tourism in Italy primarily through a network of representations abroad.

During 1986 the regulatory authority of the regions was progressively extended with the coming into force of the provisions of the Tourism Act (No. 217) of 17th May 1983. The regulatory structure is a somewhat complex one, given the fact that the Italian constitution has delegated to the local authorities both the regulatory powers and responsibility for carrying out the administrative functions relating to tourism. However, central government still retains responsibility for planning and co-ordination as well as for international relations and it exercises these functions through government services.

This situation has led, on the one hand, to a proliferation of local initiatives and, on the other, to inevitable conflicts between central and local authorities. The first of these problems has been remedied to some extent by a more targeted approach as regards planning and co-ordination, whereas the second problem had to be resolved by a court judgment regarding the constitutionality of Act 217/83. The Constitutional Court, in Decision No. 195 of 1st July 1986, ruled that the exercise of planning and co-ordination functions by the Ministry of Tourism, in accordance with the provisions of the Tourism Act, was constitutional. Although this resolved the problems of an institutional character with regard to the relations between central government and the regions, there was still the problem of the functional relationships between all of the central government services involved in tourism in one way or another, to which has recently been added the Ministry of the Environment, established by Act No. 349 of 8th July 1986.

Management of the "tourism system" within Italy's institutional framework is no easy task due to the lack of suitable "horizontal co-ordination" structures that would be able to impose some degree of uniformity on the management of its many and varied aspects. This situation has made it difficult to design and implement integrated projects such as the development of certain forms of social, cultural, rural or similar tourism. The linking of tourism and transport has proved difficult and has received little mention in the general transportation plan drawn up in 1986 by the Ministry of Transport and Civil Aviation.

In view of these problems and the fact that tourism is the single most profitable industry in Italy, the National Economic and Employment Council prepared a report pointing out the problems and recommending solutions. What this said basically was that the public and private sector structures should devote more attention to the need for a rapid improvement in the quality of Italy's tourist industry, which was showing dangerous signs of stagnation and obsolescence.

Of particular importance from an organisational standpoint are the Agencies for the Promotion of Tourism which, under the terms of Article 4 of the Tourism Act, will take over the responsibility for tourism planning and promotion from the present Provincial Tourism Organisations.

So far only 9 out of the 21 regions have brought their territorial organisation into line with the provisions of Article 4; what is more, the difference between the local situations within one and the same region has created a number of difficulties with regard to administering a system of information on the arrivals and presence of tourists in the various types of accommodation.

By and large, 1986 has been for both public and private sectors another year of reflection and increasing awareness of the role assigned to them within the present institutional structure.

Actions and measures taken in 1986

Accommodation: Italy ranks amongst the world's leaders in terms of the amount of real estate that its tourist accommodation facilities represent. What is more, the expertise acquired through years of experience in catering to the needs of guests has contributed to the particular quality of the country's tourist services and played an important part in the industry's increased productivity and competitiveness. The number of tourist facilities in operation in the country is as follows:

- Hotels: 43 000
- Other types of accommodation: 434 463
- Catering: 50 000
- Snack catering (bars, cafés, etc.): 100 000

- Other facilities (convention centres, spas, ski resorts, marinas, etc.): 5 000
- Specific services (tourist and travel agencies, convention services, currency exchange offices, individual and group transport hire, etc.): 10 000.

Italy's accommodation capacity amounts to 1.6 million beds in hotels and 3.3 million in other types of accommodation. In addition to this, there is a vast amount of accommodation on a rental or time-sharing basis, for which figures are not available, but which adds considerably to Italy's potential tourist capacity.

A breakdown of the total number of hotels by region shows that the north has 70 per cent, the centre 16 per cent, the south 10 per cent and the islands 4 per cent.

Currently 50 per cent of the hotels are classified as one-star (4th class hotels, 3rd class *pensione*) catering for tourists on a low budget, 46 per cent are in the two and three-star categories (3rd and 2nd class hotels), while the four and five-star hotels (1st class and luxury hotels) represent slightly more than 3 per cent of the total. Most of the hotels in the higher categories (57 and 52 per cent respectively) are concentrated in Northern Italy.

The most popular tourist regions in Italy are Trentino-Alto Adige, Emilia-Romagna and Veneto. Calabria has the largest surplus of hotel accommodation, whereas in the Trentino-Alto Adige Region the demand considerably outstrips the supply. The main factors contributing to these imbalances are the seasonal variations and the amount of private accommodation.

As far as the trend regarding accommodation facilities over the ten years from 1976 to 1986 is concerned, there has been a decrease in the total number of hotels (down 3 500) but an increase in the number of beds in both hotels (up 110 000) and other types of accommodation (up 500 000). The spread in terms of standard of accommodation has improved and there has been a remarkable expansion in the non-hotel segment of the market; this has been accompanied by an improvement in the productivity index for the sector as a whole in terms of a higher ratio of nights spent to available accommodation, which reached a figure of 106 (nights spent/number of beds) in 1985 compared with 91 in 1975. However, the rather unsatisfactory occupancy rate of about 35-40 per cent reveals the weak spots, which are mainly the result of the geographical imbalance of the supply and the seasonal nature of the demand.

Transport: The main shortcoming in the transport system is connections between Northern Italy and the South and the islands. Special provisions have been made to increase boat services to Sardinia and Sicily during the high season. There are still too few intercontinental flights in relation to the number of passengers, both tourists and non-tourists, which is constantly on the increase.

As regards the cost of transport, mention should be made of the special schemes introduced for both rail and air travel. The Italian State Railways now issue individual rail passes, available only to foreigners or Italians living abroad, that allow free travel over the entire network and are valid for a period of 8, 15, 21 or 30 days. Alitalia has introduced a range of special fares giving reductions of between 25 and 75 per cent on regular flights to all Italian tourist destinations and more particularly to Sardinia, for which there are preferential rates. In addition, foreign tourists using a motor car or motorcycle are able to purchase petrol coupons and vouchers for the motorways at concessionary prices.

Environment: Particular attention has been directed to the complex question of environmental protection and in 1986 it was given priority status amongst the Italian Government's general policy aims. A ministerial agency has been set up for this purpose with responsibility for the prevention of water pollution (Act No. 319 of 10th May 86), the promotion, conservation and enhancement of the country's natural heritage and the protection of natural resources from pollution.

These tasks have gained further urgency because the consequences of the Chernobyl disaster and the pollution of the sea along the resort coast have had an adverse effect on tourists' choice of destination.

In the belief that the development of tourism and protection of the environment should not be conflicting aims but rather that protection of the natural surroundings should help to make the tourist's stay more enjoyable, the Italian Government intends making future projects for the development of tourism subordinate to the higher interests of the conservation of natural, environmental and cultural resources, and to a careful assessment of their environmental impact in accordance with EEC directives.

The many measures that have been taken include a ban on plastic bags imposed by the islands in the Tyrrhenian Sea, the publication by the Ministry of various data on the degree of pollution along the coast and at seaside resorts and on radioactivity levels in the environment, and the partial adoption of EEC directives on lead-free petrol.

The number of workers in the tourism sector, including indirect employment, is now roughly 1.3 million, of whom 530 580 are self-employed.

Marketing: The public sector (regions, ENIT), the private sector (tour operators and travel agencies) and transport operators are all involved in the marketing operation: the public sector does the planning and the promotion of Italy's "brand image", while the private sector and the transport operators handle the marketing and sale of tourism "services".

In view of the need for more effective co-ordination between these three sectors, which are responsible for matching supply with demand, a series of "special projects" were launched in 1986 with the financial and technical co-operation of all the sectors concerned. In particular, the "US Plan", representing a total investment of L 9 billion, was launched with the aim of restoring the inflow of tourists from the United States.

Despite the shadow which terrorism had cast over the situation in the Mediterranean area during 1986, further progress was made in rationalising promotional and marketing efforts. In line with this, ENIT brought out brochures for a number of foreign countries and conducted major market studies on the United States and the Far East.

Technological innovation is proving of particular assistance in marketing and agency activities.

Most travel agencies and hotels are hooked up to a computerised reservations system, and there are plans to introduce a computerised market information service providing details of what is on offer and linking up tour operators and travel agents.

The marketing sector is thus now able to supply more targeted and specialised information. However, it is essential that there should be closer integration with the production sector. The central role of the reception structure, in terms of the complex interlinked system constituting the supply of tourist services, thus becomes the most urgent problem; on the other hand, the aims of a up-to-date promotional policy will increasingly concern all of the components of the supply, by virtue of the fact that they are all part of the "tourism industry".

JAPAN

While international tourism is a minor contributor to the Japanese economy, with receipts for tourism being only 0.5 per cent of exports (very much lower than in any other OECD country), it is seen as one of the best ways of combatting the current lack of understanding of

Japan abroad. The broad exchange of people flowing both inwards and outwards is probably the most effective means of promoting international co-operation and understanding. In addition, the active encouragement of Japanese travellers abroad can make a substantial contribution to reducing the large balance of payments surplus between Japan and the rest of the world; in 1985 the Japanese tourism deficit amounted to $3.7 billion. Japanese travellers abroad in 1986 exceeded 5 million for the first time, but the number of nights spent outside Japan was only 7 per cent of those spent in domestic travel. Foreign visitors to Japan declined somewhat in 1986 as a result of the rapid appreciation of the yen against most other currencies.

Government policy

The Ministry of Transport functions as the central administrative agency for the organisation of international tourism in Japan, representing the nation in international organisations and at international gatherings relating to tourism. Where domestic tourism is concerned, other governmental agencies are also involved with tourism within their respective scopes of activities, including the Environment Agency, Ministry of Health and Welfare, Ministry of Education, Ministry of Construction and National Land Agency.

The Department of Tourism within the Ministry of Transport is in charge of administrative functions relating to the development, improvement and co-ordination of the tourist industry. It has three divisions: Planning Division, Travel Agency Division and Development Division.

The Minstry is assisted by the Tourism Policy Council, made up of experienced non-governmental officials and academics, which advises the government as necessary. The Japan National Tourist Organisation (JNTO) is a separate organisation under the supervision of the Ministry of Transport, whose role is to promote overseas travel to Japan and provide information to help Japanese tourists going overseas.

The principal objectives of national and general tourism policy, as set out in the Japanese Tourism Basic Law, are to contribute towards the furtherance of international friendship, the development of the national economy and enhancement of life of the Japanese people. To achieve these objectives, the measures to be taken by the Government are summarised as follows:

- To stimulate the inflow of foreign tourists and improve the reception services for them;
- To establish tourist resorts and routes for foreigners on a comprehensive and integrated basis;
- To ensure the safety of tourists while travelling and make it more convenient for them;
- To facilitate family travel and other travel by the general public;
- To relieve excessive concentration of tourists in specific tourist resorts;
- To develop tourism in underdeveloped regions;
- To protect, cultivate and develop tourist resources; and
- To maintain the beauty of tourist resorts.

The programmes for the implementation of these objectives have been described in detail in the two previous Annual Reports. No substantial changes in the objectives of government policy or the administrative organisation of tourism in Japan took place during 1986.

Actions and measures taken in 1986

Hotel accommodation/catering: In 1986, the number of Government registered international tourist hotels increased from 532 to 549 whereas registered international tourist ryokan fell by 10 to 1 639. As of 31st December 1986, the number of registered international tourist restaurants was 145.

Environment: Since 1965, the Government of Japan has sponsored an annual "Tourism Week" with the co-operation of the Japanese National Railways, local governments and other tourism-related organisations, from 1st to 5th August. These campaigns are designed for the improvement of tourist behaviour, the protection of tourist facilities, improving the beauty of tourist resorts, and ensuring the safety of the individual tourist.

In addition to the Tourism Week, five national campaigns for the protection of natural and cultural resources take place every year, covering nature protection, tree-planting, the protection of cultural properties, fire prevention and national parks.

Vocational training: Although all vocational training in tourism is left to private enterprises, three national examinations are held annually for Guide-Interpreters, Certified General Travel Agents and Certified Domestic Travel Agents. In 1986, 304 candidates succeeded as Guide-Interpreters, 3 065 passed to become Certified General Travel Agents and 4 732 passed to become Certified Domestic Travel Agents.

Aid and incentives: The Government provided financial assistance for the construction and extension of hotels, ryokan and restaurants which agree to maintain specific standards so that international tourism promotion may be enhanced and domestic tourism requirements will be met. During the 1985 financial year, loans made by government financing institutions amounted to approximately Y 46 billion.

New developments: With the aim of implementing the recommendations of the Council for Tourism Policy in 1984, the Ministry of Transport officially designated 15 areas in March 1986 as "New Sites of Discovery" or Government-designated international tourist areas. These areas will be developed and promoted with the aim of enabling foreign visitors to discover for themselves the attractions of areas which had not previously been on foreign itineraries, partly because of lack of publicity and partly because of insufficient reception facilities for foreign travellers.

Marketing research: According to a survey of public opinion on the use of free time and travel by the Japanese, made by the Prime Minister's Office in 1986, in those cases where more than three consecutive days of holiday were available, 45.5 per cent of respondents wished to use them for travel, staying overnight. A survey on "Foreign Tourist Expenditure" made by JNTO as basic data for the promotion of foreign travellers to Japan, revealed the rapid increase in the cost of accommodation and a decrease in the amount spent on food and drink as a result of the dramatic appreciation of the yen.

Protection of the tourist as a consumer: The "Have a nice trip '87" campaign, which was aimed at preventing problems while travelling, was conducted jointly by the Ministry of Transport, local government, the Japan Association of Travel Agents (JATA) and the Japan Association of Domestic Travel Agents, from 6th to 26th March 1987. The outlines of this campaign were as follows:

– Tourists were encouraged to use registered travel agents and to be provided with full explanations of the terms and conditions of the services provided to them;

– Facilities for reporting the activities of unregistered travel agents were established in the Ministry of Transport, local governments, JATA and the Japan Association of Domestic Travel Agents, and a system of co-operation with the National Police Agency was secured; and
– Officials of the Ministry of Transport and local government inspected travel agents to ensure they were obeying the Travel Agency Law.

International co-operation: As a part of its Technical Co-operation Programme, a group training course entitled "Tourism Promotion Seminar" was sponsored by the Japan International Co-operation Agency. The seminar, in which ten persons from ten developing countries participated, was held from October to December 1986 with the collaboration of the Ministry of Transport and the JNTO. The ASEAN Promotion Centre for Trade, Investment and Tourism, which was established in Tokyo in 1981 as a contribution to regional co-operation, had a budget in 1986 of Y 633 million, of which Y 574 million was contributed by the Japanese Government. The Centre's main activities in 1986 were the organisation of seminars on Japanese tourism, the Konnichiwa ASEAN Fair, and the ASEAN Travel Trade Seminar. In response to a request from the Government of Indonesia, the Japanese Government dispatched a study team to carry out a master plan and feasibility study for tourism development projects in West Java in 1986.

LUXEMBOURG

Government policy

The National Tourist Office and the Ministry of Tourism share responsibility for tourism. The National Tourist Office, which represents the communes of tourist interest and the local tourist offices of the Grand Duchy, has general responsibility for promoting and publicising the country's tourist facilities. The Ministry of Tourism, by contrast, decides on the allocation of grants, ensures the upkeep of a number of tourist attractions of national interest and finances Luxembourg's tourism offices abroad.

Since 1973, the Luxembourg Government has sought to pursue a medium-term tourism policy, by way of a series of five-year plans to improve tourist amenities. The block appropriation for the third five-year plan covering the period 1983-1987 totalled LF 400 million.

Actions and measures taken in 1986

The hotel industry was previously somewhat behind its foreign competitors, but it has now nearly caught up, largely thanks to the special assistance provided under the various five-year plans for improving tourist infrastructures. This aid will be increased still further in the context of the fourth five-year plan covering the period 1988-1992.

The principal advantages of Luxembourg from the tourism point of view are the beauty and diversity of its countryside and historical sites. Therefore, tourism policies always take account of the need to protect nature and the environment, in order to preserve natural resources and the attractiveness of the places to be visited.

In the context of the third five-year plan the Ministry of Tourism is endeavouring to promote cultural tourism, so as to highlight the country's historical sites and enable visitors to enjoy the exceptional range of buildings (churches, castles and famous mansions).

Lastly, the Ministry of Tourism is able to grant aid to individuals, particularly those linked with agricultural undertakings, whether farmed or not, so as to help them provide accommodation for tourists. This kind of economic reconversion, giving rural houses new uses, helps to preserve or even create jobs in regions where this has become an urgent necessity.

Marketing: The various groups involved in the national tourist industry have a wide range of very different interests, but they all have one thing in common: the desire for quality, which is encouraged by the National Tourist Office on the tourism supply side.

Advertising further takes account of the recent changes in tourists' requirements and emphasises the active holidays that they can enjoy in Luxembourg, whether from the cultural, sporting or entertainment points of view. Short holidays and weekends are also promoted, particularly for springtime and autumn visitors.

The Ministry of Tourism has stepped up its attendance at foreign exhibitions and commercial fairs connected with tourism and it is widening the range of its publicity material, with particular emphasis on the provision of facilities for holding congresses.

NETHERLANDS

Tourism in the Netherlands is an important economic activity in a country with a limited surface and a small population. In 1985, total revenues from domestic and international tourism accounted for an estimated 30 billion guilders (i.e. more than 10 per cent of the private final consumption) and provided directly 238 000 man-years of labour (i.e. 5 per cent of total employment and 10 per cent of that in the service sector).

Receipts from domestic tourism (including day trips) reached 25 billion guilders in 1985, representing 6 per cent of GNP. In that year, total receipts from international tourism made up 2 per cent of total exports of goods and services and came fifth after mineral fuels (21 per cent), foodstuffs and cattle (15 per cent), chemicals (15 per cent) and machinery (12 per cent).

To determine the valued-added element of domestic tourism, 45 per cent of total turnover is taken as a benchmark by the Netherlands Central Institute of Small and Medium-sized Businesses (CIMK). Applying this rule, the value added for domestic tourism in 1985 was 11.25 billion guilders or nearly 3.5 per cent of net national income at factor costs.

Comparison with other sectors reveals that it took sixth place after manufacturing (18.7 per cent), mining and quarrying (10.0 per cent), transport and communication (6.8 per cent), building and construction (5.6 per cent) and agriculture and fisheries (4.1 per cent).

Prospects for future development: In its 1986 Tourism Trends Report, the Netherlands Research Institute for Tourism and Recreation foresaw the following trends in Dutch holiday patterns in 1987 and subsequent years:

- Increased holidays abroad;
- A rising demand for the Netherlands as a second holiday destination and a fall in its popularity as a main holiday destination;
- The segment of the Dutch population who does not take any holiday for financial reasons will remain at its present level;
- A growth in the importance of the use of cottages for holiday purposes, both at home and abroad;
- A decline in the use of camping, primarily due to the falling popularity of this type of holiday among younger couples with no children;
- A shift from visits to small and medium-sized attractions to major ones;
- A slight improvement in the use of hotels and boarding houses (particularly outside the major cities) by the domestic market.

Government policy

Tourism falls within the competence of the Ministry of Economic Affairs, under the aegis of a state secretary, a junior minister in charge of small business affairs and tourism. Together with the industry, the government co-finances the activities of the Netherlands Board of Tourism (NBT – *Nederlands Bureau voor Toerisme*), an organisation established in 1968 to handle both domestic and international tourism.

In 1979, the fast-growing balance of trade deficit in travel prompted the government to initiate a more active policy that was stated in its "Tourist Policy Paper" of 1979. It focused on three main points:

- Better quality and price control in the tourism product (infrastructure, accommodation);
- Improved service provisions to enhance presentation of the product (accessibility, information, professional training, etc.); and
- Stronger promotion of tourism.

Underlying these objectives is the idea that central government should normally limit itself to stimulating and creating favourable conditions for the development of private enterprises. Tourism has now become one of eight priority areas of government policy, that is, areas considered to be the most favourable sectors for economic activity. To retain the gains made, "Policy Paper II, 1985-89" was issued and approved by Parliament in 1985.

Local and regional tourism information offices (VVVs) co-ordinate their work closely with the NBT and an organisational structure had been made that defines more specifically the division of tasks between the NBT and the VVVs and strengthens co-operation among all these organisations. The umbrella organisation of the VVVs – the General Netherlands Association of VVV Organisations (ANVV) – was responsible for promotion of tourism to and in the Netherlands prior to the appearance of the NBT and it now only serves as the association's secretariat. This body likewise receives financing from the central government.

Another important issue for the progress of tourism policy in 1986 was that important steps were taken to improve the tourist promotion function of Dutch embassies abroad, particularly in those countries where the NBT has no branch office. In general, the Ministry of Economic Affairs, responsible for tourism policy in the Netherlands, is of the opinion that the tourism promotion capacities of the embassies are strongly under-utilized.

Actions and measures taken in 1986

The Tourist Policy Paper II mentioned above considers that the co-operation (in a structured manner) of local government authorities is essential for updating and expanding the tourism product. With the help of the Ministry for Economic Affairs, the twelve Dutch provinces have prepared tourism-recreational development plans (TROPs), that analyse provincial strengths and weaknesses and recommend proposals for systematic expansion and improvement of this product. In areas considered to have the best opportunities from a national point of view (spearhead areas), a 75 per cent state subsidy for improving the public tourism infrastructure is provided. In 1986, 52 project schemes of the provinces were received by the Ministry of Economic Affairs with a total infrastructure component of some 90 million guilders. A number of those schemes had also been presented in 1985 but had not been awarded in that year. In 1986, eight schemes were remunerated in the form of a subsidy by the Ministry to a total amount of 13.3 million guilders. Practice shows that some schemes which do not receive a subsidy from the Ministry are nevertheless, wholly or partly, carried out. This is also an aspect of the effectiveness of policy stimulation in this context.

Marketing: The strategy for the domestic market can be described as follows:

- Maintaining the number of long holidays in combination with keeping the present average length of stay;
- Increasing the number of second and/or third holidays, short ones as well as longer ones, in the off-season;
- Putting emphasis on the elderly and the lower socio-economic segments; and
- Stimulating product-development programmes, focussing on active holidays and low-budget tourism.

Marketing on the domestic market is, for the greater part, done by institutional campaigns under the slogan "A nice stay in your own country". Activities are undertaken with an accent on direct contact with the potential consumer, e.g. via house-to-house distribution of brochures. The international marketing strategy is based on three different types of markets: from neighbouring countries, from other European countries and intercontinental markets.

For long-haul markets, stress is put on the main holidays. For neighbouring countries, promotional efforts are specially directed to increase the volume of second holidays. For these countries and other European countries, the stimulation of the demand for holidays for families with children is given particular attention.

Large promotional consumer campaigns jointly with carriers and the food-processing industries are undertaken in the United States, France and Germany. The marketing strategy stresses the importance of marketing efforts as closely related as possible to the appropriate phase in the decision process, by segment of potential travellers. This results in lower costs and more effectiveness.

Protection of the tourist as a consumer: The submission to Parliament of a Bill on the travel contract as part of the New Civil Code in 1986 marked a milestone in this field of policy. The travel contract as part of civil law will certainly mean more legal security for the consumer/traveller.

Staggering of holidays: The new scheme for the staggering of summer school holidays up to the school year 1991/92 was approved by the Minister of Education and Science. A new feature of the scheme is that a change has been made in the three geographical regions

(North, Middle, South) in which the country is divided for school-holiday staggering purposes (a rotation scheme of earlier, middle and later holiday periods). The three regions have now been tailored in such a way that the population figures are, in contrast to the previous situation, more or less balanced. The effectiveness of the new summer school holiday scheme, beginning in 1986, is expected to be better than in preceding years.

NEW ZEALAND

Tourism is one of New Zealand's major foreign income earners bringing NZ$ 1.4 million to the country. Returns of the main export industries for the year ended March 1986 and expressed in New Zealand dollars were as follows:

- Dairy products: 1.9 billion
- Manufacturing: 1.7 billion
- Meat: 1.6 billion
- Tourism and travel: 1.4 billion
- Wool: 0.9 billion
- Other primary products: 0.6 billion
- Forest products: 0.5 billion
- Other animal products: 0.5 billion

A forecasting paper of International Visitor Arrivals in New Zealand was prepared in 1986. The forecasts covering the five years to 1991 for the Australian, the United States, Japanese, United Kingdom, Canadian and West German markets are a guide to the projected volume of international visitor arrivals to New Zealand and thus provide users with a guideline as to the future growth. Upper and lower projections are included as well as the base figure in an attempt to define the possible range of future growth levels in international tourism numbers.

The forecast for the next five years is 7.8 per cent compounded annually, giving over one million visitors by 1991.

Government policy

The official body for tourism in New Zealand is the New Zealand Tourist and Publicity Department (NZTP) which reports to the Minister of Tourism. The Minister also receives advice from the New Zealand Tourism Council which is a voluntary organisation made up of executives from private and public sector companies closely associated with tourism. The tourism industry has formed the New Zealand Tourist Industry Federation to represent its views to Government and other organisations who have an interest in tourism. NZTP also runs 14 travel offices in 7 locations overseas whose primary task is the marketing of New Zealand.

A new priority of identifying and removing impediments to tourism's growth and development emerged in 1986, reflecting the Government's position on freeing the economy.

Actions and measures taken in 1986

Accommodation: A surge of activity on the hotel scene was observed with 10 projects, representing 2 150 rooms, being granted approval in principle for the 10.5 per cent cash grant (which now terminates on 31 March 1988). A number of sizeable hotel/motor inn projects also opened in 1986, going a considerable way to alleviating the "accommodation gap" brought about by New Zealand's dramatic growth in overseas visitor arrivals.

Transport: Information on policy development in the air transport sector is provided in Chapter IV.

Environment: NZTP commented on and monitored all Town and Country planning documents, park management plans, and environmental legislation, where the main objective is to protect the natural environment while gaining access to it for tourists in ways that do not degrade the natural environment.

NZTP was fully involved with and supported the Wild and Scenic Rivers legislation, and successfully pushed for the inclusion of geothermal waters. Comment was also made on the draft Conservation Act.

Vocational training: The "Training Needs Analysis" study jointly funded by the Government and the Industry, designed to determine the effectiveness of existing training programmes and to identify the training needs of tourism was completed in 1985. Action has continued to be taken in 1986 to implement the recommendations of the study.

The establishment of a Tourism Training and Development Unit has been approved and is expected to begin operations early in 1987. It will serve as a centre of expertise and information for the whole industry, including industry groups, educational institutions and individual companies. The Unit will work alongside existing Training Boards and Technical Institutes in providing the necessary training and will ensure that the industry's training needs in the future are better identified and provided for.

A Government grant was made in July 1986 to the Aviation and Travel Industry Training Board for the preparation of a specialised training video as part of a major hospitality training programme for New Zealand's International Airport staff.

Aids and incentives: 1986 saw the Community and Public Sector grant scheme increased to NZ$ 2.691 million, to further aid the funding of facilities used by visitors.

The 9.5 per cent Grant-in-Lieu of Depreciation scheme for major accommodation projects in key locations was increased to 10.5 per cent and is now available to accommodation developments of 100 or more rooms located anywhere in New Zealand. The scheme was also extended by a further year to 31 March 1988.

Under the Regional Promotion Assistance scheme, the Government offers assistance for regionally based tourism marketing. The major thrust of the scheme is for grants of NZ$ 5 000 to prepare regional marketing plans.

A new Regional Development Assistance scheme offers a grant of up to 50 per cent of eligible expenditure incurred in investigating the feasibility of approved projects that are new to the region. There is no maximum grant under this scheme.

The Government initiated a subsidy scheme to encourage the erection of standardised roadside information kiosks throughout the country.

Marketing research: The main emphasis for 1986 was on the establishment of a comprehensive database covering the key indicators of both overseas and domestic tourism, the improved dissemination of more user-oriented research results and on identifying the information needs of user organisations.

NZTP and the Tourist Industry Federation were joint sponsors of a tourism research conference held in July 1986.

The major research projects undertaken in 1986 were:
- the International Visitors Product Survey;
- the International Visitors Survey; and
- the New Zealand Domestic Travel Study.

Overseas market research has also been carried out and reports have or are being written on the German, Japanese, Australian, Canadian and the United Kingdom markets. A study of the activities of International Visitors in six regions of New Zealand was also completed as were two papers on the Economic Determinants of travel prepared for NZTP by McDermott Associates.

The annual publications, New Zealand Hotel/Motel Inventory and Room Occupancy Rates (licensed) and New Zealand Visitor Statistics were again published.

Marketing strategies: 1986 saw a more intensive promotion campaign in the major markets of Australia, the United States, Japan and Europe, with a stronger emphasis placed on the consumer market.

There was a significant increase in joint trade and advertising promotion with the private sector, airlines and New Zealand exporting companies.

A policy of market diversification was carried through to foreign language promotion material, advertising, and journalist and travel agent familiarisation tours.

Major events included the Te Maori Exhibition and associated trade shows in the United States, travel agent/consumer promotion in the United Kingdom and Europe, tourism missions to South East Asia, Middle East and Scandinavia and foreign language films for the Japanese, West German and Latin American markets.

The Department's domestic travel campaign was a booklet promoting off-peak travel. An on-going regional promotion scheme has contributed to increasing the development of New Zealand's tourism product and promotion.

A New Zealand Motoring Book has been produced and is designed to help motorists experience more of New Zealand.

NORWAY

Travel is one of the secondary industries in Norway. In 1985 the hotel and restaurant sector contributed NKr 8.2 billion to the GNP, some 1.7 per cent of the total value-added in the Norwegian economy. The tourism industry as a whole, including accommodation, catering, travel agencies and that part of the transport sector directly related to tourism, employed 4 per cent of the total labour force, some 71 000 people, of whom seven out of ten are women. Of these, 56 per cent were in the accommodation and catering sector and 37 per cent in transport.

The Norwegian travel balance is strongly in deficit with receipts in 1986 being only 40 per cent of expenditure. It is estimated that 41 per cent of the adult population travelled abroad during the summer (compared to only 35 per cent in 1982). International travel expenditure makes up between 6 and 6½ per cent of total private consumption.

Government policy

On 10th October 1986, the Government presented a report on travel and tourism to the National Assembly (*Storting*) which was approved in February 1987. Some of the main points in this Report are set out below.

The travel and tourism industry shall be treated "on a par with other industries" with regard to various public loan and grant schemes. Among other things, the scope of the Norwegian Industrial Fund will be extended to include travel and tourism.

Greater efforts will be concentrated on research, guidance and studies in the field of travel and tourism. Vocational and leadership training within the industry will be given high priority.

It is the opinion of the Government that the primary objective of the travel and tourism industry should be to focus on special products and markets that can generate a "longer stay" for tourists and longer seasons. This type of strategy will enable the industry to make a greater contribution to the country's economy and employment situation.

The Government advocates establishing framework conditions and resources for the industry aimed at developing a trade that can stand on its own feet and ensure its own further growth.

"Travel and tourism – a factor in municipal and county planning". The authorities' use of public means to establish favourable conditions for new business activities within travel and tourism will be based on county plans in which the "geographical target areas" are designated and given priority. Furthermore, the authorities will base their decisions on municipal plans which, in the words of the Report, will "indicate an overall development policy, where other business activities, public infrastructure investments and services of various types are also included in the total range of activities".

Regulations for charter flights. The Government refers to the fact that international and national regulations governing charter flights may have an effect on the number of tourists travelling to Norway from abroad. In the provisions now in force, there are certain general limitations with regard to charter groups flying *to* Norway. Tour operators maintain that special marketing efforts can be made in this sector which will result in a greater number of tourists if the regulations are eased. These questions and the regulations governing charter flights between the Scandinavian countries are given favourable consideration in connection with a Report to the *Storting* regarding the concession policy for air services, which was presented at the end of 1986. The Report is taken up in more detail in Chapter IV.

Actions and measures taken in 1986

Marketing and research: The Central Bureau of Statistics has conducted a survey covering the level of holiday-taking among Norwegian adults in Norway and abroad, and the volume and value of all types of tourism trips taken by Norwegian people in 1986.

In 1986 NORTRA (Nortravel Marketing, a commercial and operative body serving as the trade's service organisation) launched the campaign "Get familiar with Norway" in order to influence the national market.

PORTUGAL

Tourism plays a major role in the country's economy and its contribution to GDP is already close to that of agriculture and fishing and civil engineering, and practically equal to that of the banking sector. Likewise, it covers over 36 per cent of the trade deficit. It is a key factor in reducing the balance of payments deficit and the second most important source of foreign currency earnings in the Portuguese economy. In terms of employment, it provides jobs for some 150 000 workers, which means that tourism, in relation to the rest of the productive sector, can be ranked as one of the industries with the highest *per capita* return in the country.

Tourism is in a constant state of flux and adjustments have to be made in order to keep pace with the developments and trends as they appear in both supply and demand. Over the past ten years we have seen major changes and trends of a qualitative character that provide some indications as to the policy that the industry should pursue. What these qualitative trends would seem to suggest is that:

– Up until 1990 tourism worldwide will expand at an average annual rate of 5.1 per cent in terms of arrivals at frontiers;
– The main destination will continue to be Europe and the Mediterranean in particular, but new destinations will make their appearance as will new tourist sources, while others will decline in importance;
– Up until the end of the 1980s, tourist expenditure worldwide is likely to increase at an average annual rate of 6.7 per cent;
– Based on the projection of past trends, it seems likely that, up until 1990, tourism in Portugal will expand at a far faster rate than tourism worldwide, as can be seen from the table showing the forecast trends in international demand over the medium term.

PORTUGAL. **Forecast trends in international demand over the medium term (1986-1990)**

	Units (thousands)		Average annual change (%) 1986-1990
	1986	1990	
Arrivals of visitors at frontiers	13 057	19 917	+ 11.1
Arrivals of tourists at frontiers	5 409	8 621	+ 12.3
Nights spent in all types of accommodation	43 910	67 078	+ 11.1
Nights spent in hotels	14 273	20 445	+ 9.4

Government policy

The overall tourism policy objectives as well as the priorities and programmes of the National Tourism Plan for the period 1986-89 were set out in the 1986 edition of the Annual Report.

However, the institutional framework and the operations of the official agencies responsible for tourism matters have undergone one or two changes. On 3rd December 1986 the Tourism Promotion Institute was set up to perform the promotional functions that were previously carried out by the Directorate-General for Tourism. It is hoped this agency will provide an institutional framework for collaboration with all the public bodies so as to prevent a dispersal of effort and increase the effectiveness of the amounts spent, thereby responding to the legitimate demands of the sectors that have for a long time been arguing in favour of such an initiative. The financial and human resources required to carry out this task will therefore be transferred from the Directorate-General for Tourism to the Institute.

As part of the plan to strengthen regional tourism structures, a new tourism region was created in April 1986: "Regiao de Turismo Dao – Lafoes".

Actions and measures taken in 1986

Development of supply: The Council of Ministers has approved Decree-Law No. 328/86 regulating accommodation and catering facilities and replacing a Decree-Law of 1959, which had become outdated. The radical changes that have taken place in the country's administrative system together with the continual expansion of tourism have led to the development of new types of tourist accommodation that were not foreseen by the earlier law.

As far as changes in the administrative structure are concerned, these have involved the creation of autonomous regions and the granting of autonomy to the communes, with the consequent devolution of powers that had previously been exercised by central government departments. The law is intended to cater for this new situation.

Without losing sight of this institutional requirement, however, it was considered essential that the law should also be designed to preserve the quality of the tourist facilities and the natural environment that constitute the essential components of Portugal's tourism supply; this it does by taking into account the consequences of decentralisation and in this respect the new Decree-Law marks a transition. The Directorate-General for Tourism retains its responsibilities with regard to hotels and hotel investment projects, from both tourism and environmental standpoints. Moreover, it is for the same reasons that, for the first time, standards have been established regarding the creation of zones that are naturally suited for tourism purposes. In the case of these standards and in the context of decentralisation, what has been established is the right to enforce strict conditions in order, on the one hand, to protect the environment and the country's existing cultural heritage and on the other, to ensure the quality of the tourist facilities that are planned. Similarly, under certain conditions it is also possible for some zones to be declared of no touristic value.

In addition, the legislative framework for the new tourist accommodation built during the 1970s and 1980s has been established. In view of the fact that tourism is an activity essential to the country's economy, the system embodied in this new law is an attempt to eliminate bureaucratic obstacles and enable those concerned to obtain a satisfactory and rapid response. For example, the whole process involved in opening new establishments is now centralised in the prefectures, which avoids having to apply to a series of departments, as was previously the case.

On 3rd September 1986 the Council of Ministers approved Decree-Law No. 264 setting out the standards governing the activities of travel agencies and bringing these into line with EEC standards, particularly as regards freedom of establishment and freedom to provide services, for which previously one of the requirements had been that the person concerned should have Portugese nationality. The changes made also include a revised classification of travel agencies into three categories. The regulatory Decree in this case (No. 22/87 of 19th March 1987) brings the operation of travel agencies into line with Community regulations.

In 1986 ENATUR (National Tourism Enterprise), which is responsible for the preservation and operation of the State-run inns (*Pousadas*), added a further three to its list: at Almeida and Marvao, both in the north of the country, and at S. Bras de Alportel in the Algarve. ENATUR has also installed swimming pools at the Sta. Luzia Hotel as well as at the *Pousadas* of Santo Antonio do Serem and Santiago do Cacem. In 1986, therefore, this State enterprise, which is the only one in the tourism sector, continued to carry out one of its main tasks, which is the construction, extension and conversion of its inns in order to meet the demands of the tourist trade.

Vocational training: The National Tourism Training Institute, which is under the authority of the Secretary of State for Tourism, has begun work on converting a large building in Coimbra for use as a hotel school and, in addition, the Institute has continued with the building of the hotel school in Estoril to cope with the industry's growing demand for training.

Environment: With a view to protection of the environment, natural resources and the country's cultural heritage, the Secretary of State for Tourism and his counterparts at the Ministries for Cultural Affairs and the Environment have signed co-operation agreements which have led to positive action being taken, such as the demolition of a number of buildings and houses erected illegally on sites of tourist or cultural interest, and which were out of keeping with their surroundings. This co-operation has also resulted in the mapping out of tourist and cultural circuits, which will help in publi-cising Portugal's heritage and in the organisation of tourists' activities and leisure.

Aid and incentives: The Secretary of State for Tourism, with the co-operation of the Tourism Fund, has introduced a low-interest loan scheme to promote new investment in the sector (including investment in new amenities) and to upgrade the supply through the rehabilitation of dilapidated or substandard facilities.

The Directorate-General for Tourism has stepped up its programme of inspection of premises and insists on the necessary work being done to bring these up to the advertised standard.

Marketing: As is done every year, surveys were carried out on the holiday habits of the Portuguese and those of foreign tourists, interviewed at the frontiers.

Portugal's tourist offices abroad continued their efforts aimed at reaching those segments of the market likely to be attracted by what is on offer during the low season, particularly in the form of events and facilities. As the result of the expansion of such facilities, and especially sports amenities, Portugal is managing to even out its high season and it has one of the highest occupancy rates among tourist countries in Europe during the winter period.

Protection of the tourist as a consumer: The government is more than ever concerned with standards of quality in the tourist industry and accordingly supports all the efforts made in this connection by the private sector and the regions. Furthermore, the new hotel schools will provide an additional supply of skilled manpower and will help to improve the general standard of tourist services.

International co-operation: An agreement regarding tourism has been signed between the Government of the State of Espirito Santo in Brazil and Portugal's Secretary of State for Tourism.

In the context of the tourism agreement between the Kingdom of Morocco and the Republic of Portugal, the second Joint Portugese-Moroccan Commission met in Rabat and practical co-operation has started in the areas of vocational training and the promotion of tourism.

SPAIN

Tourism is of major importance to the Spanish economy. For a number of years the country has been in the throes of a social and economic crisis, with unemployment rising year after year up until the second quarter of 1985, since when it has been stable at around 21 per cent of the labour force – the highest level in any OECD Member country. Throughout all these years, however, employment in tourism has increased in both absolute and relative terms, rising from 9.9 per cent of the employed population (1 140 000 jobs including direct, indirect and tourism-generated employment) in 1980 to 15 per cent (1 600 000 jobs)in 1985.

Whereas receipts from tourism represented only 3.3 per cent of GDP in 1980, by 1986 the figure had risen to 5.2 per cent. The multiplier effect of tourist expenditure raises this figure to 9.3 per cent, putting tourism in third place after trade and construction.

It is also almost entirely due to tourism, which accounts for half of all invisible earnings, that the current balance has been positive since 1984. Moreover, since 1984 the positive tourism balance has offset not only the substantial negative trade balance but also the negative balance for income from investment. Tourism is likely to make an even more substantial contribution to the external account in 1987, since the trade deficit is expected to widen still further.

By contributing to the development of certain regions, and particularly those along the coast, tourism has also been instrumental in improving the regional and per capita distribution of national income, thereby also changing the pattern of consumption of the local inhabitants and triggering off a process of acquisition of material and cultural goods.

But not all the effects of tourism are positive: the excessive building that has taken place in some areas, for example, has had an adverse impact on both the physical and the social environment. This problem of geographical and human concentration is compounded by the problem of seasonal concentration: more than 45 per cent of Spain's foreign visitors come during the third quarter of the year.

Government policy

The Ministry of Transport, Tourism and Communications (*(Ministerio de Transportes, Turismo y Comunicaciones)* is responsible for tourism policy.

Spain's present tourism policy is conditioned by a long history of State interventionism and the considerable importance of tourism in economic terms. The State has maintained close control over this activity, despite the implementation of Title VIII of the 1978 Constitution, which has meant the transfer to the governments of the seventeen Autonomous Communities of a large number of responsibilities with regard to tourism that previously had been confined solely to central government.

Article 148 of the Constitution states that the Autonomous Communities may assume powers with regard to the planning and promotion of tourism within their territory. Accordingly, they were granted the legislative, planning and administrative powers previously exercised by central government with respect to the hotel trade, travel agencies, camping sites, tourism occupa-

tions and land-use planning. On the other hand, the General Secretariat for Tourism still has responsibility for promotional activities abroad, administration of the *paradors*, loans to the industry, national registers of tourism businesses, occupations and activities, and international relations.

A reorganisation of the central tourism services was put into effect by a Decree of 19th June 1985. The General Secretariat for Tourism was made responsible for the development and implementation of national tourism policy and top-level management and supervision of tourism services. The General Secretariat comprises a General Directorate for Tourism Policy and two autonomous agencies, the National Institute for the Promotion of Tourism, whose task is to attract tourists to Spain, and the Spanish Tourism Administration, which is responsible for managing the 86 establishments making up the *parador* chain.

Spain's tourism policy has three main aims:

– To maintain Spain's share of the market by continuing to provide the same good value for money as at present;
– To improve the tourism supply by modernising accommodation and leisure facilities, and by promoting economies of scale and computerisation;
– To encourage further development of the tourism supply and leisure facilities by promoting longer tourist seasons, a better geographic spread and a diversification of the demand.

In order to achieve these aims, the General Secretariat for Tourism has concentrated its efforts on the following areas.

Diversification of the supply: The current programmes are designed to develop tourism in rural areas, tourism involving sporting or cultural activities, tourism for health purposes, for senior citizens, businessmen and conventions.

In addition to undertaking studies that will serve as the basis for a marketing strategy, it is planned to set up a computerised system of tourism information in conjunction with the regional governments, as well as a tourism documentation centre. The General Secretariat for Tourism's promotional budget for 1987 will amount to Ptas 4 billion, an increase of 20 per cent on the 1986 budget.

Modernisation of the tourism supply and services: There are plans not only for the modernisation of existing amenities and the introduction of new management techniques, but also for the construction of new leisure facilities. In addition, there are plans to provide pre-service and in-service training courses in recreational management, languages, new computer-based techniques, etc. In this connection, it should be mentioned that the Official Tourism School is under the authority of the General Directorate for Tourism Policy and the General Secretariat for Tourism.

In 1986, grants or loans totalling more than Ptas 12 billion were made for modernising existing installations or developing specific facilities. The State investment banks provide longer-term and cheaper loans to the tourism sector than to other industries. In addition, private loans may be guaranteed or subsidised by central government or the regional governments.

SWEDEN

As with the other Scandinavian countries, international tourism is not one of the most prominent of national industries, with the "travel" account receipts contributing just over one per cent to GDP. The industry caters very largely to the domestic market with less than a quarter of the nights spent in the various means of accommodation being attributable to foreign visitors. Sweden is much more a tourism generating country, with a substantial excess of expenditure abroad over receipts derived from foreign visitors (which in 1985 were only 60 per cent of expenditure).

Government policy

Tourism in Sweden comes within the overall sphere of the Ministry for Agriculture. However, in view of the growing importance of tourism, a separate Minister for Tourism, Sports and Youth, was appointed in the autumn of 1986, with responsibility for Government action in the field of tourism and recreation. Government policy in this field, which was confirmed by the Swedish Parliament in May 1984, has not been changed.

The main objectives of this policy are:

– To improve the balance of payments;
– To stimulate regional development and employment; and
– To improve tourism facilities for all residents.

It can be stated, however, that the general political awareness of the importance of tourism and recreation has increased markedly during the last few years.

Some 60 proposals relating to different items associated with tourism were introduced by members of the Swedish Parliament during the 1986-87 session. Priority has been given to the following items:

– The need for more research as well as better education and vocational training;
– Actions to facilitate tax and customs regulations for tourists and other restrictions on tourist traffic into and within the country;

– Development of the transportation system, including railway and air connections with tourist areas in northern Sweden.

The Government's guidelines state clearly that public measures must primarily be directed towards supporting initiatives taken by individual companies and by the tourist industry. The capacity of the enterprises for renewing and developing their establishments will provide the basis for their ability to compete within the tourism sector.

In order to support more effectively the realisation of the government tourism policy, the Swedish Tourist Board, to which the Government has given the responsibility of developing and co-ordinating the marketing of Sweden as a tourist destination, decided in August 1986 to change the organisational structure of the Board as well as its strategy, thus giving priority to:

– A better concentration and a more logical segmentation of its marketing activities;
– Closer co-operation with the tourist industry and the provision of better consultation services in order to reach greater profitability and a clearer definition of responsibilities;
– The creation of a more distinct profile of Sweden as an international tourist destination;
– The building up of an adequate computerised information system for market research and travel statistics.

Under the new organisation, there are now separate departments for Research and Development, Business and Product Development, Marketing Development and Consultation Services.

Actions and measures taken in 1986

Accommodation: During 1986, there was a net expansion in the hotel sector of some 3 500 rooms, 500 of which were in the three largest cities, Stockholm, Göteborg and Malmö. This resulted in an increase of the total available hotel capacity by 5.5 per cent. Accommodation in registered hotels has increased by 2.2 per cent in 1986 and, as a result, there was a decline in the average occupancy rate. The new hotel investments did not come about by Government intervention or subsidies but strictly on a free market basis. In 1986, the number of authorised camping sites increased by some 40 units (an increase of 6 per cent). In total, there are now 750 camping sites all over Sweden, and some 200 of them are open even during the winter season. The holiday-check system intended for Swedish residents, which has been discussed over the last few years, is still under consideration.

Transport: Ferry and airline transport is a very important part of Swedish tourism. Some 35 million people travel each year to and from Sweden by ferry. The supply of ferry capacity, which has increased heavily over recent years, has continued to expand in 1986, especially on the lines to and from Finland and Germany. Recent developments in Scandinavian airline policy is discussed in Chapter IV.

Aids and subsidies: The policy of granting loans and subsidies to tourist projects from Government sources has been continued in 1986. The overall purpose of these is to support both long-term and short-term employment, mainly in the northern part of the country. Tourism is regarded as a sector for which the cost/benefit ratio of assistance is very positive.

Marketing: Since 1985, an annual survey of nearly 8 000 prople has been regularly undertaken (with ten additional much smaller samples each year) to follow the changes in the holiday and recreation patterns of the Swedish population. This forms a very important data base for the co-ordinated planning of domestic market activities, which is available also for companies and organisations co-operating in the tourism industry. Sweden has made considerable recent efforts to encourage the business and conference visitors, particularly in the larger cities, but there is still a heavy emphasis on activity and touring holidays, both by land and water.

SWITZERLAND

Tourism continues to represent one of the main sources of income from trade in economic goods between Switzerland and other countries. In 1986 it accounted for about 8.4 per cent of foreign currency earnings and the total turnover from domestic and international tourism amounted to SF 17 billion or 7 per cent of gross national product.

Revenues from international tourism and transport amounted to SF 9.7 billion in 1986, ranking third as an export sector after the metal/mechanical engineering industry and chemicals, and third in terms of sector income balances with a surplus of some SF 2.8 billion.

In 1986, the hotel and catering industry provided work for some 183 000 persons, with a further 80 000 employed in tourism-related activities. Tourism thus provided a living for approximately 9 per cent of Switzerland's working population.

Prospects for development: For 1987 the forecast is for slight or moderate growth in tourism from the European countries, and in particular Germany, France and Italy, whereas it is likely to be difficult to achieve a similar result in the case of the United Kingdom due to the weakness of the pound vis-à-vis the Swiss franc. There is expected to be continued substantial demand from North America, with a possible increase of 5-10 per cent in the number of nights spent, as the result

of growth in individual travel, while the demand for package tours is likely to level off, due to the fear of terrorism. It should be noted that domestic tourism, which virtually offset the drop in foreign demand in 1986, is again expected to play an important role.

Government policy

Responsibility as regards tourism is vested, with the *Service du Tourisme*, in the *Office Fédéral de l'Industrie, des Arts et Métiers et du Travail* (OFIAMT – Federal Office for Industry, Arts and Crafts and Labour) attached to the Federal Department for the Economy. The "Swiss tourism strategy" ("*Conception suisse du tourisme*") is still the basis for tourism policy in Switzerland. The objectives set out in this strategy, which was declared mandatory in 1981 by the Government (Federal Council) in respect of the major issues as regards tourism policy, are still valid. These are contained in 53 regional development programmes and in the general land use plans of the various cantons.

When reviewing important measures with regard to tourism policy, there is constant concern to give effect to the qualitative growth called for in this strategy. In 1986, the Federal Administration drew up a number of new measures with regard to national promotion of tourism and loans to the hotel industry and holiday resorts. These incentives should in the future help to improve the standard of tourist amenities and the use made of existing facilities. With respect to regulations regarding land-use planning, protection of the environment, the grant of licences for the operation of tourist transport facilities and the sale of land to persons living abroad, the emphasis has been on an orderly development of tourism.

Actions and measures taken in 1986

Marketing: In 1986, the Confederation granted SF 21 million to the *Office National Suisse du Tourisme* (ONST), the agency responsible for promotion in the country and through its 24 representatives abroad.

On the domestic market the ONST has continued to provide a general information service using a range of media: press, radio, television, the magazine "Switzerland", electronic media and tourist information over the phone by dialling 120. Promotional activities, as is natural in a confederation, are carried out for the most part by regional and local tourist authorities, together with the private sector.

On the international level, the ONST is continuing to computerise its representations, make increasing use of electronic media and actively promote public transport. Its prime targets have been the Benelux countries, France, United Kingdom, Italy and Germany. In mid-October, five German cities were visited during the course of a large-scale public relations operation conducted by a delegation which included the ONST, the Swiss Hoteliers Association and the regional directors of tourism.

Switzerland has a tradition as a tourist country that dates back some 200 years so, started in 1986, the entire marketing campaign will take as its theme: "Two hundred years of tourism in Switzerland – A bright future for our visitors". Visitors and tourists alike have had the opportunity of reliving all sorts of pleasant experiences.

Market research: The *Fédération Suisse du Tourisme* (FST) has attempted, by means of a representative survey, to measure the perception that the Swiss have of tourism and, indirectly, their attitude toward tourists. The results show that the Swiss recognise the great importance of tourism as an economic activity, particularly as far as the mountain areas are concerned. By and large, they are aware of tourism's realities and implications. Thus, the "average Swiss" in theory accepts the need to be more pleasant to tourists.

As regards the international markets, the *Office National Suisse du Tourisme* (ONST) took part in a survey of the holiday habits of tourists from the Federal Republic of Germany vacationing in the central and eastern sections of the Alpine range (survey carried out jointly with the Bavarian, Austrian and Italian organisations). In addition, a market survey on tourists from a number of Arabic-speaking countries was carried out in conjunction with the German and Austrian tourist boards.

Aid to the hotel industry: In the context of the implementation of the Federal Act on the promotion of credit for the hotel industry and holiday resorts, the aid granted by the *Société Suisse de Crédit Hôtelier* (SCH) is for the purpose of facilitating the construction and modernisation of hotels in mountain areas. In 1986, the SCH granted loans amounting to SF 19.26 million for the modernisation of hotels and holiday resorts, the construction of new hotels, and hotel purchase; the interest rate on these loans was 5.5 per cent per annum.

For projects included in a programme of development under the Federal Act on aid to investment in mountain areas particularly worthy of support, the SCH has, in several cases, undertaken to pay part of the interest to the amount of 2 per cent per annum for an initial period of three and a maximum of five years on loans it has guaranteed.

Of the total guarantees and loans of SF 43.5 million, SF 20.5 million (47.1 per cent) were for the modernisation of hotels in tourist areas and mountain regions in accordance with the Federal Act on investment in mountain areas, SF 5.5 million (12.7 per cent) for the replacement of hotels by new constructions, SF 8.6 million (6.3 per cent), for the modernisation or creation of tourist facilities in holiday resorts, and SF 6.2 million (14.2 per cent) to finance the purchase of hotels. With the assistance of guarantees and loans by the SCH in 1986, a total volume of investments of approximately SF 350 million was financed.

Government aid is confined to loans and guarantees for bank loans. There are no government subsidies or tax incentives.

Aids to tourist infrastructure: Loans granted by the Confederation (mostly interest-free) under the Federal Act on aid to investment are designed to finance community facilities in mountain areas. Between 1975 and 1986 they totalled SF 703 million (2 548 projects). Among the projects financially supported by the Confederation, many relate to tourism infrastructure and, for the ten years up to the end of 1986, Federal lending amounted to SF 92 million. In 1986, SF 10.4 million was devoted to the construction of tourist transport infrastructure, sport facilities, museums and conference centres.

Under the Federal Act on aid to investment in mountain areas, the Confederation is authorised to support the activities of regional secretaries/organisers. Up to the end of 1986, 43 of them had obtained federal financial assistance. It should be emphasized that, in most mountain areas, tourism is an important economic sector and that the activities of the secretaries/organisers also include that of promoting the development of tourism.

Up to the end of 1986, the Federal Department for the Economy had approved 53 regional development programmes, to the implementation of which the Confederation contributed by allocating subsidies amounting to some 80 per cent of the total cost. The establishment of regional programmes is a necessary prior condition for the granting of aid enabling community facilities or the construction and modernisation of hotels in mountain areas to be financed on concessional terms. Given the importance of tourism for these regions, the development programmes invariably devote several chapters to tourism activities and deal in detail with the following aspects: analysis of the current situation, development potential and outlook, definition of objectives and choice of development projects. These development programmes cover a period of between 10 and 15 years. They include a 4 or 5-year investment programme and a financial plan. By the end of 1986, 37 of these programmes had been reviewed and approved.

Vocational training: Two Orders have been adopted regarding the minimum requirements for recognition of higher schools of tourism and higher schools of catering.

Employment: During the course of 1986 there were two factors that helped to improve the pay, conditions and social welfare of persons working in the tourism sector in general and in the hotel and catering trades in particular. Details of the improvement both in pay scales and in the protection afforded to seasonal workers and holders of short-term permits are given below.

Improvement in pay scales: In the context of the adjustment of minimum wages provided for in the collective labour agreement, the professsional associations of the hotel and catering trades established the new pay scales that would apply from 1st May 1986 to all hotel and catering workers on a fixed wage. Compared with the pay scales in force since 1st May 1985 under this agreement, these new scales represent an increase of 3.2 per cent in the nominal wage rates for the industry. Based on the results of the survey on workers' pay in the hotel and catering trades conducted in July 1986 as part of the general statistical survey on wages and salaries, average incomes rose by 2.6 per cent between July 1985 and July 1986. Taking into account the inflation rate of 0.5 per cent, this represents an increase of 2 per cent in

real terms. The rise in income for male employees (2.9 per cent) was slightly greater than that for female employees (2.3 per cent). The breakdown by type of establishment shows that levels of pay increased by 2.7 per cent in the hotel trade and by 2.3 per cent in the catering trade.

Improvement in the protection afforded to seasonal workers and holders of short-term permits: A new Order restricting the number of foreigners came into force on 1st November 1986. It provided the occasion for introducing a new provision making it a general rule for employers to produce a written contract of employment when submitting an application to hire seasonal or temporary staff. The main purpose of this is to make it easier for employment offices to monitor the conditions of hire for workers in these categories. This new regulation will mostly benefit seasonal workers and holders of short-term permits employed in the hotel and catering sector.

Protection of the tourist as a consumer: Under the Federal Act on unfair competition and the Order on price information, the Federal Court has ruled that it is a requirement that, in advertisements for holidays, the price should be marked very clearly. In order to protect consumers (and also to ensure fair competition within the industry) every travel advertisement has to state the precise destination, the duration of the holiday, the means of transport, the class of accommodation, the meals that are included in the basic price, the taxes that are payable and how long the offer lasts.

International co-operation: In the context of technical co-operation in the tourism sector, Switzerland disbursed a total of SF 2 357 000 in 1986, broken down as follows:

– Nairobi Hotel School, Kenya: SF 1 343 000;
– Training of mountain guides in Peru: SF 62 000;
– Grants for students from developing countries enrolling at the Hotel Management School at Glion, Switzerland: SF 952 000.

Transport: The development of tourist transport concessions (cablecars, gondola lifts, ski tows), was mostly confined to modernising existing facilities and increasing their carrying capacity. New concessions were granted for a cablecar and a gondola lift and several ski tows, while eight installations were replaced by more modern equipment. The tendency whereby concessions in major ski resorts are accorded only for purposes of increasing capacity has continued.

TURKEY

For Turkey, tourism, while playing a relatively small part in the overall economy, with its receipts making up only 2.1 per cent of GNP, is of major importance as a source of foreign currency. Six per cent of all foreign currency earnings are attributable to tourism and receipts from tourism make up one-fifth of the national invisibles income. Employment in the tourism sector constitutes 3.3 per cent of all registered workers but, because of the very large agricultural element, it forms a much greater part of service sector employment.

After a serious setback in 1986, it is estimated that the number of foreign arrivals will increase in 1987 to 2.8 million (a rise of some 17 per cent) and that receipts will also grow substantially to around $1.22 billion.

Government policy

The principal body responsible for tourism is the Ministry of Culture and Tourism, which carries out the general measures taken by the State Planning Organisation (DPT). There are also some other institutions that take part in tourism promotion, training and the provision of credit and loans to investors during the initial investment and operational stages. These are: the Promotion Foundation of Turkey (TUTAV), the Tourism Development and Training Foundation (TUGEV), and the Tourism Bank (*Turizm Bankasi*). However, in order to maintain cultural and historical national assets which can also have tourism functions (like accommodation facilities, restaurants, cafés, etc.), the restoration of historic buildings will continue to be carried out by the appropriate institutions.

Infrastructural investments for tourism development are provided by the government in planning areas; investments in actual facilities are left to the private sector. Tourism investments are realised in accordance with the physical plans prepared by the government and incentives are given for priority areas.

On the other hand, in order to increase the accommodation capacity in the country, public lands are rented to private investors for fairly long periods, with additional incentives to attract experienced foreign investors. Credits are given to investors during the initial investment and operational stages. The existing laws, legislation and enactments contain provisions to correct the shortcomings of certain investment activities.

By means of an active promotion and marketing policy, the number of foreign tourists coming to Turkey is expected to increase. Emphasis will be given to foreign language education and the training of experienced personnel to overcome the shortcomings in the sector. In the domestic market, there will also be certain investment facilities provided for vocational training of Turkish citizens.

New priorities which have been added to the existing objectives are the development of better international transportation facilities in Antalya and Izmir airports and the provision of the necessary support arrangements for expanding cruise tourism and yacht facilities.

Actions and measures taken in 1986

Accommodation: To implement the policy of increasing the contribution of the tourism sector to the national economy, an overall evaluation of tourism potential has been undertaken by drawing up comprehensive plans that maintain "the balance between resource preservation and utilisation". Within this overall framework, 18 separate tourism master plans, 17 of which were for coastal areas authorised as tourism investment priority regions, have been prepared and approved during the years since the early 1970s. These plans envisage a total tourist bed capacity of 615 908, including 79 328 camping spaces. The number of establishments which have been issued with tourism investment certificates and the number of establishments in operation, as at the end of 1986, is as follows:

- Establishments issued investment certificates:
  Up to 1986: 629 (99 534 beds); During 1986: 261 (39 997 beds)
- Establishments issued operation certificates:
  Up to 1986: 731 (92 129 beds); During 1986: 97 (9 764 beds)

The establishments with operation certificates include hotels, motels, holiday villages, pensions, inns and camp sites.

Environment and cultural heritage: Excavations in 67 archaeological sites and ground research in 37 regions were carried out. The restoration of touristic and cultural heritage from past civilisations was continued. This included the restoration and landscaping of the surrounding areas of five ruins, twelve castle ramparts and twenty other monuments, the restoration of fifteen buildings of civil architecture suitable for exhibition, the preparation of eight monuments and museums as exhibition sites, the maintenance and restoration of nine museums, the equipping of one museum against fire and theft and reinforcing the construction of two other museums.

Research has been done on a total of 133 area sites (67 in 1984, 48 in 1985 and 18 in 1986) and of these, the result of the work on 93 sites was evaluated and decisions taken by the Higher Council of Immovable Cultural and Natural Assets.

Special projects include the Göreme site, the Topkapi and Yildiz Palaces in Istanbul (in co-operation with UNESCO), the ancient city of Stratonikeia, the protection and development of Ankara Castle, and the restoration and landscaping of the area around Mt. Nemrut.

Vocational training: Some of the Hotel and Tourism Vocational High Schools connected with the Ministry of National Education, Youth and Sports were reorganised from the aspect of curriculum and planning by placing an emphasis on foreign languages and practical work, with the title of "Anadolu Hotel Management Vocational High Schools". For specific training in the tourism service sector, the Ministry of Culture and Tourism has planned to increase the number of Tourism Educational Centres from three to six during 1987. The Ministry is responsible for on-the-job training, by organising: a month-long course at the Tourism Educational Centres (TUREM); a 24-day course in hotels, restaurants and entertainment sites (an on-the-job training course); and a nine-month course for professional tourist guides. In 1986, 744 people graduated from on-the-job training courses and the TUREM courses are still continuing.

Aids and incentives: Investment for tourism in the scheduled areas is supported by the state in various ways, by supplying infrastructure, providing investment credits up to 75 per cent, renting land, giving tax exemptions, and customs releases. Specific infrastructure projects have included the following:

- The infrastructure works for Titreyengöl-Acisu-Sorgun Kilca were carried out;
- South Antalya (Kemer-Kiziltepe): Electricity, water supply, canalization and communication works were completed;
- Köycegiz-Iztuzu: The highway is completed and the construction of drinking-water installations have been commenced;
- The establishment and feasibility studies of infrastructure needed for tourism and urban development of the Mugla coastal area are completed;
- The studies and research for drinking-water supplies in Sarigelme are finished and the work on the highway project has also been finished; the construction of canalization of Alanya-Marmaris is being continued;
- Work concerning the storage of the coal slag of Zonguldak has been started; and
- The construction of Bodrum and Antalya marinas is in progress.

Social tourism: In the field of social tourism projects, in the Belek-Antalya area, 250 four-bed tents were added to the existing 500 three-bed tents together with all the necessary infrastructure and auxiliary units. To cover the financial cost of this project for the year 1986, TL 1 billion has been provided from the Social Housing Project Fund and TL 50 million from the 1986 budget.

A new Social Tourism Centre is being planned on a site of 300 000 square metres, allocated to the Ministry in Izmir-Seferihisar. The work has already begun.

Marketing: The Ministry of Culture and Tourism is responsible for promoting tourism activities by a variety of means, including national and international exhibitions, travel fairs, workshops and cultural festivals, film presentations and audio-visual shows. It also produces and distributes promotional literature in several languages in addition to inviting members of the foreign press, radio and television and representatives of travel agencies or tour operators to see what Turkey has to offer. The social-economic structure, preferences and habits of potential tourists in the countries marketed are taken into consideration, through Turkey's 17 foreign offices of tourism.

The Ministry, whose main target is to increase the foreign exchange receipts from tourism, undertakes advertising activities mainly in international markets rather than the national market. To achieve this goal, the Ministry has used poster campaigns and advertising in newspapers, magazines and travel trade magazines. This emphasises the country's unique combination of historical and natural beauty, its cultural heritage with the archeological ruins of ancient cities, its unpolluted seas and nature, its colourful folklore and traditional hospitality, its inexpensive and good quality shopping facilities and its delicious and varied cuisine. While advertising activities are carried out in most international markets, priority has been given to Central European and Middle East Islamic countries.

At home, promotional and advertising efforts are concentrated on the areas which have been designated Tourism Development Regions, including the coastal areas stretching from Canakkale province on the Aegean to Mersin province on the Mediterranean, the Cappodocia region in Middle Anatolia and several major cities including Istanbul, Izmir, Antalya and Ankara.

In February 1986, the Hotel and Managers' Association, in co-operation with the Ministry, arranged a Food Fair to introduce Turkish cuisine and during 1986, the Ministry arranged an International Symposium in Istanbul and Konya for the purpose of making Turkish food and drink better known. In these symposiums, extensive information about Turkey was given to a considerable number of foreign experts and foreign press representatives.

The protection of the tourist as a consumer: Market controls have been much more effective in the last few

49

years, for the benefit of the consumer. The problems of the sale of defective and over-priced souvenirs and other artifacts to tourists and the late or non-delivery of articles ordered, is being taken up as a priority matter by local administrations.

International co-operation: New cultural Exchange Programmes were signed in 1986 between Turkey and the Federal Republic of Germany, France, Spain, Korea and Morocco covering the years 1986-1988 and a Cultural Exchange Programme was signed in the same year between Turkey and Jordan covering the years 1987-1989.

In addition to the tourism agreements mentioned in the previous report, agreements now exist with Italy and the USSR. To implement these agreements, Joint Commission meetings are held periodically and protocols are signed at the end of such meetings. Tourism relations with Iran, Tunisia, Jordan, Algeria, Italy, USSR, Egypt, Yugoslavia, Syria, Bulgaria, Romania, the Federal Republic of Germany and Pakistan are also discussed within the framework of Turkey's Trade Agreements with these countries, during the meetings of the Joint Economic Commissions.

UNITED KINGDOM

Recent investigations on the tourism industry in the United Kingdom revealed that its turnover in 1984 was comparable in size to the combined sales of the electrical and electronic engineering industry and provided in 1985, either wholly or in part, just over two million jobs.

Short-term outlook: In spite of setbacks in 1986 in foreign visitor numbers, and a slight decline in earnings, the underlying trend in tourism to the United Kingdom remains upward. The recovery of North American traffic, which was apparent in the last quarter of 1986, appears to be continuing in the early months of 1987. Continued attention to the development of new facilities and attractions, improved standards of training and service, and vigorous promotion of these products to traditional and new markets, eg. the Far East, as well as the encouragement of a revival in domestic holidays, especially second holidays in the "shoulder" months, should ensure that the industry remains buoyant. Providing conditions remain stable, the British Tourist Authority is forecasting continued regular growth in numbers of around 5 per cent in 1987 and 1988, with a consequential increase in expenditure in each of these years of about 6 per cent in real terms.

Government policy

Within Government, responsibility for tourism policy within England, and the overseas promotion of Great Britain as a tourist destination, rests with the Secretary of State at the Department of Employment. The Secretaries of State for Scotland and Wales have responsibility for tourism policies within their respective territories. The Government-aided Tourist boards for England, Scotland and Wales (as well as the British Tourist Authority – which promotes Britain overseas)

were set up under the Development of Tourism Act 1969: the Northern Ireland Tourist Board was set up under separate legislation, and policy is directed by the Northern Ireland Department of Economic Development.

The Government's overall objective remains to maximise the wealth and employment opportunities offered by development of the tourism industry. It aims to do this by:

– Encouraging the growth and development of the tourism infrastructure in the United Kingdom;
– Developing the industry's competitiveness in the world market;
– Encouraging the industry to promote tourism to all areas of the country; and
– Extending the tourism season.

The Department of Employment issued a Tourism Policy Guidelines Statement in January 1986 which defined its objectives for the industry up to 1989, and set out its proposals for achieving these objectives. A target has been set to obtain an 8 per cent growth per annum in holiday tourism over the next three years, giving a total of 170 000 holiday visitors in the 1988/89 financial year. It is hoped that growth in this sector combined with increases in other tourism categories should result in the total number of visitors exceeding one million. This should generate tourism earnings in excess of £95 million and create 300 new jobs in the industry.

In July 1986 the Government produced a report, "Action for Jobs in Tourism" which detailed progress on the implementation of the "action points" identified in its earlier report on the industry "Pleasure, Leisure and Jobs" (see 1986 Annual Report) and highlighting further measures to help the tourism industry and those who work in it. The Government has continued to work towards the creation of an economic climate in which business can flourish, and has maintained its funding commitment to the tourist boards.

Funding to the British Tourist Authority and English Tourist Board has been increased by 8 per cent for 1987/88; these funds will further the Board's work to encourage the dispersal of visitors throughout the country, especially to areas of high unemployment and urban decay which are considered to have developed tourism potential, and to continue the promotion of Britain as a year-round tourist destination.

The strategies to be used to meet the objectives set out in the Northern Ireland Policy Statement include the development, through the Northern Ireland Tourist Board (NITB), of a Regional Tourism Structure; the strengthening of the marketing activities of the NITB; the holding of a biennial tourism conference and financial assistance towards the cost of developing appropriate tourism accommodation and amenity facilities.

Actions and measures taken in 1986

Transport: Information on the development in the air and road transport sectors is presented in Chapter IV.

Waterways: The British Waterways Board, which is responsible for maintaining and developing some 2 000 miles of inland waterways for recreation, amenity and conservation, has pursued a number of ventures during the past year to produce full use of the waterways system, including imaginative developments which will provide for the tourism and leisure industries. The Board works in partnership with a private operator to promote the use of the inland waterways network by overseas visitors, and considers that selective enhancement of the waterways system will help develop both domestic and foreign tourism. The Wigan Pier Heritage Centre, on the Liverpool and Leeds canal, won the British Tourist Authority's award for 1985 for most outstanding tourist attraction.

Joint ventures with the private sector have begun in 1986 to develop Woughton Marina, on the Grand Union Canal near Milton Keynes, and at the British Waterways Board site at Gloucester Docks, which includes the restoration of 14 listed buildings, and the establishment of the National Waterways Museum at Llantony. During 1986 the Board has also been exploring the idea of the formation of a Waterways Heritage Trust, which would help preserve the Board's historic buildings and structures and encourage public interest in, and enjoyment of, waterway heritage.

Tourist signposting: In a Circular to Local Authorities a new system of white on brown signing was announced, following experiments in Kent and Nottingham, and it has been widely adopted. On motor-ways, signs may now be erected to direct traffic to tourist attractions with over 150 000 visitors per annum. There is evidence that these signs are a useful form of promotion and can lead to increased visitor numbers. Signs of this colour and style can now also be used for country towns, boundary signs or to indicate roadside facilities where the use will promote tourism. In particular, this type of sign (sometimes incorporating a brief touristic message) is available to indicate tourism services in communities which are by-passed by the main roads.

Employment and vocational training: The Government has a number of employment and training schemes which are of benefit to the tourism industry; for example, the Youth Training Scheme (YTS) is making a large contribution to the training of young people for employement within the industry. Since 1 April 1986, YTS has been extended from a one-year to a two-year training scheme offering work experience combined with further education which helps young people to work towards recognised vocational qualifications. The Government has also asked the Manpower Services Commission (the body responsible for training programmes) to refocus its Adult Training Programme to take more account of the needs of small businesses and to promote enterprise and self-employment, paying particular attention to the tourism industry.

Tourism already benefits from the Government's Community Programme, an employment measure which provides work, and in many cases training for long-term unemployed people aged 18 and over on projects of benefit to the local community. This will be supplemented by additional places following the launch in October 1986 of a National initiative – "Tourism and the Community Programme".

Aids and incentives: Section 4 of the Development of Tourism Act 1969 gives the National Tourist Boards for England, Scotland and Wales the powers to provide selective financial assistance towards the provision or improvement of tourist facilities and amenities, the assistance being given on the basis of additionality.

In England, grants totalling £11.5 million were approved by the English Tourist Board (ETB) during 1985/86 in respect of 542 projects whose total capital costs amounted to £98.4 million, with a total of 1 960 jobs being directly created. For the 1986/87 financial year, the ETB were asked to give particular priority, when considering applications for assistance, to the development of tourism in those parts of the country of high unemployment which are regarded as having unexplored tourism potential.

Economic studies of the effectiveness of the Section 4 scheme were carried out during 1986, and indicate that the scheme plays a valuable role in job creation. The Government therefore decided that the scheme should continue, and a revised scheme is to be launched in 1987, with emphasis on large innovative tourism projects. In Scotland, grants under the Section 4 scheme totalling £3.7 million were approved in respect of 154 projects during 1986. The priorities for assistance were, and continue to be, projects which improve the quality of existing accommodation or provide additions to visitor attractions.

During 1986 the Northern Ireland Department of Economic Development reopened the Accommodation Grants Scheme. The Main Scheme, for projects costing in excess of £20 000, was open for a short period of time for the receipt of applications and has now closed. The Minor Scheme, for projects costing under £20 000, remains open for the receipt of applications. The grant rate for both schemes is 30 per cent of eligible costs, and projects which were selected for financial assistance under the Main Grants Scheme will result in the commitment of the Department's financial resources for the next two years.

Public infrastructure investment: During 1986 Local Authorities in Northern Ireland, with grant assistance from the Department of Economic Development and the European Community, invested approximately £2.7 million in tourist amenity infrastructure.

Marketing research: In 1986 present and potential demand in the national market was assessed through:

- The British Tourism Survey, which surveys the level of holiday-taking, both at home and abroad, by British citizens;
- The English Hotel Occupancy Survey, which collects data on the number of bed-nights in English hotels, according to the purpose of visit; and
- The National Survey of Tourism in Scotland, providing statistics on tourism expenditure, trips and bed-nights in Scotland.

Present and potential international demand was assessed by:

- The International Passenger Survey, a random sample of travellers through points of entry to identify purpose of visit, length of stay, expenditure, etc.;
- The London Visitors Survey, a survey of overseas visitors to London to examine their activities while in the capital and their opinions of the city; and
- Qualitative and quantitative research into the traffic of pure holiday visitors to Northern Ireland by the Northern Ireland Tourist Board; research centred on visitors from Britain, Europe, North America, Australia and New Zealand.

Marketing strategies: The British Tourist Authority's (BTA) promotional strategy can be defined as follows:

- Improving the seasonality of travel to Britain, increasing the proportion of traffic in off-peak periods;

- Sustaining current levels of visits and earnings from those markets in which we have a large market share;
- Developing new markets; and
- Improving the flow of tourism traffic to those areas of Britain with high unemployment which have been designated as having tourism potential.

The measures which the BTA uses to achieve these objectives encompass all marketing disciplines – advertising, public relations, information services, direct mail, leaflet and brochure publications, special promotions, travel trade exhibitions, workshops, etc.

The market segments which the BTA concentrates on in its promotion overseas of Britain are: senior citizens, the youth market, special interest and activity groups, and the business, conference and trade-fair market.

The Scottish Tourist Board (STB) continued with its promotional campaign "Surprising Scotland", designed to capture the uncommitted domestic market. The STB views the United States as potentially a very lucrative market from which to attract visitors to Scotland and during 1985 launched AMNET, a five-year project designed to build up a network of specialised travel agents in the United States who will handle and market holidays to Scotland. The STB also continues to promote Scotland in overseas markets as a complement to the activities of the BTA.

Protection of the tourist as a consumer: The proposals announced by the Government relating to *bureaux de change* operators will require the clear display of exchange rates for both buying and selling, together with details of any commission charges. The majority of operators have agreed to adhere to the draft provisions on a voluntary basis pending the enactment of legislation. The British Tourist Authority's Code of Conduct for *bureaux de change* provides additionally for transactions to be cancelled if the consumer is dissatisfied, and the code will be displayed by those operators who have agreed to conform with its provisions.

The new voluntary hotel classification scheme devised by the English Tourist Board was publicly launched at the end of 1986. The National Scheme, which awards "crowns" on a scale of 1 to 5 according to the range of services and facilities provided, will give holidaymakers a comprehensive knowledge of the facilities offered and enable them to make a comparison between participating establishments when booking.

Staggering of holidays: In its general promotion policy, the British Tourist Authority encourages visitors to come to Britain in the off-season months by underlining the fact that prices can be cheaper and that many tourist attractions are less crowded during these months. This is done in conjunction with the National Boards who promote financially attractive short breaks, such as long weekends, to encourage people to travel in the off-season.

Both the English Tourist Board and the Scottish Tourist Board continued their efforts to combat the problem of seasonality. Two important measures were the continued promotion of off-season breaks and provision of financial assistance towards the development of all-weather tourism and leisure facilities.

The statistics for December 1986 indicate that these promotional efforts are having increased success and are helping to persuade people to reconsider their holiday-taking. There has been a significant shift in the number of visitor arrivals through the year, with the numbers in the second and third quarters showing a fall whilst there was an increase in arrivals in the first and fourth quarters.

UNITED STATES

Today the United States has a service-based economy and tourism is a prime component of trade in services. The services sector accounts for more than two-thirds of the gross national product and 75 per cent of total employment. The Department of Labor has predicted that, in the next decade, nine of every ten new jobs created will be in the service industries. Among the United States' ten largest exports, tourism ranks second after chemicals as a foreign currency earner. Combining US revenues from international and domestic tourism, the tourism industry is the third largest retail industry in the US, following food stores and automobile dealers; it is a $260 billion industry, exceeding 6 per cent of GNP. Tourism ranks among the three largest industries in 39 of the 50 States and is the second largest employer in the US, employing about six million people.

International travel to the US accounts for one third of business service exports and directly generates over 300 000 jobs. In 1983, it resulted in more than $1.6 million in Federal, State and local tax revenues.

Projections of foreign arrivals for 1987 and 1988 reveal continuing increases of 4 per cent per annum to reach 23.6 million.

Government policy

The United States Travel and Tourism Administration (USTTA) was created by the National Tourism Policy Act of 1981. The USTTA, an agency of the Department of Commerce headed by an Under Secretary of sub-cabinet rank, promotes US export earning through trade in tourism. In order to increase US exports of goods and services in tourism, USTTA must encourage foreign demand, remove barriers, increase the number of small and medium size exporters, provide accurate and timely data, form partnerships with state and local governments and develop strategies for the private and public sectors. To increase the effectiveness and productivity of its efforts, USTTA develops co-operative programmes with states, cities and the private sector, enabling it to set a series of measurable goals, strategies and programmes consistent with the legislative mandate of the agency and the goals of the Department of Commerce. USTTA encourages US travel suppliers to promote and sell products, facilities and services available in the United States to the foreign travel buyer at the wholesale, retail and consumer levels. Major programmes include co-operative advertising, trade and consumer support, media services and technical marketing assistance to regions and to state and local governments. Travel development activities in countries lacking direct USTTA representation are carried out under the direction of USTTA regional directors by US and foreign commercial service officers in co-operation with "Visit USA" committees comprised of representatives of the US and foreign travel industry in those countries.

The National Tourism Policy Act also created a National Tourism Policy Council and a Travel and Tourism Advisory Board. The National Tourism Policy Council, an interagency committee which co-ordinates policies and programmes of Federal Agencies having a significant effect on tourism, met four times during the year. The meetings concentrated on effects of terrorism on tourism, problems of US-Canada motorcoach operators, barriers to tourism, air travel accessibility for handicapped persons, foreign government tourism offices in the United States, and tourism development potential in the US Pacific Territories.

The United States Travel and Tourism Advisory Board, composed of public and private industry representatives to advise the Secretary, also met four times. The Board reviewed USTTA's FY 1987 international marketing plan and co-operative advertising plan, and discussed terrorism's effect on tourism, US tourism investments abroad, tourism and the Caribbean Basin Initiative, and the German test market advertising programme.

Marketing research: The Department of Commerce, through USTTA, is required to provide tourism data to various user groups. These information consumers include international tourism organisations, other national government tourist offices, other Federal agencies and regional, state and city governments, and the many private sector elements of the US travel industry. USTTA continued a programme initiated in 1982 to gather comprehensive consumer marketing data, otherwise unavailable, on the volume and characteristics of travellers to and from the United States. An in-flight survey was distributed aboard international flights from the United States to all regions of the world. More than 30 US and foreign air carriers co-operated in the distribution of questionnaires to passengers aboard selected sample flights. The in-flight survey is partially subsidised by the sponsorship of public and private tourism agencies and companies. The quarterly reports are available on subscription from the USTTA Office of Research, Department of Commerce, Washington, D.C. 20230. The following market research reports were made available:

- "Canadian Travel to the United States": provided detailed analyses of the expenditures, destinations and trip characteristics of Canadian visitors;
- "Recap of International Travel to and from the US in 1985": provided data on the volume and expenditures of visitors to the US and US citizens travelling abroad;
- "Summary and Analysis of International Travel to the US": covered foreign visitor arrivals by month, mode of transport, country of residence, etc.
- "International Travel to and from the US, 1987 Outlook": prepared annually, it provides USTTA projections of developments in inbound and outbound tourism.
- "A Study of International Travel Markets": provides information on non-US residents' international travel habits and patterns, attitudes and preferences for foreign travel, etc.; in 1986, it covered Australia, France, Japan, the UK and Germany.

In 1986, the Office of Research, in conjunction with Tourism Canada, began a research programme studying international travel behaviour in several market countries. These studies will not only provide basic traveller information, but will yield market segmentations. This will allow for more accurate planning and targeting of industry marketing efforts in a country. The first reports will be issued in mid-1987.

Marketing objectives and strategies: USTTA mainly operates on a co-operative advertising programme basis. During 1986, USTTA co-operative advertising programmes attracted investments of over $4.8 million from public and private tourism partners to promote increased tourism to the United States. Cooper-

ative marketing programmes operated on three levels: long-term, ongoing marketing programmes to generate consumer awareness and interest and provide information on travel to the United States; short-term promotional campaigns with specific schedules, objectives and measurable results; and foreign information support programmes for the travel trade and consumers. Long-term co-operative marketing programmes educated the travel trade from the US and abroad as well as propective international visitors about travel to the United States, and laid the groundwork for future co-operative promotional campaigns. Long-term co-operative programmes, 80 per cent funded by state, city and private tourism organisations, included a range of activities, such as international site and product inspection trips by travel agent and journalist, trade seminars, workshops and travel missions. Short-term co-operative marketing campaigns were aimed at major foreign consumer groups. The fully integrated marketing mix for a campaign included sharply focused multi-media advertising, inspection trips by foreign travel agent and journalist, travel missions, consumer and trade information programmes, media events, and travel trade training workshops and seminars. Fully integrated campaigns provided states, cities and tourism organisations with a variety of ways to enter overseas markets or expand existing promotional efforts for greater penetration.

Trade support: USTTA offices in foreign markets strove to inform, educate and motivate travel wholesalers and retail agents to sell the United States as a tourism destination. This was done mainly by:

- Providing professional responses to trade inquiries and giving technical assistance in tour planning and construction;
- Conducting workshops and training programmes for foreign tourism industry staff;
- Providing assistance in the planning and organisation of US product inspection trips for the foreign travel trade; and
- Providing the foreign travel trade with basic reference materials, guides and library services, and dependable inventories of basic tourism literature for distribution to consumers at the retail level.

Other areas where USTTA was active in 1986 included consumer information, technical assistance to the public and private sectors, public information programmes through media services, and assistance to regional, state and city travel promotion organisations.

Facilitation: To aid facilitation, USTTA:

- Made recommendations on visa waiver legislation for temporary visitors;
- Advised on the expansion of pre-inspection, which is the examination by US Immigration at foreign

airports of departing passengers destined for the United States;
- Through its offices abroad, made the foreign travel trade segments aware of new procedures or publications of other government agencies dealing with the inspection of arriving visitors;

- Advised on and co-ordinated facilitation matters with city, state and US government agencies;
- Urged the increased use of symbol signs in airports and other tourism facilities; and
- Administered a corps of multilingual receptionists at US international gateway airports.

YUGOSLAVIA

Tourism is one of the branches of the economy that has been given priority in the development of Yugoslavia. The scenic beauties of the country, its diverse climate and landscape, its rich cultural and historic heritage and favourable geopolitical and communications position form the basis of this emphasis. It has been decided to formulate long-term development programmes for priority branches, which besides tourism include energy, technology, communications and agriculture, so as to make them part of national plans and policies over the long term.

With a total of 111 million bed-nights in 1986 (of which nationals accounted for 60 million), over 8 million foreign tourists annually and foreign exchange earnings of $1.34 billion, Yugoslavia has a fairly modest share of the European tourist market: the number of bed-nights accounted for 4 per cent and foreign exchange inflow for 2 per cent. Irrespective of the position of Yugoslavia in international tourism, tourism has very important current and future potential. This is confirmed by the fact that in 1985 tourism accounted for 2.9 per cent of the GNP, 4.4 per cent of the total work force (about 240 000 people), and as much as 8 per cent if tourism-related activities are included. The share of tourism in the total value of exports of goods and services was about 8 per cent.

Government policy

During the last eight years, Yugoslavia has lagged behind the other Mediterranean tourist receiving countries. This is partly because there was no clearly defined long-term, permanent orientation at the national level, and partly because tourism developed on the margin of economic activities, from which it received mainly negative impulses (inflation, the unfavourable dinar exchange rate, restrictions, etc.). Standstills also occurred due to inadequate systematic solutions and measures, resulting from insufficient development of the overall supply in terms of quantity and quality, adverse monetary trends, the lack of overall organisation of tourism and the methodology of calculating revenues.

In 1986/87, these circumstances inspired the Yugoslav government to prepare and adopt a long-term programme of tourism development entitled "Strategy for the Development of Tourism to the Year 2000". (This study was summarised in the 1986 edition of the Annual Report.) In order for tourism to take its rightful place, as an efficient and fructuous export and foreign exchange channel, it required a clear development orientation, drawing not only on domestic sources and experience, but also on trends in the international tourist market.

The general objectives of the Long-Term Programme of Economic Stabilisation are, by stimulating development in all areas, to reverse the present negative trends and lead the country into modern technology and business performance flows, with equal emphasis on self-reliance and co-operation on an international level. In the field of tourism, these objectives are translated into the full utilisation of the potentials of the country and the tourist demand in the world, i.e., the creation of a modern export market, an increased foreign exchange inflow, the development of domestic tourism as an integral part of the development of foreign tourism, the increase of employment, and the encouragement of insufficiently developed regions.

These objectives will be implemented through medium-term plans for the development of tourism, both by a joint export programme and individual programmes for each field. Particular attention is being given to improvement of the quality of tourism services and administration. Great importance is also attached to the application of integral marketing and computer technology, the training and education of personnel for work in tourism, and more sophisticated publicity and promotion activities in the foreign market.

With a view to meeting these objectives more effectively, the Yugoslav Government, during 1986, set up a special body – the Federal Committee for Tourism – which is actually a collective body composed of 24 members from all the relevant federal, state and provincial organisations, headed by a president who is a member of the Government. The other organisations in charge of tourism are: the Tourist Association of Yugoslavia, a social organisation entrusted with the organisation of foreign tourist publicity (according to the criterion that resources for such publicity should amount annually to 1 per cent of the total foreign exchange inflow in the previous year); the National Association of Travel Agencies; and the Association of the Tourist Economy, attached to the Chamber of the Economy. The Motoring Association also has a prominent role and a very extensive system of information and assistance on roads.

Actions and measures taken in 1986

Improvement of supply: The programmes include the development of nautical tourism on the Adriatic coast (and also on rivers and lakes), mountain and hunting tourism, health and recreational tourism, congress tourism and tourism in large cities. (Yugoslavia has 2 000 rivers, about 300 lakes, 2 000 hunting estates, about 500 springs of thermal and mineral water and ten modern congress centres). The aim is also to prolong the season, i.e. to make it an all-year-round destination, for which all the conditions exist in Yugoslavia owing to its climate, landscape and wide choice of attractions. Along the Adriatic coast over 150 hotels, with over 20 000 beds and over 100 indoor swimming pools with heated sea water, operate during the winter. Nudism is also developed, with over 40 official centres for nudism being visited every year by over a million tourists. There are also numerous cultural and historical monuments testifying to the turbulent history of the regions constituting present-day Yugoslavia.

To meet the growing demand during 1986, 10 000 new beds were added in hotels and 20 000 in complementary facilites. There was also a considerable growth of winter and nautical tourism. In 20 ski centres for the year 1986/87 winter season, capacity amounted to about 45 000 beds, 100 funiculars and 150 ski lifts. (Of special importance is the construction of a large ski centre on Kopaonik mountain, with 3 500 beds.) With regard to marinas, there are 36 on the Adriatic, with about 10 000 sea berths and 3 550 places for vessels on land. It is envisaged that an additional 20 000 berths will be constructed by the year 2000. New breakthroughs in transportation are also important. Yugoslav Airlines, flying to about 60 cities of the world, have opened new lines to Kuala Lumpur, Bombay, Calcutta, Beijing and Los Angeles in 1986/87. New modern planes have been purchased and the availability of air transport is improving, as is the quality of services.

In the framework of the policy of stimulating foreign tourism, there was a 5 per cent reduction in the price of petrol, new stations for lead-free petrol have been built (there are now a total of 64), and the procedure of opening new duty-free shops is under way. It is expected that some 500 will exist by the end of 1987.

International co-operation: Yugoslavia has been pursuing a policy of greater openness towards the world, and has now abolished visas for 55 countries on the basis of reciprocity. New regulations have been adopted on joint ventures which enable faster investment of foreign capital in the development of tourist-hotel capacity. It is envisaged that additional regulations will be introduced in the near future, which will remove some of the remaining unclarified issues concerning foreign investments, in order to facilitate their entrance into the Yugoslav economy. The visits of a 70-member delegation of Japanese businessmen in May 1987 and a similar group from the United States are the first serious steps towards implementing the programme of joint investments in Yugoslav tourism, which has offered 42 projects to potential foreign partners.

Yugoslavia currently has agreements for co-operation in the field of tourism with 25 countries, and has 16 tourist representation offices in 13 countries of Europe and in the United States. It is developing very intensive co-operation with its neighbours and with the other Balkan states (via the standing Balkan Conference on Tourism which meets once a year, as well as with Mediterranean and other European countries. It is the co-ordinator of tourism for the Mediterranean non-aligned countries. It is engaged in design, consultancy, management and construction of tourist, hotel and congress facilities in a number of developing countries. Yugoslavia is a member of the World Tourism Organisation and the European Travel Commission, and participates actively in the work of the OECD Tourism Committee.

Considerable efforts are being made to develop co-operation with the European Free Trade Association (EFTA) and EEC Member countries in the field of tourism. In May 1987, a group of tour operators of the EFTA Member countries paid a one-week study-business visit to Yugoslavia. Activities are under way with the EEC in linking information systems in tourism and in technical co-operation in this field.

Table 1. Travel documents required to visit Member countries

Position at 1st July 1987

Tourists from \ Country visited	Australia	Austria	Belgium	Canada	Denmark	Finland	France	Germany	Greece	Iceland	Ireland	Italy	Japan	Luxembourg	Netherlands	New Zealand	Norway	Portugal	Spain	Sweden	Switzerland	Turkey	United Kingdom[2]	United States	Yugoslavia
Australia[1]		–	–	–	–	–	V	–	–	–	–	–	V	–	–	O	–	–	V	–	–	–	–	V	V
Austria	V		IP	–	I	I	V	IP	IP	I	–	IP	–	IP	IP	–	I	I	IP	I	IP	IP	I	V	IP
Belgium	V	IP		–	I	I	IP	IP	IP	I	I	IP	–	O	IP	–	I	I	I	I	IP	IP	I	V	I
Canada[1]	V	–	–		–	–	V	–	–	–	–	–	–	–	V	–	–	V	–	–	–	–	–	O	V
Denmark[1]	V	–	I	–		O	I	I	I	O	I	I	–	I	I	–	O	I	I	O	–	–	I	V	–
Finland[3]	V	–	IP	–	O		V	–	–	O	–	–	–	–	–	–	O	–	–	O	–	–	–	V	I
France	V	IP	IP	–	I	I		IP	IP	I	I	IP	–	IP	IP	–	I	I	IP	I	IP	–	I	V	I
Germany	V	I	I	–	I	I	IP		I	I	I	I	–	I	I	–	I	I	I	I	I	I	I	V	I
Greece	V	I	I	–	I	–	IP	I		–	I	I	–	I	I	–	–	I	I	–	I	–	I	V	V
Iceland	V	–	V	–	O	O	V	–	–		–	–	–	–	–	–	O	–	–	O	–	–	–	V	I
Ireland[1]	V	–	–	–	–	–	–	–	–	–		–	–	–	–	–	–	V	–	–	–	–	O	V	–
Italy	V	I	I	–	I	–	IP	I	I	I	I		–	I	I	–	I	I	I	I	I	I	I	V	I
Japan[1]	V	–	–	–	–	–	V	–	–	–	–	–		–	–	–	–	–	–	–	–	–	–	V	–
Luxembourg	V	IP	IP	–	I	–	IP	IP	IP	I	I	I	–		IP	–	I	I	IP	I	IP	IP	I	V	I
Netherlands[1]	V	IP	IP	–	I	–	IP	IP	IP	I	I	IP	–	I		–	I	I	IP	I	IP	I	I	V	–
New Zealand[1]	–	–	–	–	–	–	V	–	–	–	–	–	–	–	–		–	V	V	–	–	–	–	V	V
Norway[1]	V	–	–	–	O	O	V	–	–	O	–	–	–	–	–	–		–	–	O	–	–	–	V	–
Portugal	V	IP	IP	V	I	–	IP	IP	IP	–	I	IP	–	IP	IP	–	–		I	–	IP	–	I	V	I
Spain	V	IP	IP	–	I	–	IP	I	I	–	I	I	–	IP	IP	–	–	I		–	IP	–	I	V	I
Sweden[1]	V	–	–	–	O	O	V	–	–	O	–	–	–	–	–	–	O	–	–		–	–	–	V	–
Switzerland	V	IP	IP	–	I	I	IP	IP	IP	I	I	IP	–	IP	IP	–	I	IP	IP	I		IP	I	V	–
Turkey	V	–	V	V	V	V	V	V	V	V	–	–	–	V	V	V	V	I	–	V	V		–	V	I
United Kingdom[1]	V	I	–	I	I	–	I	I	I	–	O	I	–	I	I	–	I	I	I	–	I	I		V	–
United States[1]	V	–	–	O	–	–	V	–	–	–	–	–	V	–	–	–	–	V	–	–	–	–	–		V
Yugoslavia	V	–	–	V	–	–	V	–	V	–	–	–	–	–	–	V	–	–	–	–	–	–	–	V	

I   Agreements under which identity cards (national cards or special tourist cards) are accepted.

IP Agreements under which passports having expired for less than five years or identity cards are accepted.

O Agreements under which control of identity documents is abolished.

– Valid passport is required.

V Visa and valid passport required for visits of any length.

1. Countries where no identity cards exist.

2. Nationals from Austria and Switzerland are required to produce a visitors' card in addition to their identity card.

3. Finnish nationals travelling outside the Nordic countries must be in possession of a valid passport.

Table 2. Currency restrictions imposed on residents of Member countries when travelling abroad

Position at 1st July 1987

Country	Credit cards	Allowances in foreign currency or travellers' cheques[1]	Additional allowance *per journey* in domestic currency
Australia	UL	Unlimited. Amounts in excess of A$ 50 000 per person *per journey* require the completion of a declaration form for taxation screening purposes.	$A 5 000 in notes or coins.
Austria		The equivalent of Sch 50 000 *per journey* is granted automatically[2].	Sch 50 000.
Belgium	UL	Unlimited.	Unlimited.
Canada	UL	Unlimited.	Unlimited.
Denmark	UL	Unlimited.	DKr 40 000.
Finland	UL	Unlimited[3].	Mk 10 000.
France	UL	The equivalent of FF 12 000 per person and *per journey*. For business purposes, a supplementary allowance of the equivalent of FF 1 000 per person and per day is granted automatically[2].	
Germany	UL	Unlimited.	Unlimited.
Greece		The equivalent of 800 ECU per person per journey for travel within the European Community and $250 per person per journey to other countries. For business educational or other purposes, higher allowances are granted upon request. For hospitalisation, unlimited amounts are granted. Use of credit cards abroad by Greek nationals limited to the equivalent of $300 per year[4].	Dr 3 000.
Iceland		The equivalent of $ 1 650 per person and *per journey*. Amount reduced if the person is taking part in an organised tour or has paid for accommodation and other expenses through a travel agency in Iceland. The allowance for children is half the authorised amounts. Credit cards use limited to $1 650 as part of the allowance.	IKr 8 000
Ireland	UL	The equivalent of Ir£ 500 *per journey* is granted automatically[2].	Ir£ 100.
Italy	UL	The equivalent of 1 250 SDRs *per person per journey*[10].	L 500 000.
Japan	UL	Unlimited.	Y 5 000 000.
Luxembourg	UL	Unlimited.	Unlimited.
Netherlands	UL	Unlimited.	Unlimited.
New Zealand	UL	Unlimited.	Unlimited.
Norway		Unlimited[6].	NKr 5 000.
Portugal		Per person and *per journey*: Esc 150 000. Authorisation required for all amounts exceeding the above limits for travel undertaken for educational, family, business or health reasons.	Esc 50 000.
Spain	UL	The equivalent per person *per journey* of Ptas 350 000 for private travel and the equivalent of Ptas 200 000 for business travel. Travel allowances for education or health are freely granted within the limits of expenses incurred[7].	Ptas 20 000.
Sweden	UL	Unlimited. For amounts in excess of the equivalent of SKr 25 000 *per journey*, a form has to be completed at time of purchase.	SKr 6 000.
Switzerland	UL	Unlimited.	Unlimited.
Turkey		The equivalent of $3 000 per person and *per journey*[5] for travellers over 18 years, and of $750 for travellers under 18 years. Business travellers may take up to the equivalent of $2 000 per trip, subject to bank approval. The use of credit cards based on foreign currency accounts is unlimited but for other accounts is limited to $1 500 per person per journey.	The equivalent of $ 1 000.
United Kingdom	UL	Unlimited.	Unlimited.
United States	UL	Unlimited[8].	Unlimited.
Yugoslavia		Unlimited provided the currency has been derived from a foreign currency bank account.	Din 2 500[9].

UL : No limits on the use of credit cards for the payment of tourism services.

1. When the allowance is limited, travel tickets (return and circular) can generally be paid for in national currency without reducing the travel allowance.
2. Additional amounts are available on request, subject to verification of the bona fide of the transaction.
3. Amounts in excess of Fmk 10 000 per journey require justification of use.
4. For travel to EEC countries, up to the equivalent of 760 European currency units.
5. An additional $1 500 may be taken provided a certificate of bank purchase is submitted. The equivalent of an additional $5 000 is authorised for health purposes.
6. In practice, NKr 20/30 000 per journey, covering only expenses relating to travel and stay. Credit card use limited to Nkr 20 000 without notice and explanation to bank concerned, only for expenses relating to travel and stay.
7. Additional amounts are granted up to Ptas 320 000 for four private journeys or more per year and up to Ptas 1 400 000 for seven business journey or more per year.
8. Amounts in exess of $5 000 must be reported to United States customs.
9. On first exit and Din 500 for subsequent occasions in the same year.
10. Justifications for use of over L 5 000 000 per year may be requested up to five years after the year in question.

Table 3. **Limitations imposed on foreign tourists concerning importation and exportation of the currency of the country visited**

Position at 1st July 1987

Country visited	Authorised importation	Authorised exportation
Australia	Unlimited	A$ 5 000
Austria	Unlimited	Sch 50 000
Belgium	Unlimited	Unlimited
Canada	Unlimited	Unlimited
Denmark	Unlimited	DKr 50 000[3]
Finland	Unlimited	Fmk 10 000[3]
France	Unlimited	F 12 000
Germany	Unlimited	Unlimited
Greece	Dr 3 000	Dr 3 000
Iceland	IKr 8 000	IKr 8 000
Ireland	Unlimited	Ir£ 100
Italy	Unlimited[5]	L 500 000
Japan	Unlimited	Y 5 000 000
Luxembourg	Unlimited	Unlimited
Netherlands	Unlimited	Unlimited
New Zealand	Unlimited	Unlimited
Norway	Unlimited	NKr 5 000
Portugal	Unlimited	Esc 100 000[3]
Spain	Unlimited	Ptas 100 000
Sweden	Unlimited	Unlimited[4]
Switzerland	Unlimited	Unlimited
Turkey	$ 1 000[1]	$ 1 000[1]
United Kingdom	Unlimited	Unlimited
United States	Unlimited	Unlimited
Yugoslavia	Din 2 500[2]	Din 2 500[2]

1. TL to the equivalent of $ 1 000.
2. Restricted to denominations of Din 100 or less. Maximum of Din 2 500 on first visit and of Din 500 on subsequent visits in the same year.
3. A higher amount if traveller can prove that the amount does not exceed the sum imported in national or foreign currency.
4. Amounts in excess of the equivalent of SKr 6 000 require justification of their purchase abroad.
5. The importation of amounts of L 5 000 000 by non-residents or L 500 000 by residents is subject to a verification procedure.

II

INTERNATIONAL TOURIST FLOWS IN MEMBER COUNTRIES

This chapter brings together, in the form of summary tables, all the most recent data available on international tourist flows to OECD Member countries (broken down by region) and to Yugoslavia. Monthly data for the main generating countries together with annual information by country of origin of tourists or visitors are set out in the Statistical Annex.

Section A outlines the recent trend in international tourism in the OECD area for the period 1980-1985, providing a perspective for developments in 1986, the latest year for which data are available.

Section B describes the trend in international tourist flows in 1986, country by country. The data cover:

i) *arrivals at frontiers* either of *tourists* (i.e. persons spending more than one night in the country) or, when this is not available, of *visitors* (tourists and excursionists); and

ii) the *number of nights spent* by foreign tourists *in hotels and similar establishments* (generally speaking, hotels, motels, inns and boarding houses) and *in all means of accommodation* without distinction. For further details of the types of accommodation that these statistics include in each country, please refer to Table C in the introduction to the Statistical Annex.

Finally, Section C assesses international flows from the four main generating countries, France, Germany, the United Kingdom and the United States.

A. THE RECENT TREND IN INTERNATIONAL TOURISM IN THE OECD AREA (1980-1985)

From the start of the decade until 1983, international tourism stood up fairly well in the generally adverse economic climate, with demand towards the OECD area levelling off somewhat. By late 1983 there were signs of a recovery, and this in fact occurred in 1984-1985. However, that broad summary conceals a number of special features which are discussed below.

In 1985 the most significant expansion was once more in tourist movements towards the Member countries of the Pacific basin. They grew by 11 % (compared with 5 % for the OECD area as a whole) to reach a total of 4.1 million. This rise was partly due to the increasing rate of growth in visitors from the United States, who at present make up nearly 20 % of visitor arrivals at frontiers. Among European countries, the only significant source of visitors in the Pacific region is the United Kingdom (which contributes between 7 and 14 % of the market, depending on host country),

due to historical and cultural links. Tourist flows from France, though increasing steadily, are mainly to Japan, where about 40 000 French visitors (out of 53 000 for the region) were recorded in 1985.

The two OECD Member countries in North America received 34.2 million foreign tourists in 1985. Naturally enough, they are each other's "best customers". US tourists made up 88 per cent of arrivals in Canada and Canadians contributed 52 % (declining since 1983) of those in the United States. Other important markets for the United States are Mexico (13 %), Japan (7 %) and the United Kingdom (4 %). The French take only sixth place, with 1.6 % of the market (after Germany's 2 %); the exchange controls introduced in 1983 brought their numbers down significantly, but 1984, in spite of increasingly unfavourable exchange rates, saw an 8 % rise.

Main generating markets in the OECD area
(Indices : 1980 = 100)

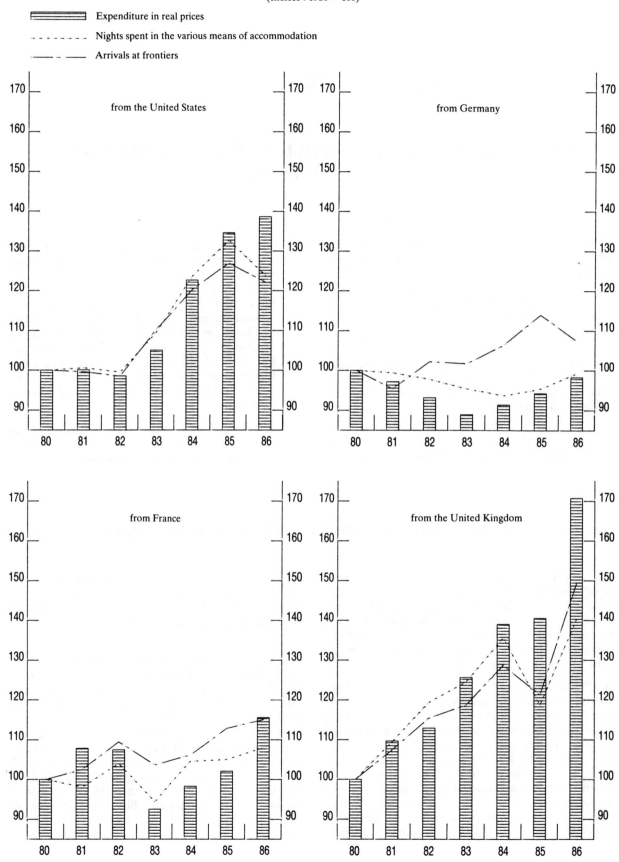

62

1985 was a record year in Europe, from the stand-points both of intra-regional travel (which makes up 80 % of tourist movements in the region) and of the number of transatlantic visitors. According to the European Tourism Commission (ETC), Europe received nearly 8.6 million visitors from outside Europe, and between them they spent more than $8.3 billion. Looking at a map of favourite destinations for intra-European tourism, the most striking fact is that Germans form the first or at least the second most important market for virtually all European countries. In spite of the preponderance of the German market, the Scandinavian countries, the Netherlands, Austria and Switzerland have all seen their numbers of German visitors fall since 1983, while the countries in the Mediterranean basin have all seen substantial increases, from 8 % for France to 71 % for Turkey.

There was a switch away from Scandinavia in 1985 by tourists from the rest of Europe, apart from the United Kingdom. This was not offset by the large number of transatlantic visitors, particularly from the United States, or by the increase in tourists from other Nordic countries.

The countries of Europe all benefited, to varying degrees, from the overall rise in international tourism and in particular, with favourable exchange rates and low air fares, from the very large increase in Americans. In 1985 they became the most important group of clients for the European hotel industry, making up 21 % of the market, according to Horwath & Horwath International, placing them ahead of the British and the Germans. But data show that from June 1985 there was a downward trend in this market, a movement which was accelerated by the combined influence of the Group of Five measures at the end of September 1985 and the threats to the safety of travellers.

The Mediterranean basin has been experiencing rapid development for several years. Apart from the three traditional major hosts in this region (Italy with 53.6 million visitors in 1985, Spain with 43.2 million and France with 36.8 million tourists), the other countries have seen a substantial expansion in tourist arrivals since 1980: Turkey + 103 % (including 61 % since

1983), Portugal + 84 %, Greece + 37 % and Yugoslavia + 32 % (and 42 % from the low point in 1982). After the sharp fall in the number of Yugoslav tourists as a result of exchange restrictions imposed during 1982, they are now returning to their two main destinations, Turkey (where they now make up 14 % of the market) and Greece (where they form 5 %). The French, who were also affected by strict exchange controls in 1983, cut back on their foreign travel in that year; all the Mediterranean countries, other than Portugal, had substantially fewer French visitors. By 1984 they were back, and in some countries in fact increased their market share.

Unlike in other Mediterranean countries, in Italy the number of tourists fell overall in the period 1980-1983, mainly due to a trend away from Italy by the Germans, who make up its principal market. This was not balanced by increasing numbers of Swiss and Austrians. Italy saw an upturn in tourist flows, British visitors excepted, only in 1984.

The United Kingdom market is the one which saw the most impressive growth among the four main generating countries. Over these five years, visitors from the United Kingdom went up by 110 % in Portugal, 102 % in Turkey, 92 % in Yugoslavia, 73 % in Greece and 70 % in France. Spain, which had seen a rise of 68 % between 1980 and 1984, lost a million British visitors in 1985 (a 17 % fall from the previous year) as a result of a number of attacks on British tourists which received considerable prominence in the British press. The government's deregulation policy appears to be one of the main elements in this quite spectacular rise in the number of British travellers going to many countries, most notably in the Mediterranean region [according to *British Tourism Survey – Yearly*, the main international destinations for the British are Spain (31 % of departures in 1985), France (13 %), Greece (8 %) and Italy (5 %)]. Increased airline competition has led to a wide choice of charters at low prices, and this has significantly influenced British holiday patterns, as the upward development of foreign travel has shown, compared with all travel over the same period (21 % in 1980, 28 % in 1985).

B.   INTERNATIONAL TOURISM TRENDS IN 1986, COUNTRY BY COUNTRY

Since mid-1985 a number of factors have disrupted the development of international tourism worldwide, and in the OECD area in particular. It is not possible to quantify the impact of each in isolation, but three factors have to be mentioned: fears of terrorist threats to personal safety in Europe, the consequences of the Chernobyl accident, and the continuing decline in the

dollar exchange rate against European currencies. There were substantial changes in the destinations chosen by North American and Japanese tourists, resulting in lower numbers going to Europe and more US tourists in Canada, Australia and New Zealand. Larger numbers of Europeans visited non-European destinations than in the previous year, and intra-

European traffic was also higher, with more travel to the Mediterranean area, to the detriment of the Scandinavian countries.

Arrivals at frontiers: Of the 19 Member countries in Europe, only 12 collect data or provide estimates on tourist or foreign visitor movements at frontiers. Data concerning the number of arrivals have been removed from Table 1 for Austria and Germany; these countries record traveller arrivals at frontiers, a much broader category than is used for analysing tourist flows since it includes travellers in transit. Their data are shown for information in Table 6 in the Statistical Annex. In addition, Norway has not collected these data since 1st January 1984. The collection of data on tourist movements at frontiers may well become less common in the future with the steps Member countries are taking to promote unimpeded movement of residents within the OECD area, especially when travelling for tourism purposes.

For the 14 countries, taken overall, which collected data or provided estimates (Switzerland) on international tourist flows at frontiers over the last four years, the rate of growth has slackened, from + 5 % in 1985 to + 3 % in 1986 (Table 1).

Table 1. **Change in growth rate of number of arrivals of foreign tourists at frontiers[1]**

	T/V	% 84/83	% 85/84	% 86/85	1986 Millions of arrivals
Austria					
Belgium					
Denmark					
Finland					
France	T	4.0	3.9	–1.8	36.1
Germany					
Greece	T	15.6	19.0	6.9	7.0
Iceland	T	9.8	14.4	16.5	0.1
Ireland[2]	V			–5.1	1.8
Italy	V	5.5	9.1	–0.6	53.3
Luxembourg					
Netherlands					
Norway					
Portugal	T	10.9	21.1	8.4	5.4
Spain	V	4.0	0.7	9.6	47.4
Sweden					
Switzerland[3]	T	3.0	0.4	–3.4	11.5
Turkey	V	29.7	23.8	–8.4	2.4
United Kingdom	V	9.5	6.1	–4.9	13.8
EUROPE[1]		5.6	5.8	1.6	
Canada	T	3.9	1.5	18.6	15.6
United States	T	–4.0	1.0	4.7	22.0
NORTH AMERICA[1]		–1.1	1.2	10.1	
Australia	V	7.5	12.6	25.1	1.4
New Zealand	T	36.1	24.3	17.6	0.6
Japan	V	7.2	10.3	–11.4	2.1
AUSTRALASIA-JAPAN[1]		9.9	12.5	2.7	
OECD[1]		4.5	5.1	3.0	
Yugoslavia	V	5.3	18.5	5.9	24.7

V Visitors.
T Tourists.
1. Overall trend for all countries with data available from 1983 to 1986.
2. New series from 1986; 1985 figures are revised.
3. Estimates.

North America shows the strongest rise, 10 %, a trend reversal that began to emerge in late 1985 when disturbances in Europe and the depreciation of the dollar made North American destinations more attractive for European tourists and for others, including US citizens, drawn by promotion drives to take advantage of Canada's proximity and visit Expo'86 in Vancouver. In Member countries in the Pacific area, growth continued at a more modest pace on account of the historic fall in Japan in 1986 (– 11 %), which was largely due to the continuing appreciation of the yen from September 1985 onwards and the exceptional levels reached with Expo'85 at Tsukuba.

In Europe, where ten countries only provide frontier data, the rise fell back to 2 % in 1986, compared with 6 % in the previous year. The continued rise in international flows within Europe helped keep the trend positive in spite of the lower numbers of North American and Japanese tourists. Reference should be made, however, to significant downturns in Turkey (– 8 %, against + 24 %) and in the United Kingdom (– 5 %, against + 6 %).

Nights spent in hotels and similar establishments: Thirteen European countries have data for nights spent by foreign tourists in hotels and similar establishments for the period 1983-1986. In 1986 the upward trend resumed, + 3 %, compared with – 2 % in the previous year (Table 2). That was largely due to increases in just four countries, all in the Mediterranean area: 13 % in Turkey, 11 % in Spain, 10 % in Portugal and 2 % in Italy. The sharpest falls were noted in France (Ile-de-France, – 17 %), Norway (– 11 %) and Sweden (– 7 %).

Nights spent in all accommodation: Fourteen European countries, with Canada, record nights spent by foreigners in all means of accommodation for the period 1983-1986. Taken overall, the upward trend has slackened pace since 1984, being 1 % in 1986 compared with 3 % and 4 % in the previous years (Table 3).

When Canada is taken out we find no growth in 1986 in Europe, which has the world's largest host countries in terms of nights spent in accommodation: France, with 332 million nights (+ 1 % in 1986); the United Kingdom, with 156 million (a substantial fall, 7 %); Italy, with 100 million (+ 4 %); and Austria, with 85 million (virtually static, + 0.4 %). The increases in half the Member countries in Europe were relatively modest, but offset the loss of 12 million nights in the United Kingdom, which recorded the largest fall.

Australia: Visitor arrivals reached 1.4 million in 1986, 25 % up on the previous year and showing rapid and continuing growth since 1981, when there had been a slight fall of 1 %. The adjoining area of the Pacific basin and Asia, the source of 69 % of international arrivals, showed the sharpest rises: New Zealand (37 %), Japan (35 %), the United States (25 %) and

Table 2. **Change in growth rate of nights spent by foreign tourists in hotels and similar establishments**[1]

	% 84/83	% 85/84	% 86/85	1986 Millions of beds-nights
Austria	1.0	−1.7	−0.1	54.5
Belgium	6.7	5.3	−4.4	5.3
Denmark	2.4	−0.4	−5.5	4.3
Finland	2.5	−0.7	−3.6	2.0
France[2]	7.8	1.2	−17.2	15.0
Germany[3]		7.4	−1.8	23.5
Greece	19.4			
Iceland				
Ireland				
Italy	−0.5	1.1	2.1	65.1
Luxembourg	2.4	5.3	−2.7	0.9
Netherlands	8.8	3.2	−2.3	6.6
Norway[3]		7.3	−11.2	3.3
Portugal	11.5	17.4	10.4	14.3
Spain	11.7	−11.4	11.1	87.7
Sweden	8.5	8.1	−6.7	3.3
Switzerland	1.7	0.7	−3.7	19.6
Turkey	30.4	30.7	13.3	5.0
United Kingdom				
EUROPE[1]	5.4	−2.2	2.6	
Canada				
United States				
NORTH AMERICA				
Australia	−9.2	20.0		
New Zealand				
Japan				
AUSTRALASIA-JAPAN[1]				
OECD[1]	5.4	−2.2	2.6	
Yugoslavia	17.0	14.1	0.9	27.5

1. Overall trend for all countries with data available from 1983 to 1986.
2. Concerns Ile-de-France region only.
3. New series from 1984.

Table 3. **Change in growth rate of nights spent by foreign tourists in all means of accommodation**[1]

	% 84/83	% 85/84	% 86/85	1986 Millions of beds-nights
Austria	−0.8	−1.9	0.4	85.4
Belgium	4.5	5.3	−0.2	9.8
Denmark	−4.4	−1.5	−5.1	8.5
Finland				
France	3.9	3.1	0.7	332.2
Germany[2]		7.4	−1.0	27.8
Greece	20.4	8.1	−0.5	35.3
Iceland				
Ireland	2.9	−2.2	0.8	19.0
Italy	−2.2	1.0	4.1	100.1
Luxembourg	18.9	−10.5	7.4	2.4
Netherlands	12.5	2.8		
Norway	5.0	1.9	−4.1	5.0
Portugal	6.9	17.1	12.4	16.8
Spain	10.9			
Sweden[3]	3.7	−0.7	−4.2	7.2
Switzerland	−2.8	0.6	−0.7	34.9
Turkey	31.2	31.0	21.8	5.9
United Kingdom	6.6	8.5	−7.1	155.7
EUROPE[1]	3.5	3.6	−0.4	
Canada	9.4	0.3	18.6	91.5
United States				
NORTH AMERICA				
Australia	−13.2	6.7		
New Zealand				
Japan				
AUSTRALASIA-JAPAN				
OECD[1]	4.0	3.3	1.2	
Yugoslavia	19.6	20.2	1.1	51.4

1. Overall trend for all countries with data available from 1983 to 1986.
2. New series from 1984.
3. Change of coverage in 1985.

non-Member Asian countries (25 %). Although New Zealand's share of all visitors fell back, from 35 % in 1979 to 24 % in 1986, it is still the largest market, followed by the United States (17 %), the United Kingdom (12 %) and Japan (10 %). The Japanese market is expected to become the third largest source very soon, with its rapid expansion placing it ahead of the United Kingdom.

The encouraging results for Australia in 1986 are the outcome of a mix of factors affecting international tourism: a combination of caution and hesitancy in selecting destinations, the wider effects of the Chernobyl accident, considerable exchange rate fluctuations, and uncertainty about the possible effects of the disequilibrium in world trade. Further contributing elements were the ripples from promotion drives over the last few years, creating greater awareness of Australia's attractions on major markets. The devaluation of the Australian dollar also had an appreciable impact on demand from some markets, in particular New Zealand where it effectively meant a 12 % fall in 1986 after one of 24 % in the previous year. Last, the expansion of international air transport and more attractive air fares assisted the development of the most important markets.

Austria: Since 1981, when nights spent in all forms of accommodation reached a record level (92.5 million), relatively small but repeated falls brought the total back to 85.4 million. In 1986 total demand held steady at that level through a 2 % increase from Europe, which accounts for virtually all (95 %) nights, 65 % coming from the German market, by far Austria's main source (+ 1 % in 1986, a trend reversal from 1985 which had shown a 3 % fall). The lower numbers of North American visitors consequently had little effect in Austria, though they were down 38 % (making 2 % of the total).

Belgium: For the first time in the 1980s, nights spent by foreign tourists in approved hotels showed a fall, of 4 %, compared with a 5 % rise in the previous year. In addition, nights spent in all forms of accommodation marked time, after the 5 % increase in 1985. Greater use of non-hotel accommodation by European tourists helped to produce this result, in particular Netherlands residents who account for 34 % of all nights spent in Belgium. North American tourists more generally use hotels, and this sector most felt the decline in their numbers, down 22 % (against a 13 % rise in 1985).

65

Canada: In 1986 Canada recorded 40.5 million visitor arrivals, 13 % up on 1985. Of this figure, 39 % were tourist arrivals, spending around 92 million nights in all, a 19 % increase over the previous year. Analysis of changes in the American market, far the largest one with 70 % of nights, shows a higher volume of tourists (+ 18 %) in 1986, while the numbers of excursionists also rose but less markedly (+ 9 %). In terms of nights, that represented a 9.5 million increase, contributing over two-thirds to the overall growth in foreign tourism. Other important markets showed a reversal of demand from virtually all European Member countries, in particular three making up 11 % of the total: the United Kingdom (+ 25 %, against – 11 % in 1985), Germany (+ 21 %, against – 10 %) and France (+ 32 %, against – 3 %). The growing significance of markets in non-Member countries of Asia and Oceania should be noted; their share has doubled since the start of the decade and reached 4.3 % in 1986.

All these record results were due to a considerable extent to Expo'86 in Vancouver; growth in international tourism would otherwise have been more modest, an estimated 5 %. This was compounded by the competitiveness of the Canadian dollar against European currencies, the yen and the US dollar, the favourable economic conditions in the most important generating countries, and the postponement or cancellation of travel to Europe by US tourists.

Denmark: With 4.3 million nights recorded in all forms of accommodation (hotels throughout the year, camping sites between April and September), in 1986 Denmark showed a second consecutive fall, – 5 % (against – 2 % in the previous year). That is due to successive declines from all markets since 1984, apart from Sweden (+ 15 %) and Norway (+ 5 %), these two countries representing 30 % of the foreign clientele. There were significant falls from the major market, Germany (around 40 % of the total, down 11 % over the same period).

These results are the outcome of a number of factors which discouraged foreign tourists from visiting Europe in 1986, notably the accident at Chernobyl. The fallback in international demand, especially from the United States and Japanese markets, led to harsh competition from Mediterranean destinations which reacted by lowering prices substantially, thereby making Scandinavian destinations uncompetitive on both European and overseas markets. The appreciation of the Danish kroner against a large number of currencies, notably the US dollar and sterling, also helped to reduce competitiveness.

Finland: Since the start of the 1980s, international demand from Finland's closest neighbours (Germany, Norway and Sweden) has progressively fallen while rising from other parts of Europe (Italy and the United Kingdom, for example) and overseas, producing an overall increase of 10 % between 1980 and 1986.

Over that period the volume of nights spent by nationals rose more substantially (+ 33 %), raising total demand for hotel accommodation only to 8.9 million nights in 1986.

After a downturn in 1985, the number of nights spent by foreign tourists in hotels and similar establishments fell by 4 % to the 1982 level of 2 million. This result is due to the repeated fall in demand from three of Finland's four main sources, Sweden (26 % of the total), Germany (12 %) and Norway (7 %). The third largest market, the United States, showed a trend reversal, down 14 % (compared with the 18 % increase in the previous year). The trend was general, in particular on promising markets such as Japan, for which the volume of nights had doubled between 1980 and 1985 to around 45 000, 2 % of that year's total; it fell back by 13 % by 1986. These adverse results were amply offset by 3 % growth in domestic demand in 1986 over the previous year.

France: Provisional figures for 1986 show a 2 % fall in the number of international tourist visits (36.1 million) while the number of nights held steady at 332 million, much the same as in 1985. These figures, it should be noted, are based on an update of the findings of the 1982 frontier survey.

In 1986 the fall in nights was particularly large in approved hotels in the Paris area (– 17 %); the capital undoubtedly suffered from the wave of terrorism in France, leading to government measures to ensure the safety of residents and travellers, including the requirement for entry visas introduced on 16th September 1986.

The fall in international tourism came largely from the American market (8 % of stays in 1985, down 40 % in 1986). Tourists from European Member countries, on the other hand, held steady, up 2 %.

France's seven immediate neighbours (the United Kingdom, Belgium, Luxembourg, Germany, Switzerland, Italy and Spain) represent a little over two-thirds of its foreign clientele, with 29 million visits in 1986. They are not just captive markets, but faithful visitors who come back regularly. Between 1980 and 1985 the Belgian and Luxembourg market declined sharply (– 47 %) and now accounts for only 9 % of all visits (against 20 % in 1980). On the other hand, Germany held its leading position with a 16 % increase in stays, while countries such as the United Kingdom and Switzerland showed increases of 69 % and 64 % respectively. Before the disruption of 1986, visitors from the United States had risen from 1.2 to 2.8 million in five years, very largely due to an attractive exchange rate. It should further be noted that visits from the Scandinavian countries had risen almost fivefold in five years, from 130 000 in 1980 to 775 000 in 1985.

Germany: The new statistical series since 1984 does not permit comparisons with earlier periods. After 7 %

rises in 1985, nights spent in hotels and in all forms of accommodation fell by 2 % and 1 % respectively in 1986. This decline is due essentially to lower demand from non-European countries, in particular in North America, Asia and Oceania. Increases were noted for all European countries, and in all forms of accommodation where they account for 65 % of demand there was a 7 % increase, including + 6 % for the Netherlands (19 % of the total) and + 4 % for the United Kingdom (9 %).

Greece: Tourist arrivals at frontiers advanced at a slower pace, up 7 % compared with 19 % in the previous year, to total over 7 million arrivals in 1986. To this can be added some 314 000 cruise passenger arrivals, sharply down from the figure of over half a million at the start of the decade.

Since 1st July 1986 nationals of EEC countries entering Greece need no longer complete the special visitor's card, so the usual breakdown by country of origin for tourists from this area can no longer be provided. The Secretariat has made estimates for the three main European generating countries, on the basis of survey findings in the countries of origin, France, Germany and the United Kingdom.

In 1986 tourist flows from Europe rose, with the single exception of Switzerland, down 24 %. Among the major markets there was further growth for the United Kingdom (+ 11 %, and 21 % of the total), and France (+ 6 %, 7 % of the total) and a steady level from Germany, representing 15 % of the total Greek market.

Iceland: The feature of developments in 1986 was a sharp increase in frontier arrivals, + 17 %, for a total of 113 500 nights (compared with rises of 14 % and 10 % in the two previous years). The only data available at the time of going to press concern the four main international tourism generating countries in the OECD area (see Table 5). They show that these countries represent 57 % of all arrivals, and all increased in 1986 over the previous year; in declining order of market share, they are the United States (+ 3 %), the United Kingdom (+ 10 %), Germany (+ 44 %) and France (+ 25 %).

Ireland: A new statistical series on frontier arrivals has been introduced and comparisons cannot be made with earlier years, apart from 1985 for which estimates were prepared on the same basis. The new method allows more accurate evaluation of the origin of international tourist flows at frontiers, by recording arrivals of overseas visitors only, and excluding land frontier crossings. The figures recorded up to 1984 were 9.9 million; the figures for 1985 and 1986 are 1.9 and 1.8 million respectively. The new statistical base shows that the largest flows are still from the United Kingdom with 60 % of the total, followed by the United States with 16 %. The falls from these two markets (down 2 %

and 21 % respectively) were the reasons why 1986 showed an overall decline of 5 % from the previous year.

In terms of nights, these two markets are again the most important ones, with 51 % and 22 % respectively of the total for all forms of accommodation. With Germany and France they provide 85 % of tourists. After the decline in the previous year (– 2 %), 1986 saw resumed growth, + 1 %. The falling numbers from the United States and France (– 20 % and – 4 % respectively) were offset by larger numbers from Germany (+ 5 %) and the United Kingdom (+ 2 %).

Italy: Visitor arrivals at frontiers totalled 53.3 million in 1986, 1 % down on the previous year and the first fall since the 9 % decline in 1981. 46 % of this total, or 24.7 million arrivals, were tourists.

The development of international tourism in Italy is most clearly seen in terms of nights spent; for all forms of accommodation they passed the 100 million mark in 1986, up 4 % (against + 1 % in the previous year). The rise was more modest in hotels alone (+ 2 %, against + 1 %), indicating an increase in the use of accommodation other than hotels by foreign tourists.

Germany continues to be the dominant market, with 45 % of all nights spent in all forms of accommodation, while Italy's neighbours share a further 21 % (split equally among Austria, France and Switzerland). In 1986 European demand rose 9 % overall, with numbers from Germany up 8 % and from neighbouring countries 5 %. Looking outside Europe, there was a trend reversal for North America (– 41 %, against + 7 %) and an increase from non-Member countries (+ 5 %). Tourists from Japan also increased, by 13 %, Italy being one of the few exceptions to the pattern virtually everywhere else in Europe in 1986.

Japan: The number of foreign visitor arrivals fell by 11 % in 1986 to 2.1 million. The essential reason is the reversal in the previous year's favourable trend in the main markets, Asia-Oceania (- 14 %, against + 10 % in 1985) and Europe (– 13 %, against + 12 %). The fall in American visitors was less marked, – 1 % (against + 9 %).

These results are the outcome of the continuing appreciation of the yen, which started in September 1985, and the exceptional inflows for Expo'85 at Tsukuba.

Luxembourg: Nights spent in all forms of accommodation totalled 2.4 million in 1986, 7 % up on the previous year. The only breakdowns available at the time of going to press are for the four main OECD generating countries, which account for 19 % of the total market (see Table 5). In 1986 falls were recorded for the United States (– 24 %) and Germany (– 5 %), with increases for the United Kingdom (+ 7 %) and France (+ 2 %).

Netherlands: At the time of going to press the data on nights cover the first six months of 1986 only. However an overall estimate for the full year shows a 2 % fall in hotels and similar establishments. For the main generating markets which constitute 61 % of the total, provisional data suggest increases from Germany (+ 9 %) and France (+ 5 %) and decreases from the United Kingdom (– 3 %) and the United States (– 30 %) (see Table 5).

New Zealand: The increase in tourist arrivals at frontiers continued in 1986, up 18 % against 24 % and 36 % in the two previous years. The arrivals total passed the half-million mark; despite losing 10 percentage points since the start of the decade, Australia is still the leading market with 37 % of the total. Over that period the American and Japanese markets increased their shares, each gaining 6 percentage points to 23 % and 10 % of the total respectively. In 1986 these two markets each increased by 27 %, while the total for Australia fell by 11 %.

Norway: Nights in hotels alone totalled 3.3 million in 1986, a trend reversal of – 11 %, compared with + 7 % in the previous year. A new statistical series produced since 1984 does not permit comparison with earlier periods. For all forms of accommodation (hotels, camping sites and youth hostels), the fall in 1986 was less significant (– 4 %).

In the hotel sector demand declined from all markets with just two exceptions, which had little impact on the overall trend since they represent only 6 % of the total: Finland (+ 9 %) and France (+ 8 %). There were very sharp declines in two major markets, the United States (– 36 %, 13 % of the total) and the United Kingdom (– 19 %, 11 % of the total).

Portugal: Since the start of the 1980s all indicators of international tourism development have been moving up, far above the average for Europe over the same period. In 1986 tourist arrivals at frontiers rose by 8 % and visitor arrivals by 12 %, while nights spent in hotels rose by 10 % and nights in all forms of accommodation by 12 %. These figures show a slight increase in arrivals by excursionists, who made up 59 % of passengers at frontiers in 1986, as well as a rise in demand for non-hotel accommodation.

At frontiers, where European countries provide 92 % of all tourist arrivals, increases were substantial, particularly for the United Kingdom, + 31 %. In all forms of accommodation the same trends are apparent, with the United Kingdom market, which accounts for 36 % of the total, rising by 18 %, followed by Spain (+ 15 %, 10 % of the total) and Germany (14 %, 15 % of the total).

Among the non-European clientele there was a 27 % fall from the American market, but a 5 % rise from Latin America and an 8 % increase from Japan, one of the few exceptions to the adverse trends across Europe in 1986.

Spain: Numbers of visitor arrivals at frontiers continue to advance with a very marked increase in 1986, + 10 % over the previous year for a total of 47.4 million. It is estimated that 63 % of these arrivals, or 29.9 million, were tourists. In the major markets there were trend reversals in the cases of the United Kingdom and Portugal (+ 28 % and + 23 % respectively, compared with – 17 % and – 7 % in 1985) and further increases in the cases of France (+ 3 %, after + 10 %) and Germany (+ 5 %, after + 8 %).

For tourist accommodation, the only data systematically recorded are for hotels, giving an incomplete picture of the trend in international demand in Spain. 1986 saw a return to the position of two years before, since the 11 % rise cancelled out the similar loss in 1985. This is due essentially to the return of British tourists, who had switched away from Spain in large numbers following publicity given to incidents affecting the safety of tourists in 1985. The 35 per cent rise in 1986 more than offset the 29 % fall in the previous year. There was also a spectacular reduction in tourists from the United States, – 42 %, one of the sharpest falls in Europe for the US market in 1986 (though it represents only 2 % of the total for Spain).

Sweden: International demand in terms of nights fell back by 7 % in hotels (against + 8 %) and by 4 % (against – 1 %) in all means of accommodation. The second successive fall in all forms of accommodation was due to widespread successive falls in virtually all markets, in particular the major ones, Germany (18 % of the total), the Netherlands (5 %) and the United Kingdom[5] %). The exceptions here were Denmark (+ 3 %, against 16 %), Finland (+ 3 %, against + 16 %), and Italy (+ 6 %, against + 7 %).

Switzerland: In 1986 Swiss and foreign tourists spent a total of 74.9 million nights in Switzerland, or around 64 000 more than in 1985. This figure, the fifth highest annual total, is 5.5 % below the 1981 record of 79.1 million nights, but 3 % above the average over the last 10 years. Increases were chiefly in non-hotel accommodation, with some 39.4 million nights, about 700 000 or 1.8 % more than in 1985. Hotels, on the other hand, recorded some 35.5 million nights, some 533 000 or 1,5 % less than in the previous year. The fall may be considered relatively small, given the substantial decline in US visitors (– 36 %). The figures for hotels would have been worse, in fact, without the rise in domestic demand (+ 2 %) and in demand from European Member countries (+ 4 %), where three markets make up 51 % of all international demand: Germany with 32 %, the United Kingdom with 10 % and France with 9 %.

Turkey: Numbers of frontier arrivals by travellers fell back for the first time since 1982, when a relatively modest fall (– 1 %) had been recorded. In 1986 there were 8 % fewer arrivals, and a total of 2.4 million. However, the most significant data for international

68

tourism are for accommodation where the rise continued, + 22 % with a total of 5.9 million nights, 85 % of which were in hotels proper (+ 13 % in 1986).

The rises with the most impact were from Germany and France, given the importance of these markets (48 % of the total). Nights spent by German tourists in all forms of accommodation increased by 73 %, while nights spent by French tourists rose by 26 %. Falls were noted in the United States (– 18 %) and Austrian (– 28 %) markets.

United Kingdom: After the exceptional year of 1985 following three successive years of rapid growth, 1986 saw a 5 % decline to 13.8 million frontier arrivals. A similar trend was observed for nights, down 12 million or 7 %. In the latter case every quarter was affected, but the largest falls were noted in the period April-June, down 14 %, including – 31 % from the United States and – 12 % from Germany. The position stabilised in the third quarter, down only – 3 % over the equivalent 1985 period.

The data for arrivals and nights are taken from the same survey; it was found that Europeans came in larger numbers (+ 4 %), though they stayed for shorter periods (– 2 %). That was the case for the French and Irish, traditional visitors to the United Kingdom, while the Germans formed an exception, arrivals up 7 % and nights up 11 %. Outside Europe the situation deteriorated with a trend reversal for North American visitors (– 19 % in 1986, against + 15 % in the previous year) and Australian tourists (– 9 %, against + 15 %).

United States: After several years of declining figures since the record year of 1981 with 23.5 million arrivals, international tourism sprang back in 1986 with a 5 % rise and a total of 22 million. This was due to the impact of favourable economic conditions in the main generating markets, greater purchasing power of foreign currencies against the dollar, inflation continuing at a relatively low level, and competitive air fares on international routes.

After the slight decline in the previous year, the main market, Canada with 50 % of all tourist arrivals, showed a modest rise in 1986 (+ 1 %) to return to the 1984 level. A substantial fall occurred in the second largest market, Mexico, 10 % of the total and – 13 % in 1986. However overseas markets showed the strongest growth, up 18 % over 1985. Visitors from Europe and South America were more numerous, showing increases of 28 % and 21 % respectively. The chief rises were observed from Brazil (+ 34 %), the United Kingdom (+ 32 %), Germany (+ 32 %), France (+ 31 %), Italy (+ 22 %) and Japan (+ 12 %).

Yugoslavia: Since 1982 when all the indicators moved down, growth in international tourism has continued at a slower pace in 1986 with + 6 % frontier arrivals (against + 19 % in the previous year), + 1 % in hotel nights (against + 14 %), and + 1 % nights in all forms of accommodation (against + 20 %).

For nights spent in hotels, a new statistical series with a breakdown by country of origin has been available since 1985 only, ruling out comparisons with earlier periods. With the series for nights in all forms of accommodation, where data breakdowns are available for a longer period, 1986 shows a marked slowdown in European demand making up 85 % of the clientele: that was the case with Germany (+ 2 %, against + 21 %) and the United Kingdom (+ 7 %, against + 39 %), while Austria and Italy reversed the favourable trend in the previous year (– 2 % and – 7 % respectively, against + 32 % and + 19 %).

C. MAIN GENERATING MARKETS

International tourist flows from France, Germany, the United Kindgom and the United States make up 46 % of frontier arrivals and 56 % of nights in the OECD area as a whole. In 1986 the data available broadly indicate an increase in tourism from the United Kingdom and France, a decline from the United States, and a mixed picture for Germany.

Arrivals at frontiers: Table 4 shows the trend in arrivals at frontiers in fourteen Member countries, from the four main tourism generators. In 1986 there were rises of 2 % from France and 16 % from the United Kingdom, while falls are recorded for Germany (– 6 %) and the United States (– 4 %). With the French and German markets, the impact of these falls fell significantly on Europe, particularly Italy for which they are major sources (down 2 %, and 18 % respectively), while German arrivals in France fell as well (– 4 %, 24 % of the total). British tourists visited all countries in greater numbers, except for Ireland (– 2 %) and Japan (– 22 %). United States visitors shunned Europe (down 30 %), where in 1985 they had made up 6 % of the overall market, and crossed the Canadian frontier in larger numbers (+ 18 %).

Nights spent in accommodation: Seventeen European countries and Canada provide data on nights spent by foreign tourists, broken down by country of origin. For 1986 the figures show more nights spent in the various means of accommodation by the Germans (+ 3 %), the British (+ 15 %) and the French (+ 3 %), and a 10 % fall for US visitors (Table 5).

All the European countries showed historic falls in the number of nights spent by US visitors, down 42 % in Spain for example, 41 % in Austria and 37 % in Yougoslavia. On the other hand, US visitors spent 18 % more nights in Canada than in the previous year.

For the other three main generating countries there was a general fall in German and British demand in Scandinavia, Belgium and the Netherlands and lower numbers of French visitors to Ireland and the United Kingdom, which both normally receive substantial numbers.

Table 4. **Change in growth rate of number of arrivals at frontiers from the four main generating countries**

	T/V	Total Variation % 86/85	From France		From Germany		From United Kingdom		From United States	
			Relative share % 85	Variation % 86/85	Relative share % 85	Variation % 86/85	Relative share % 85	Variation % 86/85	Relative share % 85	Variation % 86/85
Austria										
Belgium										
Denmark										
Finland										
France (R)	T	−1.8			23.7	−3.5	16.0	7.5	7.6	−40.0
Germany										
Greece[1] (N)	T	6.9	6.7	6.2	16.0	0.0	20.2	11.0	7.1	−56.1
Iceland (N)	T	16.5	4.6	25.3	9.7	44.4	10.0	5.6	32.5	3.4
Ireland (R)	V	−5.1	4.9	−7.5	5.0	1.0	57.8	−1.6	19.8	−21.2
Italy (N)	V	−0.6	16.2	−1.6	21.8	−18.4	3.3	15.6	3.4	−13.2
Luxembourg										
Netherlands										
Norway										
Portugal (N)	T	8.4	6.4	6.4	7.4	3.6	15.1	31.4	3.3	−30.6
Spain (N)	V	9.6	25.4	2.5	13.1	5.2	11.6	27.7	2.3	−22.8
Sweden										
Switzerland										
Turkey (N)	V	−8.4	5.7	−4.0	11.5	29.6	4.8	23.7	7.5	−59.4
United Kingdom (R)	V	−4.9	11.2	8.0	10.2	7.0			21.9	−27.8
EUROPE		1.8	13.6	1.4	17.9	−6.7	9.7	15.7	6.1	−29.7
Canada (R)	T	18.6	0.8	30.8	1.2	26.7	2.4	27.2	87.8	17.7
United States (R)	T	4.7	1.6	31.0	2.4	31.6	4.1	31.7		
NORTH AMERICA		10.1	1.3	30.9	1.9	30.4	3.4	30.5	33.8	17.7
Australia (R)	V	25.1	1.1	15.8	3.3	12.3	13.4	14.7	17.2	24.9
New Zealand (R)	T	17.6	0.3	20.8	1.7	14.9	7.0	19.5	21.1	26.5
Japan (N)	V	−11.4	1.7	−11.0	2.1	1.1	7.9	−22.3	24.0	−1.0
AUSTRALASIA-JAPAN		2.7	1.3	−4.2	2.4	6.8	9.4	−3.1	21.7	8.2
OECD		3.2	11.3	1.9	14.9	−5.8	8.7	16.3	11.1	−3.8
Yugoslavia (N)										

V   Visitors.
T   Tourists.
(R) Tourist count by country of residence.
(N) Tourist count by country of nationality.
1.   For 1986, Secretariat estimates for France, Germany and the United Kingdom.

Table 5. **Change in growth rate of nights spent in the various means of accommodation from the four main generating countries**

	H/A	Total Variation % 86/85	From France		From Germany		From the United Kingdom		From the United-States	
			Relative share % 85	Variation % 86/85	Relative share % 85	Variation % 86/85	Relative share % 85	Variation % 86/85	Relative share % 85	Variation % 86/85
Austria (R)	A	0.4	2.9	9.0	65.2	1.1	5.0	1.5	2.8	−40.7
Belgium (R)	A	−0.2	9.6	2.9	15.4	−0.3	12.6	−6.8	9.1	−10.3
Denmark (N)	A	−5.1	1.6	−8.6	38.8	−5.8	4.5	−7.9	6.6	−26.8
Finland (R)	H	−3.6	2.8	−6.0	13.0	−8.5	5.2	−4.5	8.8	−13.7
France (R)	A	0.7			23.2	0.0	16.1	10.5	9.4	−25.0
Germany (R)	A	−1.0	4.6	3.9			8.8	4.0	18.1	−25.5
Greece (N)										
Iceland										
Ireland (R)	A	0.8	5.8	−4.1	6.7	5.4	50.9	1.8	21.7	−19.6
Italy (N)	A	4.1	7.5	6.4	43.4	8.2	6.2	20.1	7.6	−43.9
Luxembourg (R)	A	7.4	4.0	1.6	7.5	−4.7	3.1	6.9	4.8	−24.1
Netherlands (R)	H	−2.3	6.0	4.7	20.4	8.6	19.2	−3.1	16.0	−30.4
Norway (N)	H	−11.2	2.7	7.7	13.7	−2.8	12.1	−18.8	17.3	−36.0
Portugal (N)	A	12.4	6.9	17.4	15.0	13.9	34.1	17.8	5.4	−36.7
Spain (N)	H	11.1	7.6	3.5	29.9	−0.1	31.7	35.2	3.2	−41.5
Sweden (N)	A	−4.2	1.9	9.8	17.9	−3.8	4.6	−3.7	6.7	−31.8
Switzerland (R)	A	−0.7	7.1	6.2	41.2	1.9	7.8	6.1	10.1	−34.5
Turkey (N)	A	21.8	13.4	26.4	24.2	73.4	5.4	32.9	5.6	−17.8
United Kingdom (R)	A	−7.1	7.6	−5.3	8.7	11.1			18.6	−21.2
EUROPE		0.5	4.1	2.1	26.6	2.9	12.5	14.9	10.2	−26.3
Canada (R)	A	18.6	1.8	31.8	2.9	20.6	6.0	24.5	69.8	17.6
United States										
NORTH AMERICA										
Australia	A		1.3		5.2		10.3		22.2	
New Zealand										
Japan										
AUSTRALASIA-JAPAN										
OECD		2.0	3.9	3.2	24.7	3.1	12.0	15.3	14.9	−10.1
Yugoslavia (N)	A	1.1	3.0	−6.7	38.2	1.6	9.8	7.3	1.2	−36.5

H   Hotels and similar establishments.
A   All means of accommodation.
(R) Tourist count by country of residence.
(N) Tourist count by country of nationality.

III

THE ECONOMIC IMPORTANCE OF INTERNATIONAL TOURISM IN MEMBER COUNTRIES

This chapter brings together the most recent data available concerning international tourist receipts and expenditure in the 24 Member countries of the OECD area and its constituent regions, as well as in Yugoslavia. As far as possible, these data exclude receipts and expenditure relative to international fare payments unless otherwise stated (see Statistical Annex).

Part A of this chapter covers a) receipts, first in national currencies and US dollars (both in current terms) and then in real terms, discounting the effects both of inflation and exchange rate movements against the dollar, and b) expenditure in current terms in national currencies and US dollars. Lastly, c) presents the resultant "tourism balance sheet" in dollars. The accompanying tables must be interpreted with due regard for the steep appreciation of most national currencies in Member countries against the dollar, which was one of the striking features of 1986. Last year the only countries whose national currencies did not appreciate against the dollar were Australia, Canada, Greece, Iceland, Turkey and Yugoslavia. (See Statistical Annex for further details).

Part B compares these data with the main macroeconomic indicators such as Gross Domestic Product, private final consumption, and exports and imports of goods and services up to 1985, the most recent year for which data were available for all OECD Member countries.

Part C which, in the 1986 edition, provided some information on the importance of tourism as an economic activity in a number of OECD Member countries, has now been incorporated by country in Chapter I.

The problem of comparability of international tourist receipts and expenditure has been recognised by the Tourism Committee as one of the top priorities for the work of its Statistical Working Party. This body has completed a study on the issue, along similar lines to that on "international comparability of arrivals and nights." These two documents are available on request from the Secretariat. Proposals for improving this situation are also expected to be put forward in the near future.

A. INTERNATIONAL TOURIST RECEIPTS AND EXPENDITURE

The year 1986 was marked by various events that were beyond the control of the tourism authorities in Member countries although they certainly influenced the development of international tourism in the OECD area. These events included the considerable fluctuations in exchange rates which affected one of the main indicators, i.e. tourist receipts and expenditure. Contrary to the situation prevailing from 1981, the fall in the dollar (the common unit of account used to measure the performance of world foreign trade) distorted the results given by this indicator in 1986 and, in certain cases,

considerably inflated the figures for international tourist receipts and expenditure.

Thus, despite the varying results for receipts in national currency terms and current prices (since nine countries posted decreases), the total figure in current dollars for all the countries was up 24 % from the previous year. This can be partially explained by the fact that the rises in value due to exchange rate fluctuations often exceeded the declines in national currency terms. A similar movement occurred in expenditure, which was up 31 % in dollars.

Table 1. **International tourist receipts and expenditure in national currencies**

In millions

	Currency	Receipts			Expenditure		
		1985	1986	%86/85	1985	1986	%86/85
Austria	Schilling	105 186	105 782	0.6	56 333	64 228	14.0
Belgium-Luxembourg	Franc	98 700	101 400	2.7	121 700	129 000	6.0
Denmark	Krone	14 048	14 230	1.3	14 864	17 095	15.0
Finland	Markka	3 107	3 026	−2.6	4 820	5 425	12.6
France	Franc	71 231	66 361	−6.8	40 889	44 217	8.1
Germany	Deutsche Mark	17 336	16 997	−2.0	43 077	44 879	4.2
Greece	Drachma	196 794	255 953	30.1	50 953	69 388	36.2
Iceland	Krona	1 742			3 190		
Ireland	Pound	519	492	−5.2	402	510	26.9
Italy	Lira	16 721 972	14 691 006	−12.1	4 360 273	4 112 283	−5.7
Netherlands	Guilder	4 975	4 668	−6.2	10 353	10 852	4.8
Norway	Krone	6 493	7 333	12.9	14 812	17 954	21.2
Portugal	Escudo	191 765	234 487	22.3	40 040	49 347	23.2
Spain	Peseta	1 374 682	1 671 927	21.6	170 000	210 400	23.8
Sweden	Krona	10 187	10 993	7.9	16 902	20 021	18.5
Switzerland	Franc	7 775	7 625	−1.9	5 930	6 075	2.4
Turkey	Lira	768 223	821 481	6.9	169 880	208 677	22.8
United Kingdom	Pound	5 451	5 403	−0.9	4 876	5 925	21.5
Canada	Dollar	4 236	5 353	26.4	5 634	5 968	5.9
United States	Dollar	11 675	12 913	10.6	16 482	17 627	6.9
Australia	Dollar	1 554	2 044	31.5	2 727	2 880	5.6
New Zealand[1]	Dollar	561			842		
Japan	Yen	269 870	243 144	−9.9	1 138 453	1 202 946	5.7
Yugoslavia	Dinar	195 016	292 306	49.9			

Notice: for statistical coverage, see notes in tables on Payments in annex.
1. New Zealand : New series from 1986.

Table 2. **International tourists receipts and expenditure in current dollars**

Rounded figures in million dollars

	Receipts			Expenditure		
	1985	1986	%86/85	1985	1986	%86/85
Austria	5 085.1	6 928.3	36.2	2 723.4	4 206.7	54.5
Belgium	1 660.8	2 269.2	36.6	2 047.9	2 886.9	41.0
Denmark	1 326.0	1 759.2	32.7	1 403.0	2 113.3	50.6
Finland	501.4	596.8	19.0	777.9	1 069.9	37.5
France	7 928.6	9 580.2	20.8	4 551.3	6 383.4	40.3
Germany	5 889.1	7 825.9	32.9	14 633.5	20 663.5	41.2
Greece	1 425.5	1 835.1	28.7	369.1	497.5	34.8
Iceland	41.9			76.8		
Ireland	548.8	659.0	20.1	425.1	683.1	60.7
Italy	8 757.6	9 852.8	12.5	2 283.6	2 758.0	20.8
Netherlands	1 497.4	1 905.6	27.3	3 116.2	4 430.0	42.2
Norway	755.5	992.0	31.3	1 723.6	2 428.9	40.9
Portugal	1 128.5	1 582.5	40.2	235.6	333.0	41.3
Spain	8 083.7	11 945.2	47.8	999.7	1 503.2	50.4
Sweden	1 184.2	1 543.2	30.3	1 964.8	2 810.5	43.0
Switzerland	3 163.9	4 239.9	34.0	2 413.1	3 378.0	40.0
Turkey	1 478.6	1 227.9	−17.0	327.0	311.9	−4.6
United Kingdom	6 995.1	7 920.5	13.2	6 257.2	8 685.8	38.8
EUROPE	57 410.0	72 663.3	26.6	46 251.8	65 143.7	40.8
Canada	3 101.4	3 852.7	24.2	4 125.0	4 295.4	4.1
United States	11 675.0	12 913.0	10.6	16 482.0	17 627.0	6.9
NORTH AMERICA	14 776.4	16 765.7	13.5	20 607.0	21 922.4	6.4
Australia	1 085.4	1 366.3	25.9	1 904.7	1 925.2	1.1
New zealand[1]	277.1			415.8		
Japan	1 130.9	1 442.8	27.6	4 770.9	7 138.3	49.6
AUSTRALASIA-JAPAN	2 216.4	2 809.2	26.7	6 675.7	9 063.5	35.8
OECD	74 402.7	92 238.2	24.0	73 534.4	96 129.6	30.7
Yugoslavia	1 050.2	1 105.1	5.2			

1. New Zealand: New series from 1986.

a) *International tourist receipts*

Receipts in *national currencies* were up from 1985 in nine Member countries. Substantial increases were recorded in Australia (32 %), Greece (30 %), Canada (26 %), Spain (22 %) and Portugal (22 %). But the situation deteriorated for the first time since the start of the decade in many countries, with decreases of 12 % in Italy, 10 % in Japan, 7 % in France, 6 % in the Netherlands and 2 % in Switzerland (Table 1).

For the reasons stated previously, when these receipts are expressed *in current dollars*, the common unit of account used in the "Travel" account of the balance of payments, an increase is observed in every country, except for Turkey (– 17 %) (Table 2). On this basis, it is also found that the four leading international tourist receiving countries in terms of receipts have remained the same for many years, accounting for 48 % of the total in the OECD area; these are, in order of rank, the United States, Spain, Italy and France which together accounted for $44.3 billion in receipts in 1986.

In the OECD area as a whole, receipts *in current dollars* continued to rise, after declining slightly between 1981 and 1983, and came to $92.2 billion in 1986, or 24 % more than in the previous year. According to provisional data published by the World Tourism Organisation (WTO), this figure represented 71 % of the 1986 world total ($130 billion) (Diagram 1).

In *real terms*, these receipts remained at the 1985 level in which year there had been a rise of 5 % (Table 3). The falls were noted in Europe and in Japan with the most important declines in Turkey (– 20 %), Italy (– 17 %) and Japan (– 10 %). On the other hand, the most vigorous expansions were recorded in Canada, Australia and Spain with + 21 %, + 20 % and + 12 % respectively. This result was due to the drop of 4 % in Europe where the relative share has made up three-quarters of the OECD total for over two decades. But the 1.5 point gain by the Australasia/Japan region, which accounted for 2.2 % of total receipts in 1980 (Diagram 2), should also be noted.

Table 3. **Trends in international tourist receipts in real prices [1]**

	1981 = 100					Relative share in percentage of total	
	1982	1983	1984	1985	1986	1985	1986
Austria	98.7	95.1	96.3	96.9	96.0	6.9	6.8
Belgium-Luxembourg	112.5	127.3	131.2	128.5	130.2	2.2	2.2
Denmark	110.3	113.4	119.3	119.4	116.8	1.7	1.7
Finland	85.2	77.9	77.5	77.2	72.6	0.7	0.6
France	126.3	138.0	155.3	157.9	144.0	10.4	9.6
Germany	94.4	97.0	104.8	115.7	113.9	8.1	8.0
Greece	82.2	69.6	84.1	94.5	100.7	2.0	2.1
Iceland	129.1	154.5	190.0	231.0		0.1	0.0
Ireland	127.7	127.5	134.5	151.6	138.6	0.7	0.7
Italy	112.2	118.5	117.4	118.8	98.4	11.8	9.8
Netherlands	95.3	94.3	107.4	106.1	99.5	2.0	1.9
Norway	96.1	92.1	94.8	108.0	113.5	1.0	1.1
Portugal	91.7	97.4	113.7	130.1	142.4	1.5	1.6
Spain	109.5	122.5	139.5	141.9	158.5	10.7	12.0
Sweden	119.0	139.8	145.7	148.2	152.8	1.6	1.6
Switzerland	97.4	102.1	111.1	111.9	109.3	4.3	4.2
Turkey[2]	112.2	130.4	288.2			2.0	1.6
United Kingdom	99.1	119.2	131.1	147.0	140.5	9.3	8.9
EUROPE	105.1	111.7	121.2	127.4	122.9	76.9	74.5
Canada	89.5	89.4	99.7	109.5	132.9	4.2	5.2
United States	90.8	80.3	76.9	76.5	82.8	15.3	16.6
NORTH AMERICA	90.6	81.8	80.7	81.8	91.0	19.5	21.8
Australia	102.2	100.9	99.1	116.3	139.7	1.7	2.1
New Zealand[3]	88.9	97.7	137.5	122.8		0.4	0.3
Japan	112.8	114.8	132.6	151.6	135.8	1.5	1.4
AUSTRALASIA-JAPAN	104.6	105.5	115.3	129.6	134.8	3.6	3.7
OECD	101.1	103.3	109.9	115.0	114.6	100.0	100.0
Yugoslavia	72.6	86.3	126.7	108.3	86.1		

1. After correcting for the effects of inflation in each country. For the regional and OECD totals, the receipts of the individual countries are weighted in proportion to their share in the total expressed in dollars.
2. New series from 1984.
3. New series from 1986

International tourist receipts

Diagram 1.   **Importance of the OECD area in the world total in 1986[1]**
(in current dollars)

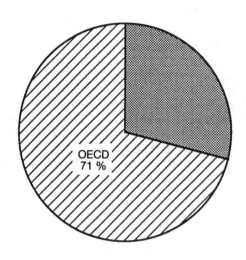

1.   Provisional data.

Diagram 2.   **Shares of the various regions within the OECD area**
(in real terms, 1980)

1980

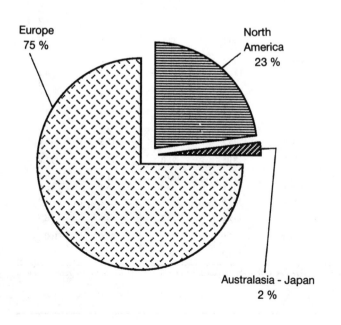

Europe
75 %

North
America
23 %

Australasia - Japan
2 %

1986

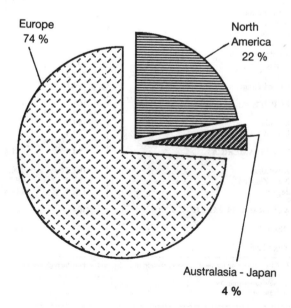

Europe
74 %

North
America
22 %

Australasia - Japan
4 %

b) International tourist expenditure

All countries posted increases in expenditure in *national currencies* in 1986, except for Italy (– 6 % from the previous year) (Table 1). A recent development that will in time affect the world position of certain tourist generating countries should be noted: the speed-up observed in Japan since 1983 with an increase of 3 % in that year and progress of 4 %, 4 % and 6 % in the subsequent years.

The expenditure of Member countries in *current dollars* was up in almost every case in 1986, the only exception being Turkey where a 5 % decline was recorded from the previous year (Table 2). Overall, expenditure increased by 31 % to reach $96.1 billion in 1986. If Member countries are classified as sources of international tourism on the basis of expenditure in current dollars, the progress of the Japanese market is to be noted, for it now ranks fourth, ahead of France but behind Germany, the United States and the United Kingdom. These five countries together accounted for 63 % of the total expenditure of OECD Member countries.

c) Tourism balance sheet

After being more or less in equilibrium since 1982, the tourism balance sheet for the OECD area deteriorated in 1986 with a deficit of $3.9 billion (Table 4). The

Table 4. **Tourism balance sheet**
In billions of current dollars

	1984	1985	1986
EUROPE			
Receipts	54.1	57.4	72.7
Expenditure	43.9	46.3	65.1
Balance[1]	10.2	11.2	7.5
NORTH AMERICA			
Receipts	14.2	14.8	16.8
Expenditure	19.4	20.6	21.9
Balance[1]	–5.2	–5.8	–5.2
AUSTRALASIA-JAPAN[2]			
Receipts	2.1	2.2	2.8
Expenditure	6.7	6.7	9.1
Balance[1]	–4.7	–4.5	–6.3
OECD[2]			
Receipts	70.4	74.4	92.2
Expenditure	70.1	73.5	96.1
Balance[1]	0.3	0.9	–3.9

1. Minus signs indicate deficits. Due to rounding of figures, balances are not always equal to difference between receipts and expenditures.
2. Excluding New Zealand (new series from 1986) and Iceland.

surplus in European OECD countries as a whole partly offset the deficits in the other regions. With 79 % of total receipts and 68 % of total expenditure, Europe's figures for these two items were up 27 % and 41 % respectively from the previous year, which gave a surplus of $7.5 billion. Contrary to the situation between 1982 and 1985, this sum was not sufficient to offset the traditional deficits of the other regions which include three of the six largest generating markets in terms of dollars, i.e. the United States, Japan and Canada.

B. THE ECONOMIC IMPORTANCE OF THE "TRAVEL ACCOUNT" IN THE BALANCE OF PAYMENTS

For many years the Tourism Committee has been studying the best way of relating the international tourism trend to the main economic indicators. Pending the outcome of certain work to improve the quality and comparability of data on services (see in particular that of the Tourism Committee discussed in Chapter V), it seemed necessary to stay with the approach used in earlier editions.

It should be stated that the figures as contained in the OECD databanks have been used so as to allow comparisons with data already collected for the OECD area. Since some statistics are based on methods differing from those used by the Tourism Committee, reference should be made to the OECD publications for further details. This explains, for example, the use of the term "travel account" in the balance of payments as, in some cases, it has been found that the data provided by the central banks differed from those obtained by means of the Tourism Committee's annual questionnaire. As the 1986 data on the indicators used are not yet available

for all Member countries, the fullest possible series has been used, i.e. the one for the year 1985.

In addition, to show the importance of tourism more clearly in the Member countries' balances of payments, payments for "international passenger transport" should be taken into account. However, as shown by the relevant table in the Annex to the publication, fewer than half the Member countries are in possession of this information coming under the balance of payments "transport account".

a) Ratio of "travel account" receipts to Gross Domestic Product

In the absence of a full series for all Member countries on the Gross National Product, the Gross Domestic Product can be used for comparisons between countries and between sectors in the same country. In this context a more accurate measurement of the contribution by tourism should include residents' tourist expenditure. For the time being, however, these data are available only in a small number of countries, so their use would be limited and therefore not representative of the situation in the OECD area as a whole.

For the past ten years this ratio has been almost 1 % for the OECD area as a whole, with the "Europe" region up 0.5 points to 2 % in 1985. Between 1983 and 1985 the largest increases were recorded in the less developed area of OECD: in Turkey (from 0.8 to 2.1), in Greece (from 3.4 to 4.4) and in Portugal (from 4.1 to 5.5) (Table 5).

Table 5. **Ratio of the "Travel" account receipts to the gross domestic product (%)**

	1983	1984	1985
Austria	7.9	7.9	7.7
Belgium-Luxembourg	2.1	2.2	2.1
Denmark	2.3	2.4	2.3
Finland	1.0	1.0	0.9
France	1.4	1.6	1.6
Germany	0.8	0.9	0.9
Greece	3.4	3.9	4.3
Iceland	1.1	1.4	1.6
Ireland	2.7	2.7	3.0
Italy	2.2	2.1	2.0
Netherlands	1.1	1.2	1.2
Norway	1.2	1.2	1.3
Portugal	4.1	5.0	5.5
Spain	4.4	5.0	4.9
Sweden	1.2	1.2	1.2
Switzerland	4.2	4.5	4.4
Turkey	0.8	1.1	2.1
United Kingdom	1.3	1.4	1.6
EUROPE	**1.8**	**1.9**	**2.0**
Canada	1.0	1.0	1.1
United States	0.3	0.3	0.3
NORTH AMERICA	**0.4**	**0.4**	**0.4**
Australia	0.7	0.6	0.7
New Zealand	1.0	1.4	1.3
Japan	0.1	0.1	0.1
AUSTRALASIA-JAPAN	**0.2**	**0.2**	**0.2**
OECD	**0.9**	**0.9**	**0.9**

Source: OECD, Balance of Payments Division and *National Accounts of OECD Member Countries.*

b) Ratio of "travel account" expenditure to private final consumption

The comment made in Section B. *a)* on the use and availability of data on tourist spending by residents also applies to the calculation of the ratio of expenditure to private final consumption.

On the basis of available data, this ratio has been on an uptrend for ten years in Europe where it has risen from 2.2 to 2.7. The largest increases between 1983 and 1985 were also recorded in Europe, with Iceland up 1.2 point, Switzerland 0.6 and Turkey 0.5 (Table 6).

Table 6. **Ratio of the "Travel" account expenditure to the private final consumption (%)**

	1983	1984	1985
Austria	7.5	7.2	7.3
Belgium-Luxembourg	4.0	3.9	4.0
Denmark	4.0	4.2	4.4
Finland	2.3	2.5	2.7
France	1.3	1.4	1.4
Germany	4.0	4.0	4.1
Greece	1.6	1.6	1.7
Iceland	4.6	5.6	5.8
Ireland	4.2	4.1	4.1
Italy	0.7	0.8	0.7
Netherlands	4.1	4.1	4.2
Norway	6.4	6.2	6.4
Portugal	1.6	1.7	1.7
Spain	0.9	0.8	0.9
Sweden	3.4	3.5	3.8
Switzerland	4.6	4.9	5.2
Turkey	0.3	0.7	0.8
United Kingdom	2.3	2.4	2.3
EUROPE	**2.6**	**2.6**	**2.6**
Canada	2.6	2.6	2.6
United States	0.6	0.6	0.6
NORTH AMERICA	**0.8**	**0.8**	**0.8**
Australia	1.8	2.0	2.0
New Zealand	3.2	3.5	3.0
Japan	0.6	0.6	0.6
AUSTRALASIA-JAPAN	**0.8**	**0.8**	**0.8**
OECD	**1.4**	**1.4**	**1.4**

Source: OECD, Balance of Payments Division and *National Accounts of OECD Member Countries.*

c) Share of "travel account" receipts in exports of goods and services

The share of receipts in the exports of goods and services of OECD Member countries as a whole has remained at 4 % for many years. Between 1983 and 1985, substantial increases were recorded, particularly in Turkey (from 5.3 % to 9.6 %) and in Greece (from 16.4 % to 20.1 %), while the share was down by 2 points in Austria and by 1 point in Italy (Table 7).

For better comparisons using this economic performance indicator, changes in the share of receipts in exports of goods are often used, thus excluding services, for which the statistical content is often uncertain or relates to accounting operations that have nothing to do with measuring the results in economic terms. This kind of calculation leads to some interesting comparisons at world level. For instance, recent data published by the WTO on this subject show that at world level this share has remained at above 5 % since the start of the decade, with some progress since 1983 (from 5.2 to 5.7 % in 1985). The figure is slightly higher in the case of the OECD area but has tended to taper off and came to 6.1 % in 1985, with European Member countries accounting for 7.9 %. Of the latter, three major receiving countries have seen marked fluctuations in this percentage since 1980: Austria which was up 4.9 points to 28.7 % in 1985, Greece which was down 13.9 points to 33.3 % and Portugal down 5.2 points to 19.9 %.

Table 7. **Share of "Travel" account receipts in exports of goods and services**

	1983	1984	1985
Austria	18.8	17.7	16.8
Belgium-Luxembourg	2.2	2.1	2.0
Denmark	5.8	5.8	5.5
Finland	3.2	3.0	3.0
France	5.0	5.2	5.2
Germany	2.6	2.6	2.7
Greece	16.4	17.9	20.1
Iceland	2.4	3.2	3.5
Ireland	4.7	4.3	4.5
Italy	9.3	8.6	8.1
Netherlands	1.8	1.8	1.7
Norway	2.5	2.4	2.5
Portugal	13.3	13.5	14.2
Spain	21.0	21.1	21.1
Sweden	3.0	3.0	3.0
Switzerland	9.1	8.9	8.6
Turkey	5.3	5.6	9.6
United Kingdom	3.3	3.2	3.5
EUROPE	5.2	5.2	5.2
Canada	3.5	3.3	3.5
United States	3.4	3.2	3.3
NORTH AMERICA	3.5	3.2	3.3
Australia	4.3	3.8	4.0
New Zealand	3.4	4.3	3.8
Japan	0.5	0.5	0.5
AUSTRALASIA-JAPAN	1.0	1.0	1.0
OECD	4.2	4.1	4.1

Source: OECD, Balance of Payments Division.

d) Share of "travel account" expenditure in the imports of goods and services

The share of travel expenditure in imports of goods and services is 4 % for the OECD area as a whole. The countries with the biggest differences between 1983 and 1985 are Austria (from 10.5 to 9.0 %) and Iceland (from 5.8 to 7.0 %) (Table 8).

However, taking only the imports of goods into account, it is 6 % for OECD Member countries as a whole. Since the start of the decade this percentage has risen, especially in Iceland (by 8.6 points), Norway (by 3.3) and Finland (by 2.2), while the opposite was seen in New Zealand (down 3.3 points).

Table 8. **Share of "Travel" account expenditure in imports of goods and services**

	1983	1984	1985
Austria	10.5	9.2	9.0
Belgium-Luxembourg	2.7	2.5	2.5
Denmark	5.2	5.1	5.3
Finland	3.8	4.2	4.5
France	2.9	2.9	3.0
Germany	7.8	7.4	7.4
Greece	3.3	3.1	3.1
Iceland	5.8	6.9	7.0
Ireland	3.7	3.2	3.1
Italy	1.9	2.0	1.7
Netherlands	4.2	3.9	3.9
Norway	7.1	6.6	7.0
Portugal	2.3	2.3	2.4
Spain	2.5	2.3	2.7
Sweden	4.5	4.7	5.0
Switzerland	7.0	6.9	7.1
Turkey	1.1	2.1	2.2
United Kingdom	3.5	3.3	3.3
EUROPE	4.5	4.3	4.3
Canada	5.7	5.0	4.9
United States	3.7	3.4	3.6
NORTH AMERICA	4.0	3.7	3.8
Australia	5.8	5.7	5.2
New Zealand	5.3	5.1	4.5
Japan	2.8	2.6	2.9
AUSTRALASIA-JAPAN	3.3	3.3	3.3
OECD	4.2	4.0	4.1

Source: OECD, Balance of Payments Division.

IV

TRANSPORT

Tourism and civil air transport are closely interdependent. Both have experienced spectacular growth and development since the end of the Second World War. Indeed, international tourism as we know it today would be literally impossible without highly developed air transport facilities serving an ever-growing range of destinations. Equally, the airlines of the world derive the greater part of their revenue from leisure travellers. Growth has been spurred on by the dramatic reduction in the true cost of air travel – now about half what it was some 20 years ago. The scheduled airlines, alert to the price-sensitivity of the holiday market, have progressively introduced a variety of innovative promotional fares.

The airline industry has expanded into the hotel accommodation and tour operating sectors. Furthermore, the substantial expenditure by airlines on advertising and sales promotion helps to publicise tourism destinations over and above the resources of local or national tourism authorities. The air transport and tourism sectors thus share a strong mutual interest.

According to the report on economic trends in air transport assembled by the 156 states members of the International Civil Aviation Organisation (ICAO), air transport has performed better in the last ten years than the general economy and should continue to do so through the next decade. The comparatively favourable position of air transport in terms of production and revenue is attributable in part to the fact that the price of air services did not increase as rapidly as either per capita income or the price index. The average annual rate of increase in the air passenger fare per kilometre, for example, was 3.6 per cent against 7.2 per cent for per capita income in developed market economies.

Historically, the ability of the air transport industry to offer transportation at unit prices which have increased less than those for other goods and services is attributed to improved productivity, made possible by technological innovation. By way of example, productivity per airline employee rose at an average annual rate of 7.3 per cent between 1975 and 1985, while labour productivity in manufacturing in developed market economies increased by 3.2 per cent per year.

In the near future it is expected that the scheduled air traffic growth rate of 7 per cent a year over the past decade will continue. International scheduled passenger traffic is forecast to grow at an average rate of 8 per cent per year and domestic scheduled passenger traffic at 6 per cent per year. The slower growth of domestic traffic is due to the fact that 77 per cent of all domestic scheduled passenger traffic is accounted for by the already highly developed domestic systems in the USA and USSR, where future growth rates are expected to be moderate.

In 1986 the average real growth of some 2.5 per cent in the GNP of the industrialised countries was down on the 3 per cent and 4.75 per cent recorded in 1985 and 1984 respectively, and tourism was also faced with several unpredictable events such as terrorist activity, Chernobyl and a drop in the value of the American dollar. However, according to the preliminary information assembled by ICAO, despite such negative factors, because of renewed upward growth during the autumn months, the continuous increasing trend of revenue passenger-kilometres could be maintained overall in 1986.

This upward trend has been reinforced in the beginning of 1987. According to the twenty members of the Association of European Airlines (AEA), AEA member airlines achieved an 11 per cent upturn in passenger traffic for February 1987, resulting in a record load factor for this time of year of 59.7 per cent. A similar passenger result was recorded on the North Atlantic where, as a result of double-digit growth by ten members coupled with moderate capacity increases, the overall load factor rose to 55.4 per cent from 51.5 in 1986. Geographical Europe and Asian routes also saw load factor increases during February.

As far as safety is concerned, information assembled by ICAO shows that sixteen airline accidents killed 330 passengers on scheduled flights in 1986, a sharp drop from the 1985 record of 22 fatal accidents and 1 066 deaths.

Some influential judgements were issued in 1986. These included the "Nouvelles Frontières" case considered by the European Court concerning the competition policy of European civil aviation, the judgement by the US Supreme Court accepting the right of individual states to tax international aviation operations, and the rejection by the Italian Constitutional Court of the limits of liability for passengers as expressed by the Warsaw Convention.

Following the "*Nouvelles Frontières*" case, the Commission of the European Communities has vigorously encouraged both EC governments and their airlines in the direction of free competition of air transport. In May 1987 it finally decided to pursue its legal action against Lufthansa, Alitalia and Olympic Airways, the national airlines of Germany, Italy and Greece respectively, over alleged infringement of EEC competition rules. The decision marks a significant stepping up of the Commission's attack on the deep-rooted EEC airline cartels.

In response to these initiatives by the Commission, after a number of meetings, the Ministers of Transport of the European Communities agreed on the common criteria of the awarding of discount and deep-discount, which can be 55 per cent of the normal price of an economy-class ticket.

In response to the agreement by the Ministers of Transport, the 22 member states of the European Civil Aviation Conference (ECAC) have finalised two new international agreements in April 1987 and they were signed in June. The first of these agreements, dealing with tariffs, provides for two zones of automatic approval for discount and deep-discount fares. It gives the ability to an airline unilaterally to propose tariffs to governments, without the necessity of agreeing them first with other airlines, and incorporates a new quick arbitration process to resolve tariff disputes. This agreement replaces the International Tariffs Agreement of 1967, which was also developed under the auspices of ECAC and which has provided the framework within which air fares have been established over the past twenty years.

The second agreement relates to capacity sharing and effectively puts an end to insistence by some states that in each bilateral market their airlines should have a 50 per cent share of total capacity between two countries. This agreement will cover a two-year experimental period, with provision for further flexibility in the third year.

Both agreements provide for review of the experimental elements, within 18 months to two years of their coming into force. Protocols to be signed on the same occasion by those signatories which are also members of the EEC will avoid any conflict between the provisions of the agreements and the law of the European Communities as regards relations between EEC Member States. The new agreements and protocols were signed at a Diplomatic Conference being held in conjunction with ECAC's sixteenth intermediate session, which took place in June 1987.

In the United States, as a result of the progressive deregulation which has lasted from the late 1970s, air transport productivity has been much improved and as a result, air fares have declined. However, at the same time, the concentration has also much increased. It is clear that the US has entered the second stage of deregulation which involves the more difficult task of how competition can be maintained under conditions of developing oligopoly.

The most significant development for rail transport was the agreement between France and the United Kingdom to construct a railway tunnel to connect their countries, a decision that is not only historic in that the plans for such a tunnel, which have been put forward so many times, seem at last to be moving forward, but also illustrates a development in the pattern of thinking in Europe of the rail versus road debate. A fixed rail link brings the United Kingdom closer to the Continent, not only in the direct practical sense but also in the sense that it symbolises a greater commitment to European transport integration.

Among the world cruising markets, the Mediterranean was seriously affected in 1986 by travellers' concern over threats to security. Even in 1987, the influence has been maintained. According to a leading Greek cruising company, by the beginning of March 1987 there had been only 5 000 bookings from US tourists, only an eighth of what would have been expected before 1986. On the other hand, because of the transfer of a number of cruise ships from the Mediterranean and other European areas to the Caribbean, the competition is at present stronger than ever before in that market.

A. AIR TRANSPORT: EVOLUTION OF TRAFFIC

a) *World air traffic*

During the earlier part of 1986, as a result of the combined impact of the decline in dollar exchange rates, fears over security and the accident at Chernobyl, international scheduled air traffic turned downwards. According to the 151 members of the International Air Transport Association (IATA), on IATA international scheduled services (from January to July 1986), revenue passenger-kilometres fell by more than 1 per cent compared to the same period in 1985. Furthermore, the available seat-kilometres continued to increase, by 5.8 per cent, so the passenger load factor decreased very substantially.

Despite these setbacks, the trend turned upwards again during the autumn months and, overall, a slight increase of the volume of passenger-kilometres was recorded in 1986. Information assembled by ICAO for international scheduled services shows that nearly 200 million passengers were carried in 1986. However, in terms of passenger-kilometres, traffic increased by only 1 per cent while capacity (available seat-kilometres) increased by 4 per cent, which resulted in the passenger load factor dropping by 2 points to 63 per cent (see Table 1). Preliminary estimates indicate that there was an increase of 8 per cent in international charter passenger-kilometres.

Table 1. **Development of world scheduled passenger traffic**

Year	Number of passengers		Passenger-kilometres		Seat-kilometres		Passenger load factor (%)
	In millions	Annual variation (%)	In billions	Annual variation (%)	In billions	Annual variation (%)	
1977	610	6	818	7	1 346	6	61
1978	679	11	936	14	1 451	8	65
1979	754	11	1 060	13	1 607	11	66
1980	748	–1	1 089	3	1 724	7	63
1981	752	1	1 119	3	1 756	7	64
1982	765	2	1 142	2	1 794	2	64
1983	797	4	1 119	4	1 852	3	64
1984	846	6	1 277	7	1 970	6	65
1985	897	6	1 367	7	2 078	5	66
1986[1]	950	6	1 442	5	2 213	6	65

1. Provisional data.
Source: International Civil Aviation Organisation (ICAO).

In 1986, the scheduled airlines of ICAO contracting states had estimated operating results of $4.5 billion on revenues of $123 billion. The industry has now achieved positive financial results for three years in succession, although the net profit (which is not yet available) is likely to be lower than in 1985.

Among the many factors which make up unit costs, jet fuel represents about 20 per cent of airlines' total operating costs (second only to staff costs for most carriers), and it amounts to some US$ 10 billion per year for international scheduled services by IATA airlines. The dramatic drop in crude oil prices from 1985 has been reflected in jet fuel prices in almost all competitive markets, especially Australia, Europe, the Far East and North America where, by the middle of 1986, airlines were able to buy fuel for as little as US cents 45-50 per gallon. As a result, latest estimates by IATA show that total fuel costs to the airlines in 1986 will be about one-third less than last year.

Despite such lower fuel costs, other elements such as insurance costs, user charges on airlines and the new administrative burden for collecting taxes imposed on passengers, pushed unit costs up about 5 per cent in 1986 over 1985.

At first, as far as insurance is concerned, airlines renewing their insurance in the first half of 1986 experienced increases of over 10 per cent on hull rates, while some of them faced rises of more than 50 per cent in liability rates. Furthermore, most airlines have had their cover reduced in one form or another. In May 1986, the airlines had a cancellation and re-rating of their war risk cover imposed on them as well as the introduction of a terrorist surcharge.

Secondly, there have been significant changes in the user charges environment in recent years. There is a growing tendency to make airports autonomous bodies responsible for their own management and, therefore, for earning sufficient revenue to pay their costs. This trend is expected to accelerate, resulting in increasing pressure on the airlines to pay more for airport services; and in the field of air navigation charges and facilities, there are strong moves towards 100 per cent cost recovery.

Lastly, in the same context, airlines increasingly became required to collect taxes or charges imposed on passengers. The cost and administrative burden of collection falls on the airlines. In cases where a tax or charge is imposed purely on departing passengers, there are certain local facilitation concerns and a necessity for reporting and accounting of the tax or charge. Where the tax is required to be collected by airlines outside the jurisdiction of the taxing authority, the administrative burden and cost of collecting and remitting the tax becomes considerably greater, especially for airlines operating in a large number of jurisdictions.

In conclusion, IATA estimates that the combined effect of these changes in traffic, capacity, yield and unit cost, along with a small increase in combined total interest charges and increasing personnel expenditure, will be a loss of between $ 600-800 million for 1986, the worst net result since 1982.

b) North Atlantic air traffic

Information assembled by IATA shows that more than 21 million passengers were flown on North Atlantic routes by all operators in 1986, a decrease of 9 per cent over 1985 (Table 2). Scheduled traffic fell by 6 per cent and non-scheduled traffic was also cut dramatically by 38 per cent over 1985.

Table 2. **Trend of North Atlantic air traffic**

IATA and non-IATA

Number of passengers carried in both directions
in 1986: 21 083 000

	83/82 %	84/83 %	85/84 %	86/85 %
Scheduled	6.4	12.5	7.6	–5.9
Non-scheduled	5.7	13.6	–9.4	–37.6
Total	6.3	12.6	5.6	–8.9

Source :   International Air Travel Association (IATA).

As the data by major groupings of routes in Table 3 shows, apart from scheduled services to and from Canada, all services decreased in 1986. However, as far as scheduled services are concerned, this negative trend was reversed from November (Table 4). On the other hand, charter services maintained their decreasing long-term trend, because of increasingly competitive scheduled services. Compared to the decline of passengers to and from the United States, Canada's was moderate, mainly as a result of the impact of Expo '86.

Because the increasing trend in capacity had been maintained until the middle of the year, in 1986 as a whole the capacity increased by 2.0 per cent, so that the average passenger load factor fell to 63.6 per cent, 4.4 points lower than 1985. However, as a result of the decrease of the capacity during the second half of 1986, the average passenger load factor started to creep up again during the last quarter. Concerning charter services, the decline in demand was closely reflected in capacity reductions and the average passenger load factor remained almost the same as in 1985.

c) Air traffic between Europe and the Far East

According to IATA, passenger-kilometres flown between Europe and the Far East, in 1986, increased by 4.2 per cent over 1985 to 47.7 billion. However, available seat-kilometres rose even faster by 11.7 to 72.1 billion. As a result, the very high passenger load factor

Table 3. **North Atlantic air traffic in both directions**

IATA and non-IATA

	1984 Relative share %	1984/83 Variation %	1985 Relative share %	1985/84 Variation %	1986 Relative share %	1986/85 Variation %
North Atlantic						
Scheduled	87.9	12.5	90.2	7.6	93.6	–5.9
Non-scheduled	12.1	13.6	9.8	–9.4	6.4	–37.6
Total	100.0	12.6	100.0	5.6	100.0	–8.9
Of which:						
United States						
Scheduled	75.5	12.1	77.5	7.6	79.5	–6.9
Non-scheduled	8.2	25.2	6.4	–15.5	3.8	–42.8
Total	83.7	13.3	83.9	5.4	83.3	–9.5
Canada						
Scheduled	11.0	14.0	11.4	9.0	12.8	1.6
Non-scheduled	3.9	–5.4	3.4	4.7	2.6	–28.0
Total	14.9	8.3	14.8	8.0	15.4	–5.1
Beyond						
scheduled	1.4	20.0	1.3	–6.2	1.3	–10.0
Non-scheduled	0.0		0.0		0.0	
Total	1.4	20.0	1.3	–6.0	1.3	–10.2

Source: International Air Transport Association (IATA).

Table 4. **North Atlantic air traffic in both directions**

IATA and non-IATA

Percentage variations 1985-1986

Month	Number of passengers			Number of seats			Load factor		
	Total	Scheduled flights	Non-scheduled flights	Total	Scheduled flights	Non-scheduled flights	Total	Scheduled flights	Non-scheduled flights
January	5.8	6.4	−13.5	13.4	14.0	−11.6	−4.2	−4.1	−1.9
February	4.4	4.6	−6.7	14.3	14.7	−7.1	−4.9	−4.9	0.4
March	−1.8	−1.1	−21.3	19.2	20.3	−20.1	−13.5	−13.7	−1.4
April	−10.5	−11.3	2.7	10.6	10.9	3.7	−13.5	−14.0	−0.8
May	−17.7	−16.2	−32.5	3.4	6.2	−31.5	−14.1	−14.3	−1.3
June	−21.0	−17.0	−46.9	−8.1	−3.2	−45.9	−10.6	−10.6	−1.6
July	−16.7	−11.3	−46.4	−8.6	−2.6	−46.6	−6.8	−6.6	0.3
August	−8.5	−2.5	−40.9	−8.2	−3.1	−40.9	−0.2	0.4	0.0
September	−9.8	−6.4	−35.9	−9.2	−6.5	−34.6	−0.5	0.1	−1.7
October	−6.4	−4.9	−27.9	−8.1	−6.9	−29.7	1.2	1.4	2.1
November	3.0	3.5	−17.4	−0.9	−0.5	−26.0	2.2	2.2	9.3
December	5.2	6.7	−41.3	−0.5	0.4	−43.1	3.4	3.7	2.7
TOTAL	−8.9	−5.9	−37.6	−1.0	2.0	−37.3	−5.5	−5.2	−0.4

Source: International Air Transport Association (IATA).

attained on this route area in recent years fell from 70.9 per cent in 1985 to 66.2 per cent in 1986. The Polar route was particularly affected with its load factor falling from 73.2 per cent to 64.8 per cent.

d) Air traffic in Europe

IATA reported that there was no appreciable growth on intra-European routes in passenger-kilometres for its member airlines in 1986. The passenger load factor fell to 60.6 per cent in 1986 from 63.1 per cent in 1985, as the available seat-kilometres increased during the year to 90.5 billion.

e) Air traffic to and from Japan

In 1986, total passenger traffic on routes to and from Japan was 17.5 million, 3.7 per cent more than in the previous year. The movement of Japanese nationals on these routes was 10.3 million, 12.6 per cent more than in 1985. There were no major fluctuations in the distribution of total traffic between the major regional groupings as identified in Table 5.

However, foreign passengers between major regional groupings and Japan (except South America) decreased 7 per cent over the previous year. Japanese nationals travelling between Oceania and Japan showed a considerable increase during 1986.

Table 5. **International air traffic to and from Japan by scheduled flights**

In thousands

Region/country	Total passenger traffic						Japanese nationals					
	1985		1986		1986/85		1985		1986		1986/85	
	Volume %	Relative share %	Volume %	Relative share %	Variation %		Volume %	Relative share %	Volume %	Relative share %	Variation %	
Canada/United States[1]	5 400	32.1	5 754	33.0	6.6		2 938	32.2	3 304	32.1	12.5	
South America[2]	68	0.4	81	0.5	19.1		38	0.4	44	0.4	15.8	
Oceania	319	1.9	381	2.2	19.4		214	2.4	284	2.3	32.7	
Asia	9 545	56.7	9 755	55.9	2.2		4 887	53.5	5 579	54.3	14.2	
Middle East/Africa	105	0.6	77	0.4	−26.7		51	0.5	39	0.4	−23.5	
Europe	1 393	8.3	1 406	8.0	0.9		1 001	11.0	1 033	10.0	3.2	
TOTAL[3]	16 831	100.0	17 454	100.0	3.7		9 129	100.0	10 283	100.0	12.6	

1. Hawaï, Guam and Saipan included.
2. Mexico included.
3. Transit passengers included.
Source: Ministry of Justice, Immigration Department.

f) Air traffic to and from Australia

Data provided in Table 6 on air traffic to and from Australia in 1984, 1985 and 1986 is not directly comparable with similar information published in earlier editions. This is due to the fact that the previous data was based on city pair air traffic information provided by the Department of Aviation whereas it now originates from the Australian Bureau of Statistics which provides a more accurate indication of the ultimate origin or destination of the travellers.

In 1986, the number of passengers travelling to and from Australia by air increased by 11.4 per cent with strong growth on many major routes. Travel to and from Asia and America became relatively more significant while travel to and from the United Kingdom was relatively less important.

Table 6. **International air traffic to and from Australia**

Country/Region	Overseas visitors (Arrivals)			Australian residents (Departures)		
	1984 %	1985 %	1986 %	1984 %	1985 %	1986 %
Africa	1.4	1.4	1.4	1.4	1.3	1.2
America	15.3	15.6	16.1	15.4	15.7	16.4
North America	14.4	14.6	15.1	14.5	14.7	15.4
Asia	28.0	28.3	29.4	26.9	27.8	29.3
South East Asia	14.0	13.7	14.2	13.4	13.5	14.0
East Asia	11.1	11.7	12.4	10.7	11.6	12.6
Europe	26.6	26.8	25.5	27.1	27.1	25.1
United Kingdom	14.0	13.9	13.2	14.6	14.0	13.0
Other Europe	12.5	12.9	12.3	12.5	13.0	12.2
Oceania[2]	28.5	27.7	27.4	28.8	27.6	27.3
Other countries	0.2	0.2	0.2	0.4	0.5	0.7
TOTAL (%)	100.0	100.0	100.0	100.0	100.0	100.0
TOTAL (in thousands of passengers)	2 530.5	2 794.2	3 122.0	2 490.1	2 687.3	2 983.7

1. Not comparable to data published in earlier editions.
2. New Zealand included.
Source: Australian Bureau of Statistics, and Department of Aviation.

B. AIR TRANSPORT: POLICY DEVELOPMENTS

Passenger services: The IATA Multilateral Interline Traffic Agreement – Passenger, and the many related standard industry forms, procedures and specifications, form the basic structure of the worldwide interline system. The interline agreement and these standards, which are in the form of resolutions and recommended practices, are constantly under review and refinement.

In 1986, a number of challenging issues and industry problems concerning reservations, ticketing, passenger processing, baggage tracing and management have been dealt with, recognising the increasing importance and opportunities of automation. Among those, some typical topics can be raised as follows.

In response to pressure from consumer groups, a task force was appointed to study ways to reduce the number of no-show passengers and thereby to reduce carriers' reliance on tactics such as overbooking. In turn this should reduce the number of passengers denied boarding. The task force made a number of recommendations for improvement which were considered at the annual meeting of the Passenger Services Committee in September 1986.

A completely revolutionary method of fare basis coding for passenger tickets has been developed. The revised system will be more logical for computerised ticketing systems and will simplify the deciphering of the fare basis on tickets by both passengers and airline staff. It will provide considerable cost savings and greater accuracy in the areas of revenue accounting and statistics. The revised fare basis coding system was presented for adoption at the September 1986 joint ATC/IATA meeting of the Passenger Service Conference.

A standard industry boarding pass has been developed which can be handled in either a manual or automated environment. The standard boarding pass will enable airlines to use shared boarding pass printers at airports and will permit the issue of through-interline boarding passes. This will improve passenger service and reduce passenger queues at connecting airports. The standard boarding pass will also facilitate automated boarding control and passenger/baggage matching for security purposes.

The IATA/SITA Primary Baggage Tracing System (Bagtrac) now has 106 participating carriers and continues to be a valuable tool for interline baggage tracing. To further improve the effectiveness of the system, a series of ten Bagtrac workshops will be held throughout Africa and the Middle East during 1987 in conjunction with the Baggage Improvement Programme.

Noise certification standards: In the current discussions between ECAC, EEC and the United States, noise certification standards which will be used as a basis to apply operating bans or restrictions on aircraft already in service, are being proposed, which may come into effect as early as 1st January 1988.

While in a global context only a small number of old-type jet aircraft would be affected at certain airports, the restrictions would impose a heavy economic burden on airlines of some developing countries which cannot afford to replace or upgrade their fleets before that date. At the 26th ICAO Assembly, the Assembly urged states imposing such noise restrictions to grant temporary exemptions for up to two years. The ICAO Council was instructed to study as a matter of urgency the economic implications of further limitations on operations of the quieter subsonic jets (those generally produced after 1977) and to report to the next session.

Security: Acts of international terrorism against civil aviation have continued, both in the air and on the ground. In order to oppose more effectively these acts, the ICAO Council revised Annex 17 of the Chicago Convention in December 1985. This revision, which tightened aviation security, became applicable worldwide on 19th May 1986. In its triennial report, the ICAO Council also urged all States to insert in their bilateral agreements on air services a clause on aviation security.

At the 26th Session of the ICAO Assembly in October 1986, the Assembly adopted a resolution to develop a draft instrument which would extend the provisions of existing ICAO Conventions on unlawful seizure of aircraft and acts against the safety of civil aviation to criminal acts at airports serving international civil aviation. The existing Conventions (The Hague and Montreal), which have been ratified by 130 States, require the prosecution or extradition of offenders without exception as well as the imposition of severe penalties. The Assembly called upon the Council to include the preparation of an additional draft instrument by the Legal Committee as a matter of the highest

priority with a view to its adoption at a Diplomatic Conference before the end of 1987. The Assembly also condemned once again all terrorist acts directed against international civil aviation "wherever and by whoever they are perpetrated" and instructed the Council to continue giving top priority to aviation security.

Concerning the financial burden on developing States of implementing the more stringent provisions of the recently revised Annex 17 and the need for increased technical assistance in the field of aviation security, on the initiative of the Government of Canada, in co-operation with ICAO, a $10 million assistance programme was established to improve the level of airport and aircraft security in developing nations.

IATA also expanded the Intensified Aviation Security Programme. This provides for airport surveys by small groups of airline experts co-ordinated by the secretariat. More than 24 airports received visits in 1986, ranging from major international gateways to smaller airports catering largely to seasonal holiday traffic. IATA has also worked to secure implementation by governments of the new Security Annex to the Chicago Convention. Pressure was also maintained to ensure that the terms of the three security conventions – Tokyo, The Hague and Montreal – are observed. Work with the Airport Associations Co-ordinating Council is continuing and joint policies covering baggage, cargo and ramp security, high-risk designation and inadmissible passengers have been developed. When converted into practice, these policies are designed to result in tighter security and safer air travel. They have been presented both within ICAO and in Europe within ECAC, as well as being used as a basis for discussion with national authorities.

The 19 member countries of the European Conference of Ministers of Transport (ECMT) adopted a resolution on aviation security at the 63rd Session of the Council in May 1986. It decided:

- To strengthen their co-operation in the sphere of aviation security, especially within ECAC and ICAO;
- To continue to make every effort to improve security in airports in their countries;
- To strengthen co-operation at all levels and, more particularly, to exchange information relating to security and technological developments in connection with aircraft and airport security; etc.

In the air navigation field, ICAO refined and improved the provisions concerning the interception of aircraft. This effort resulted in the unanimous adoption by an Extraordinary (25th) Session of the Assembly of an amendment (Article 3 bis) to the Chicago Convention which prohibits the use of weapons against civil aircraft in flight. At the same time, the Air Navigation Commission undertook a detailed review of interception procedures and developed comprehensive amendments involving several Annexes to the Chicago Convention and Procedures for Air Navigation Services which were adopted or approved by the Council on 10th March 1986 and have since come into effect.

Elderly and disabled passengers: At the 26th ICAO Assembly, the Council was directed to complete as soon as possible a review of problems of elderly and disabled air travellers worldwide to determine what measures could be taken to improve their access to airports and services. In adopting this resolution, the Assembly took note that a growing segment of air travellers were elderly or disabled people who could not take advantage of air transport because of many unnecessary barriers.

Europe: On 30th April 1986, the European Court of Justice issued its decision in the *"Nouvelles Frontières"* case. The facts that were at the origin of the judgement related to the failure of the travel operator "Nouvelles Frontières" to comply with the fares authorised by the French government under the Civil Aviation Code. The case had been referred by the Paris Police Court for a preliminary ruling: the European Court had to decide whether national regulations on the authorisation of fares were in conformity with the Treaty of Rome. The European Court clarified that air transport remains, as for other modes of transport, subject to the general rules of the Treaty, including the competition rules, but pending the adoption of a Council regulation, the application of the competition rules is left to the Member States and the EEC Commission.

In July 1986 the European Commission used the Nouvelles Frontières decision as a lever to send letters to ten European carriers, notifying them that, in its view, their present tariff, capacity and pooling practices contravened the Rome Treaty. All the airlines concerned replied to the July letters, and with the exception of British Caledonian, will inform the Commission in early 1987 of the remedial measures they intend to take.

On 19th December 1986, representatives from several ECAC states, including certain members of the EC, signed a series of memoranda of understanding on capacity share and tariffs, although not on market entry. In the proposals, capacity shares would be widened to a margin of up to 55/45 per cent for the first two years, increasing thereafter by only 1 per cent in the third year if a more liberal accord is not agreed after 18 months. However, the memoranda include some restrictions. For example, on discount fares there are three mandatory conditions: return trip or circle starting and finishing at the same location, a minimum stay of not less than six days, and a maximum stay of six months. For deep discount fares, the three mandatory conditions apply and airlines have also to include one of five others. The most restrictive of these five conditions would allow ticket purchase only on the day prior to departure for both inbound and outbound travel.

The competition commissioner for the European Commission has deemed the ECAC agreement inadequate for EC states wishing exemption from the competition rules of the Treaty of Rome, and EC signatories to the ECAC memoranda have signed a separate memorandum recognising that the ECAC agreement cannot prevail if there is a conflict with EC law.

There was one area of general agreement in the EC Council of Ministers in 1986, on a plan to ease capacity sharing agreements in bilateral agreements among EC Member States. The ministers in December accepted in principle a compromise plan to provide for a minimum 55/45 per cent capacity division, which would loosen those bilateral agreements which presently provide for a rigid 50/50 capacity share. Interpretations differ, however, on whether the flexibility will apply on a city/city or a country/country basis. In the third year of the agreement, the capacity split would be eased to 60/40 per cent, pending a review after 18 months.

The ministers failed to reach agreement, however, on the issue of market entry and liberalisation of the system for Europe's regional carriers. Since these two questions are related, there is reason to believe that they will be considered together in any final package that emerges from the council. As of 1st January 1987, there was apparently a consensus in favour of allowing "multiple designation" of carriers on a country/country basis, a provision already permitted in many bilaterals. However, on the more controversial issue of multiple designation between cities, several countries continue to insist on restrictive conditions, notably a certain existing volume of traffic on the route and/or a minimum frequency of flights.

The most difficult question remains tariff flexibility, and the only concrete result in 1986 was not in the direction of increased liberalisation; there was a consensus not to allow "zones of flexibility" around normal economy or business class fare on EC routes, as the United Kingdom had originally proposed. The AEA estimated that 43 per cent of European scheduled passengers were still travelling on full fares in 1985.

A new Memorandum of Understanding on North Atlantic pricing was signed on 13th February 1987 by the authorities of 13 member states of ECAC and the United States of America. Three other member states are expected to sign shortly. Like earlier similar arrangements between ECAC states and the United States of America (the most recent of which was due to expire at the end of April 1987), the new Memorandum provides for the responsible authorities of the states concerned to grant automatic approval to North Atlantic fares filed by airlines within specified pricing zones. Those authorities also undertake not to prevent any carrier from participating in multilateral tariff co-ordination while the arrangement is in force.

The pricing-zone system in the new Memorandum is based on an agreed reference fare for each route. A zone of automatic approval is then established within an agreed percentage range of that reference level for each of five main fare types (first class, business class, economy, discount and deep discount).

Compared with the previous arrangements, it is worth noting that the pricing zones/reference fares have been adjusted to take into account recent cost trends. The signatories have also agreed on new provisions allowing for consultations to take place at any time on matters related to North Atlantic air transport.

Australia: The Government continued to approve capacity increases for international airlines on routes experiencing growth in demand. New routes and services were also approved where it could be demonstrated that sufficient to justify the introduction of regular scheduled services on new routes, the Government has encouraged the introduction of programmess of charter flights to experiment with market demand, whilst meeting the need for direct air links.

Subsequent to the decision by an Australian domestic tribunal to remove the exemption granted under Australia's competition law for certain IATA practices and arrangements in that country, the Australian Trade Practices Commission, in December 1985, issued a final determination regarding IATA's activities. This determination authorises IATA to continue all its activities in Australia other than requiring its member airlines or their agents to apply the fares and commissions which have been agreed by the Tariff Co-ordinating Conferences or preventing these airlines or their agents from advertising the fares which they are actually offering.

The Independent Air Fares Committee conducted a major Cost Allocation Review of the two domestic trunk airlines, in order to assess only those costs that are efficiently incurred by the airlines, for the purposes of determining core air fares. The Committee also authorised a number of discount fares proposed by trunk and regional carriers, aimed at developing of tourist markets.

The Independent Review of Economic Regulation of Domestic Aviation presented its report to the Federal Government in December 1986. The Government has called for public comment on the various options for future regulatory measures, with a view to early decision in 1987. The balance of public opinion to date favours some lessening of regulation to stimulate increased competition among domestic trunk airline services. The Review follows a number of similar reviews of regulatory controls of aviation services conducted in 1985 and 1986 by State Governments, which have resulted in varying degrees of greater competition within those States.

In the 1986/87 Budget, funding of A$109 million was announced for major airport facilities upgrading. Major airport redevelopment continued at Brisbane, and the new Perth International Terminal building was commissioned in October 1986 in time for a large influx of passengers arriving for the America's Cup race series. The Government announced a A$23 million redevelopment project for Sydney International Terminal, which presently handles about 54 per cent of Australia's international air passenger traffic. The Budget allocation for airports included A$9.5 million for property acquisitions for a site for a second Sydney Airport.

Progress continued on the formation of the Federal Airports Corporation, which is expected to become operational in the near future and will assume responsibility for managing and developing major airports. The Government decided to establish a statutory authority called the Civil Aviation Corporation to provide and operate airways systems throughout Australia. The Government also continued to implement revised charging arrangements for airport and airways services, designed to facilitate transfer of responsibilities to these Corporations and to better administer cost recovery policies.

These measures are intended to place the provision of aviation facilities on a more commercial footing, making them more responsive to public needs and to encourage greater industry participation in future investment decisions.

Canada: *National transportation act*: One of the most significant events over the past year has been the tabling by the Minister of Transport of a revised National Transportation Act (Bill C-18) in November 1986. This Bill proposes significant revisions to Canada's transportation policy and reflects not only the proposals in the position paper "Freedom to Move" (July 1985) but the consultations which followed.

For the air mode, the regime in international air services is set down in legislation for the first time and embodies current practices. As for domestic air services, economic regulatory reform is extensive. A modified regulatory regime has been retained for the remote and northern parts of Canada. In the south, very little economic regulation will remain. For example, entry of carriers to domestic routes will be subject to simplified requirements of Canadian ownership (75 per cent), proper operational certification and adequate liability insurance. Exit from a given route requires only 60 days' notice. Regulatory review of tariffs will cease, and will be replaced by an obligation to publish all tariffs including a base fare. On complaint, unreasonable base fare increases will be subject to review and possible roll back.

Domestically, the end result is expected to be increased competition with a wider range of price and service options, substitution of turbo-prop aircraft for jet services in certain local and regional markets offering greater frequencies of departure, emergence of new carriers and continued development of inter-carrier alliances, as well as mergers and acquisitions.

Canada-USA air transport agreement: Discussions are currently in progress between Canada and the United States of America concerning a new Air Transport Agreement. However, the different approaches for achieving a more open regulatory system in the two countries have not been resolved. Canada continues to favour an exchange of cabotage rights and has submitted a draft text of a new agreement setting out its position.

The Exchange of Notes on regional, local and commuter air services of August 1984 has, however, permitted the development of new services between pairs of cities not designated as routes under the main agreement. These are of shorter distance and limited to aircraft of less than 60 passengers.

The experimental programme whereby unrestricted access was permitted to Montreal-Mirabel and the San Jose, California airports remains in place. Few carriers have taken advantage of the more flexible fare pricing system allowed.

International co-operation: In 1986, Canada concluded five new or revised bilateral air transport agreements. These cover Chile, the Dominican Republic, Portugal, Thailand and India. These agreements are representative of the growing relationship between Canada and major world airline markets, and will further the development of new links in trade and tourism.

Facilitation: Industry facilitation activity has resulted in the development of new legislation which will benefit airlines serving that country to the extent of C$4 million per annum. The savings come from the reduction in detention penalties imposed on carriers in connection with passengers deemed inadmissible on arrival. Previously the detention periods were open-ended and could exceed one year. A limit of 3 days has now been agreed.

Federal Republic of Germany: The German Federal Cartel Office has started investigating possible fare price-fixing by Lufthansa, the country's national airline, in May 1987. The investigation is being undertaken separately from the continuing efforts by the European Commission to bring more competition into the EC's airline industry. The Cartel Office has started looking into the arrangements under which Lufthansa sets its European air fares.

Greece: With the aim of improving the safety standards of flights and speeding up services rendered to travellers, development work continued at Athens Main Airport and the airports of Rhodes, Heraklion, Corfu, Mykonos, Skiathos, Kavala, Chania and Santorini. New terminal buildings are under construction at the airports of Kefalonia and Mitilini.

Within the framework of the implementation of the Government's policy for decentralisation and regional development, the runway at Kithira airfield has been extended and a similar extension on Chios is under study. Airfields on Naxos and Syros are also under construction.

Italy: The Italian Constitutional Court decided that the limits of liability for passengers as expressed by the Warsaw Convention cannot be enforced in Italy as a matter of domestic law because they no longer satisfy modern requirements. This decision potentially exposes carriers operating to and from Italy, and those selling tickets in Italy, to unlimited liability for claims concerning personal injury or death.

The Warsaw Convention is the main legal basis of the liability relationship between air carriers and their customers. However, the modernisation of the Convention has become progressively more urgent. An instrument for such modernisation exists in the form of the Montreal Protocols of 1975. Unfortunately, these have to be ratified by 30 states before they come into force and less than ten have so far done so.

A series of IATA missions to governments has been undertaken to promote ratification of the Montreal Protocols. These delegations have discussed with government officials the problems involved in ratification and pressed them to start ratification procedures urgently. Formal missions have been undertaken to Ireland, Australia and Hungary. Informal contacts have also been made with the Canadian Government.

Japan: Deregulation and privatisation: In June 1986, the Council for Transport Policy issued a report concerning "The Future Administration Policy of the Air Transport Industry". According to the report, the main objectives of future policy would be the improvement of passengers' interest by promoting competition among carriers, to the extent that this would not prejudice the safety of operations. In concrete terms, it recommended the establishment of several international Japanese carriers, the complete privatisation of Japan Airlines and the promotion of competition on domestic routes.

As a result of this report, the Ministry of Transport (MOT) licensed All Nippon Airlines to operate international scheduled flights and it encouraged the operation of a second company on several domestic routes. Japan Airlines will be completely privatised in 1987. As a result of the new competitive climate, international scheduled operations began on eleven new routes, including Tokyo-Washington.

Concerning fares, MOT has taken positive initiatives for granting discount fares, and a number of such fares were introduced on domestic routes. Because of the rapid appreciation of the yen against the dollar, fares from Japan became much higher than fares to Japan on the same route. In order to adjust such a difference, the MOT permitted airlines to reduce fares from Japan to Europe and the US.

Development of airports: The main international airports in Japan, Tokyo/Narita, Tokyo/Haneda and Osaka/Itami, are facing severe capacity problems. The MOT has introduced a fifth five-year airport development plan covering the period 1986-1990 at a total cost of 1 920 billion yen. The main objectives of this plan are, firstly, the construction of a new international airport at Kansai, and secondly, the enlargement of both Tokyo/Narita and Tokyo/Haneda.

New Zealand: A new competition law, the Commerce Act, was passed in 1986 which prohibits arrangements that might have the effect of substantially reducing competition in a given market. The legislation contains transitional provisions, exempting until 28th February 1987, those arrangements in air transport which would otherwise be in contravention of the relevant sections of the legislation. During the transitional period, the New Zealand authorities reviewed the situation to establish the extent to which airline practice should be exempted by statute on a more lasting basis. Representations were made by the airline industry to the New Zealand authorities to permit continuation of multilateral tariff co-ordination and other industry level activities. It was recognised that the current international aviation environment involves the Government in being party to a number of international air service agreements with other states, and that these agreements generally require or permit discussions between the airlines on tariffs and capacity matters. It was also accepted that airlines need, from time to time, to consult on questions of fare levels and provision of complementary services. As a result of the review, the Civil Aviation Amendment Act was passed in February 1987 exempting international aviation agreements or understandings from the relevant sections of the Commerce Act, provided they are approved by the Minister of Civil Aviation and Meteorological Services as being in line with fair market practices and New Zealand's international obligations.

Since the release of the revised External Aviation Policy in December 1985, new or additional services have commenced with Argentina, Japan, Canada, Australia, the United Kingdom, the Cook Islands, Singapore, Hong Kong and the United States, and new services to West Germany and Thailand are scheduled to commence before the end of 1987.

Norway: A recent Government report has concluded that present international and national regulations governing charter flights may have an adverse effect on the number of tourists travelling to Norway from abroad. In the provisions now in force, there are certain general limitations with regard to charter groups flying to Norway. Tour operators maintain that if the regulations are eased, special marketing efforts can be made in this sector which will result in a greater number of tourists. These questions and possible changes in the regulations governing charter flights between the Scandinavian countries were taken up in this report, which considered the overall concession policy for air services. This report was presented to the Storting at the end of 1986.

Scandinavia: In May 1986, the transport ministers of Denmark, Norway and Sweden approved the continuation of some of the monopoly privileges requested by SAS, but agreed that other air transport operations in the region should be deregulated. SAS, which is part-owned by the three governments, opposed deregulation as a threat to its expansion plans. Even the ministers' moderate proposals could, in its view, reduce revenue and damage scheduled air traffic.

The transport ministers recommended extending by 10 years to 2005, SAS's near-monopoly as international carrier for the three Nordic countries, whereas SAS wished it to be extended to 2010. It considered that such an extension was crucial for raising SKr 30 billion to modernise its fleet in the coming decade.

The ministers also proposed the elimination of several traffic and competition curbs within Scandinavia. The changes include total deregulation of air freight operations, charter traffic between Scandinavian capitals, and traffic on secondary routes between capitals and smaller cities throughout Scandinavia. At present, SAS can veto competition even on domestic routes it does not fly, on the grounds that passengers could be diverted from existing SAS routes.

United Kingdom: Airports: The Government's airport policy is intended to ensure that there should be sufficient capacity at the London airports to handle the expected increase in overseas visitors. At Heathrow, Terminal 4 was opened in April 1986 and this will enable an eventual increase in the total capacity of the airport from 30 million passengers per annum (mppa) to 38 mppa, while the North Terminal at Gatwick (which will provide a phased increase in capacity from 16 mppa to 25 mppa) is expected to be in operation by the summer of 1988. The Government has also approved a major development at Stansted Airport, the first stage of which will increase capacity there to 7.8 mppa by the early 1990s.

The British Airports Authority (BAA) had already implemented over half the recommendations for improved competition called for by the Monopolies and Mergers Commission (MMC). In December 1985, the MMC released the findings of a detailed "efficiency unit" of BAA, carried out under Item 11 of the Competition Act 1980. The MMC concluded that the commercial activities of BAA, which operates Heathrow, Gatwick and several other major UK airports, are not run in a way that acts against the public interest. However, it made a total of 34 recommendations for change, many of which directly relate to competition. The MMC concentrated on four specific issues: the scope for increasing competition at the point of sale; the procedure for awarding concession contracts; control of the standard of service provided by concessionaires; and the administration of leases.

Deregulation: Under the pressure of deregulation and increased competition, there have been considerable improvements in real labour costs, in relation to seat kilometres capacity, at both British Caledonian and British Airways (–62.7 per cent and –38 per cent respectively since 1978). Productivity measured in ton-kilometres per aircraft (TKAs) has risen 40 per cent at British Airways since 1982; the number of employees has dropped by 24 per cent. As far as regional airlines are concerned, the liberal entry conditions which have been offered for new entrants has resulted in there now being some 30 small carriers, eight of which entered scheduled service in the year ending October 1986.

The UK, in March 1986, invoked its so-called "blocking legislation", the Protection of Trading Interests Act, against two private anti-trust suits brought in United States courts in connection with the collapse of Laker Airways in 1982. One was by a travel company, the other by a group of former employees of Laker Airways, both alleging loss of income as a result of an alleged conspiracy. In so doing it prohibited airlines doing business in the UK from providing information held in the United Kingdom which is relevant to the two suits.

Compensation: The UK may take unilateral action to raise the level of compensation for air crash victims, if higher levels cannot be agreed internationally. The Minister for Aviation told the Air Transport Users' Committee in London, in July 1986, that the current international limits under the Warsaw Convention were too low – roughly £12 000 for death. The Government would like to see this limit raised to about £76 000, which is the same as that which already applies to UK airlines as a condition of their air transport licences.

United States: The trend to oligopoly: The great wave of deregulation during the late 1970s and early 1980s was based on the belief that replacement of the dead hand of regulation with the invisible hand of the free market would spur competition, enhance productivity and reduce prices. For example, between 1978 and 1984 unit labour costs, in relation to capacity available, declined 33.7 per cent which reflects changes in the US airline labour force caused by mergers, two-tier wage settlements and lay-offs. Airline fares, when adjusted for inflation, have fallen by 13 per cent since 1978. On the other hand, as a result of the wave of mergers in 1986, several major airlines have vanished and the six biggest US airlines have increased their combined share of the market to 84 per cent (compared to 73 per cent in 1978).

The regional airlines have grown faster under deregulation than any other sector of the US airline industry; they carried 8 per cent of total US domestic traffic in 1985, amounting to 27.3 million passengers (4.5 per cent up on 1984). However, even if the regionals gain access to hub airports (see below) they are still at a major disadvantage against larger airlines. While regional traffic is up, the number of small carriers has been decreasing by around 10 per cent per year. Department of Transportation figures show that there were 179 regional carriers in October 1986, down from 254 at the height of deregulation. Many of these carriers have been bought out by the majors: 10 of the top 20 regionals are now either wholly or partly owned by larger airlines. The US Regional Airlines Association (RAA) concluded that it has been becoming virtually impossible for a commuter airline to be profit-making (on the American scale) without linking up with a major in some way. The system most frequently applied is "code sharing" which involves the small one's fleet wearing the big one's livery and being used as its feeder network.

Within the United States, non-scheduled services have virtually disappeared since 1978. Furthermore, non-scheduled traffic on the North Atlantic declined from 12.1 per cent of the market in 1984 to 6.4 per cent in 1986, with the increased competition from scheduled services.

Hub-and-spoke systems: The most significant result of route deregulation has been the accelerated development of hub-and-spoke systems. These systems feed passengers from various cities into a centralised airport (hub), where they connect to other flights for destinations beyond the hub. This system has become the most important and successful strategy for major airlines.

Firstly, they allow a form of diversification resulting from carriers being able to serve many more origin and destination markets on a connect or through basis than could possibly be served if they flew simply point-to-point.

Secondly, the system in a sense "pools" capacity, by allowing medium and small cities to have frequent daily services to many destinations, through the use of direct flights to a single hub. This allows carriers to tailor their capacity to the demand at a given city by adjusting these multiple frequencies slightly up or down. Such adjustments are practically impossible in a "one market one flight" type of scheduling.

Thirdly, the systems are much more efficient ways to carry traffic since in general hub services operate at higher load factors than most point-to-point services.

The systems, however, have become competitive barriers almost as formidable as those erected by earlier regulations. The ability to feed passengers from one flight to another allows major carriers to dominate traffic at most large hubs. United Airlines in Pittsburgh and TWA in St. Louis control more than 80 per cent of the flow through those hubs. As a result, entry becomes very difficult for new entrants to most major markets.

Computer reservation systems: Automated reservation systems were initially introduced by large airlines, which were able to meet the heavy investment costs necessary to facilitate the transaction of reservations by their own sales staff on their own services. As their systems grew and the technology developed, these airlines were able to include access by travel agents and offer other airlines the opportunity to participate in their systems.

Airlines and travel agents have taken increasing advantage of the large productivity gains offered by use of Computer Reservation Systems (CRSs), rather than the relatively cumbersome procedure of using printed airline tariff guides and the telephone, and a large majority of sales transactions by agents are made using CRSs. With the impetus of deregulation, the proportion of tickets sold through agents has risen from around 40 per cent in 1978 to well over 70 per cent at present; 9 out of 10 tickets sold by agents currently are being transacted through CRSs.

As a result, airlines without access to advanced computer and communications systems are finding themselves increasingly at a considerable disadvantage. However, investment in computer systems can be extremely expensive, and participation in another's facility (where feasible) is frequently under terms and conditions which favour that other carrier. Because of the very high investment required in automation technology, a situation is being created in which it will become increasingly difficult for all but a handful of carriers to compete effectively in marketing their product. There are essentially six operators providing CRS services, five of which are airlines. Two of the airline-operated CRSs have over 60 per cent of the CRS market in the United States.

Following studies by various government departments, the US Department of Transportation announced in September 1986 that it would undertake a review of the existing rules. The Department of Transportation has, in the meantime, persuaded CRS operators voluntarily to apply the anti-bias rules for all displays of information.

On the initiative of IATA, a group of airlines operating to, from or within the United States (some 30 in total at present, including US and other airlines) was set up in 1984 to study the feasibility of developing a jointly-operated "Neutral Industry Booking System (NIBS)". Negotiations with existing CRS operators regarding either outright purchase by the NIBS group or shared ownership with the NIBS group have so far been inconclusive.

Taxation: A worldwide policy of reciprocal exemption from taxes on fuel, lubricants and other consumable technical supplies assures equitable treatment for all international airlines. This policy enables international air transport to avoid multiple taxation in the many jurisdictions through which it operates.

However, in June 1986, the United States Supreme Court upheld the right of the State of Florida to impose an excise tax on aviation fuel sold to non-US airlines. The Court concluded that the US Federal Government had not displaced the ability of states to impose taxes on airline operations.

Florida's action had a snowball effect and other states and local jurisdictions wasted little time in following its example: the State of Massachusetts imposed an aviation fuel tax, the State of Illinois removed an exemption from taxes on fuel and in-flight meals previously granted to foreign airlines and the City of Chicago introduced an aviation fuel tax. According to IATA, there remain few states in the US which exempt the fuel used by international air transport from taxation.

With such proliferation of US state taxes on international air transport – contrary to ICAO's objectives – there clearly exists the danger that other ICAO states may decide to impose their own taxation on US international carriers operating in foreign jurisdictions, a move which may well herald the end of an agreement which has served the international airline industry since the 1930s.

C. RAIL TRANSPORT

Europe: *The European dimension and future prospects of the railways:* In January 1986, ECMT organised in Paris an international seminar on the topic: "The European dimension and future prospects of the railways". Discussions covered:

– Actions recommended by international organisations and adaptation of the railways to economic changes;
– Possibilities opened up by high speeds;

– Contribution of computer technologies; and
– Operating constraints.

One aspect of the problem on which attention focused was the decline in the railway's share of the international transport market, in spite of the growing integration of European countries resulting from the expansion of trade between them.

As far as the short-term measures which would be needed to improve international rail transport were concerned, there was unanimous agreement on the need for increased co-operation between networks. There are indeed many ways in which international train services can be made more attractive (joint marketing and accounting policies, harmonized tariff structures etc.), the overall aim being to enable the railways to act as a single operator towards customers. Qualitative improvements in international rail transport could be made by eliminating unnecessary stops, raising maximum speeds, improving connections, separating international services from domestic services, and inter-industry co-operation to facilitate exchanges between networks. To this end, it was recommended that joint working parties be set up by railways connected by major traffic corridors. All these measures are in line with the recommendations adopted by the ECMT in this field.

Economic changes were analysed. The railways no longer provide universal geographical coverage and their services are now only competitive in certain markets. Financial dependence on governments and the lack of a clear definition of the railways' role have contributed to the distortion of investment decisions and, at a more general level, the allocation of resources.

High-speed traffic on the railway network of Europe: In April 1986, the ECMT organised an international seminar on the topic of high-speed traffic on the European rail network.

The main points covered at the seminar were: technical aspects of new lines, the possibility of making the transition from a number of high-speed lines in Europe to a European high-speed network, demand evaluation and, finally, forms of co-operation among the railways.

On the technical side, the projects for mixed high-speed lines (passengers and freight) gave rise to some queries as to whether the fullest advantage can be derived from the investment made, and attention was drawn to the problem of passenger and freight trains crossing in tunnels. The choice of mixed lines also calls for a compromise with respect to the technical parameters for the track if both heavy freight trains and high-speed trains are to use it. Construction and maintenance costs are higher than those for specialised lines, so the return on projects may not be affected to the same extent.

As regards magnetic levitation, this technology offers considerable scope: a significant increase in speed as compared with the most sophisticated rail/wheel systems and lower operating and maintenance costs than high-speed rail as matters now stand.

Where detrimental effects on the environment are concerned, it was pointed out that the techniques developed on the basis of the research done have meant that the noise generated externally by high-speed trains

is no greater than that of ordinary trains travelling at their commercial speed.

The example of the French *"train à grande vitesse"* (TGV) shows that it is essential to plan lines which link up major centres of economic activity with substantial two-way traffic in order to ensure that the investment shows a high rate of return. Not many routes meet this condition, so the level of the return on the investments can be used as a basis for establishing priorities and determining the stages for completion of the work.

The overall cost of the Paris-Brussels-Cologne/Amsterdam project is estimated at 3 billion Ecus to reduce the journey time by about one half. Construction of the Paris-Lille section of the line would show an economic return, but it would seem that the Brussels, Cologne or Amsterdam sections cannot attract sufficient traffic. The prospect of a Channel Tunnel will probably increase the disparities in rates of return on the sections, disparities that are clearly the main obstacle to the implementation of the project.

Eurotunnel: France and the United Kingdom decided to construct a railway-only tunnel to connect their countries. The cross-Channel link will provide the means of connecting the United Kingdom and continental cities by land transport, an important factor at a time when so many plans are in hand to revitalise the railways by stepping up speeds.

It is, of course, common knowledge that the Paris-Lyons TGV connection provides the most profitable high-speed service in Europe, largely owing to the fact that the line connects two densely populated cities which are a suitable distance apart for a fast train, conditions that are not met by many pairs of cities. Paris/London clearly is such a pair and, while there are unresolved problems on the Dover-London section for a really high-speed train connection, the Channel Tunnel offers interesting possibilities for a fast land transport connection between the two capitals, while also improving the prospects for extending the network to Brussels, Cologne and Amsterdam and probably to other areas. In short, the decision to build a fixed-link across the Channel may provide a major incentive for the development of land transport infrastructure in Europe.

In May 1987, the Eurotunnel company reached a compromise with British Rail and the French railways to end a dispute over the level of payments which threatened the progress of the financing of the Channel Tunnel. Both sides made concessions during the negotiations in London and Paris over Eurotunnel demands that the railways pay more for using the tunnel, to reflect their intended speed increases and to help provide a more attractive package to raise bank finance. As a result of the compromise, the European Investment Bank decided to finance a £1 billion loan for the tunnel as part of the overall investment still required.

Other important European rail developments include the progress being made in France towards the construction of the TGV Atlantique with interesting innovations in the technology employed, the trial runs on the first section of the experimental high speed train at Fulda in Germany, which reached a speed of 345 km per hour, and the approval, in Spain, of plans for improvements to the rail connection between Madrid and Cordoba, with trains travelling at between 200 and 250 km per hour. In Italy, new sections of the "direttissima" between Rome and Florence were opened, which provide the possibility of higher speeds and greater capacity, and in Switzerland, the "Rail 2000" plan was formally adopted which envisages extensions to the existing network.

Australia: Following a review of transcontinental passenger rail operations, State and Federal rail authorities have established a joint marketing authority to promote and sell interstate rail travel. Further consideration is being given to restructuring of inter-service

pasenger rail operations with the aim of improving services and containing operating costs.

Canada: On 24th February 1986 a legislative blueprint for rail passenger services in Canada – the National Rail Passenger Transportation Bill – was tabled in the House of Commons; however, in late August 1986, it failed to pass the necessary procedural stages. It is the desire of Transport Canada to reintroduce the bill into Parliament in early 1987.

The proposed Act is designed to provide VIA Rail with a clear legislative mandate, to introduce a new simplified costing regime and more effective compensation arrangement for VIA's relationship with Canadian National and Canadian Pacific, and to provide an effective legislative basis for the continued improvement and development of rail passenger services. Tourism Canada continues to play an advocacy role with Transport Canada on rail passenger matters seen as vital to Canada's continued emergence as a major international travel destination.

D. ROAD TRANSPORT

Europe: Investment in transport infrastructures: The increase in trade between countries calls for adequate transport infrastructures. Despite the considerable improvements in rail, waterway and road infrastructures in recent decades, the land transport system unquestionably has certain deficiencies which severely hamper the development of transport in Europe. Given the foreseeable growth in traffic, such difficulties are likely to increase over the next few years unless certain new infrastructures are constructed and others modernised.

In order to ascertain the facts with regard to this trend, which is a decisive factor in shaping the future investment policy, the Council of Ministers of the ECMT decided in 1984 to set up an ad hoc Group on investment in the transport sector. In 1986, a preliminary draft report was drawn up which essentially shows that the overall level of investment in road and inland waterway infrastructures in the ECMT member countries fell on average by almost 30 per cent in real terms between 1975 and 1984, whereas the total investment in rail infrastructure remained more or less unchanged during the same period. The study also shows that, while total expenditure on the maintenance of infrastructures has increased by more than 18 per cent in real terms since 1975, this increase has not kept pace with that in the volume of traffic.

Road Safety Year: 1986 was declared "Road Safety Year" by the European Communities. There were a great many activities of various kinds organised by the

various EEC Member States with a view to mobilising public awareness and channelling and co-ordinating the efforts of the various authorities concerned. The different projects are expected to have encouraged progress in a sphere which is of vital importance in human terms in addition to its economic and social implications.

Transport for disabled persons: A growing concern for those who have difficulty in travelling is apparent world-wide. It is now recognised that mobility is one of the most vital elements in the integration of disabled people in everyday life. It is also quite clear that the problem is not marginal since it affects a substantial and growing portion of the population. Indeed, it is estimated that in Western Europe, over 40 million people have difficulty in moving about.

In early 1986, the ECMT published the report "Transport for Disabled People – International Comparisons of Practice and Policy with Recommendations for Change". The report deals in detail with such issues as:

– The numbers and nature of disabled people;
– The use and licensing of cars for disabled people;
– The responsibility for local transport provision;
– The costs of transport for disabled people;
– The policies in Member countries.

Traffic information: ECMT is examining the exchange of traffic information between road authorities and road users. The particular work is concentrating on agreeing a system of coding of traffic and weather information which will allow this to be transmitted digitally and "translated" by in-car equipment in a standard way. In this work close co-operation is being maintained with the European Broadcasting Union and with industry.

Gasoline prices: To illustrate the effects upon travellers using their private cars, as a majority of tourists do, Table 7 shows gasoline prices in US dollars per litre in 1986 and indices (1980 = 100) of how gasoline prices in national currencies have changed over the last five years in OECD Member countries.

Australia: Federal Government grants to the States and the Northern Territory for road works amounted to A$1 245 million in the 1986/87 Budget. The "Australian Land Transport Program" is primarily directed towards continuing financial assistance to State and local government authorities to construct and maintain roads. The "Australian Bicentennial Roads Development Program" is intended to accelerate the development of the nation's road system to a high standard by 1988. Both programmes are financed by a dedicated levy on fuel excise. In October 1986, the final section of Highway 1 was completed, enabling travellers to drive around Australia completely on sealed highways for the first time.

United Kingdom: As part of the follow-up to the publication of "Pleasure, Leisure and Jobs" described in the previous Annual Report, the Department of Transport published, in March 1986, a consultation report and information leaflet "Tourist Coaches in London – Access and Parking". The report highlighted a number of problems facing local authorities and tourist coaches in London and identified a number of measures to improve the situation.

To implement the report, a number of new facilities were introduced, including some new on-street spaces. In Westminster, some spaces could be paid for by using a pre-purchased magnetic "coach card". In addition, coach helpers were introduced, through the Community Programme, to provide information to coach drivers on parking facilities near major tourist attractions. Despite these initiatives there was an overall loss of coach parking spaces in London in 1986. Studies showed that insufficient use was made by coaches of parking facilities in London which require payment.

The long-term solution is the provision of more coach parking spaces, both on and off-street, though these are unlikely to be provided if the existing spaces are not properly utilised. The Department is encouraging local authorities to make better use of existing facilities. The industry is also considering drawing up a code of practice, setting out guidelines for coach operators and their drivers.

Table 7. **Changes in the prices of premium gasoline**

Country	Prices per litre in dollars 1985	Price indices in national currencies (1980 = 100)				
		1981	1982	1983	1984	1985
Australia	0.348	127.2	143.3	155.7	172.5	170.5
Austria	0.624	130.3	127.7	131.4	137.2	109.8
Belgium	0.572	129.0	136.1	137.6	145.0	110.6
Canada	0.347	170.5	183.5	194.3	201.1	184.7
Denmark	0.794	130.8	133.7	132.0	135.9	141.6
Finland	0.624	120.4	127.6	131.4	134.2	109.6
France	0.681	130.9	141.0	152.7	167.0	139.5
Germany	0.496	119.5	117.9	120.3	122.0	92.4
Greece	0.557	128.7	147.6	163.1	191.9	229.5
Ireland	0.794	160.3	184.7	194.7	207.5	185.3
Italy	0.858	147.1	167.4	184.3	189.0	182.9
Japan	0.730	110.4	103.9	97.4	95.5	83.7
Luxembourg	0.469	140.1	145.8	149.8	152.8	117.4
Netherlands	0.608	121.4	120.9	126.0	128.2	103.8
New Zealand	0.432	139.2	144.3	162.4	189.4	168.5
Norway	0.642	123.6	132.7	140.2	140.8	127.8
Portugal	0.761	138.5	181.6	217.8	250.6	259.2
Spain	0.586	131.5	159.3	172.2	172.2	151.9
Sweden	0.582	134.4	142.0	143.0	158.0	140.8
Switzerland	0.563	109.1	105.3	104.8	109.1	87.6
United Kingdom	0.544	129.0	138.5	143.5	153.0	131.1
United States	0.245	104.3	99.7	97.9	96.3	74.7

Source: OECD, International Energy Agency.

E. THE CRUISE INDUSTRY

a) General trends in 1986

After a period of rapid growth in the early eighties, the world cruise market suffered overall a substantial setback. Passenger volumes declined significantly, particularly for East Mediterranean itineraries, as a result of the security problems perceived by potential United States cruise passengers in the wake of the "Achille Lauro" affair and the attacks on aircraft and airfields. However, some of the passengers who abandoned holiday plans in the Mediterranean booked instead on ships operating out of southern United States ports to the Caribbean and in the Pacific.

The South American market has regained strength. Passenger volumes are now reaching the levels of the early eighties. However, the major earthquake in the Western parts of Mexico at the end of 1985 caused a setback in this important winter cruise market and a reduction in the number of vessels scheduled in that area thereafter. Some of the US West Coast vessels were transferred into the Caribbean together with vessels being re-routed from the Mediterranean. In addition, already existing Caribbean operators brought several new ships into service. All these events brought considerable extra capacity into this area and competition between lines during 1986 and early 1987 is stronger than ever before.

Adverse weather conditions for several years in

succession resulted in a reduction in the number of vessels scheduled for North European cruising in 1986. In addition, the Chernobyl incident caused a reduction in cruise tourism throughout Europe during the 1986 season.

b) The evolution of the world cruise fleet

According to Fearnleys, a leading Norwegian ship broking company, the total number of cruise ships in the world fleet fell by one unit during 1986. (A "cruise ship" is defined as "a trading, oceangoing passenger vessel over 5 000 gross register tons, suitable to cater for holidaymakers, with insignificant or no cargo space"). On the other hand, the total gross tonnage of the cruise fleet rose by 5 per cent over 1985, to 1.76 million, and the available capacity for passengers also rose by 2.6 per cent, to 66 600 berths (Table 8). This is a reflection of the trend towards the introduction of bigger vessels to the market whilst smaller vessels have been laid up or sold for other purposes than pure cruising. There is a distinct difference in the size of vessels built before and after 1980. The average passenger capacity per ship built before 1980 is 717, whereas for ships built between 1980 and 1986 it is 1 099. Nevertheless, the world cruise fleet still contains a large number of old ships, with an average fleet age of nearly 23 years.

Table 8. **Development of world cruise fleet**[1]

| Year | Existing total fleet | | Capacity ('000) | | New buildings | | Lost or scrapped | |
	Number of ships	Gross tonnage ('000)	Number of passengers	Number of cabins	Number of ships	Gross tonnage (000')	Number of ships	Gross tonnage ('000)
1977	70	1 313	48.0	25.7				
1978	71	1 342	49.3	26.4				
1979	75	1 419	51.6	27.6	1	8	2	58
1980	75	1 372	51.6	26.8				
1981	76	1 397	52.6	27.4	2	49	1	9
1982	82	1 571	58.1	30.2	3	102		
1983	85	1 620	61.5	31.6	1	34	2	22
1984	89	1 745	65.7	33.7	3	118	1	16
1985	87	1 679	64.9	33.1	1	46		
1986	86	1 764	66.6	34.0	3	109		

1. The following types of passenger vessels are excluded:
   - with insignificant or no sleeping facilities;
   - built before 1945 if not extensively refitted after 1960;
   - operating regular ferry or liner services during a major part of the year;
   - cargo passenger vessels;
   - East European vessels; and
   - car ferries.

Source: Fearnleys.

c) New trends in cruise shipping

Under the present condition of excessive competition, the passenger demand is not sufficient to match currently offered capacity, and rebating has been widely introduced in an attempt to fill the surplus ship capacity. In the US market, this type of market influence is the rule rather than the exception. As a result of six to seven years of ongoing rebating of different type and nature in the cruise industry, public awareness of the possibilities of shopping around for fares below those advertised appears to have become a fact of life. All cruise lines are participating to a larger or smaller extent.

The image of "old style" vessels has grown even for the furnishings of newbuildings, and the "art deco" style of the 1920s is reappearing. Top-price yacht-style cruising was recently introduced, but such relatively small vessels have proved to be less profitable than projected, the reason being lack of marketing capabilities and high daily running costs necessary on high-cost, limited passenger capacity type of vessels.

Conversions are being contemplated for numerous over-aged vessels, both small and large. However, relatively few of these projects seem to materialise, probably due to the apparently uncontrollable acceleration of conversion costs, experienced on several vessels converted during recent years.

A major study for the introduction of a very large combined passenger vessel and activity centre is being conducted through the Phoenix or World City project. Being able to accommodate about 5 000 persons, three times larger than that of the world's largest existing cruise ship, this concept could offer completely new prospects for seaborne activity.

Some of the 25 Russian-flag vessels over 5 000 grt are seasonably chartered to western tour operators. In addition, some of the Russian vessels are scheduled for summer cruises from western ports mostly in the Mediterranean, but the number of such cruises are very few, and it seems safe to conclude that most of Russian-flag capacity is basically reserved for the home trades.

d) Developments in individual Member countries

Canada: Vancouver now ranks among the five most popular cruise ports in the western hemisphere, receiving about 15 per cent of the worldwide total of 2.5 million passengers in 1986. There were 240 sailings with over 325 000 passengers from Vancouver to the Inside Passage and Alaska during 1986, very substantially more than in 1985. The magnificent facilities at this port, however, are capable of handling more than 800 000 passengers per year.

The new passenger cruise ship terminal at Canada Place in downtown Vancouver which became operational in April 1986 is designed to accommodate the largest ocean-going cruise vessels, and is considered by many authorities to be one of the most advanced cruise terminals in the world. The new facilities at Canada Place plus Ballantyne Pier now have a capacity of five vessels per day.

Greece: Greek cruise shipping suffered a reduction of 80 per cent in US tourists in 1986. For the past two years, Greek cruise-ship operators have found that the impact of security fears has had a disastrous effect on bookings. Fierce competition from other international cruise-ship operators has also had a profound effect on the already difficult market. Many foreign operators have been able to cut costs through the use of lower paid crews, whereas Greek-flag vessels are obliged by law to employ not more than 40 per cent non-Greek seamen on board.

A series of harbour developments have been continued by the central and regional planning services of the competent bodies (Ministry of Public Works, etc.). In an effort to improve the infrastructure for the reception of pleasure craft, a programme of improvements to yacht marinas continued. Certain stages of the projects for creating new large marinas (such as those at Rhodes, Cos, Kefalonia, Paxos, Zakynthos, Chios, Ikaria and Alexandroupolis) have been completed.

Japan: The coastal shipping lines transported 154 million passengers (5 733 million passenger-kilometres) during the 1985 financial year. As of April 1986, there were 1 292 passenger routes in operation, utilising 2 349 vessels of nearly a million gross tons in total. The great majority of these services are not, however, primarily intended for purely tourism purposes.

NOTE

We would like to express our thanks to the following organisations which have provided us with a certain amount of information and statistical data which has helped in the drafting of this Chapter:

International Civil Aviation Organisation (ICAO)
European Conference of Ministers of Transport (ECMT)
European Civil Aviation Conference (ECAC)
International Air Transport Association (IATA)
Association of European Airlines (AEA)

We would also like to acknowledge the use of material from "The World Cruise Fleet, January 1987", produced by Fearnleys, Oslo.

V

TOURISM AND THE NATIONAL ACCOUNTS: THE NORDIC COUNTRIES' EXPERIENCE

A. THE OECD APPROACH

The extensive work on trade in services undertaken in OECD from 1982 in fulfilment of a series of mandates given by the Council at Ministerial level has brought out the importance of having a sound statistical base in this field. In their 1986 Communiqué, OECD Ministers "stressed the need to intensify and broaden ongoing conceptual analytical and statistical work" on trade in services. As one of the most important and growing service sectors, tourism and its statistical measurement have therefore been identified as one of the areas needing improvement. This has been stressed on different occasions by the Tourism Committee, which has requested its Statistical Working Party to study ways and means of enabling the provision of appropriate background material on which to base policy-making discussions and decisions.

It is in this context that the Statistical Working Party decided to investigate the relationship of tourism to the overall economic structure, using the System of National Accounts (SNA). By taking an internationally recognised framework such as the SNA, it enabled tourism activities to be measured, employing the same definitions and classifications as for the rest of the economy. This new approach was not intended, however, to replace the traditional assembling of readily available statistics, e.g. those on arrivals and nights, but was pursued in order to complement it by furnishing a better assessment of the role of tourism in national economies.

The task was assigned to a Group of experts composed of Member countries' specialists serving in their personal capacity and representing different areas: overall economic statistics (including National Accounts), tourism, and central banks. The Group studied the possibility of including tourism statistics in the SNA on the basis of a proposal submitted by an expert from a Member country. The World Tourism Organisation (WTO), which had undertaken research in this field[1], was also invited to participate in the meetings, held in 1985 and 1986, which were organised with the collaboration of the OECD Economics and Statistics Department.

The questionnaire developed by the Group of Experts uses the definition and classifications of the SNA. It is composed of five tables requesting four types of information: on *production* of goods and services by tourism industries and other producers, e.g. producers of government services or non-profit institutions serving households (Tables 1 and 2); on *consumption expenditures*, by resident and non-resident tourists, as defined by WTO (Table 3); on *capital formation*, by industries and other producers (Table 4); and on *employment* in tourist industries and other producers (Table 5). "Tourism industries" are activities which are directly influenced by expenditure by tourists and are classified according to fourteen categories within the International Standard Industrial Classification (ISIC). The current definitions are reproduced at the end of this chapter.

So far, the work of the Group has been directed towards examining:

- The usefulness and objectives of such an exercise for policy-making in tourism and for the achievement of international comparability;
- The ways of improving the questionnaire used for collecting data, with particular regard to the ability of Member countries to complete it;
- The content of Member countries' replies to the questionnaire, including their comments on problems encountered and suggestions for amelioration; and
- The possibility of OECD making an input to the ongoing UN work on the revision of the ISIC from the point of view of identifying tourist activities.

While the Tourism Committee has decided to maintain this activity as part of its long-term programme of work, some countries have found this approach immediately appropriate at a time when they are considering ways and means of improving their tourism statistical measurement. This is the case for the Nordic countries which, at the initiative of Sweden, were granted additional resources by the Nordic Council of Ministers to take an active part in the OECD tourism project. The Nordic Member countries comprise Denmark, Finland, Iceland, Norway and Sweden. Their experience is described below.

B.   THE NORDIC COUNTRIES' EXPERIENCE

Relevant economic data on tourism is increasingly in demand. The OECD project for reporting such data in terms of the System of National Accounts has therefore met with great interest in the Nordic countries. Statistics Sweden therefore applied for and was granted resources by the Nordic Council of Ministers to study the conditions necessary to illustrate the economic importance of tourism using the principles outlined in the OECD project. The study was to be based on material produced by the Nordic countries in reply to the 1985 pilot questionnaire designed by the OECD Group of experts. The study was to include:

– Tentative estimates on the basis of existing statistics;
– Supplementary "estimates" based on evaluations provided by specialists in various industries, as well as other information drawn from the National Accounts;
– Documentation on the need for supplementary data, necessary for the production of estimates.

The Nordic project was commenced in December 1985, and the results of the first tentative estimates were presented in a report in March 1987. The actual values produced at this stage were felt to be of an interim nature and are therefore not included in the present chapter. The following sections are directed to a consideration of the overall methodological approach that might be used in the future.

Aim of the project

The overall aim of the project was to increase the availability, comparability and information value of the Nordic statistics on tourism. To achieve this, the statistics produced have to be based on similar definitions and terminology used in all the Nordic countries. Thus, it means that the methodological work conducted in any of these countries is applicable to all of them. The similarities between the Nordic countries in respect of both the structure of the economy and the type of statistics available made such a project fully realistic.

Experiences of the first round of tentative estimates

The general view expressed was that it was difficult, and for some fields even impossible, to provide the data requested. It was, however, generally recognised that economic data on tourism will be increasingly demanded and that the matter will become of growing interest. All the Nordic countries also seemed to believe that better and more reliable data will be available in the future and that the estimates can be improved.

All Nordic countries have advanced systems of national accounts, which conform to the recommendations of the SNA. In Denmark, Finland and Norway the input-output tables have been integrated in the national accounts systems, while in Sweden such integration is in progress. The comparability between the countries in respect of the national accounts is therefore good. It is not possible from the present Nordic national accounts to obtain data on purchases made by tourists. Even if the systems are improved and the input-output tables are integrated, it will still be a matter of making estimates. These may, however, be of high quality, and they can be made comparable. Another general view voiced by the Nordic countries was that good comparability calls for more precise definitions than those provided in the OECD questionnaire. It was also felt that some of the tables cover a field much larger than tourism and that thereby their value is considerably reduced.

Estimation methods for the various tables – problems and suggestions

Table 1, "Supply and use of commodities characteristic of tourism industries" describes total supply and use of commodities at the "commodity level" in tourism industries. Such a presentation includes all activities in each of nine 3-digit ISIC categories and excludes all others. These nine industries belong to three ISIC two-digit categories: 63 (restaurants and hotels), 71 (transport and storage) and 94 (recreational and cultural services). For the Nordic countries it is difficult to obtain data for restaurants and hotels and recreational services at the 3-digit level. On the other hand, for all the countries, transport can be specified at a more detailed level than that contained in the table.

In Table 1, "Total uses" (which should equal total supply) is to be broken down by: "Purchased by tourists", and "Other uses". "Purchased by tourists" is to be broken down by: "Residents", and "Non-residents". However, in the National Accounts, items purchased by tourists fall into both intermediate and final consumption. No breakdown of tourism by intermediate and final consumption is made in the Nordic national accounts. The data in columns "Purchased by resident tourists" and "Purchased by non-resident tourists" will therefore have to be estimated. It is suggested that the estimations should be based on the approach used by Norway and Sweden, which means that the industries concerned (ISIC 63, 71 and 94) are broken down as far as permitted by the national accounts systems. The tourism shares are then estimated by means of other available information.

The following estimation methods are suggested:
- A standardised breakdown of the services in restaurants and hotels is made so that restaurants account for two-thirds and hotels for one-third of the activities. The breakdown is made by means of the Population and Housing Census and of data drawn from the VAT returns.
- The proportion of the restaurant industry output associated with tourism is estimated by means of the accommodation statistics. These provide a basis for assumptions on the number of meals eaten by tourists at restaurants. The cost of such meals is drawn from the consumer price index.
- The wide definition of tourism applied makes it reasonable to classify 98 per cent of the hotel industry output as tourism.
- Land transport is first broken down by, for example, railways, buses/coaches and taxis. A distinction is subsequently made between passenger traffic and freights. For railways, the proportion of tourism is estimated by means of the type of tickets sold. For buses and coaches, a distinction is first made between inter-city traffic and other traffic, and the proportion of tourism is then estimated. In the national accounts the taxi output value is broken down by intermediate and final consumption. For each sector the proportion of tourism has to be roughly estimated.
- Water transport output is first broken down by freight and passenger transport. The passenger share is then broken down by final consumption and exports. Estimates of tourism have to be determined by means of special studies.
- The air transport output value is broken down by receipts from passengers and other receipts, with the interest subsequently focussed on the passenger receipts (source: Nordic national accounts). The

SNA permits a breakdown of the receipts from passengers by intermediate consumption, final consumption and exports. Owing to the wide definition, the tourism share of air transport ought to be close to 100 per cent. Norway constitutes an exception, with its large proportion of coastal air traffic classifiable as business travelling and not as tourism. The tourism share is broken down by residents and non-residents by means of a subdivision of the passenger receipts into intermediate and final consumption on the one hand and exports on the other. For Denmark, Norway and Sweden the results largely depend on the returns submitted by the Scandinavian Airlines System. It is therefore of utmost importance that the same principles are followed in all the countries.
- ISIC 719, services allied to transport, includes travel agency activities. In order to avoid double-counting, domestic output in this case should be calculated net, with intermediary services therefore excluded. An alternative is to report package tours at their gross value and make a corresponding reduction in the value for transport and other industries (to be treated as intermediate consumption). Other items to be included are road and bridge tolls, parking and garage charges, and car rentals.
- For transport, the column "Purchased by tourists, residents" should include receipts credited to companies in their own country, even if the destination is another country. For example, expenditure by Norwegian tourists on board Norwegian cruise liners should be entered under "Residents", even if the ship is bound for the Caribbean Islands. This conforms to the principles of the SNA in respect to seamen serving aboard their own nation's ships in foreign trade.
- For the Nordic countries, with their high rate of charter flights, item 713, Air Transport, will accordingly show a very high value in the "Residents" column. To avoid a misinterpretation of the column total, it is proposed that the Nordic countries append a note showing the proportion due to charter transports.
- A breakdown of ISIC 94, Recreational and Cultural Services, to the 3-digit level has proved almost impossible. In the estimation, it therefore seems better to start from 94 and then remove items which are of minor interest from the tourism point of view, such as radio and TV, authors' services, lottery operations etc. More interesting items, from a tourism point of view, are for instance amusement and animal parks, museums, castles, major sports events and theatrical performances. However, at many leisure areas, for example those in Copenhagen and Stockholm, the majority of visitors are from the local population. If no special studies are available, the tourism proportion will therefore have to be roughly estimated by each individual country.

Table 1. **Supply and use of commodities characteristic of tourism industries at market prices**

In current prices

ISIC[1]	Total supply		Total supply and uses	Total uses		
	Domestic production	Imports		Purchased by tourists		Other uses
				Residents	Non-residents	
Industries						
631 Restaurants, cafés, etc.						
632 Hotels, camps, etc.						
711 Land transport,						
of which:						
7111 Railway transport						
7112 Road passenger transport						
7113 Other passenger land transport						
7116 Supporting services to land transport						
712 Water transport,						
of which:						
7121 Ocean & coastal water transport						
7122 Inland water transport						
713 Air transport,						
of which:						
7131 Air transport carriers						
7191 Services incidental to transport						
94 Recreational & cultural services						
Other producers						
94 Recreational & cultural services						
TOTAL TOURISM INDUSTRIES						
Memorandum item: Total economy						

1. ISIC: International Standard Industrial Classification.

In Table 2, "Derivation of value added in tourism industries", the present design does not cause any problem. On the other hand the table gives little information about the tourism contribution to the value added. In view of this it will probably be necessary to revise this table extensively, and for this reason, no suggestions of estimation methods are given.

In Table 3, "Final consumption expenditure of tourists according to types of goods and services", has caused the Nordic countries great difficulties. However, there is a unanimous opinion that the table is of great informative value. Total expenditure for foreign tourists has been drawn from the statistics on travel currency. It is proposed that this should be continued. The breakdown by various items of expenditure is proposed to be made on the basis of regional studies, even if these are marred by some uncertainty. It is difficult to obtain reliable information about tourism expenditure for resident tourists. The sources suggested are household expenditure surveys and holiday surveys. These surveys are undertaken at regular intervals and cover only final consumption. They also only indicate totals.

One problem is which items should be defined as tourism expenditure. The classifications and definitions suggested for the Nordic countries are listed below:

– The definition of "tourism expenditure" ought to be very wide for non-resident tourists. On the basis of the total given by the revenue item on the travel currency statistics, all expenditure regardless of size is to be included, as long as it is intended for final consumption. For example, diamonds and cars for private use should be included, whereas combine harvesters ordered during the trip for use on the farm should be excluded.

– On the other hand, the definition of "tourism expenditure" ought to be very narrow for resident tourists. Only special expenditure arising while travelling is to be included. Costs of tents, skis and other sports equipment, special clothing etc. should not be included. These costs should be considered in estimates of the size of the leisure activities sector but are not to be regarded as tourism expenditure.

– Costs of owning a week-end cottage (e.g. purchase/operating costs, equipment, fuel costs for travelling to and from the place) are not to be included, whereas the costs of renting a week-end

Table 2. **Derivation of value added in tourism industries at market prices**

In current prices

ISIC[1]	Gross output (equals domestic production)	less Intermediate consumption	equals Gross value added	Of which:			
				Compensation of employees	Operating surplus	Consumption of fixed capital	Indirect taxes less subsidies
Industries							
631 Restaurants, cafés, etc.							
632 Hotels, camps, etc.							
711 Land transport,							
of which:							
7111 Railway transport							
7112 Road passenger transport							
7113 Other passenger land transport							
7116 Supporting services to land transport							
712 Water transport,							
of which:							
7121 Ocean & coastal water transport							
7122 Inland water transport							
713 Air transport,							
of which:							
7131 Air transport carriers							
7191 Services incidental to transport							
94 Recreational & cultural services							
Other producers							
94 Recreational & cultural services							
TOTAL TOURISM INDUSTRIES							
Memorandum item: Total economy							

1. ISIC: International Standard Industrial Classification.

cottage (on an occasional basis) should be included.

- Costs of food, beverages, tobacco, and clothing and footwear for resident tourists (items 1.1-1.4 and 2 in Table 3) are not to be included. The extra costs added to these items owing to the fact that a person is a tourist can be considered negligible at the total level. These items are of interest only at a local level.

- The expenditure of resident tourists should only be broken down into a few categories, such as restaurants, hotels and transport. If the estimations are based on a total, this classification should mean that the residual left after the breakdown falls under the item "goods and services n.e.s.".

- For these limited categories of restaurants, hotels and transport, it is proposed that the expenditure of resident tourists be reported separately for a) final consumption, b) intermediate consumption, and c) public administration.

- The expenditure of resident tourists should, as far as possible, adhere to the definitions applied in the SNA for final consumption. Expenditure for charter flights and coaches from a person's own country might be separately reported in a note, to give an idea of the tourism in his own country.

- On the demand side in Table 3, restaurants and hotels ought to be separately reported. This is feasible, while it is much more difficult to do the same on the supply side (Table 1).

The aim of Table 4, "Gross fixed capital formation by tourism industries", is to give an idea of the magnitude of the investments made in the tourism sector, in respect of both buildings and machinery. Table 4 has caused no great problems for the Nordic countries, as the data has been available in the national accounts. The problems mentioned are of a general nature and concern the breakdown by ISIC categories. The main criticism of Table 4 is that the table in its present form does not measure what it is supposed to measure, viz. the magnitude of investments in the tourism industries. The major objections are that:

Table 3. **Consumption expenditure of tourists according to types of goods and services**

In current prices

SNA Table 6.1		Non-resident tourists	Resident tourists			*Memorandum item:* Total final consumption expenditure
			Household	Government	Business	
1.1	Food					
1.2,1.3	Beverages					
1.4	Tobacco					
2	Clothing and footwear					
3	Gross rents, fuel and power					
4.5	Household operation					
5.1,5.2, 5.3,5.4	Medical goods and services					
6.1	Personal transport equipment					
6.2	Operation of personal transport equipment					
6.3	Purchased transport					
6.4	Communications					
7.1,7.3	Recreational goods					
7.2	Entertainment, recreational and cultural services					
7.4	Education					
8.3.1	Restaurants and cafés					
8.3.2	Hotels and similar lodging services					
8.4	Package tours					
8.1,8.2, 8.5,8.6	Miscellaneous goods and services					
	Other goods and services n.e.s.					
TOTAL						

- Investments in buildings are often made within special real estate companies and are not reported under ISIC 63, 71 or 94;
- Machinery investments too are often made within special leasing companies and are reported under ISIC 83;
- Large parts of the ISIC 71 investments have very little to do with tourism but concern transportation of goods.

The table should be given a different design, so that the investments are associated with the industry using them and not with their owners. Furthermore, the value of leasing contracts should be considered on a par with investments. Investments not at all related to tourism, for example, investments in lorries and merchant vessels, should be excluded. For some parts of the transport sector it might, however, be very difficult to distinguish investments associated with freight from investments for passenger traffic. Pending information about the design of the next survey, no suggestions are made on estimation methods.

Table 5, "Employment in tourism industries" is to describe the employment situation in the tourism industries. The table is intended to illustrate the average number of persons engaged, both the total number and the number of employees. Also included is the total number of man-hours worked by employees. The general views expressed on Tables 2 and 4 apply to Table 5 as well, viz. that the presentation covers much more than tourism and that therefore the data has lost much of its value. Norway has estimated the proportion of the total employment generated by tourism by applying to the various categories the same tourism ratios as those obtained in Table 1. This is appropriate for the categories where fixed assets and output for tourism agree with all other output. Examples are restaurants and hotels and air transport. It is more dubious for sectors including both passengers and goods. If the OECD Group of Experts does not amend the table or provide special instructions for its use, it is proposed that the Nordic countries follow the example of Norway and make an attempt to estimate the tourist shares. Even if this results in very rough estimates, it is still preferable to the information yielded by the present table. To facilitate comparability, sources and definitions should be reported to show how the employment data has been obtained. In ISIC 63 and 94, there is a large proportion of seasonal labour. These industries also have a high rate of employee turnover.

Table 4. Gross fixed capital formation by tourism industries
In current prices

ISIC[1]	Gross fixed capital formation
Industries	
631 Restaurants, cafés, etc.	
632 Hotels, camps, etc.	
711 Land transport, *of which:*	
7111 Railway transport	
7112 Road passenger transport	
7113 Other passenger land transport	
7116 Supporting services to land transport	
712 Water transport, *of which:*	
7121 Ocean and coastal water transport	
7122 Inland water transport	
713 Air transport, *of which:*	
7131 Air transport	
7191 Services incidental to transport	
94 Recreational & cultural services	
Other producers	
94 Recreational & cultural services	
TOTAL TOURISM INDUSTRIES	
Memorandum item: Total economy	

1. ISIC: International Standard Industrial Classification.

Table 5. Employment in tourism industries:

ISIC[1]	Average number of persons engaged		Total man-hours worked by employees
	All persons	Employees	
Industries			
631 Restaurants, cafés, etc.			
632 Hotels, camps, etc.			
711 Land transport, *of which:*			
7111 Railway transport			
7112 Road passenger transport			
7113 Other passenger land transport			
7116 Supporting services to land transport			
712 Water transport, *of which:*			
7121 Ocean and coastal water transport			
7122 Inland water transport			
713 Air transport, *of which:*			
7131 Air transport			
7191 Services incidental to transport			
94 Recreational & cultural services			
Other producers			
94 Recreational & cultural services			
TOTAL TOURISM INDUSTRIES			
Memorandum item: Total economy			

1. ISIC: International Standard Industrial Classification.

Proposed overall measures

It seems advisable to allocate resources to the national accounts units or other appropriate units at the central bureaux of statistics to make it possible to carry out estimations while the system development is in progress.

One way of obtaining an expenditure total for resident tourists is to utilise the household expenditure surveys. These could be supplemented with a data collection during holidays, similar to the collection during the rest of the year. Preferably, a special questionnaire (for example the Danish version) should be used to facilitate a breakdown by various expenditure items. Also, the Nordic household expenditure surveys ought to be co-ordinated in respect of both the date of performance and the questions.

To obtain an expenditure total for non-resident tourists, it is proposed that data on purchases within the country be collected at borders and airports from tourists returning home. This total would subsequently be compared with the statistics on travel currency.

As a supplement to the household expenditure surveys and the border surveys, special (interview) surveys are proposed, in which tourists are asked about their expenditure during their holidays. It is important that these are carried out during the holiday and not on a later occasion, as experience shows that even after a day or two it is difficult to remember how the expenditure was distributed on various items.

Interview surveys can be very expensive. It is therefore important to be flexible and take advantage of various possibilities, for example:

- To include questions about expenditure structure when tourists and travellers are interviewed in other contexts ("omnibus surveys");
- To encourage universities which include tourism in their courses to conduct regional surveys. The statistical central bureaux could assist in the planning, data processing and analyis of the findings, while the universities could take on the data collection and checking and, if necessary, the encoding.

In the national accounts, the aim should be to attain as detailed a presentation as possible for categories 63, restaurants and hotels, 71, transport, and 94, recreational and cultural services, with special estimates of the tourism shares. For instance, in the transport category, passenger transport and goods transport should be distinguishable, and in the restaurant category, staff canteens should be separable from other restaurants. An ideal would be input-output tables where tourism is reported as an economic activity in its own right.

C. CONCLUSIONS

Although it might be too early to draw any final conclusions from the "Nordic Experience" with application to the OECD Member countries as a whole, the outcome gives a strong impetus to the development of this project since it has shown that the approach can make a significant contribution to meeting the need for a better grasp of the economic contribution that tourism makes to the national economies. It should also be noted that in the overall approach in the OECD towards improving statistics in the various sectors of trade in services, tourism is the only one where concrete work on integration with the SNA is going on.

While it has been difficult for all Member countries to reply in detail to the questionnaire drawn up by the Group of Experts, it has, however, met with considerable interest in certain Member countries where such an approach was being considered. This is the case in particular for Canada, where an integrated system is being developed, for France, which is considering how to improve its satellite account, and for Spain, which has been using input-output tables since 1974. The work undertaken in the Nordic countries will assist the Group of experts in making the project more generally applicable and the results obtained more useful and comparable.

The integration of tourism in the SNA is a long-term project. However, the Tourism Committee of the OECD has recognised that it should be one of the continuing objectives of the work of the Committee and its subsidiary bodies. The importance of the work undertaken in the statistical field has been recently endorsed by the Committee and the widening of the scope of activities in this sector is envisaged during the coming years.

NOTE

1. Determination of the importance of tourism as an economic activity within the framework of the national accounting system, Madrid, 1983.

PRESENT CLASSIFICATION OF THE TOURIST INDUSTRIES IN THE INTERNATIONAL STANDARD INDUSTRIAL CLASSIFICATION OF ALL ECONOMIC ACTIVITIES (ISIC)

631 *Restaurants, cafés and other eating and drinking places*

Retail establishments selling prepared foods and drinks for immediate consumption, such as restaurants, cafés, lunch counters and refreshment stands. Catering is included in this group. Also included are dining-car services in railroad trains and other passenger transport facilities which are operated as an independent business; and canteens and eating facilities in plants and offices which can be separately reported. Restaurant facilities operated in connection with the provision of lodgings are classified in group 6320 (Hotels, rooming houses, camps and other lodging places).

632 *Hotels, rooming houses, camps and other lodging places*

The provision, on a fee basis, of lodging, camping space and camping facilities, whether open to the general public or restricted to members of a particular organisation. Restaurant facilities operated in connection with the provision of lodgings are included in this group.

711 *Land Transport*

7111 *Railway transport*

Companies furnishing transportation by interurban and suburban railroads; and services allied to railway transportation, such as sleeping-car services, railway express, and switching and other terminal services. Also included are dining-car services in railroad trains not operated as independent businesses; and the building, overhaul and repair of railway rolling stock and the construction and maintenance of railway right-of-way and buildings by railway transport companies which it is not possible to report separately. Excluded from this group are units operated by railroad companies which are primarily engaged in providing telegraph services (classified in group 7200); in operating hotels (classified in group 6320); and in providing water transport (classified in the appropriate group of 712).

7112 *Urban, suburban and interurban highway passenger transport*

Interurban and suburban bus and coach lines; and urban passenger transportation whether by electric railway, trolley coach, bus, tramways or subway. The operation of associated terminals, maintenance and service facilities is included. Urban transit systems may also include ferries and any other means of transport forming part of an integrated system of urban passenger transport.

7113 *Other passenger land transport*

Passenger transportation services, not elsewhere classified, such as sightseeing buses, limousines to airports or stations, school buses, taxicabs; and animal-drawn vehicles for the transport of passengers or freight. The rental of automobiles with drivers is also included. The provision of ambulance services is classified in group 9331 (Medical, dental and other health services).

7116 *Supporting services to land transport*

Services in support of land transport, such as the operation of toll roads, highway bridges, vehicular tunnels and parking lots and structures; the rental of railroad cars and of automobiles and trucks without drivers. Storage or warehousing of motor vehicles (dead storage) is classified in group 7192; and the rental of automobiles or trucks with drivers is classified in groups 7113 or 7114 respectively.

712   Water transport

7121   *Ocean and coastal water transport*

The operation of vessels for transport of freight and passengers overseas and coastwise.

7122   *Inland waterway transport*

The operation of vessels for the transport of freight and passengers by rivers, canals and other inland waterways. Included are ferries operated across rivers, domestic lakes and within harbours.

713   *Air transport*

7131   *Air transport carriers*

The transport by air of passengers and freight, whether by regular services or by private charter.

7191   *Services incidental to transport*

Services incidental to transport, such as forwarding; packing and crating; arrangement of transport (including travel agencies); inspection, sampling and weighing; ship and aircraft brokers. The operation of stock yards which provide pens, feed and selling areas for livestock temporarily held, either pending sale or in transit to or from the market, is also included.

94   *Recreational and Cultural Services*

Motion picture and other entertainment services:

Motion picture production
Motion picture distribution and projection
Radio and television broadcasting
Theatrical producers and entertainment services
Authors, music composers and other independent artists not elsewhere classified
Libraries, museums, botanical and zoological gardens, and other cultural services not elsewhere classified
Amusement and recreational services not elsewhere classified.

STATISTICAL ANNEX

NOTES

This Annex reproduces the main tourism statistical series available in Member countries. For 1986, data are frequently provisional. It illustrates recent tourism developments in the OECD (over a two or three-year period). However, in the near future, the Committee will be making generally available a statistical compendium covering a longer historical time series. This will give a broader perspective on the evolution of national and international tourism.

Some of the data contained in the text itself may not always correspond exactly to that included in the Annex: the discrepancies can be explained by a different statistical coverage (e.g. the use of GNP instead of GDP) or by the use of material of a more analytical nature (data derived from gross figures).

Finally, certain tables are prepared from data available for other OECD work (e.g. Balance of Payments and National Accounts), in some cases, these statistics, which have been standardised to follow existing international guidelines, may differ from the ones supplied by countries in response to the annual questionnaire of the Tourism Committee.

Three tables of general interest for the use of the statistical series are presented at the beginning of the Annex:

A. Classification of travellers;
B. Series available by country;
C. Types of establishments covered by the statistics.

In July 1981, a Resolution was passed by the Tourism Committee concerning the improvement of international comparability of tourism statistics published by OECD Member countries. Some of its main items are reproduced in an Appendix which will appear at the end of the Report.

Geographic coverage:

Belgium-Luxembourg: Balance of payments statistics refer to the Belgo-Luxembourg Economic Union.

Other OECD-Europe: include OECD European countries for which no breakdown is available.

Other European countries: include non-OECD European countries for which no breakdown is available.

Origin country unspecified: includes non-OECD countries which cannot be broken down into any specific large geographic region (Other European countries, Latin America, Asia-Oceania, Africa).

SOURCES

The principal national bodies for each OECD Member country dealing with tourism statistics are as follows:

Australia

Australian Bureau of Statistics
Australian Tourist Commission
Reserve Bank of Australia

Austria

Osterreichisches Statistisches Zentralamt
Osterreichische Nationalbank

Belgium

Institut National de Statistiques
Banque nationale de Belgique
Institut Belgo-Luxembourgeois du Change

Canada

Statistics Canada, International Travel Section

Denmark

Danmarks Statistik
Danmarks National Bank

Finland

Central Statistical Office
Bank of Finland

France

Ministère de l'Industrie, des P et T et du Tourisme,
Direction de l'industrie touristique
Banque de France

Germany

Statistisches Bundesamt
Deutsche Bundesbank

Greece

National Statistical Service of the National Tourist
Organisation of Greece
Bank of Greece

Iceland

Icelandic Immigration Authorities
Iceland Tourist Board
Central Bank of Iceland

Ireland

Central Statistics Office
Irish Tourist Board (Bord Failte)

Italy

Istituto Centrale di Statistica
Banca d'Italia

Japan

Ministry of Transport, Department of Tourism
Japan National Tourist Organisation
Bank of Japan

Luxembourg

Service Central de la Statistique et des Etudes
Economiques (STATEC)
Institut Belgo-Luxembourgeois du Change

Netherlands

Ministry of the Economy, Central Bureau of
Statistics
Dutch Central Bank

New Zealand

New Zealand Tourist and Publicity Department
Reserve Bank of New Zealand

Norway

Central Bureau of Statistics
Bank of Norway

Portugal

Direcçao-Geral de Turisme
Instituto Nacional de Estatistica
Banco de Portugal

Spain

Instituto Nacional de Estadisticas
Banco de Espana

Sweden

Central Bureau of Statistics
Swedish Tourist Board
Central Bank of Sweden

Switzerland

Office Fédéral de la Statistique, Section du
Tourisme

Turkey

Ministry of Culture and Tourism
Central Bank

United Kingdom

Department of Employment, Office of Population
Censuses and Surveys
British Tourist Authority

United States

Department of Commerce, United States Travel and
Tourism Administration (USTTA)
Department of Commerce, Bureau of Economic
Analysis

Yugoslavia

Federal Bureau of Statistics
National Bank of Yugoslavia

A. Classification of travellers

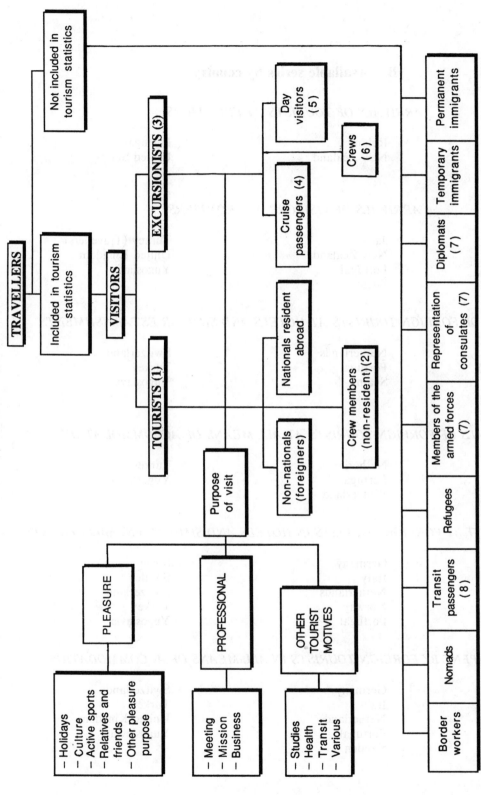

TRAVELLERS

- Included in tourism statistics
- Not included in tourism statistics

VISITORS

- TOURISTS (1)
- EXCURSIONISTS (3)

TOURISTS (1) — Purpose of visit:

- PLEASURE
  - Holidays
  - Culture
  - Active sports
  - Relatives and friends
  - Other pleasure purpose
- PROFESSIONAL
  - Meeting
  - Mission
  - Business
- OTHER TOURIST MOTIVES
  - Studies
  - Health
  - Transit
  - Various

- Non-nationals (foreigners)
- Nationals resident abroad
- Crew members (non-resident) (2)

EXCURSIONISTS (3)

- Cruise passengers (4)
- Day visitors (5)
- Crews (6)

Not included in tourism statistics:

Border workers | Nomads | Transit passengers (8) | Refugees | Members of the armed forces (7) | Representation of consulates (7) | Diplomats (7) | Temporary immigrants | Permanent immigrants

1. Visitors who spend at least one night in the country visited.
2. Foreign air or ship crews docked or in lay over and who use the accommodation establishments of the country visited.
3. Visitors who do not spend the night in the country visited although they may visit the country during one day or more and return to their ship or train to sleep.
4. Normally included in excursionists. Separate classification of these visitors is nevertheless recommended.
5. Visitors who come and leave the same day.
6. Crews who are not residents of the country visited and who stay in the country for the day.
7. When they travel from their country of origin to the duty station and vice-versa (including household servants and dependants accompanying or joining them).
8. Who do not leave the transit area of the airport or the port. In certain countries, transit may involve a stay of one day or more. In this case, they should be included in the visitors statistics.

Source: World Tourism Organisation.

113

B. Available series by country

ARRIVALS OF TOURISTS AT FRONTIERS

Canada	Iceland	Portugal
France	New Zealand	United States
Greece		

ARRIVALS OF VISITORS AT FRONTIERS

Australia	Japan	Turkey (Travellers)
Canada	New Zealand	United Kingdom
Ireland	Portugal	Yugoslavia
Italy	Spain	

ARRIVALS OF FOREIGN TOURISTS AT HOTELS AND SIMILAR ESTABLISHMENTS

Austria	Netherlands	Switzerland
France (Ile de France)	Portugal	Turkey
Germany	Spain	Yugoslavia
Italy		

ARRIVALS OF FOREIGN TOURISTS AT ALL MEANS OF ACCOMMODATION

Austria	Netherlands	Turkey
Germany	Portugal	Yugoslavia
Italy	Switzerland	

NIGHTS SPENT BY FOREIGN TOURISTS IN HOTELS AND SIMILAR ESTABLISHMENTS

Austria	Germany	Spain
Belgium	Italy	Sweden
Denmark	Netherlands	Switzerland
Finland	Norway	Turkey
France (Ile de France)	Portugal	Yugoslavia

NIGHTS SPENT BY FOREIGN TOURISTS IN ALL MEANS OF ACCOMMODATION

Austria	Germany	Switzerland
Belgium	Italy	Turkey
Canada	Netherlands	United Kingdom
Denmark	Portugal	Yugoslavia
France	Sweden	

C. Types of accommodation covered by the statistics

Countries	Hotels and similar establishments					Supplementary means of accommodation							
	Hotels[1]	Motels	Boarding houses	Inns	Others[2]	Youth hostels	Camping and caravaning sites	Holiday villages[3]	Mountain huts and shelters	Rented rooms, houses and flats	Sanatoria, health establishments	Recreation homes for children	Others[4]
Australia	x	x	x		x	x	x	x		x			x
Austria[5]	x					x	x	x	x	x	x	x	x
Belgium	x				x		x			x	x	x	x
Canada	x	x					x						x
Denmark[5]	x	x				x	x						x
Finland	x				x		x						
France	x						x						
Germany	x		x	x		x	x	x			x		x
Italy	x		x	x	x	x	x	x			x		x
Netherlands	x		x		x	x	x			x			
Norway[5]	x				x	x	x						
Portugal	x	x	x	x	x		x					x	
Spain	x	x					x						
Sweden	x	x	x			x	x	x		x			
Switzerland	x	x		x		x	x			x	x		x
Turkey	x	x	x	x			x	x	x				
Yugoslavia	x	x	x	x	x	x	x	x	x	x	x		x

Countries not listed in this table do not dispose of data by type of accommodation.

1. "Hotels" include:
   Germany: hotels serving breakfast only; Switzerland: boarding houses.

2. Other "Hotels and similar establishments" include:
   Australia: hotels and motels without facilities in most rooms and not necessarily providing meals and liquor; Belgium: non-licensed establishments; Finland: lodging houses and part of youth hostels, holiday villages and boarding houses; Netherlands: youth hostels in Amsterdam; Portugal: holiday flats and villages; Sweden: boarding houses, inns and resort hotels.

3. "Holiday villages" include:
   Germany: Mountain huts and shelters.

4. Other "supplementary of accommodation" include:
   Australia: rented farms, house-boats, rented camper-vans, boats, cabin cruisers, camping outside commercial grounds; Belgium: youth hostels, holiday villages and social tourism establishments; Canada: homes of friends or relatives, camping outside commercial grounds; private cottages, commercial cottages and others (universities, hostels); Germany: recreation and holiday homes, institutions providing educational services; Italy: recreation homes for children, mountain huts and shelters, holiday homes and religious establishments; Switzerland: dormitories in (recreation homes for children, tourist camps, mountain huts and shelters, holiday villages); Yugoslavia: children and student homes, sleeping cars, cabins on ships.

5. Totals available without breakdown for "hotels and similar establishments".

1. Tourism from European Member countries[1]

	Arrivals at frontiers[2]			Arrivals at all means of accommodation[3]			Nights spent in all means of accommodation[4]		
	Volume 1986 ('000)	% 86/85	% 85/84	Volume 1986 ('000)	% 86/85	% 85/84	Volume 1986 ('000)	% 86/85	% 85/84
Austria				13 415.4	3.4	− 0.6	80 989.0	1.8	− 2.3
Belgium							8 106.9	1.1	3.5
Denmark							7 312.9	− 2.4	− 1.4
Finland							1 357.2	− 3.4	− 2.4
France	30 420.0	1.9	2.8	30 420.0	1.9	2.8	256 715.0	4.7	1.0
Germany				7 980.9	5.1	5.4	18 080.4	7.0	5.8
Greece	4 065.7	−16.2	21.8						
Iceland			12.8						
Ireland	1 269.0	− 1.9	−86.2						
Italy	43 538.6	− 4.1	7.7	15 092.6	9.0	2.3	86 928.5	8.9	0.8
Luxembourg						8.1			5.5
Netherlands						2.3			1.9
Norway							2 313.3	− 5.9	5.9
Portugal	4 955.8	10.8	22.0	3 047.8	14.8	16.4	15 256.5	17.3	17.4
Spain	42 346.6	11.5	0.6			− 7.0	80 581.0	13.1	−12.5
Sweden							6 012.4	− 1.1	− 2.3
Switzerland				6 697.8	4.7	− 0.6	28 866.2	4.1	0.0
Turkey	1 223.0	12.8	23.0	1 459.0	27.2	41.5	4 472.8	37.2	48.3
United Kingdom	8 119.6	4.2	4.5				71 579.0	− 2.1	9.5
Canada	1 099.7	25.8	− 6.1				15 159.2	22.2	− 7.4
United States	3 627.1	52.1	32.8						
Australia	334.2	16.0	9.9						23.6
New Zealand	71.8	21.6	8.6						
Japan	341.6	−13.0	11.7						
Yugoslavia				6 848.6	0.1	19.5	43 475.1	0.8	22.7

1. Derived from tables by receiving country(see corresponding notes).
2. *Tourist or visitor arrivals.* When both available : *tourist arrivals.*
3. Arrivals *in all means of accommodation* or *in hotels and similar establishments.* When both available: arrivals *in all means of accommodation.*
4. Nights spent *in all means of accommodation* or *in hotels and similar establishments.* When both available: nights spent *in all means of accommodation.*

2. Tourism from Canada and the United States[1]

	Arrivals at frontiers[2]			Arrivals at all means of accommodation[3]			Nights spent in all means of accommodation[4]		
	Volume 1986 ('000)	% 86/85	% 85/84	Volume 1986 ('000)	% 86/85	% 85/84	Volume 1986 ('000)	% 86/85	% 85/84
Austria				586.0	−45.9	6.9	1 618.5	−38.3	8.7
Belgium							888.1	−11.1	20.8
Denmark							436.4	−26.8	7.7
Finland							184.9	−13.9	16.0
France	2 054.0	−36.9	11.6	2 054.0	−36.9	11.6	29 086.0	−22.6	15.0
Germany				2 028.0	−28.5	5.3	4 135.5	−24.4	8.3
Greece	279.3	−50.9	2.1						
Iceland			16.3						
Ireland	326.0	−19.1	24.4						
Italy	1 929.5	−11.6	3.4	1 626.0	−49.2	6.5	4 787.0	−41.3	6.5
Luxembourg						18.8			15.6
Netherlands						2.1			2.1
Norway							411.2	−36.0	14.6
Portugal	186.6	−20.2	7.4	273.6	−31.7	13.2	884.7	−26.8	21.3
Spain	946.7	−20.4	8.9			−89.3	1 826.6	−39.6	4.9
Sweden							366.0	−31.1	14.6
Switzerland				1 104.4	−38.0	5.6	2 642.2	−32.7	8.0
Turkey	92.7	−57.4	− 5.9	84.2	−11.6	11.5	239.7	−16.0	4.8
United Kingdom	2 831.2	−25.4	14.0				32 764.0	−18.7	14.8
Canada	13 608.4	17.7	2.3				63 320.8	17.6	1.6
United States	10 942.8	0.6	− 0.9						
Australia	292.4	23.2	21.8						27.2
New Zealand	157.2	23.6	28.6						
Japan	607.4	− 1.9	9.7						
Yugoslavia				181.6	−34.7	6.8	475.2	−32.8	− 0.4

1. Derived from tables by receiving country(see corresponding notes).
2. *Tourist or visitor arrivals.* When both available : *tourist arrivals.*
3. Arrivals *in all means of accommodation* or *in hotels and similar establishments.* When both available: arrivals *in all means of accommodation.*
4. Nights spent *in all means of accommodation* or *in hotels and similar establishments.* When both available: nights spent *in all means of accommodation.*

3. Tourism from Australia, New Zealand and Japan[1]

	Arrivals at frontiers[2]			Arrivals at all means of accommodation[3]			Nights spent in all means of accommodation[4]		
	Volume 1986 ('000)	% 86/85	% 85/84	Volume 1986 ('000)	% 86/85	% 85/84	Volume 1986 ('000)	% 86/85	% 85/84
Austria				187.0	− 8.6	14.3	401.6	− 5.9	13.8
Belgium							98.9	0.7	10.8
Denmark							70.1	−10.1	− 1.9
Finland							38.6	−12.7	5.5
France	800.0	− 7.9	7.8	800.0	− 7.9	7.8	5 705.0	− 4.8	6.3
Germany				631.4	− 1.6	16.4	1 118.5	− 0.5	15.9
Greece	201.3	− 6.2	17.0						
Iceland			30.0						
Ireland	31.0	− 8.8	0.0						
Italy	715.2	3.2	− 1.3	596.2	− 1.7	4.5	1 349.5	− 5.5	2.6
Luxembourg									
Netherlands						12.9			19.3
Norway							46.0	−28.5	2.2
Portugal	38.7	9.7	13.9	48.0	− 0.8	13.0	112.6	− 6.1	11.5
Spain	189.2	− 5.0	11.2			20.3	421.9	7.9	15.3
Sweden							54.7	− 8.7	− 0.3
Switzerland				477.3	− 0.2	6.5	877.1	− 2.3	6.6
Turkey	43.6	10.6	28.1	53.1	39.8	44.9	117.3	41.6	57.8
United Kingdom	764.5	− 0.3	2.0				15 350.0	− 8.7	8.8
Canada	299.4	30.3	5.4				2 922.5	44.9	− 2.3
United States	2 035.2	17.3	23.4						
Australia	482.3	36.7	9.5						−10.4
New Zealand	264.3	− 4.4	18.2						
Japan	57.7	−23.0	9.6						
Yugoslavia				45.5	12.7	332.6	95.1	9.9	228.6

1. Derived from tables by receiving country(see corresponding notes).
2. *Tourist or visitor arrivals*. When both available : *tourist arrivals*.
3. Arrivals *in all means of accommodation* or *in hotels and similar establishments*. When both available: arrivals *in all means of accommodation*.
4. Nights spent *in all means of accommodation* or *in hotels and similar establishments*. When both available: nights spent *in all means of accommodation*.

4. Tourism from all OECD countries[1]

	Arrivals at frontiers[2]			Arrivals at all means of accommodation[3]			Nights spent in all means of accommodation[4]		
	Volume 1986 ('000)	% 86/85	% 85/84	Volume 1986 ('000)	% 86/85	% 85/84	Volume 1986 ('000)	% 86/85	% 85/84
Austria				14 188.3	− 0.5	0.2	83 009.1	0.5	− 1.9
Belgium							9 094.0	− 0.2	5.2
Denmark							7 749.3	− 4.2	− 0.8
Finland							1 580.7	− 5.0	− 0.1
France	33 274.0	− 2.0	3.7	33 274.0	− 2.0	3.7	291 506.0	0.9	2.7
Germany				10 640.3	− 3.9	6.0	23 334.4	− 0.7	6.8
Greece	4 546.3	−19.3	19.3						
Iceland			14.2						
Ireland	1 626.0	− 6.0	−82.3						
Italy	46 183.3	− 4.3	7.3	17 314.9	− 1.9	3.1	93 065.0	4.1	1.4
Luxembourg						10.0			7.0
Netherlands						2.6			2.3
Norway							2 770.5	−12.5	7.5
Portugal	5 181.1	9.3	21.1	3 369.3	8.5	15.9	16 253.9	13.4	17.7
Spain	43 482.4	10.4	0.9			−14.8	82 829.4	11.0	−11.8
Sweden							6 433.1	− 3.6	− 1.1
Switzerland				8 279.5	− 4.4	1.0	32 385.5	− 0.5	1.1
Turkey	1 359.4	1.3	17.3	1 596.3	24.7	38.8	4 829.8	33.1	43.8
United Kingdom	11 715.3	− 5.2	7.1				119 693.0	− 8.1	11.0
Canada	15 007.5	18.5	1.8				81 402.5	19.3	− 0.3
United States	16 605.1	10.7	5.8						
Australia	1 108.9	26.3	12.7						11.6
New Zealand	493.2	6.6	19.5						
Japan	1 006.7	− 7.4	10.4						
Yugoslavia				7 075.7	− 1.2	19.4	44 045.5	0.3	22.4

1. Derived from tables by receiving country(see corresponding notes).
2. *Tourist or visitor arrivals*. When both available : *tourist arrivals*.
3. Arrivals *in all means of accommodation* or *in hotels and similar establishments*. When both available: arrivals *in all means of accommodation*.
4. Nights spent *in all means of accommodation* or *in hotels and similar establishments*. When both available: nights spent *in all means of accommodation*.

5. Tourism from non-Member countries [1]

	Arrivals at frontiers [2]			Arrivals at all means of accommodation [3]			Nights spent in all means of accommodation [4]		
	Volume 1986 ('000)	% 86/85	% 85/84	Volume 1986 ('000)	% 86/85	% 85/84	Volume 1986 ('000)	% 86/85	% 85/84
Austria				904.0	− 8.8	13.1	2 394.2	− 2.4	0.1
Belgium							721.8	0.1	6.8
Denmark							761.9	−13.6	− 8.0
Finland							441.0	1.8	− 3.0
France	2 438.0	− 1.9	5.3	2 438.0	− 1.9	5.3	37 030.0	− 1.0	5.5
Germany				1 576.8	− 2.6	8.1	4 477.7	− 2.2	10.2
Greece	1 023.7	8.9	17.4						
Iceland			12.6						
Ireland	46.0	4.5	51.7						
Italy	7 140.6	33.0	28.6	2 055.6	1.7	− 6.8	7 055.6	4.5	− 2.9
Luxembourg						7.2			1.9
Netherlands						0.7			0.9
Norway							527.2	− 3.5	6.2
Portugal	228.1	− 7.5	21.7	185.8	− 8.4	6.9	534.5	−10.7	4.9
Spain	3 730.2	1.0	− 1.4			2.3	4 868.3	14.1	− 2.9
Sweden							738.8	− 9.2	3.4
Switzerland				878.0	1.0	− 4.4	2 543.1	− 3.4	− 4.8
Turkey	1 023.0	−19.0	31.0	404.3	−10.7	1.8	1 112.2	−11.0	4.2
United Kingdom	2 057.0	− 3.3	0.9				36 001.0	− 3.7	0.7
Canada	613.8	20.5	− 4.2				10 068.0	13.3	5.3
United States	5 398.3	− 3.0	−16.0						
Australia	320.5	21.3	12.0						− 7.8
New Zealand	73.0	294.2							
Japan	1 054.8	−14.9	10.1						
Yugoslavia				1 388.4	8.7	4.0	7 354.1	6.4	8.0

1. Derived from tables by receiving country(see corresponding notes).
2. *Tourist* or *visitor arrivals*. When both available : *tourist arrivals*.
3. Arrivals *in all means of accommodation* or *in hotels and similar establishments*. When both available: arrivals *in all means of accommodation*.
4. Nights spent *in all means of accommodation* or *in hotels and similar establishments*. When both available: nights spent *in all means of accommodation*.

6. Tourism from all countries [1]

	Arrivals at frontiers [2]			Arrivals at all means of accommodation [3]			Nights spent in all means of accommodation [4]		
	Volume 1986 ('000)	% 86/85	% 85/84	Volume 1986 ('000)	% 86/85	% 85/84	Volume 1986 ('000)	% 86/85	% 85/84
Austria [5]	140 940.0	7.4	1.5	15 092.3	− 1.0	0.9	85 403.4	0.4	− 1.9
Belgium							9 815.8	− 0.2	5.3
Denmark							8 511.2	− 5.1	− 1.5
Finland							2 021.7	− 3.6	− 0.7
France	36 080.0	− 1.8	3.9	36 080.0	− 1.8	3.9	332 208.0	0.7	3.1
Germany [5]	163 414.0	4.6	−13.5	12 217.2	− 3.7	6.2	27 812.1	− 1.0	7.4
Greece	7 024.8	6.9	19.0				35 331.1	− 0.5	8.1
Iceland	113.5	16.5	14.4						
Ireland	1 814.0	− 5.1		1 878.0	− 3.4	5.8	18 971.9	0.8	− 2.2
Italy	53 323.9	− 0.6	9.1	19 370.4	− 1.5	2.0	100 120.7	4.1	1.0
Luxembourg				711.0	3.3	0.1	2 356.3	7.4	−10.5
Netherlands						2.6	6 591.7	− 2.3	3.2
Norway				1 637.5	−15.3	10.8	3 297.7	−11.2	7.3
Portugal	5 409.2	8.4	21.1	3 555.1	7.5	15.3	16 788.3	12.4	17.1
Spain	47 388.8	9.6	0.7	13 587.3	9.2	− 4.6	87 697.7	11.1	−11.4
Sweden				522.5			7 171.9	− 4.2	− 0.7
Switzerland [6]	11 500.0	− 3.4	0.4	9 157.5	− 3.9	0.5	34 928.6	− 0.7	0.6
Turkey [5]	2 391.1	− 8.4	23.8	2 000.5	15.4	26.8	5 942.0	21.8	31.0
United Kingdom	13 772.3	− 4.9	6.1				155 694.0	− 7.1	8.5
Canada	15 621.3	18.6	1.5	15 621.3	18.6	1.5	91 470.5	18.6	0.3
United States	22 003.4	4.7	1.0						
Australia	1 429.4	25.1	12.6						6.7
New Zealand	566.2	17.6	24.3						
Japan	2 061.5	−11.4	10.3						
Yugoslavia	24 747.0	5.9	18.5	8 464.0	0.3	16.8	51 399.5	1.1	20.2

1. Derived from tables by receiving country. See corresponding notes, except for the countries mentioned in notes 5 and 6 below.
2. *Tourist* or *visitor arrivals*. When both available : *tourist arrivals*.
3. Arrivals *in all means of accommodation* or *in hotels and similar establishments*. When both available: arrivals *in all means of accommodation*.
4. Nights spent *in all means of accommodation* or *in hotels and similar establishments*. When both available: nights spent *in all means of accommodation*.
5. *Traveller* arrivals at frontiers.
6. *Tourist* arrivals at frontiers : estimates.

7. Expenditure of US residents travelling abroad

In millions of dollars

	1983	1984	1985	1986
Expenditure abroad[1]	13 556	15 449	16 482	17 627
Canada[2]	2 160	2 416	2 694	3 242
Mexico	3 618	3 599	3 531	3 879
Of which: Persons visiting Mexican border only	1 996	2 087	2 048	2 215
Overseas areas	7 778	9 434	10 257	10 506
Of which: Europe and Mediterranean area[3]	4 201	5 171	5 857	5 315
Of which: European Member countries	3 747	4 689	5 379	..
Caribbean and Central America	1 428	1 786	1 830	2 077
Of which: Bermuda	203	217	249	..
Bahamas	367	393	417	..
Jamaica	181	185	187	..
Other British West Indies	218	399	382	..
Dutch West Indies	188	213	236	..
South America	408	357	365	407
Other overseas countries	1 741	2 120	2 205	2 707
Of which: Japan	276	400	458	738
Hong Kong	195	258	255	..
Australia – New Zealand	456	545	607	..
Fare payments	..	..	..	..
Foreign-flag carriers	5 484	6 502	7 313	6 842
US-flag carriers	..	..	..	..

.. Data not available.
1. Excludes travel by military personnel and other Government employees stationed abroad, their dependents and United States citizens residing abroad; includes shore expenditure of United States cruise travellers.
2. Excluding fare payments and crew spending.
3. Fore more data concerning Europe and Mediterranean area and individual Member countries in Europe, see Table 8.
Source: US Department of Commerce, Bureau of Economic Analysis.

8. Number and expenditure of US residents travelling overseas

Countries visited	Number of travellers In thousands[1]			Total expenditure Millions of dollars[2]			Average expenditure per traveller		
	1983	1984	1985	1983	1984	1985	1983	1984	1985
European Member countries	8 678	10 526	11 625	3 747	4 689	5 379	432	445	463
Of which: Austria	524	631	643	142	182	191	271	288	296
Belgium-Luxembourg	333	426	468	61	73	94	172	172	201
Denmark	252	333	379	70	100	120	275	299	315
France	1 205	1 494	1 586	567	705	770	470	472	485
Germany	1 064	1 438	1 673	396	570	672	373	396	402
Greece	364	293	287	213	157	148	585	537	517
Ireland	169	211	288	80	100	138	472	472	478
Italy	834	1 151	1 021	461	661	619	553	574	607
Netherlands	498	553	671	122	137	168	246	247	250
Norway	166	168	209	57	72	92	345	426	439
Portugal	93	143	135	26	40	36	278	282	268
Spain	365	534	404	198	312	229	540	584	568
Sweden	237	218	257	68	79	88	285	361	342
Switzerland	753	964	1 081	279	336	369	371	348	342
United Kingdom	1 821	1 969	2 523	1 007	1 165	1 645	553	592	652
Europe and Mediterranean area[3]	4 780	5 760	6 457	4 201	5 171	5 857	882	897	907
Caribbean and Central America	2 989	3 313	3 497	1 428	1 786	1 830	452	511	496
South America	535	557	553	408	357	365	724	641	661
Other overseas countries	1 324	1 622	1 802	1 741	2 120	2 205	1 306	1 307	1 222
TOTAL	9 628	11 252	12 309	7 778	9 434	10 257	798	830	825

1. Excludes travel by military personnel and other Government employees stationed abroad, their dependents and United States citizens residing abroad and cruise travellers.
2. Includes shore expenditure of cruise travellers; excludes fares.
3. Includes all European countries Algeria, Cyprus, Egypt, Israël, Lebanon, Lybia, Malta, Morocco, Syria, Tunisia and Turkey.
Source: US Department of Commerce, Bureau of Economic Analysis, based on data of the US Department of Justice, Immigration and Naturalization Service.

AUSTRALIA

ARRIVALS OF FOREIGN VISITORS AT FRONTIERS[1]
(by month)

	Total number 1986	% Variation over 1985	% of 1985 total	From New Zealand	% Variation over 1985	From United States	% Variation over 1985
January	98 000	18.6	6.9	15 500	23.0	17 500	36.7
February	118 000	19.4	8.3	15 900	28.2	20 900	25.9
March	129 500	22.9	9.1	23 800	42.5	20 100	10.4
April	110 600	31.8	7.7	22 500	41.5	25 800	36.5
May	91 700	21.1	6.4	32 900	45.6	13 700	10.5
June	94 800	25.7	6.6	33 700	33.7	13 300	13.7
July	109 500	31.8	7.7	38 300	53.2	16 900	29.0
August	105 100	26.8	7.4	32 800	43.2	15 500	7.6
September	95 000	22.9	6.6	26 600	33.7	16 000	18.5
October	130 300	23.3	9.1	29 200	28.6	26 300	17.4
November	156 700	28.5	11.0	28 800	37.1	32 600	33.1
December	190 100	26.7	13.3	36 700	28.8	26 900	49.4
Total	1 429 300	25.1	100.0	336 700	37.2	245 500	24.9

(by country of residence)

	1985	Relative share	1986	Relative share	% Variation over 1985
Austria	4 200	0.4	5 100	0.4	21.4
Belgium	2 300	0.2	2 500	0.2	8.7
Denmark	5 100	0.4	6 300	0.4	23.5
Finland	2 100	0.2	3 100	0.2	47.6
France	12 000	1.1	13 900	1.0	15.8
Germany[2]	37 300	3.3	41 900	2.9	12.3
Greece	6 600	0.6	6 400	0.4	-3.0
Iceland	100	0.0	100	0.0	0.0
Ireland	5 500	0.5	7 400	0.5	34.5
Italy	14 500	1.3	17 300	1.2	19.3
Luxembourg	100	0.0	200	0.0	100.0
Netherlands	15 400	1.3	15 900	1.1	3.2
Norway	2 400	0.2	3 200	0.2	33.3
Portugal	900	0.1	900	0.1	0.0
Spain	1 700	0.1	2 200	0.2	29.4
Sweden	9 700	0.8	14 200	1.0	46.4
Switzerland	14 300	1.3	16 900	1.2	18.2
Turkey	400	0.0	700	0.0	75.0
United Kingdom	153 400	13.4	176 000	12.3	14.7
Other OECD-Europe					
Total Europe	288 000	25.2	334 200	23.4	16.0
Canada	40 900	3.6	47 000	3.3	14.9
United States	196 500	17.2	245 400	17.2	24.9
Total North America	237 400	20.8	292 400	20.5	23.2
Australia					
New Zealand	245 300	21.5	336 700	23.6	37.3
Japan	107 600	9.4	145 600	10.2	35.3
Total Australasia and Japan	352 900	30.9	482 300	33.7	36.7
Total OECD Countries	878 300	76.9	1 108 900	77.6	26.3
Yugoslavia (S.F.R.)	5 600	0.5	6 400	0.4	14.3
Other European countries	17 500	1.5	19 600	1.4	12.0
of which: Bulgaria	100	0.0			
Czechoslovakia	600	0.1			
Hungary	1 000	0.1	1 100	0.1	10.0
Poland	3 000	0.3	3 100	0.2	3.3
Rumania	200	0.0			
USSR	1 000	0.1	1 100	0.1	10.0
Latin America	7 100	0.6	9 400	0.7	32.4
Asia-Oceania	212 700	18.6	260 700	18.2	22.6
Africa	17 300	1.5	19 600	1.4	13.3
Origin country undetermined	4 100	0.4	4 800	0.3	17.1
Total Non-OECD Countries	264 300	23.1	320 500	22.4	21.3
TOTAL	1 142 600	100.0	1 429 400	100.0	25.1

1. Includes a small number of "in transit" passengers who leave the port or airport, but do not necessarily stay overnight in Australia.
2. Germany includes Federal and Democratic Republics.

AUSTRIA

ARRIVALS OF FOREIGN TOURISTS IN HOTELS
(by month)

	Total number 1986	% Variation over 1985	% of 1985 total	From Germany	% Variation over 1985	From United States	% Variation over 1985
January	759 367	1.8	7.1	449 701	3.8	25 418	− 3.6
February	935 943	4.8	8.7	436 034	5.3	27 686	− 4.4
March	1 050 017	23.3	9.8	626 336	22.6	36 607	− 7.7
April	516 824	−14.6	4.8	223 574	−20.6	26 374	−40.8
May	868 995	2.1	8.1	468 568	13.3	36 863	−60.8
June	935 349	−19.2	8.7	446 146	−16.6	49 300	−66.2
July	1 388 272	− 7.0	12.9	606 456	3.0	63 095	−60.7
August	1 563 492	− 2.2	14.5	742 345	2.1	51 813	−56.0
September	1 142 803	− 4.0	10.6	599 016	2.5	59 094	−55.7
October	662 215	− 1.2	6.2	373 017	6.9	39 993	−50.7
November	292 570	2.4	2.7	154 341	6.8	16 711	−27.8
December	649 674	7.3	6.0	353 798	9.2	25 162	−16.3
Total	10 765 521	− 1.7	100.0	5 479 332	3.3	458 116	−50.5

(by country of residence)

	1985	Relative share	1986	Relative share	% Variation over 1985
Austria					
Belgium [1]	233 973	2.1	227 302	2.1	−2.9
Denmark	124 369	1.1	131 672	1.2	5.9
Finland	39 174	0.4	40 800	0.4	4.2
France	525 910	4.8	574 618	5.3	9.3
Germany (F.R.)	5 305 944	48.5	5 479 332	50.9	3.3
Greece	47 657	0.4	40 815	0.4	−14.4
Iceland [2]					
Ireland	6 229	0.1	7 402	0.1	18.8
Italy	472 412	4.3	573 659	5.3	21.4
Luxembourg [1]					
Netherlands	738 637	6.7	732 879	6.8	−0.8
Norway	51 396	0.5	58 444	0.5	13.7
Portugal	9 497	0.1	9 685	0.1	2.0
Spain	101 399	0.9	98 835	0.9	−2.5
Sweden	217 813	2.0	238 682	2.2	9.6
Switzerland	432 795	4.0	459 646	4.3	6.2
Turkey	22 905	0.2	22 900	0.2	−0.0
United Kingdom	697 191	6.4	673 727	6.3	−3.4
Other OECD-Europe					
Total Europe	9 027 301	82.5	9 370 398	87.0	3.8
Canada	79 234	0.7	61 537	0.6	−22.3
United States	925 603	8.5	458 116	4.3	−50.5
Total North America	1 004 837	9.2	519 653	4.8	−48.3
Australia [3]	79 020	0.7	68 365	0.6	−13.5
New Zealand [3]					
Japan	125 598	1.1	118 585	1.1	−5.6
Total Australasia and Japan	204 618	1.9	186 950	1.7	−8.6
Total OECD Countries	10 236 756	93.5	10 077 001	93.6	−1.6
Yugoslavia (S.F.R.)	85 017	0.8	90 656	0.8	6.6
Other European countries	289 873	2.6	276 814	2.6	−4.5
of which: Bulgaria	9 009	0.1			
Czechoslovakia	27 647	0.3			
Hungary	223 464	2.0			
Poland	17 139	0.2			
Rumania	3 806	0.0			
USSR	8 808	0.1			
Latin America	91 179	0.8	103 387	1.0	13.4
Asia-Oceania	104 599	1.0	109 387	1.0	4.6
Africa	29 545	0.3	22 041	0.2	−25.4
Origin country undetermined	110 930	1.0	86 235	0.8	−22.3
Total Non-OECD Countries	711 143	6.5	688 520	6.4	−3.2
TOTAL	10 947 899	100.0	10 765 521	100.0	−1.7

1. Luxembourg included in Belgium.
2. Iceland included in "Other European countries".
3. New Zealand included in Australia.

AUSTRIA

ARRIVALS OF FOREIGN TOURISTS IN REGISTERED TOURIST ACCOMMODATION
(by month)

	Total number 1986	% Variation over 1985	% of 1985 total	From Germany	% Variation over 1985	From United States	% Variation over 1985
January	1 040 595	1.1	6.9	667 647	2.0	28 745	− 0.7
February	1 371 630	5.1	9.1	706 089	5.7	30 442	− 3.9
March	1 480 645	28.0	9.8	982 790	28.0	39 378	− 4.5
April	627 622	−18.2	4.2	302 674	−26.2	28 689	−38.4
May	1 051 803	3.4	7.0	611 710	13.5	39 982	−59.2
June	1 230 719	−18.7	8.2	638 477	−18.0	55 754	−63.8
July	2 327 894	− 3.7	15.4	1 100 000	3.4	74 275	−57.8
August	2 461 015	− 1.1	16.3	1 326 988	1.5	59 262	−54.1
September	1 452 029	− 2.6	9.6	837 045	2.6	63 484	−54.3
October	800 284	− 1.2	5.3	479 449	5.0	42 826	−49.8
November	324 672	1.2	2.2	176 714	3.8	18 371	−25.9
December	923 375	8.3	6.1	564 036	10.0	28 264	−15.4
Total	15 092 283	− 0.5	100.0	8 393 619	3.0	509 472	−48.4

(by country of residence)

	1985	Relative share	1986	Relative share	% Variation over 1985
Austria					
Belgium [1]	339 113	2.2	329 554	2.2	−2.8
Denmark	182 972	1.2	194 481	1.3	6.3
Finland	39 174	0.3	40 800	0.3	4.2
France	664 933	4.4	722 937	4.8	8.7
Germany (F.R.)	8 145 318	53.4	8 393 619	55.6	3.0
Greece	51 305	0.3	44 679	0.3	−12.9
Iceland [2]					
Ireland	6 229	0.0	7 402	0.0	18.8
Italy	534 756	3.5	641 313	4.2	19.9
Luxembourg [1]					
Netherlands	1 247 378	8.2	1 243 350	8.2	−0.3
Norway	51 396	0.3	58 444	0.4	13.7
Portugal	9 497	0.1	9 685	0.1	2.0
Spain	101 399	0.7	98 835	0.7	−2.5
Sweden	279 317	1.8	304 534	2.0	9.0
Switzerland	497 955	3.3	530 175	3.5	6.5
Turkey	22 905	0.2	22 900	0.2	−0.0
United Kingdom	795 973	5.2	772 650	5.1	−2.9
Other OECD-Europe					
Total Europe	12 969 620	85.1	13 415 358	88.9	3.4
Canada	94 762	0.6	76 545	0.5	−19.2
United States	987 722	6.5	509 472	3.4	−48.4
Total North America	1 082 484	7.1	586 017	3.9	−45.9
Australia [3]	79 020	0.5	68 365	0.5	−13.5
New Zealand [3]					
Japan	125 598	0.8	118 585	0.8	−5.6
Total Australasia and Japan	204 618	1.3	186 950	1.2	−8.6
Total OECD Countries	14 256 722	93.5	14 188 325	94.0	−0.5
Yugoslavia (S.F.R.)	99 152	0.7	107 702	0.7	8.6
Other European countries	362 484	2.4	351 646	2.3	−3.0
of which: Bulgaria	10 812	0.1			
Czechoslovakia	35 332	0.2			
Hungary	281 811	1.8			
Poland	20 746	0.1			
Rumania	4 975	0.0			
USSR	8 808	0.1			
Latin America	91 179	0.6	103 387	0.7	13.4
Asia-Oceania	190 245	1.2	116 093	0.8	−39.0
Africa	29 545	0.2	22 041	0.1	−25.4
Origin country undetermined	218 503	1.4	203 089	1.3	−7.1
Total Non-OECD Countries	991 108	6.5	903 958	6.0	−8.8
TOTAL	15 247 830	100.0	15 092 283	100.0	−1.0

1. Luxembourg included in Belgium.
2. Iceland included in "Other European countries".
3. New Zealand included in Australia.

AUSTRIA

NIGHTS SPENT BY FOREIGN TOURISTS IN HOTELS
(by month)

	Total number 1986	% Variation over 1985	% of 1985 total	From Germany	% Variation over 1985	From United States	% Variation over 1985
January	5 079 914	− 4.1	9.3	3 126 527	− 3.5	110 374	− 7.7
February	6 141 950	3.4	11.3	2 910 269	2.9	127 571	− 3.9
March	6 433 705	22.0	11.8	4 412 108	23.1	138 457	− 7.3
April	2 198 439	−21.9	4.0	1 203 698	−32.5	62 918	−36.9
May	2 918 997	5.6	5.4	1 827 027	12.2	76 336	−59.1
June	4 026 990	−17.8	7.4	2 393 120	−19.8	104 321	−62.7
July	7 555 742	− 2.4	13.9	4 407 029	0.7	148 017	−56.9
August	8 588 965	0.7	15.8	5 544 458	3.2	134 342	−51.1
September	5 364 441	1.0	9.8	3 574 608	3.2	132 795	−50.6
October	2 127 096	1.8	3.9	1 343 161	6.5	87 330	−48.1
November	769 382	0.4	1.4	429 865	3.3	42 540	−25.1
December	3 326 734	5.3	6.1	2 005 228	7.2	89 378	−13.1
Total	54 532 355	− 0.1	100.0	33 177 098	1.1	1 254 379	−42.5

(by country of residence)

	1985	Relative share	1986	Relative share	% Variation over 1985
Austria					
Belgium [1]	1 440 483	2.6	1 366 486	2.5	−5.1
Denmark	615 769	1.1	642 086	1.2	4.3
Finland	142 149	0.3	153 839	0.3	8.2
France	1 911 014	3.5	2 121 711	3.9	11.0
Germany (F.R.)	32 802 153	60.1	33 177 098	60.8	1.1
Greece [2]	126 661	0.2	110 748	0.2	−12.6
Iceland [2]					
Ireland	26 223	0.0	37 679	0.1	43.7
Italy	1 084 824	2.0	1 319 797	2.4	21.7
Luxembourg [1]					
Netherlands	5 079 537	9.3	5 036 307	9.2	−0.9
Norway	176 317	0.3	205 825	0.4	16.7
Portugal	18 574	0.0	20 897	0.0	12.5
Spain	210 646	0.4	215 381	0.4	2.2
Sweden	975 545	1.8	1 056 407	1.9	8.3
Switzerland	1 524 916	2.8	1 623 722	3.0	6.5
Turkey	52 821	0.1	53 386	0.1	1.1
United Kingdom	3 744 144	6.9	3 825 162	7.0	2.2
Other OECD-Europe					
Total Europe	49 931 776	91.5	50 966 531	93.5	2.1
Canada	200 122	0.4	165 178	0.3	−17.5
United States	2 182 863	4.0	1 254 379	2.3	−42.5
Total North America	2 382 985	4.4	1 419 557	2.6	−40.4
Australia [3]	192 853	0.4	171 379	0.3	−11.1
New Zealand [3]					
Japan	234 070	0.4	230 233	0.4	−1.6
Total Australasia and Japan	426 923	0.8	401 612	0.7	−5.9
Total OECD Countries	52 741 684	96.6	52 787 700	96.8	0.1
Yugoslavia (S.F.R.)	213 484	0.4	238 871	0.4	11.9
Other European countries	647 818	1.2	644 283	1.2	−0.5
of which: Bulgaria	26 152	0.0			
Czechoslovakia	65 297	0.1			
Hungary	451 341	0.8			
Poland	65 387	0.1			
Rumania	10 783	0.0			
USSR	28 858	0.1			
Latin America	185 122	0.3	208 419	0.4	12.6
Asia-Oceania	349 902	0.6	324 304	0.6	−7.3
Africa	128 359	0.2	89 247	0.2	−30.5
Origin country undetermined	321 500	0.6	239 537	0.4	−25.5
Total Non-OECD Countries	1 846 185	3.4	1 744 661	3.2	−5.5
TOTAL	54 587 869	100.0	54 532 361	100.0	−0.1

1. Luxembourg included in Belgium.
2. Iceland included in "Other European countries".
3. New Zealand included in Australia.

AUSTRIA

NIGHTS SPENT BY FOREIGN TOURISTS IN REGISTERED TOURIST ACCOMMODATION
(by month)

	Total number 1986	% Variation over 1985	% of 1985 total	From Germany	% Variation over 1985	From United States	% Variation over 1985
January	7 342 980	– 4.7	8.6	4 877 881	– 4.6	124 096	– 7.7
February	9 131 036	3.9	10.7	4 699 512	3.8	140 825	– 4.7
March	9 581 046	26.6	11.2	7 111 012	28.5	148 485	– 5.8
April	3 077 195	–25.1	3.6	1 874 024	–35.1	69 016	–34.3
May	3 788 479	6.8	4.4	2 558 345	12.5	83 934	–57.3
June	5 735 272	–20.0	6.7	3 700 367	–23.2	119 112	–60.2
July	14 459 264	– 1.5	16.9	8 755 554	0.4	177 768	–53.9
August	15 752 382	1.7	18.4	11 100 728	3.5	157 900	–48.8
September	7 781 877	2.2	9.1	5 657 996	3.7	145 079	–49.3
October	2 778 073	1.5	3.3	1 886 390	4.9	94 279	–46.8
November	904 000	– 0.7	1.1	530 965	1.0	46 422	–24.1
December	5 061 732	6.4	5.9	3 302 634	8.2	101 887	–12.8
Total	85 393 336	0.4	100.0	56 055 408	1.1	1 408 803	–40.7

(by country of residence)

	1985	Relative share	1986	Relative share	% Variation over 1985
Austria					
Belgium [1]	2 244 744	2.6	2 162 888	2.5	–3.6
Denmark	858 757	1.0	907 485	1.1	5.7
Finland	142 149	0.2	153 839	0.2	8.2
France	2 478 962	2.9	2 702 647	3.2	9.0
Germany (F.R.)	55 431 560	65.2	56 055 408	65.6	1.1
Greece	137 593	0.2	122 741	0.1	–10.8
Iceland [2]					
Ireland	26 223	0.0	37 679	0.0	43.7
Italy	1 264 367	1.5	1 518 736	1.8	20.1
Luxembourg [1]					
Netherlands	9 176 892	10.8	9 175 793	10.7	–0.0
Norway	176 317	0.2	205 825	0.2	16.7
Portugal	18 574	0.0	20 897	0.0	12.5
Spain	210 646	0.2	215 381	0.3	2.2
Sweden	1 245 320	1.5	1 350 657	1.6	8.5
Switzerland	1 875 959	2.2	1 997 796	2.3	6.5
Turkey	52 821	0.1	63 386	0.1	20.0
United Kingdom	4 232 906	5.0	4 297 861	5.0	1.5
Other OECD-Europe					
Total Europe	79 573 790	93.5	80 989 019	94.8	1.8
Canada	245 932	0.3	209 691	0.2	–14.7
United States	2 376 876	2.8	1 408 803	1.6	–40.7
Total North America	2 622 808	3.1	1 618 494	1.9	–38.3
Australia [3]	192 853	0.2	171 379	0.2	–11.1
New Zealand [3]					
Japan	234 070	0.3	230 233	0.3	–1.6
Total Australasia and Japan	426 923	0.5	401 612	0.5	–5.9
Total OECD Countries	82 623 521	97.1	83 009 125	97.2	0.5
Yugoslavia (S.F.R.)	287 474	0.3	328 573	0.4	14.3
Other European countries	835 831	1.0	842 463	1.0	0.8
of which: Bulgaria	33 551	0.0			
Czechoslovakia	85 900	0.1			
Hungary	590 182	0.7			
Poland	84 048	0.1			
Rumania	13 292	0.0			
USSR	28 858	0.0			
Latin America	185 122	0.2	208 419	0.2	12.6
Asia-Oceania	375 019	0.4	348 341	0.4	–7.1
Africa	128 359	0.2	89 247	0.1	–30.5
Origin country undetermined	640 524	0.8	577 185	0.7	–9.9
Total Non-OECD Countries	2 452 329	2.9	2 394 228	2.8	–2.4
TOTAL	85 075 850	100.0	85 403 353	100.0	0.4

1. Luxembourg included in Belgium.
2. Iceland included in "Other European countries".
3. New Zealand included in Australia.

BELGIUM

NIGHTS SPENT BY FOREIGN TOURISTS IN HOTELS
(by month)

	Total number 1986	% Variation over 1985	% of 1985 total	From Netherlands	% Variation over 1985	From United States	% Variation over 1985
January	251 768	4.4	4.8	28 314	− 0.8	38 492	11.1
February	275 948	4.3	5.2	36 654	2.8	38 077	13.3
March	384 166	8.8	7.3	42 771	4.0	44 823	− 7.3
April	416 160	−12.6	7.9	45 075	−17.3	50 021	−12.0
May	571 441	− 1.9	10.8	64 352	12.9	56 999	−27.9
June	514 569	−12.6	9.7	54 055	− 6.9	61 571	−32.2
July	567 966	− 8.6	10.7	87 895	4.4	56 697	−35.2
August	599 294	− 9.2	11.3	79 833	2.4	54 620	−33.5
September	550 860	− 5.2	10.4	64 145	7.0	67 457	−26.8
October	495 849	− 4.5	9.4	75 503	7.9	58 224	−29.5
November	375 566	0.5	7.1	47 141	5.5	41 801	−16.3
December	288 810	4.9	5.5	50 973	8.1	31 467	− 8.5
Total	5 292 397	− 4.4	100.0	676 711	2.7	600 249	−22.2

(by country of residence)

	1985	Relative share	1986	Relative share	% Variation over 1985
Austria	50 784	0.9	49 149	0.9	−3.2
Belgium					
Denmark	53 395	1.0	57 146	1.1	7.0
Finland [1]					
France	576 834	10.4	592 496	11.2	2.7
Germany (F.R.)	746 951	13.5	761 452	14.4	1.9
Greece	62 895	1.1	55 617	1.1	−11.6
Iceland [1]					
Ireland	28 283	0.5	28 357	0.5	0.3
Italy	219 867	4.0	217 880	4.1	−0.9
Luxembourg	76 980	1.4	79 543	1.5	3.3
Netherlands	658 740	11.9	676 711	12.8	2.7
Norway	42 301	0.8	43 399	0.8	2.6
Portugal	42 695	0.8	49 710	0.9	16.4
Spain	145 941	2.6	150 442	2.8	3.1
Sweden	77 619	1.4	80 888	1.5	4.2
Switzerland	85 486	1.5	84 053	1.6	−1.7
Turkey	15 347	0.3	15 431	0.3	0.5
United Kingdom	1 050 809	19.0	976 216	18.4	−7.1
Other OECD-Europe					
Total Europe	3 934 927	71.1	3 918 490	74.0	−0.4
Canada	92 732	1.7	72 702	1.4	−21.6
United States	771 965	13.9	600 249	11.3	−22.2
Total North America	864 697	15.6	672 951	12.7	−22.2
Australia [2]					
New Zealand [2]					
Japan	94 191	1.7	95 327	1.8	1.2
Total Australasia and Japan	94 191	1.7	95 327	1.8	1.2
Total OECD Countries	4 893 815	88.4	4 686 768	88.6	−4.2
Yugoslavia (S.F.R.)					
Other European countries	123 624	2.2	120 796	2.3	−2.3
of which: Bulgaria					
Czechoslovakia					
Hungary					
Poland					
Rumania					
USSR	7 844	0.1			
Latin America	90 187	1.6	94 734	1.8	5.0
Asia-Oceania	212 847	3.8	192 916	3.6	−9.4
Africa	215 684	3.9	197 183	3.7	−8.6
Origin country undetermined					
Total Non-OECD Countries	642 342	11.6	605 629	11.4	−5.7
TOTAL	5 536 157	100.0	5 292 397	100.0	−4.4

1. Included in "Other European countries".
2. Included in "Asia-Oceania".

BELGIUM

NIGHTS SPENT BY FOREIGN TOURISTS IN REGISTERED TOURIST ACCOMMODATION
(by month)

	Total number 1986	% Variation over 1985	% of 1985 total	From Netherlands	% Variation over 1985	From United States	% Variation over 1985
January	374 023	15.8	3.8	106 591	12.4	57 771	62.5
February	400 156	15.0	4.1	121 197	17.9	58 360	69.1
March	517 654	17.5	5.3	115 290	14.0	59 445	19.8
April	554 407	−12.1	5.6	110 846	−13.7	66 264	2.3
May	982 673	2.0	10.0	292 632	4.3	73 304	−16.9
June	941 779	−11.7	9.6	269 176	− 2.5	77 690	−24.6
July	1 901 138	− 5.0	19.4	1 033 073	6.8	76 015	−27.5
August	1 683 124	4.4	17.1	612 705	6.3	70 696	−28.1
September	881 541	− 2.8	9.0	226 428	1.7	82 768	−23.6
October	682 769	− 0.4	7.0	184 264	2.2	73 107	−23.1
November	473 514	0.9	4.8	106 562	− 0.7	57 543	− 9.5
December	422 991	7.0	4.3	144 316	11.7	47 445	1.6
Total	**9 815 769**	**− 0.3**	**100.0**	**3 323 080**	**4.9**	**800 408**	**−10.3**

(by country of residence)

	1985	Relative share	1986	Relative share	% Variation over 1985
Austria	60 976	0.6	56 630	0.6	−7.1
Belgium					
Denmark	65 596	0.7	71 924	0.7	9.6
Finland [1]					
France	945 197	9.6	972 144	9.9	2.9
Germany (F.R.)	1 516 985	15.4	1 512 155	15.4	−0.3
Greece	65 749	0.7	57 542	0.6	−12.5
Iceland [1]					
Ireland	33 051	0.3	32 953	0.3	−0.3
Italy	250 002	2.5	247 856	2.5	−0.9
Luxembourg	169 815	1.7	178 215	1.8	4.9
Netherlands	3 166 687	32.2	3 323 080	33.9	4.9
Norway	91 618	0.9	57 014	0.6	−37.8
Portugal	51 635	0.5	70 966	0.7	37.4
Spain	167 689	1.7	174 247	1.8	3.9
Sweden	87 422	0.9	93 175	0.9	6.6
Switzerland	93 764	1.0	91 938	0.9	−1.9
Turkey	16 396	0.2	16 890	0.2	3.0
United Kingdom	1 234 696	12.6	1 150 214	11.7	−6.8
Other OECD-Europe					
Total Europe	8 017 278	81.5	8 106 943	82.6	1.1
Canada	105 945	1.1	87 716	0.9	−17.2
United States	892 542	9.1	800 408	8.2	−10.3
Total North America	998 487	10.2	888 124	9.0	−11.1
Australia [2]					
New Zealand [2]					
Japan	98 203	1.0	98 906	1.0	0.7
Total Australasia and Japan	98 203	1.0	98 906	1.0	0.7
Total OECD Countries	**9 113 968**	**92.7**	**9 093 973**	**92.6**	**−0.2**
Yugoslavia (S.F.R.)					
Other European countries	142 297	1.4	149 501	1.5	5.1
of which: Bulgaria					
Czechoslovakia					
Hungary					
Poland					
Rumania					
USSR	8 485	0.1			
Latin America	99 136	1.0	105 172	1.1	6.1
Asia-Oceania	235 430	2.4	225 171	2.3	−4.4
Africa	241 419	2.5	240 028	2.4	−0.6
Origin country undetermined	2 717	0.0	1 924	0.0	−29.2
Total Non-OECD Countries	**720 999**	**7.3**	**721 796**	**7.4**	**0.1**
TOTAL	**9 834 967**	**100.0**	**9 815 769**	**100.0**	**−0.2**

1. Included in "Other European countries".
2. Included in "Asia-Oceania".

CANADA

ARRIVALS OF FOREIGN TOURISTS AT FRONTIERS
(by month)

	Total number 1986	% Variation over 1985	% of 1985 total	From United Kingdom	% Variation over 1985	From United States	% Variation over 1985
January	412 000	15.7	2.6	9 000	4.7	354 700	17.1
February	460 100	13.0	2.9	8 300	6.4	405 300	13.8
March	598 600	14.9	3.8	13 400	9.8	518 300	15.5
April	660 600	− 1.5	4.2	16 000	8.8	561 600	− 3.0
May	1 463 800	26.3	9.3	42 700	26.3	1 276 300	27.0
June	2 003 900	16.4	12.8	55 100	26.4	1 731 700	15.4
July	2 979 300	22.1	19.0	73 800	36.4	2 608 500	20.7
August	3 120 800	19.5	19.9	76 900	36.8	2 749 900	17.9
September	1 699 200	32.4	10.9	49 100	28.2	1 469 800	32.3
October	1 039 900	15.0	6.6	25 100	30.1	901 800	13.3
November	599 600	4.6	3.8	14 200	16.4	516 900	3.3
December	622 800	12.6	4.0	22 500	20.3	515 600	11.3
Total [1]	15 660 600	18.6	100.0	406 100	27.1	13 610 400	17.8

(by country of residence)

	1985	Relative share	1986	Relative share	% Variation over 1985
Austria	14 000	0.1	17 200	0.1	22.9
Belgium	15 200	0.1	19 700	0.1	29.6
Denmark	14 500	0.1	18 800	0.1	29.7
Finland	10 300	0.1	12 900	0.1	25.2
France	107 300	0.8	140 300	0.9	30.8
Germany (F.R.)	156 500	1.2	198 300	1.3	26.7
Greece	14 200	0.1	15 900	0.1	12.0
Iceland	900	0.0	1 200	0.0	33.3
Ireland	11 100	0.1	14 500	0.1	30.6
Italy	55 200	0.4	65 200	0.4	18.1
Luxembourg	900	0.0	1 000	0.0	11.1
Netherlands	58 400	0.4	68 600	0.4	17.5
Norway	9 000	0.1	13 100	0.1	45.6
Portugal	14 200	0.1	19 500	0.1	37.3
Spain	11 800	0.1	15 000	0.1	27.1
Sweden	19 000	0.1	21 700	0.1	14.2
Switzerland	44 700	0.3	53 700	0.3	20.1
Turkey	2 800	0.0	3 600	0.0	28.6
United Kingdom	314 000	2.4	399 500	2.6	27.2
Other OECD-Europe					
Total Europe	874 000	6.6	1 099 700	7.0	25.8
Canada					
United States	11 557 500	87.8	13 608 400	87.1	17.7
Total North America	11 557 500	87.8	13 608 400	87.1	17.7
Australia	69 700	0.5	77 000	0.5	10.5
New Zealand	14 200	0.1	25 300	0.2	78.2
Japan	145 800	1.1	197 100	1.3	35.2
Total Australasia and Japan	229 700	1.7	299 400	1.9	30.3
Total OECD Countries	12 661 200	96.1	15 007 500	96.1	18.5
Yugoslavia (S.F.R.)	9 300	0.1	10 400	0.1	11.8
Other European countries	46 300	0.4	46 500	0.3	0.4
of which: Bulgaria	400	0.0	500	0.0	25.0
Czechoslovakia	4 000	0.0	5 700	0.0	42.5
Hungary	6 100	0.0	7 200	0.0	18.0
Poland	26 100	0.2	25 700	0.2	−1.5
Rumania	1 500	0.0	1 200	0.0	−20.0
USSR	8 200	0.1	6 200	0.0	−24.4
Latin America [2]	95 800	0.7	114 800	0.7	19.8
Asia-Oceania	223 900	1.7	303 700	1.9	35.6
Africa	40 000	0.3	43 400	0.3	8.5
Origin country undetermined	94 200	0.7	95 000	0.6	0.8
Total Non-OECD Countries	509 500	3.9	613 800	3.9	20.5
TOTAL [1]	13 170 700	100.0	15 621 300	100.0	18.6

1. Discrepancies between data by month and by country of origin arise because monthly figures are estimates.
2. Including Mexico.

CANADA

ARRIVALS OF FOREIGN VISITORS AT FRONTIERS
(by month)

	Total number 1986	% Variation over 1985	% of 1985 total	From United Kingdom	% Variation over 1985	From United States	% Variation over 1985
January	1 681 600	17.3	4.2	9 700	3.2	1 621 100	17.7
February	1 654 300	11.7	4.1	8 800	3.5	1 596 600	11.9
March	2 213 200	10.7	5.5	14 300	10.0	2 125 600	10.6
April	2 284 900	2.6	5.6	17 400	0.0	2 175 100	2.5
May	3 571 500	15.0	8.8	45 800	24.8	3 361 900	14.7
June	4 636 500	10.3	11.5	58 600	25.5	4 340 400	9.5
July	6 501 400	12.3	16.1	79 200	37.3	6 095 600	11.2
August	6 713 200	13.6	16.6	83 400	38.3	6 304 400	12.5
September	3 874 200	16.2	9.6	53 700	29.1	3 617 100	15.1
October	2 934 500	13.7	7.3	28 400	34.0	2 776 400	12.8
November	2 182 100	9.1	5.4	15 900	20.5	2 089 000	8.7
December	2 211 900	18.8	5.5	24 100	24.2	2 096 300	18.6
Total	40 459 300	12.6	100.0	439 300	27.3	38 199 500	12.0

(by country of residence)

	1985	Relative share	1986	Relative share	% Variation over 1985
Austria	16 500	0.0	19 700	0.0	19.4
Belgium	16 700	0.0	21 700	0.1	29.9
Denmark	16 800	0.0	21 300	0.1	26.8
Finland	12 100	0.0	15 000	0.0	24.0
France	117 200	0.3	155 900	0.4	33.0
Germany (F.R.)	182 000	0.5	235 900	0.6	29.6
Greece	15 600	0.0	17 500	0.0	12.2
Iceland	1 200	0.0	1 400	0.0	16.7
Ireland	12 800	0.0	16 300	0.0	27.3
Italy	65 200	0.2	80 500	0.2	23.5
Luxembourg	1 000	0.0	1 100	0.0	10.0
Netherlands	63 900	0.2	75 700	0.2	18.5
Norway	10 100	0.0	14 500	0.0	43.6
Portugal	14 700	0.0	19 600	0.0	33.3
Spain	13 700	0.0	18 200	0.0	32.8
Sweden	22 100	0.1	25 000	0.1	13.1
Switzerland	49 100	0.1	59 600	0.1	21.4
Turkey	3 100	0.0	4 000	0.0	29.0
United Kingdom	345 100	1.0	439 300	1.1	27.3
Other OECD-Europe					
Total Europe	978 900	2.7	1 242 200	3.1	26.9
Canada					
United States	34 117 400	95.0	38 199 500	94.4	12.0
Total North America	34 117 400	95.0	38 199 500	94.4	12.0
Australia	76 500	0.2	85 700	0.2	12.0
New Zealand	15 700	0.0	27 400	0.1	74.5
Japan	174 500	0.5	235 200	0.6	34.8
Total Australasia and Japan	266 700	0.7	348 300	0.9	30.6
Total OECD Countries	35 363 000	98.4	39 790 000	98.3	12.5
Yugoslavia (S.F.R.)	9 700	0.0	10 800	0.0	11.3
Other European countries	51 100	0.1	48 000	0.1	−6.1
of which: Bulgaria	400	0.0	500	0.0	25.0
Czechoslovakia	4 300	0.0	5 900	0.0	37.2
Hungary	6 200	0.0	7 500	0.0	21.0
Poland	29 700	0.1	26 400	0.1	−11.1
Rumania	1 500	0.0	1 300	0.0	−13.3
USSR	9 000	0.0	6 400	0.0	−28.9
Latin America [1]	110 500	0.3	129 900	0.3	17.6
Asia-Oceania	250 700	0.7	334 700	0.8	33.5
Africa	41 800	0.1	44 700	0.1	6.9
Origin country undetermined	98 400	0.3	101 700	0.3	3.4
Total Non-OECD Countries	562 200	1.6	669 800	1.7	19.1
TOTAL	35 925 200	100.0	40 459 800	100.0	12.6

1. Including Mexico.

CANADA

NIGHTS SPENT BY FOREIGN TOURISTS IN TOURIST ACCOMMODATION[1]

	Total number 1986	% Variation over 1985	% of 1985 total	From United Kingdom	% Variation over 1985	From United States	% Variation over 1985
January February March	6 882 600	12.0	7.5	390 400	34.6	3 892 500	1.6
April May June	23 186 000	22.9	25.3	1 757 500	23.2	15 204 800	23.5
July August September	49 842 700	21.9	54.5	2 849 600	26.3	36 609 300	20.9
October November December	11 559 100	2.8	12.6	739 500	16.3	7 014 100	− 5.4
Total	91 470 400	18.6	100.0	5 737 000	24.5	62 720 700	16.5

(by country of residence)

	1985	Relative share	1986	Relative share	% Variation over 1985
Austria	190 800	0.2	226 300	0.2	18.6
Belgium	187 500	0.2	259 100	0.3	38.2
Denmark	204 500	0.3	221 700	0.2	8.4
Finland	99 700	0.1	145 600	0.2	46.0
France	1 372 100	1.8	1 807 900	2.0	31.8
Germany (F.R.)	2 260 800	2.9	2 727 200	3.0	20.6
Greece	313 000	0.4	357 800	0.4	14.3
Iceland	7 100	0.0	8 600	0.0	21.1
Ireland	157 800	0.2	179 400	0.2	13.7
Italy	755 400	1.0	836 400	0.9	10.7
Luxembourg	9 700	0.0	13 900	0.0	43.3
Netherlands	916 600	1.2	969 500	1.1	5.8
Norway	113 600	0.1	128 200	0.1	12.9
Portugal	282 400	0.4	414 300	0.5	46.7
Spain	135 100	0.2	191 500	0.2	41.7
Sweden	159 200	0.2	207 200	0.2	30.2
Switzerland	575 600	0.7	660 000	0.7	14.7
Turkey	51 900	0.1	67 600	0.1	30.3
United Kingdom	4 608 800	6.0	5 737 000	6.3	24.5
Other OECD-Europe					
Total Europe	12 401 600	16.1	15 159 200	16.6	22.2
Canada					
United States	53 822 600	69.8	63 320 800	69.2	17.6
Total North America	53 822 600	69.8	63 320 800	69.2	17.6
Australia	901 100	1.2	1 041 800	1.1	15.6
New Zealand	187 000	0.2	353 200	0.4	88.9
Japan	928 600	1.2	1 527 500	1.7	64.5
Total Australasia and Japan	2 016 700	2.6	2 922 500	3.2	44.9
Total OECD Countries	68 240 900	88.5	81 402 500	89.0	19.3
Yugoslavia (S.F.R.)	326 400	0.4	213 200	0.2	−34.7
Other European countries	2 215 500	2.9	2 349 200	2.6	6.0
of which: Bulgaria					
Czechoslovakia					
Hungary					
Poland					
Rumania					
USSR					
Latin America [2]	1 174 600	1.5	1 272 200	1.4	8.3
Asia-Oceania	3 165 700	4.1	3 912 000	4.3	23.6
Africa	695 200	0.9	809 200	0.9	16.4
Origin country undetermined	1 307 400	1.7	1 512 200	1.7	15.7
Total Non-OECD Countries	8 884 800	11.5	10 068 000	11.0	13.3
TOTAL	77 125 700	100.0	91 470 500	100.0	18.6

1. Covers all forms of accommodation, including homes of friends or relatives.
2. Including Mexico.

DENMARK

NIGHTS SPENT BY FOREIGN TOURISTS IN HOTELS
(by month)

	Total number 1986	% Variation over 1985	% of 1985 total	From Germany	% Variation over 1985	From United States	% Variation over 1985
January	130 700	−16.3	3.0	20 400	− 0.5	13 800	9.5
February	137 800	− 9.1	3.2	15 100	− 2.6	15 100	5.6
March	213 100	6.4	4.9	39 500	34.8	18 600	6.9
April	227 200	−14.7	5.2	35 100	−29.9	21 400	− 6.1
May	388 100	− 6.4	8.9	81 200	− 1.5	39 100	−26.9
June	537 000	−10.7	12.4	110 400	−14.7	61 200	−34.7
July	962 900	− 1.8	22.2	190 200	3.4	70 000	−38.5
August	773 000	− 6.8	17.8	232 000	−10.8	77 500	−28.0
September	363 700	− 5.7	8.4	101 000	2.2	46 200	−31.4
October	260 100	− 1.0	6.0	53 300	7.7	24 100	−28.7
November	192 600	− 2.0	4.4	20 800	− 3.3	17 100	−24.3
December	152 100	4.2	3.5	31 600	20.2	10 000	−27.0
Total	4 338 300	− 5.5	100.0	930 600	− 3.8	414 100	−27.7

(by country of nationality)

	1985	Relative share	1986	Relative share	% Variation over 1985
Austria [1]					
Belgium [1]					
Denmark					
Finland	122 800	2.7	112 700	2.6	−8.2
France	84 200	1.8	76 600	1.8	−9.0
Germany (F.R.)	967 200	21.1	930 700	21.5	−3.8
Greece [1]					
Iceland [1]					
Ireland [1]					
Italy	78 600	1.7	78 400	1.8	−0.3
Luxembourg [1]					
Netherlands	98 000	2.1	93 800	2.2	−4.3
Norway	712 300	15.5	751 100	17.3	5.4
Portugal [1]					
Spain [1]					
Sweden	893 500	19.5	942 100	21.7	5.4
Switzerland [1]					
Turkey [1]					
United Kingdom	333 300	7.3	311 700	7.2	−6.5
Other OECD-Europe					
Total Europe	3 289 900	71.7	3 297 100	76.0	0.2
Canada					
United States	573 000	12.5	414 200	9.5	−27.7
Total North America	573 000	12.5	414 200	9.5	−27.7
Australia					
New Zealand					
Japan	78 000	1.7	70 100	1.6	−10.1
Total Australasia and Japan	78 000	1.7	70 100	1.6	−10.1
Total OECD Countries	3 940 900	85.8	3 781 400	87.2	−4.0
Yugoslavia (S.F.R.)					
Other European countries	243 500	5.3	237 400	5.5	−2.5
of which: Bulgaria					
Czechoslovakia					
Hungary					
Poland					
Rumania					
USSR					
Latin America					
Asia-Oceania					
Africa					
Origin country undetermined	406 300	8.9	319 500	7.4	−21.4
Total Non-OECD Countries	649 800	14.2	556 900	12.8	−14.3
TOTAL	4 590 700	100.0	4 338 300	100.0	−5.5

1. Included in "Other European countries".

DENMARK

NIGHTS SPENT BY FOREIGN TOURISTS IN REGISTERED TOURIST ACCOMMODATION [1]
(by month)

	Total number 1986	% Variation over 1985	% of 1985 total	From Germany	% Variation over 1985	From United States	% Variation over 1985
January	130 700	−16.3	1.6	20 400	−0.5	13 800	9.5
February	137 800	−9.1	1.7	15 100	−2.6	15 100	5.6
March	213 100	6.4	2.6	39 500	34.8	18 600	6.9
April	267 400	−16.7	3.3	70 600	−29.8	21 600	−5.3
May	577 400	−3.8	7.1	241 500	−0.9	39 400	−27.0
June	948 300	−6.9	11.7	363 000	−4.8	62 400	−34.8
July	2 859 600	−1.0	35.3	1 114 000	4.1	73 100	−37.6
August	1 877 600	−11.8	23.2	995 800	−18.1	79 700	−27.6
September	475 000	−3.6	5.9	197 200	3.2	46 600	−31.2
October	260 100	−1.0	3.2	53 300	7.7	24 100	−28.7
November	192 600	−2.0	2.4	20 800	−3.3	17 100	−24.3
December	152 100	4.2	1.9	31 600	20.2	10 000	−27.0
TOTAL [1]	8 091 700	−5.5	100.0	3 162 800	−6.0	421 500	−27.6

(by country of nationality)

	1985	Relative share	1986	Relative share	% Variation over 1985
Austria					
Belgium					
Denmark					
Finland	220 158	2.5	212 648	2.5	−3.4
France	143 870	1.6	131 504	1.5	−8.6
Germany (F.R.)	3 478 210	38.8	3 275 704	38.5	−5.8
Greece					
Iceland					
Ireland					
Italy	120 841	1.3	117 668	1.4	−2.6
Luxembourg					
Netherlands	670 771	7.5	598 256	7.0	−10.8
Norway	1 075 139	12.0	1 109 097	13.0	3.2
Portugal					
Spain					
Sweden	1 377 714	15.4	1 492 960	17.5	8.4
Switzerland					
Turkey					
United Kingdom	407 223	4.5	375 085	4.4	−7.9
Other OECD-Europe					
Total Europe	7 493 926	83.5	7 312 922	85.9	−2.4
Canada					
United States	595 803	6.6	436 384	5.1	−26.8
Total North America	595 803	6.6	436 384	5.1	−26.8
Australia					
New Zealand					
Japan					
Total Australasia and Japan					
Total OECD Countries	8 089 729	90.2	7 749 306	91.0	−4.2
Yugoslavia (S.F.R.)					
Other European countries					
of which: Bulgaria					
Czechoslovakia					
Hungary					
Poland					
Rumania					
USSR					
Latin America					
Asia-Oceania					
Africa					
Origin country undetermined	881 819	9.8	761 935	9.0	−13.6
Total non-OECD Countries [2]	881 819	9.8	761 935	9.0	−13.6
TOTAL [3]	8 971 548	100.0	8 511 241	100.0	−5.1

1.   Monthly figures includes nights at hotels for the whole year and nights in camping sites from April to September and annual figures include in addition nights at youth hostels. These represent 383 241 nights in 1986 and 394 448 nights in 1985. Camping sites represent 3 779 500 nights for 1986 and 3 986 400 nights for 1985.
2.   Includes nights spent by foreign tourists from a number of Member countries.

FINLAND

NIGHTS SPENT BY FOREIGN TOURISTS IN HOTELS
(by month)

	Total number 1986	% Variation over 1985	% of 1985 total	From Sweden	% Variation over 1985	From United States	% Variation over 1985
January	95 048	3.4	4.7	25 059	0.3	6 828	7.7
February	100 930	11.6	5.0	26 750	23.9	6 292	5.8
March	106 349	− 9.4	5.3	27 714	−10.0	8 569	− 0.6
April	111 294	4.8	5.5	32 982	− 2.3	8 252	2.2
May	165 479	− 6.5	8.2	53 797	6.2	12 102	−13.7
June	256 777	−10.6	12.7	56 804	− 0.9	22 616	−26.0
July	324 286	−16.0	16.0	78 891	−13.2	25 308	−35.0
August	299 643	− 6.5	14.8	68 804	− 5.6	27 456	−14.6
September	197 434	11.8	9.8	50 806	8.6	17 699	− 2.0
October	151 233	11.6	7.5	44 943	10.7	12 174	22.5
November	128 019	2.6	6.3	40 896	3.5	6 903	− 3.3
December	85 171	2.3	4.2	25 218	− 0.7	5 268	5.4
Total	**2 021 663**	**− 3.6**	**100.0**	**532 664**	**− 0.5**	**159 467**	**−13.7**

(by country of residence)

	1985	Relative share	1986	Relative share	% Variation over 1985
Austria	22 791	1.1	23 505	1.2	3.1
Belgium	13 920	0.7	12 180	0.6	−12.5
Denmark	55 555	2.6	53 875	2.7	−3.0
Finland					
France	57 854	2.8	54 377	2.7	−6.0
Germany (F.R.)	273 417	13.0	250 083	12.4	−8.5
Greece [1]					
Iceland	5 891	0.3	6 454	0.3	9.6
Ireland [2]					
Italy	47 021	2.2	50 577	2.5	7.6
Luxembourg [1]					
Netherlands	40 402	1.9	36 985	1.8	−8.5
Norway	157 566	7.5	147 183	7.3	−6.6
Portugal [3]					
Spain [3]	17 555	0.8	17 712	0.9	0.9
Sweden	535 169	25.5	532 664	26.3	−0.5
Switzerland	69 692	3.3	68 286	3.4	−2.0
Turkey [1]					
United Kingdom [2]	108 258	5.2	103 347	5.1	−4.5
Other OECD-Europe					
Total Europe	1 405 091	67.0	1 357 228	67.1	−3.4
Canada	29 917	1.4	25 439	1.3	−15.0
United States	184 798	8.8	159 467	7.9	−13.7
Total North America	214 715	10.2	184 906	9.1	−13.9
Australia					
New Zealand					
Japan	44 180	2.1	38 550	1.9	−12.7
Total Australasia and Japan	44 180	2.1	38 550	1.9	−12.7
Total OECD Countries	**1 663 986**	**79.3**	**1 580 684**	**78.2**	**−5.0**
Yugoslavia (S.F.R.)					
Other European countries [1]	329 555	15.7	342 845	17.0	4.0
of which: Bulgaria [4]	5 841	0.3	5 570	0.3	−4.6
Czechoslovakia	13 402	0.6	18 072	0.9	34.8
Hungary	18 657	0.9	18 687	0.9	0.2
Poland	16 583	0.8	16 059	0.8	−3.2
Rumania [4]					
USSR	248 192	11.8	252 386	12.5	1.7
Latin America [5]					
Asia-Oceania [5]					
Africa [5]					
Origin country undetermined [5]	103 560	4.9	98 134	4.9	−5.2
Total Non-OECD Countries	**433 115**	**20.7**	**440 979**	**21.8**	**1.8**
TOTAL	**2 097 101**	**100.0**	**2 021 663**	**100.0**	**−3.6**

1. Greece, Luxembourg and Turkey included in "Other European countries".
2. Ireland included in United Kingdom.
3. Portugal included in Spain.
4. Rumania included in Bulgaria.
5. Latin America, Asia-Oceania and Africa included in "Origin country undetermined".

FRANCE

ARRIVALS OF FOREIGN TOURISTS AT FRONTIERS[1]

	Total number 1986	% Variation over 1985	% of 1985 total	From Germany	% Variation over 1985	From United States	% Variation over 1985
January							
February							
March							
April							
May							
June							
July							
August							
September							
October							
November							
December							
Total							

(by country of residence)

	1985	Relative share	1986	Relative share	% Variation over 1985
Austria	464 000	1.3	400 000	1.1	−13.8
Belgium[3]	3 117 000	8.5	3 099 000	8.6	−0.6
Denmark	353 000	1.0	378 000	1.0	7.1
Finland[2]	421 000	1.1	450 000	1.2	6.9
France					
Germany (F.R.)	8 723 000	23.7	8 417 000	23.3	−3.5
Greece[5]					
Iceland[5]					
Ireland[4]					
Italy	2 646 000	7.2	2 798 000	7.8	5.7
Luxembourg[3]					
Netherlands	3 655 000	9.9	4 012 000	11.1	9.8
Norway[2]					
Portugal[5]					
Spain	995 000	2.7	1 043 000	2.9	4.8
Sweden[2]					
Switzerland	3 603 000	9.8	3 524 000	9.8	−2.2
Turkey[5]					
United Kingdom[4]	5 862 000	16.0	6 299 000	17.5	7.5
Other OECD-Europe[5]	301 000	0.8	368 000	1.0	22.3
Total Europe	30 140 000	82.0	30 788 000	85.3	2.1
Canada	477 000	1.3	386 000	1.1	−19.1
United States	2 778 000	7.6	1 668 000	4.6	−40.0
Total North America	3 255 000	8.9	2 054 000	5.7	−36.9
Australia	341 000	0.9	292 000	0.8	−14.4
New Zealand[6]					
Japan	528 000	1.4	508 000	1.4	−3.8
Total Australasia and Japan	869 000	2.4	800 000	2.2	−7.9
Total OECD Countries	34 264 000	93.2	33 642 000	93.2	−1.8
Yugoslavia (S.F.R.)					
Other European countries	157 000	0.4	171 000	0.5	8.9
of which: Bulgaria					
Czechoslovakia					
Hungary					
Poland					
Rumania					
USSR					
Latin America[7]	590 000	1.6	696 000	1.9	18.0
Asia-Oceania[6],[8]	142 000	0.4	135 000	0.4	−4.9
Africa	1 244 000	3.4	1 120 000	3.1	−10.0
Origin country undetermined[9]	351 000	1.0	316 000	0.9	−10.0
Total Non-OECD Countries	2 484 000	6.8	2 438 000	6.8	−1.9
TOTAL	36 748 000	100.0	36 080 000	100.0	−1.8

1. Estimates of number of "trips", the same person coming perhaps several times in one year.
2. Norway and Sweden included in Finland.
3. Luxembourg included in Belgium.
4. Ireland included in United Kingdom.
5. Other OECD-Europe includes: Greece, Iceland, Portugal and Turkey.
6. New Zealand includes Oceania.
7. Includes Latin and Central America.
8. Asia only.
9. Near and Middle East.

FRANCE[1]

ARRIVALS OF FOREIGN TOURISTS IN HOTELS
(quarterly)

	Total number 1986	% Variation over 1985	% of 1985 total	From Germany	% Variation over 1985	From United States	% Variation over 1985
January February March	1 298 668	9.8	22.3	133 458	23.3	157 190	−8.0
April May June	1 702 361	−16.8	29.2	234 793	−15.0	228 592	−49.7
July August September	1 701 023	−23.0	29.2	176 044	−26.1	249 216	−53.9
October November December	1 126 969	−24.3	19.3	116 640	−33.2	121 652	−52.9
Total	5 829 021	−15.9	100.0	660 935	−17.1	756 650	−46.9

(by country of residence)

	1985	Relative share	1986	Relative share	% Variation over 1985
Austria	36 984	0.5	32 305	0.6	−12.7
Belgium[3]	229 636	3.3	216 894	3.7	−5.5
Denmark	82 458	1.2	79 102	1.4	−4.1
Finland[2]	193 303	2.8	207 300	3.6	7.2
France					
Germany (F.R.)	797 106	11.5	660 935	11.3	−17.1
Greece					
Iceland					
Ireland[4]					
Italy	487 690	7.0	496 086	8.5	1.7
Luxembourg[3]					
Netherlands	297 233	4.3	290 726	5.0	−2.2
Norway[2]					
Portugal					
Spain	217 272	3.1	234 479	4.0	7.9
Sweden[2]					
Switzerland	288 386	4.2	269 446	4.6	−6.6
Turkey					
United Kingdom[4]	880 303	12.7	743 986	12.8	−15.5
Other OECD-Europe[5]	101 466	1.5	84 117	1.4	−17.1
Total Europe	3 611 837	52.1	3 315 376	56.9	−8.2
Canada	209 825	3.0	151 277	2.6	−27.9
United States	1 423 997	20.6	756 650	13.0	−46.9
Total North America	1 633 822	23.6	907 927	15.6	−44.4
Australia	79 121	1.1	64 546	1.1	−18.4
New Zealand[6]	14 582	0.2	11 909	0.2	−18.3
Japan	470 298	6.8	447 659	7.7	−4.8
Total Australasia and Japan	564 001	8.1	524 114	9.0	−7.1
Total OECD Countries	5 809 660	83.9	4 747 417	81.4	−18.3
Yugoslavia (S.F.R.) Other European countries of which: Bulgaria Czechoslovakia Hungary Poland Rumania USSR	47 234	0.7	43 832	0.8	−7.2
Latin America[7]	198 644	2.9	223 384	3.8	12.5
Asia-Oceania[8]	127 371	1.8	127 916	2.2	0.4
Africa	410 808	5.9	348 659	6.0	−15.1
Origin country undetermined[9]	334 181	4.8	337 760	5.8	1.1
Total Non-OECD Countries	1 118 238	16.1	1 081 551	18.6	−3.3
TOTAL	6 927 898	100.0	5 828 968	100.0	−15.9

1. Data concern Ile de France region only.
2. Norway, Sweden included in Finland.
3. Luxembourg included in Belgium.
4. Ireland included in United Kingdom.
5. Other OECD-Europe includes: Greece, Iceland, Portugal and Turkey.
6. New Zealand includes Oceania.
7. Includes Latin and Central America.
8. Asia only.
9. Includes Near and Middle East (178 506 arrivals in 1986 and 203 973 in 1985).

FRANCE[1]

NIGHTS SPENT BY FOREIGN TOURISTS IN HOTELS
(quarterly)

	Total number 1986	% Variation over 1985	% of 1985 total	From Germany	% Variation over 1985	From United States	% Variation over 1985
January February March	3 272 242	7.0	21.7	318 541	21.4	401 867	−14.1
April May June	4 327 865	−21.0	28.8	590 740	−15.7	603 336	−51.6
July August September	4 554 221	−21.7	30.3	426 886	−27.6	666 348	−54.0
October November December	2 891 979	−24.2	19.2	270 151	−35.4	330 017	−52.2
Total	15 046 307	−17.2	100.0	1 606 318	−18.5	2 001 568	−48.1

(by country of residence)

	1985	Relative share	1986	Relative share	% Variation over 1985
Austria	96 201	0.5	88 640	0.6	−7.9
Belgium[3]	463 972	2.6	435 942	2.9	−6.0
Denmark	326 008	1.8	327 985	2.2	0.6
Finland[2]	571 007	3.1	601 239	4.0	5.3
France					
Germany (F.R.)	1 970 279	10.8	1 606 318	10.7	−18.5
Greece					
Iceland					
Ireland[4]					
Italy	1 337 332	7.4	1 338 212	8.9	0.1
Luxembourg[3]					
Netherlands	756 259	4.2	731 242	4.9	−3.3
Norway[2]					
Portugal					
Spain	576 248	3.2	630 269	4.2	9.4
Sweden[2]					
Switzerland	762 440	4.2	688 553	4.6	−9.7
Turkey					
United Kingdom[4]	2 171 564	12.0	1 714 266	11.4	−21.1
Other OECD-Europe[5]	304 537	1.7	259 201	1.7	−14.9
Total Europe	9 335 847	51.4	8 421 867	56.0	−9.8
Canada	561 332	3.1	395 188	2.6	−29.6
United States	3 853 024	21.2	2 001 568	13.3	−48.1
Total North America	4 414 356	24.3	2 396 756	15.9	−45.7
Australia	214 861	1.2	181 317	1.2	−15.6
New Zealand[6]	34 088	0.2	28 718	0.2	−15.8
Japan	1 029 780	5.7	1 021 145	6.8	−0.8
Total Australasia and Japan	1 278 729	7.0	1 231 180	8.2	−3.7
Total OECD Countries	15 028 932	82.7	12 049 803	80.1	−19.8
Yugoslavia (S.F.R.) Other European countries	143 288	0.8	133 230	0.9	−7.0
of which: Bulgaria					
Czechoslovakia					
Hungary					
Poland					
Rumania					
USSR					
Latin America[7]	597 217	3.3	712 172	4.7	19.2
Asia-Oceania[8]	292 257	1.6	256 959	1.7	−12.1
Africa	1 151 053	6.3	1 005 647	6.7	−12.6
Origin country undetermined[9]	953 667	5.2	888 490	5.9	−6.8
Total Non-OECD Countries	3 137 482	17.3	2 996 498	19.9	−4.5
TOTAL	18 166 414	100.0	15 046 301	100.0	−17.2

1. Data concern Ile de France region only.
2. Norway, Sweden included in Finland.
3. Luxembourg included in Belgium.
4. Ireland included in United Kingdom.
5. Other OECD-Europe includes: Greece, Iceland, Portugal and Turkey.
6. New Zealand includes Oceania.
7. Includes Latin and Central America.
8. Asia only.
9. Includes Near and Middle East (572 597 arrivals in 1986 and 655 432 in 1986).

FRANCE

NIGHTS SPENT BY FOREIGN TOURISTS IN TOURIST ACCOMMODATION [1]

	Total number 1986	% Variation over 1985	% of 1985 total	From Germany	% Variation over 1985	From United States	% Variation over 1985
January							
February							
March							
April							
May							
June							
July							
August							
September							
October							
November							
December							
Total							

(by country of residence)

	1985	Relative share	1986	Relative share	% Variation over 1985
Austria	2 812 000	0.9	2 691 000	0.8	−4.3
Belgium [3]	27 047 000	8.2	27 099 000	8.2	0.2
Denmark	4 341 000	1.3	5 134 000	1.5	18.3
Finland [2]	4 147 000	1.3	4 319 000	1.3	4.1
France					
Germany (F.R.)	76 406 000	23.2	76 388 000	23.0	−0.0
Greece					
Iceland [2]					
Ireland [4]					
Italy	20 724 000	6.3	23 146 000	7.0	11.7
Luxembourg [3]					
Netherlands	31 293 000	9.5	34 580 000	10.4	10.5
Norway [2]					
Portugal					
Spain	5 940 000	1.8	6 338 000	1.9	6.7
Sweden [2]					
Switzerland	19 545 000	5.9	18 422 000	5.5	−5.7
Turkey					
United Kingdom [4]	53 053 000	16.1	58 598 000	17.6	10.5
Other OECD-Europe [5]	3 486 000	1.1	3 672 000	1.1	5.3
Total Europe	248 794 000	75.4	260 387 000	78.4	4.7
Canada	6 650 000	2.0	5 884 000	1.8	−11.5
United States	30 938 000	9.4	23 202 000	7.0	−25.0
Total North America	37 588 000	11.4	29 086 000	8.8	−22.6
Australie [6]	2 282 000	0.7	2 011 000	0.6	−11.9
New Zealand					
Japan	3 713 000	1.1	3 694 000	1.1	−0.5
Total Australasia and Japan	5 995 000	1.8	5 705 000	1.7	−4.8
Total OECD Countries	292 377 000	88.7	295 178 000	88.9	1.0
Yugoslavia (S.F.R.)					
Other European countries	2 877 000	0.9	3 087 000	0.9	7.3
of which: Bulgaria					
Czechoslovakia					
Hungary					
Poland					
Rumania					
USSR					
Latin America [7]	6 305 000	1.9	7 117 000	2.1	12.9
Asia-Oceania [8]	1 280 000	0.4	1 219 000	0.4	−4.8
Africa	22 452 000	6.8	21 464 000	6.5	−4.4
Origin country undetermined [9]	4 484 000	1.4	4 143 000	1.2	−7.6
Total Non-OECD Countries	37 398 000	11.3	37 030 000	11.1	−1.0
TOTAL	329 775 000	100.0	332 208 000	100.0	0.7

1. Based on an update of the findings of the 1982 frontier survey.
2. Iceland, Norway and Sweden included in Finland.
3. Luxembourg included in Belgium.
4. Ireland included in United Kingdom.
5. Other OECD-Europe includes: Greece, Portugal and Turkey.
6. Australia includes Oceania.
7. Includes Latin and Central America.
8. Asia only.
9. Includes Near and Middle East.

GERMANY (F.R.)[1]

ARRIVALS OF FOREIGN TOURISTS IN HOTELS[2]
(by month)

	Total number 1986	% Variation over 1985	% of 1985 total	From Netherlands	% Variation over 1985	From United States	% Variation over 1985
January	521 440	5.1	4.6	73 107	2.7	92 661	5.3
February	636 944	6.2	5.7	113 176	9.9	96 825	5.0
March	725 070	4.9	6.4	77 285	13.7	126 420	− 7.5
April	844 625	1.6	7.5	77 922	0.6	135 115	−16.9
May	1 066 175	− 7.0	9.5	122 661	1.6	164 229	−38.3
June	1 147 728	−14.1	10.2	159 285	− 3.9	192 118	−43.8
July	1 472 773	− 8.7	13.1	236 807	− 1.4	203 088	−44.5
August	1 349 342	− 7.0	12.0	201 237	− 4.5	180 232	−38.9
September	1 301 717	− 8.8	11.6	158 741	− 3.6	207 388	−36.7
October	1 009 493	− 5.7	9.0	111 407	2.1	176 327	−30.1
November	669 801	7.2	5.9	53 376	6.3	113 599	− 2.0
December	522 478	3.8	4.6	69 466	15.4	88 353	− 1.0
Total	11 267 586	− 4.4	100.0	1 454 470	0.9	1 776 355	−29.9

(by country of residence)

	1985	Relative share	1986	Relative share	% Variation over 1985
Austria	436 814	3.7	452 839	4.0	3.7
Belgium	376 645	3.2	387 688	3.4	2.9
Denmark	549 777	4.7	580 455	5.1	5.6
Finland	121 353	1.0	131 593	1.2	8.4
France	594 722	5.0	613 039	5.4	3.1
Germany (F.R.)					
Greece	85 895	0.7	81 791	0.7	−4.8
Iceland	14 518	0.1	15 247	0.1	5.0
Ireland	24 269	0.2	24 912	0.2	2.6
Italy	524 549	4.4	566 637	5.0	8.0
Luxembourg	52 718	0.4	53 627	0.5	1.7
Netherlands	1 443 282	12.2	1 461 823	12.9	1.3
Norway	250 129	2.1	291 213	2.6	16.4
Portugal	30 328	0.3	30 997	0.3	2.2
Spain	177 967	1.5	187 578	1.7	5.4
Sweden	584 496	5.0	685 463	6.1	17.3
Switzerland	520 263	4.4	550 419	4.9	5.8
Turkey	72 820	0.6	74 410	0.7	2.2
United Kingdom	1 110 364	9.4	1 122 306	9.9	1.1
Other OECD-Europe					
Total Europe	6 970 909	59.0	7 312 037	64.8	4.9
Canada	184 518	1.6	153 530	1.4	−16.8
United States	2 537 543	21.5	1 769 815	15.7	−30.3
Total North America	2 722 061	23.1	1 923 345	17.0	−29.3
Australia	104 729	0.9	91 223	0.8	−12.9
New Zealand	14 611	0.1	9 135	0.1	−37.5
Japan	474 345	4.0	478 810	4.2	0.9
Total Australasia and Japan	593 685	5.0	579 168	5.1	−2.4
Total OECD Countries	10 286 655	87.1	9 814 550	86.9	−4.6
Yugoslavia (S.F.R.)	128 813	1.1	143 421	1.3	11.3
Other European countries	330 050	2.8	327 093	2.9	−0.9
of which: Bulgaria	15 457	0.1			
Czechoslovakia	46 383	0.4			
Hungary	56 651	0.5			
Poland	60 821	0.5			
Rumania	12 535	0.1			
USSR	22 572	0.2			
Latin America	216 560	1.8	204 206	1.8	−5.7
Asia-Oceania	528 895	4.5	537 091	4.8	1.5
Africa	147 575	1.3	133 092	1.2	−9.8
Origin country undetermined	167 208	1.4	130 238	1.2	−22.1
Total Non-OECD Countries	1 519 101	12.9	1 475 141	13.1	−2.9
TOTAL	11 805 756	100.0	11 289 691	100.0	−4.4

1. Includes West Berlin. Discrepancies between data by month and by country of origin arise because the latter (more representative) are assembled at a later stage.
2. Arrivals at hotels (including "bed and breakfast"), boarding houses and inns.

GERMANY (F.R.)[1]

ARRIVALS OF FOREIGN TOURISTS IN REGISTERED TOURIST ACCOMMODATION[2]
(by month)

	Total number 1986	% Variation over 1985	% of 1985 total	From Netherlands	% Variation over 1985	From United States	% Variation over 1985
January	554 091	5.6	4.5	86 969	5.5	96 114	5.2
February	698 941	6.0	5.7	145 639	11.0	99 176	4.6
March	781 772	6.5	6.4	91 377	19.1	131 547	− 5.8
April	904 483	1.3	7.4	92 420	− 1.9	141 232	−16.3
May	1 147 845	− 6.0	9.4	147 128	5.4	170 936	−37.7
June	1 242 059	−13.5	10.2	182 962	− 4.4	204 202	−42.8
July	1 643 505	− 7.4	13.5	293 948	− 0.4	218 102	−43.0
August	1 482 586	− 6.1	12.2	237 500	− 3.4	190 379	−38.2
September	1 380 563	− 8.5	11.3	180 610	− 2.7	213 879	−36.4
October	1 089 865	− 4.9	8.9	137 248	3.9	182 532	−29.9
November	707 505	7.4	5.8	62 643	8.8	118 365	− 1.9
December	561 821	5.2	4.6	84 032	16.9	92 340	− 0.2
Total	12 195 036	− 3.7	100.0	1 742 476	2.3	1 858 804	−29.2

(by country of residence)

	1985	Relative share	1986	Relative share	% Variation over 1985
Austria	450 574	3.6	467 950	3.8	3.9
Belgium	402 478	3.2	417 097	3.4	3.6
Denmark	614 839	4.8	654 775	5.4	6.5
Finland	132 859	1.0	142 946	1.2	7.6
France	651 717	5.1	672 897	5.5	3.2
Germany (F.R.)					
Greece	87 654	0.7	84 275	0.7	−3.9
Iceland	16 278	0.1	17 883	0.1	9.9
Ireland	28 142	0.2	29 275	0.2	4.0
Italy	542 130	4.3	588 691	4.8	8.6
Luxembourg	56 055	0.4	56 715	0.5	1.2
Netherlands	1 706 906	13.5	1 749 511	14.3	2.5
Norway	266 705	2.1	310 411	2.5	16.4
Portugal	33 421	0.3	33 977	0.3	1.7
Spain	188 199	1.5	198 752	1.6	5.6
Sweden	611 682	4.8	717 300	5.9	17.3
Switzerland	544 827	4.3	575 475	4.7	5.6
Turkey	76 458	0.6	78 442	0.6	2.6
United Kingdom	1 179 126	9.3	1 184 524	9.7	0.5
Other OECD-Europe					
Total Europe	7 590 050	59.8	7 980 896	65.3	5.1
Canada	205 038	1.6	175 802	1.4	−14.3
United States	2 630 553	20.7	1 852 229	15.2	−29.6
Total North America	2 835 591	22.4	2 028 031	16.6	−28.5
Australia	134 150	1.1	122 561	1.0	−8.6
New Zealand	19 104	0.2	14 525	0.1	−24.0
Japan	488 582	3.9	494 333	4.0	1.2
Total Australasia and Japan	641 836	5.1	631 419	5.2	−1.6
Total OECD Countries	11 067 477	87.2	10 640 346	87.1	−3.9
Yugoslavia (S.F.R.)	132 787	1.0	148 083	1.2	11.5
Other European countries	369 024	2.9	371 985	3.0	0.8
of which: Bulgaria	16 025	0.1			
Czechoslovakia	49 174	0.4			
Hungary	62 218	0.5			
Poland	74 425	0.6			
Rumania	13 133	0.1			
USSR	24 278	0.2			
Latin America	226 254	1.8	216 131	1.8	−4.5
Asia-Oceania	547 297	4.3	557 805	4.6	1.9
Africa	159 906	1.3	142 822	1.2	−10.7
Origin country undetermined	183 629	1.4	140 024	1.1	−23.7
Total Non-OECD Countries	1 618 897	12.8	1 576 850	12.9	−2.6
TOTAL	12 686 374	100.0	12 217 196	100.0	−3.7

1. Includes West Berlin. Discrepancies between data by month and by country of origin arise because the latter (more representative) are assembled at a later stage.
2. Arrivals at hotels and similar establishments, holiday villages, sanatoria and recreation and holiday homes.

GERMANY (F.R.)[1]

NIGHTS SPENT BY FOREIGN TOURISTS IN HOTELS[2]
(by month)

	Total number 1986	% Variation over 1985	% of 1985 total	From Netherlands	% Variation over 1985	From United States	% Variation over 1985
January	1 122 436	5.1	4.8	143 298	2.6	199 045	2.9
February	1 414 579	5.3	6.0	271 762	16.6	202 009	– 3.8
March	1 508 206	5.8	6.4	150 175	18.8	249 403	–10.3
April	1 731 213	3.8	7.4	156 952	– 0.1	275 939	–14.9
May	2 232 131	– 0.3	9.5	268 622	5.8	336 514	–31.7
June	2 256 933	–12.2	9.6	350 448	– 2.0	368 509	–39.7
July	2 986 650	– 5.9	12.7	603 870	3.9	390 231	–40.5
August	2 844 042	– 3.8	12.1	501 629	3.3	359 394	–36.3
September	2 690 592	– 5.7	11.5	348 920	– 0.5	411 084	–32.4
October	2 083 306	– 5.2	8.9	239 651	4.5	354 107	–26.1
November	1 439 543	11.4	6.1	102 243	10.3	255 801	5.5
December	1 137 048	5.0	4.8	161 227	15.1	193 503	4.4
Total	23 446 679	– 1.8	100.0	3 298 797	4.8	3 595 539	–25.8

(by country of residence)

	1985	Relative share	1986	Relative share	% Variation over 1985
Austria	858 535	3.6	890 930	3.8	3.8
Belgium	818 252	3.4	859 200	3.7	5.0
Denmark	934 095	3.9	1 019 220	4.3	9.1
Finland	214 852	0.9	239 037	1.0	11.3
France	1 114 651	4.7	1 162 686	5.0	4.3
Germany (F.R.)					
Greece	201 627	0.8	199 112	0.8	–1.2
Iceland	31 074	0.1	34 531	0.1	11.1
Ireland	55 099	0.2	55 686	0.2	1.1
Italy	1 005 754	4.2	1 100 322	4.7	9.4
Luxembourg	134 223	0.6	143 489	0.6	6.9
Netherlands	3 152 571	13.2	3 316 589	14.1	5.2
Norway	405 936	1.7	463 948	2.0	14.3
Portugal	63 852	0.3	68 214	0.3	6.8
Spain	344 014	1.4	372 758	1.6	8.4
Sweden	907 984	3.8	1 050 945	4.5	15.7
Switzerland	1 060 976	4.4	1 140 365	4.9	7.5
Turkey	165 769	0.7	182 776	0.8	10.3
United Kingdom	2 277 775	9.5	2 378 761	10.1	4.4
Other OECD-Europe					
Total Europe	13 747 039	57.5	14 678 569	62.5	6.8
Canada	340 220	1.4	299 218	1.3	–12.1
United States	4 846 727	20.3	3 585 433	15.3	–26.0
Total North America	5 186 947	21.7	3 884 651	16.5	–25.1
Australia	190 736	0.8	171 271	0.7	–10.2
New Zealand	25 784	0.1	18 554	0.1	–28.0
Japan	825 788	3.5	839 238	3.6	1.6
Total Australasia and Japan	1 042 308	4.4	1 029 063	4.4	–1.3
Total OECD Countries	19 976 294	83.6	19 592 283	83.5	–1.9
Yugoslavia (S.F.R.)	295 942	1.2	325 515	1.4	10.0
Other European countries	961 352	4.0	1 021 677	4.4	6.3
of which: Bulgaria	39 664	0.2			
Czechoslovakia	104 032	0.4			
Hungary	131 873	0.6			
Poland	275 190	1.2			
Rumania	33 991	0.1			
USSR	65 912	0.3			
Latin America	437 863	1.8	446 638	1.9	2.0
Asia-Oceania	1 434 528	6.0	1 423 219	6.1	–0.8
Africa	414 573	1.7	375 219	1.6	–9.5
Origin country undetermined	374 711	1.6	287 982	1.2	–23.1
Total Non-OECD Countries	3 918 969	16.4	3 880 250	16.5	–1.0
TOTAL	23 895 263	100.0	23 472 533	100.0	– 1.8

1. Includes West Berlin. Discrepancies between data by month and by country of origin arise because the latter (more representative) are assembled at a later stage.
2. Nights spent in hotels (including "bed and breakfast"), boarding houses and inns.

GERMANY (F.R.)[1]

NIGHTS SPENT BY FOREIGN TOURISTS IN REGISTERED TOURIST ACCOMMODATION[2]
(by month)

	Total number 1986	% Variation over 1985	% of 1985 total	From Netherlands	% Variation over 1985	From United States	% Variation over 1985
January	1 276 374	4.4	4.6	212 637	5.3	208 387	− 0.9
February	1 757 764	5.7	6.3	470 657	17.3	209 320	− 3.7
March	1 736 788	7.8	6.3	214 431	23.8	264 306	− 8.3
April	1 968 272	2.1	7.1	236 677	− 4.5	293 677	−13.9
May	2 550 076	0.4	9.2	404 293	6.4	352 166	−31.3
June	2 647 095	−11.6	9.5	525 443	− 3.9	394 683	−38.9
July	3 937 651	− 2.8	14.2	1 132 216	6.5	423 598	−39.3
August	3 485 459	− 3.0	12.5	819 518	2.4	384 500	−35.5
September	3 043 314	− 5.6	11.0	506 475	− 0.5	428 062	−32.1
October	2 438 255	− 4.0	8.8	393 995	5.6	371 095	−25.8
November	1 600 591	11.2	5.8	145 102	13.7	271 003	5.8
December	1 334 695	6.9	4.8	251 465	16.5	205 622	5.7
Total	27 776 334	− 1.0	100.0	5 312 909	5.4	3 806 419	−25.2

(by country of residence)

	1985	Relative share	1986	Relative share	% Variation over 1985
Austria	907 098	3.2	940 908	3.4	3.7
Belgium	942 348	3.4	1 008 438	3.6	7.0
Denmark	1 228 913	4.4	1 356 726	4.9	10.4
Finland	240 517	0.9	261 238	0.9	8.6
France	1 294 241	4.6	1 345 326	4.8	3.9
Germany (F.R.)					
Greece	210 064	0.7	209 101	0.8	−0.5
Iceland	47 786	0.2	48 131	0.2	0.7
Ireland	62 754	0.2	64 599	0.2	2.9
Italy	1 058 306	3.8	1 165 248	4.2	10.1
Luxembourg	153 848	0.5	161 160	0.6	4.8
Netherlands	5 053 815	18.0	5 336 089	19.2	5.6
Norway	438 309	1.6	527 922	1.9	20.4
Portugal	76 977	0.3	83 643	0.3	8.7
Spain	378 795	1.3	412 105	1.5	8.8
Sweden	971 512	3.5	1 128 223	4.1	16.1
Switzerland	1 176 447	4.2	1 250 003	4.5	6.3
Turkey	181 577	0.6	203 939	0.7	12.3
United Kingdom	2 479 414	8.8	2 577 554	9.3	4.0
Other OECD-Europe					
Total Europe	16 902 721	60.2	18 080 353	65.0	7.0
Canada	380 297	1.4	339 652	1.2	−10.7
United States	5 091 998	18.1	3 795 838	13.6	−25.5
Total North America	5 472 295	19.5	4 135 490	14.9	−24.4
Australia	238 717	0.9	223 506	0.8	−6.4
New Zealand	32 549	0.1	26 614	0.1	−18.2
Japan	852 957	3.0	868 420	3.1	1.8
Total Australasia and Japan	1 124 223	4.0	1 118 540	4.0	−0.5
Total OECD Countries	23 499 239	83.7	23 334 383	83.9	−0.7
Yugoslavia (S.F.R.)	311 612	1.1	343 478	1.2	10.2
Other European countries	1 314 745	4.7	1 388 725	5.0	5.6
of which: Bulgaria	41 778	0.1			
Czechoslovakia	115 002	0.4			
Hungary	164 022	0.6			
Poland	458 748	1.6			
Rumania	40 606	0.1			
USSR	74 887	0.3			
Latin America	471 107	1.7	485 208	1.7	3.0
Asia-Oceania	1 507 662	5.4	1 505 991	5.4	−0.1
Africa	458 767	1.6	416 877	1.5	−9.1
Origin country undetermined	516 059	1.8	337 451	1.2	−34.6
Total Non-OECD Countries	4 579 952	16.3	4 477 730	16.1	−2.2
TOTAL	28 079 191	100.0	27 812 113	100.0	−1.0

1. Includes West Berlin. Discrepancies between data by month and by country of origin arise because the latter (more representative) are assembled at a later stage.
2. Nights spent in hotels and similar establishments, holiday villages, sanatoria, and recreation and holiday homes.

GREECE

ARRIVALS OF FOREIGN TOURISTS AT FRONTIERS[1]
(by month)

	Total number 1986	% Variation over 1985	% of 1985 total	From United Kingdom[5]	% Variation over 1985	From United States	% Variation over 1985
January	103 016	7.5	1.5	8 593	− 5.2	8 860	−39.8
February	108 420	16.0	1.5	7 934	2.5	7 797	−39.2
March	273 070	17.9	3.9	25 290	35.2	13 702	−50.7
April	432 669	− 2.2	6.2	69 109	0.3	14 483	−66.1
May	816 528	9.2	11.6	221 025	27.5	17 784	−71.7
June	883 720	− 0.4	12.6	252 090	25.1	28 913	−66.5
July	1 293 722	7.2	18.4			36 617	−49.8
August	1 314 860	8.3	18.7			26 789	−43.7
September	895 069	− 0.1	12.7			17 761	−56.0
October	520 567	12.2	7.4			12 845	−60.1
November	186 497	28.2	2.7			9 268	−34.7
December	196 621	31.6	2.8			9 848	−15.3
Total	7 024 759	6.9	100.0	1 475 477	11.0	204 667	−56.1

(by country of nationality)

	1985	Relative share	1986	Relative share	% Variation over 1985
Austria	282 468	4.3	292 720	4.2	3.6
Belgium [2]	89 056	1.4			
Denmark	160 792	2.4			
Finland	141 689	2.2	166 892	2.4	17.8
France [5]	441 141	6.7	468 499	6.7	6.2
Germany [5]	1 050 078	16.0	1 050 078	14.9	0.0
Greece					
Iceland [3]					
Ireland	39 032	0.6			
Italy	364 177	5.5			
Luxembourg [2]					
Netherlands	280 309	4.3			
Norway	144 152	2.2	156 891	2.2	8.8
Portugal	9 029	0.1			
Spain	40 791	0.6			
Sweden	223 956	3.4	248 756	3.5	11.1
Switzerland	205 662	3.1	157 412	2.2	−23.5
Turkey	48 784	0.7	48 977	0.7	0.4
United Kingdom [5]	1 329 259	20.2	1 475 477	21.0	11.0
Other OECD-Europe			1 454 773	20.7	
Total Europe	4 850 375	73.8	5 520 475	78.6	13.8
Canada	102 552	1.6	74 612	1.1	−27.2
United States	466 155	7.1	204 667	2.9	−56.1
Total North America	568 707	8.7	279 279	4.0	−50.9
Australia	121 894	1.9	116 272	1.7	−4.6
New Zealand [4]					
Japan	92 802	1.4	85 075	1.2	−8.3
Total Australasia and Japan	214 696	3.3	201 347	2.9	−6.2
Total OECD Countries	5 633 778	85.7	6 001 101	85.4	6.5
Yugoslavia (S.F.R.)	350 735	5.3	466 467	6.6	33.0
Other European countries	255 970	3.9	255 989	3.6	0.0
of which: Bulgaria	40 834	0.6	37 036	0.5	−9.3
Czechoslovakia	12 214	0.2	12 797	0.2	4.8
Hungary	19 483	0.3	18 764	0.3	−3.7
Poland	59 472	0.9	59 862	0.9	0.7
Rumania	7 154	0.1	7 057	0.1	−1.4
USSR	7 738	0.1	7 102	0.1	−8.2
Latin America	50 772	0.8	42 176	0.6	−16.9
Asia-Oceania [4]	168 103	2.6	173 130	2.5	3.0
Africa	114 139	1.7	85 433	1.2	−25.2
Origin country undetermined	496	0.0	483	0.0	−2.6
Total Non-OECD Countries	940 215	14.3	1 023 678	14.6	8.9
TOTAL	6 573 993	100.0	7 024 779	100.0	6.9

1. Excluding Greek nationals residing abroad and cruise passengers who numbered 465 435 (-7.7%) in 1985 and 314 236 (-32.5%) in 1986.
2. Belgium includes Luxembourg.
3. Included in "Other European countries".
4. "Asia-Oceania" includes New Zealand.
5. For 1986, Secretariat estimates from household surveys conducted in those countries.

ICELAND

ARRIVALS OF FOREIGN TOURISTS AT FRONTIERS[1]

ARRIVALS OF FOREIGN TOURISTS AT FRONTIERS[1]
(by month)

	Total number 1986	% Variation over 1985	% of 1985 total	From Germany	% Variation over 1985	From United States	% Variation over 1985
January	3 306	8.3	2.9	126	10.5	1 332	2.6
February	3 209	38.7	2.8	90	5.9	1 189	25.7
March	3 822	− 5.2	3.4	237	53.9	1 313	18.8
April	5 746	8.7	5.1	378	112.4	2 190	19.7
May	8 342	22.0	7.3	1 589	181.2	2 371	− 1.5
June	16 678	12.4	14.7	2 301	28.4	3 721	− 7.0
July	26 830	18.4	23.6	4 384	39.8	5 811	5.0
August	18 660	12.6	16.4	2 777	21.9	4 468	− 4.3
September	9 955	21.5	8.8	1 065	112.6	3 063	− 6.2
October	7 749	32.8	6.8	311	− 9.9	3 444	20.7
November	5 151	21.5	4.5	175	78.6	2 216	13.2
December	4 081	13.6	3.6	168	− 2.9	1 582	−10.2
Total	113 529	16.5	100.0	13 601	44.4	32 700	3.4

(by country of nationality)

	1985	Relative share	1986	Relative share	% Variation over 1985
Austria	2 235	2.3			
Belgium	594	0.6			
Denmark	9 946	10.2			
Finland	2 596	2.7			
France	4 483	4.6			
Germany (F.R.)	9 419	9.7			
Greece	66	0.1			
Iceland					
Ireland	320	0.3			
Italy	1 170	1.2			
Luxembourg	142	0.1			
Netherlands	1 653	1.7			
Norway	7 665	7.9			
Portugal	76	0.1			
Spain	457	0.5			
Sweden	8 167	8.4			
Switzerland	2 744	2.8			
Turkey	16	0.0			
United Kingdom	9 720	10.0			
Other OECD-Europe					
Total Europe	61 469	63.1			
Canada	1 286	1.3			
United States	31 633	32.5			
Total North America	32 919	33.8			
Australia	414	0.4			
New Zealand	122	0.1			
Japan	716	0.7			
Total Australasia and Japan	1 252	1.3			
Total OECD Countries	95 640	98.1			
Yugoslavia (S.F.R.)	157	0.2			
Other European countries	422	0.4			
of which: Bulgaria	12	0.0			
Czechoslovakia	56	0.1			
Hungary	31	0.0			
Poland	116	0.1			
Rumania	3	0.0			
USSR	204	0.2			
Latin America	334	0.3			
Asia-Oceania					
Africa					
Origin country undetermined	890	0.9			
Total Non-OECD Countries	1 803	1.9			
TOTAL	97 443	100.0			

1. Excluding shore excursionists.

IRELAND

ARRIVALS OF FOREIGN VISITORS AT FRONTIERS[1]

	Total number 1986	% Variation over 1985	% of 1985 total	From United Kingdom	% Variation over 1985	From United States	% Variation over 1985
January							
February							
March							
April							
May							
June							
July							
August							
September							
October							
November							
December							
Total	1 814 000	− 5.1	100.0	1 086 000	− 1.6	298 000	−21.2

(by country of residence)

	1985	Relative share	1986	Relative share	% Variation over 1985
Austria					
Belgium					
Denmark					
Finland					
France	93 000	4.9	86 000	4.7	−7.5
Germany (F.R.)	96 000	5.0	97 000	5.3	1.0
Greece					
Iceland					
Ireland					
Italy					
Luxembourg					
Netherlands					
Norway					
Portugal					
Spain					
Sweden					
Switzerland					
Turkey					
United-Kingdom [2]	1 104 000	57.8	1 086 000	59.9	−1.6
Other OECD-Europe	137 000	7.2	142 000	7.8	3.6
Total Europe	1 430 000	74.8	1 411 000	77.8	−1.3
Canada	25 000	1.3	28 000	1.5	12.0
United States	378 000	19.8	298 000	16.4	−21.2
Total North America	403 000	21.1	326 000	18.0	−19.1
Australia [3]	34 000	1.8	31 000	1.7	−8.8
New Zealand [3]					
Japan [4]					
Total Australasia and Japan	34 000	1.8	31 000	1.7	−8.8
Total OECD Countries	1 867 000	97.7	1 768 000	97.5	−5.3
Yugoslavia (S.F.R.)					
Other European countries					
of which: Bulgaria					
Czechoslovakia					
Hungary					
Poland					
Rumania					
USSR					
Latin America					
Asia-Oceania					
Africa					
Origin country unspecified [4]	44 000	2.3	46 000	2.5	4.5
Total Non-OECD Countries	44 000	2.3	46 000	2.5	4.5
TOTAL	1 911 000	100.0	1 814 000	100.0	−5.1

1. Visitors arrivals on overseas routes only.
2. New series from 1986 (see note 1); 1985 figures are revised.
3. New Zealand included in Australia.
4. Origin country unspecified includes Japan.

ITALY

ARRIVALS OF FOREIGN VISITORS AT FRONTIERS[1]
(by month)

	Total number 1986	% Variation over 1985	% of 1985 total	From Germany	% Variation over 1985	From United States	% Variation over 1985
January	2 537 245	11.2	4.8	336 258	31.7	82 867	8.3
February	2 432 163	1.8	4.6	322 942	0.0	70 151	− 9.1
March	3 269 381	6.0	6.1	670 647	21.4	100 770	− 1.7
April	3 249 843	−17.0	6.1	507 578	−39.9	104 499	−16.1
May	4 518 108	4.8	8.5	989 452	0.4	121 553	−19.4
June	4 721 360	− 9.8	8.9	925 979	−25.1	149 618	−32.3
July	7 092 348	−10.6	13.3	1 406 287	−29.7	234 998	−22.2
August	8 492 980	− 5.4	15.9	1 806 079	−21.3	215 768	−17.7
September	5 624 454	6.8	10.5	1 064 421	−13.4	168 524	−14.3
October	4 249 211	10.7	8.0	668 709	−20.7	133 609	0.0
November	3 395 310	12.7	6.4	389 551	−26.8	106 040	14.6
December	3 732 503	10.1	7.0	467 537	−24.7	103 145	8.2
Total	53 314 906	− 0.6	100.0	9 555 440	−18.4	1 591 542	−13.2

(by country of nationality)

	1985	Relative share	1986	Relative share	% Variation over 1985
Austria	5 265 085	9.8	5 413 624	10.2	2.8
Belgium	795 832	1.5	1 038 993	1.9	30.6
Denmark	458 074	0.9	764 001	1.4	66.8
Finland	261 612	0.5	304 625	0.6	16.4
France	8 708 159	16.2	8 570 229	16.1	−1.6
Germany (F.R.)	11 717 155	21.8	9 555 440	17.9	−18.4
Greece	414 845	0.8	418 560	0.8	0.9
Iceland [2]					
Ireland	103 870	0.2	106 441	0.2	2.5
Italy					
Luxembourg	134 967	0.3	154 892	0.3	14.8
Netherlands	1 660 220	3.1	1 743 102	3.3	5.0
Norway	252 802	0.5	288 603	0.5	14.2
Portugal	209 545	0.4	192 987	0.4	−7.9
Spain	505 531	0.9	537 695	1.0	6.4
Sweden	492 990	0.9	835 093	1.6	69.4
Switzerland	12 465 534	23.2	11 299 825	21.2	−9.4
Turkey	173 129	0.3	266 680	0.5	54.0
United Kingdom	1 770 713	3.3	2 047 774	3.8	15.6
Other OECD-Europe					
Total Europe	45 390 063	84.6	43 538 564	81.6	−4.1
Canada	348 567	0.6	337 939	0.6	−3.0
United States	1 834 420	3.4	1 591 542	3.0	−13.2
Total North America	2 182 987	4.1	1 929 481	3.6	−11.6
Australia	276 663	0.5	233 642	0.4	−15.5
New Zealand	81 331	0.2	80 326	0.2	−1.2
Japan	335 190	0.6	401 278	0.8	19.7
Total Australasia and Japan	693 184	1.3	715 246	1.3	3.2
Total OECD Countries	48 266 234	90.0	46 183 291	86.6	−4.3
Yugoslavia (S.F.R.)	3 075 251	5.7	3 880 658	7.3	26.2
Other European countries	656 333	1.2	1 297 593	2.4	97.7
of which: Bulgaria					
Czechoslovakia					
Hungary					
Poland					
Rumania					
USSR	25 283	0.0	25 463	0.0	0.7
Latin America	488 304	0.9	445 198	0.8	−8.8
Asia-Oceania	152 208	0.3	152 202	0.3	−0.0
Africa	112 287	0.2	90 651	0.2	−19.3
Origin country undetermined	883 791	1.6	1 274 277	2.4	44.2
Total Non-OECD Countries	5 368 174	10.0	7 140 579	13.4	33.0
TOTAL	53 634 408	100.0	53 323 870	100.0	−0.6

1. Includes 53% of excursionists.
2. Included in "Other European countries".

144

ITALY

ARRIVALS OF FOREIGN TOURISTS IN HOTELS
(by month)

	Total number 1986	% Variation over 1985	% of 1985 total	From Germany	% Variation over 1985	From United States	% Variation over 1985
January	470 344	4.4	3.1	115 090	12.9	57 947	– 3.3
February	581 620	5.4	3.8	147 538	11.2	55 612	– 3.9
March	1 128 813	17.1	7.4	427 157	39.7	97 919	–16.7
April	1 118 557	–17.0	7.3	325 386	–18.0	99 089	–46.1
May	1 785 737	0.8	11.7	625 783	28.4	116 288	–62.9
June	1 582 480	–20.6	10.4	455 172	–13.8	131 375	–70.3
July	2 013 706	–10.7	13.2	502 713	8.9	160 530	–65.9
August	2 023 347	– 6.4	13.3	635 134	6.5	124 323	–61.9
September	2 035 829	– 2.3	13.4	621 616	8.4	189 838	–50.7
October	1 436 487	– 2.5	9.4	443 946	11.7	155 327	–47.1
November	567 597	– 0.5	3.7	94 243	7.6	68 730	–33.1
December	499 356	7.0	3.3	101 279	5.4	60 826	– 9.2
Total	15 243 873	– 5.3	100.0	4 495 057	7.9	1 317 804	–53.3

(by country of nationality)

	1985	Relative share	1986	Relative share	% Variation over 1985
Austria	806 895	5.0	890 689	5.8	10.4
Belgium	317 258	2.0	347 447	2.3	9.5
Denmark	110 608	0.7	122 500	0.8	10.8
Finland	94 183	0.6	92 940	0.6	–1.3
France	1 651 989	10.3	1 756 969	11.5	6.4
Germany (F.R.)	4 164 722	26.1	4 495 057	29.5	7.9
Greece	153 385	1.0	140 039	0.9	–8.7
Iceland [1]					
Ireland	43 405	0.3	45 517	0.3	4.9
Italy					
Luxembourg	26 700	0.2	30 370	0.2	13.7
Netherlands	262 342	1.6	277 163	1.8	5.6
Norway	68 217	0.4	83 438	0.5	22.3
Portugal	45 458	0.3	50 701	0.3	11.5
Spain	533 380	3.3	570 311	3.7	6.9
Sweden	189 457	1.2	214 630	1.4	13.3
Switzerland	919 514	5.8	971 112	6.4	5.6
Turkey	52 810	0.3	50 776	0.3	–3.9
United Kingdom	1 055 445	6.6	1 165 772	7.6	10.5
Other OECD-Europe					
Total Europe	10 495 768	65.7	11 305 431	74.2	7.7
Canada	267 326	1.7	205 808	1.4	–23.0
United States	2 820 366	17.6	1 317 804	8.6	–53.3
Total North America	3 087 692	19.3	1 523 612	10.0	–50.7
Australia	268 110	1.7	222 214	1.5	–17.1
New Zealand					
Japan	277 728	1.7	322 606	2.1	16.2
Total Australasia and Japan	545 838	3.4	544 820	3.6	–0.2
Total OECD Countries	14 129 298	88.4	13 373 863	87.7	–5.3
Yugoslavia (S.F.R.)	150 481	0.9	164 693	1.1	9.4
Other European countries	243 764	1.5	249 046	1.6	2.2
of which: Bulgaria					
Czechoslovakia					
Hungary					
Poland					
Rumania					
USSR	22 453	0.1	23 461	0.2	4.5
Latin America	424 462	2.7	601 325	3.9	41.7
Asia-Oceania	85 999	0.5	208 778	1.4	142.8
Africa	69 049	0.4	51 639	0.3	–25.2
Origin country undetermined	878 361	5.5	594 529	3.9	–32.3
Total Non-OECD Countries	1 852 116	11.6	1 870 010	12.3	1.0
TOTAL	15 981 414	100.0	15 243 873	100.0	–4.6

1. Included in "Other European countries".

ITALY

ARRIVALS OF FOREIGN TOURISTS IN REGISTERED TOURIST ACCOMMODATION
(by month)

	Total number 1986	% Variation over 1985	% of 1985 total	From Germany	% Variation over 1985	From United States	% Variation over 1985
January	511 060	4.3	2.6	134 253	10.4	60 020	−3.0
February	639 968	5.1	3.3	175 072	7.4	57 838	−3.0
March	1 312 648	24.9	6.8	550 642	53.1	102 218	−15.0
April	1 238 652	−16.3	6.4	383 461	−18.6	103 954	−44.9
May	2 147 789	6.4	11.1	859 465	35.8	123 271	−61.4
June	2 034 840	−18.3	10.5	667 210	−15.2	140 973	−69.0
July	3 141 695	−3.5	16.2	939 006	14.6	174 249	−64.5
August	3 121 667	−2.1	16.1	1 203 599	7.3	137 526	−59.8
September	2 526 329	0.8	13.0	889 035	10.5	198 214	−49.7
October	1 568 286	−1.5	8.1	516 911	12.6	160 225	−46.5
November	589 722	−1.2	3.0	98 696	5.1	71 293	−33.1
December	537 771	6.3	2.8	119 165	3.6	63 721	−8.5
Total	19 370 427	−2.1	100.0	6 536 515	9.9	1 393 502	−52.1

(by country of nationality)

	1985	Relative share	1986	Relative share	% Variation over 1985
Austria	1 120 795	5.7	1 237 667	6.4	10.4
Belgium	396 607	2.0	441 987	2.3	11.4
Denmark	180 266	0.9	213 573	1.1	18.5
Finland	110 984	0.6	111 394	0.6	0.4
France	1 983 682	10.1	2 097 602	10.8	5.7
Germany (F.R.)	5 949 547	30.2	6 536 515	33.7	9.9
Greece	166 799	0.8	151 291	0.8	−9.3
Iceland [1]					
Ireland	50 838	0.3	54 982	0.3	8.2
Italy					
Luxembourg	32 455	0.2	37 501	0.2	15.5
Netherlands	483 810	2.5	531 138	2.7	9.8
Norway	89 091	0.5	106 734	0.6	19.8
Portugal	57 804	0.3	63 293	0.3	9.5
Spain	610 064	3.1	643 656	3.3	5.5
Sweden	244 543	1.2	285 590	1.5	16.8
Switzerland	1 117 291	5.7	1 169 860	6.0	4.7
Turkey	56 786	0.3	56 007	0.3	−1.4
United Kingdom	1 192 632	6.1	1 353 793	7.0	13.5
Other OECD-Europe					
Total Europe	13 843 994	70.4	15 092 583	77.9	9.0
Canada	292 060	1.5	232 542	1.2	−20.4
United States	2 907 222	14.8	1 393 502	7.2	−52.1
Total North America	3 199 282	16.3	1 626 044	8.4	−49.2
Australia	321 309	1.6	264 423	1.4	−17.7
New Zealand					
Japan	285 320	1.5	331 813	1.7	16.3
Total Australasia and Japan	606 629	3.1	596 236	3.1	−1.7
Total OECD Countries	17 649 905	89.7	17 314 863	89.4	−1.9
Yugoslavia (S.F.R.)	162 849	0.8	181 866	0.9	11.7
Other European countries	311 666	1.6	322 644	1.7	3.5
of which: Bulgaria					
Czechoslovakia					
Hungary					
Poland					
Rumania					
USSR	23 536	0.1	24 274	0.1	3.1
Latin America	448 902	2.3	632 045	3.3	40.8
Asia-Oceania	91 627	0.5	221 417	1.1	141.7
Africa	76 409	0.4	58 080	0.3	−24.0
Origin country undetermined	929 580	4.7	639 512	3.3	−31.2
Total Non-OECD Countries	2 021 033	10.3	2 055 564	10.6	1.7
TOTAL	19 670 938	100.0	19 370 427	100.0	−1.5

1. Included in "Other European countries".

ITALY

NIGHTS SPENT BY FOREIGN TOURISTS IN HOTELS
(by month)

	Total number 1986	% Variation over 1985	% of 1985 total	From Germany	% Variation over 1985	From United States	% Variation over 1985
January	1 992 038	4.2	3.1	769 873	4.2	172 811	− 5.8
February	2 545 951	9.0	3.9	899 750	11.7	171 680	− 2.4
March	4 305 890	26.1	6.6	2 225 154	47.1	268 878	−16.2
April	3 717 247	−16.9	5.7	1 474 533	−20.8	255 610	−41.3
May	6 313 325	8.6	9.7	2 861 639	27.6	285 483	−59.2
June	7 484 252	−11.0	11.5	3 087 375	−13.3	336 293	−64.3
July	10 654 378	0.4	16.4	3 845 576	5.9	420 469	−60.1
August	10 541 075	3.1	16.2	4 571 485	8.6	337 441	−55.2
September	9 294 132	5.7	14.3	4 109 402	9.6	486 279	−43.9
October	4 979 219	3.9	7.6	2 037 184	12.6	385 996	−43.6
November	1 640 443	0.2	2.5	341 866	6.3	183 920	−35.2
December	1 654 848	5.3	2.5	491 902	3.2	165 736	− 6.6
Total	65 122 798	1.8	100.0	26 715 739	7.2	3 470 596	−47.2

(by country of nationality)

	1985	Relative share	1986	Relative share	% Variation over 1985
Austria	3 741 227	5.9	4 006 129	6.2	7.1
Belgium	1 588 948	2.5	1 765 733	2.7	11.1
Denmark	486 206	0.8	593 060	0.9	22.0
Finland	479 950	0.8	502 461	0.8	4.7
France	5 261 270	8.2	5 660 003	8.7	7.6
Germany (F.R.)	24 918 807	39.1	26 715 739	41.0	7.2
Greece	353 153	0.6	326 994	0.5	−7.4
Iceland [1]					
Ireland	155 357	0.2	184 517	0.3	18.8
Italy					
Luxembourg	173 064	0.3	207 211	0.3	19.7
Netherlands	1 127 807	1.8	1 279 459	2.0	13.4
Norway	308 438	0.5	376 028	0.6	21.9
Portugal	114 244	0.2	129 885	0.2	13.7
Spain	1 039 464	1.6	1 159 892	1.8	11.6
Sweden	775 647	1.2	890 770	1.4	14.8
Switzerland	4 235 880	6.6	4 637 292	7.1	9.5
Turkey	139 801	0.2	139 281	0.2	−0.4
United Kingdom	4 909 986	7.7	5 774 722	8.9	17.6
Other OECD-Europe					
Total Europe	49 809 249	78.1	54 349 176	83.5	9.1
Canada	670 203	1.1	527 919	0.8	−21.2
United States	6 577 523	10.3	3 470 596	5.3	−47.2
Total North America	7 247 726	11.4	3 998 515	6.1	−44.8
Australia	622 001	1.0	505 454	0.8	−18.7
New Zealand					
Japan	583 130	0.9	654 297	1.0	12.2
Total Australasia and Japan	1 205 131	1.9	1 159 751	1.8	−3.8
Total OECD Countries	58 262 106	91.3	59 507 442	91.4	2.1
Yugoslavia (S.F.R.)	363 590	0.6	380 047	0.6	4.5
Other European countries	923 653	1.4	1 039 870	1.6	12.6
of which: Bulgaria					
Czechoslovakia					
Hungary					
Poland					
Rumania					
USSR	65 843	0.1	74 096	0.1	12.5
Latin America	1 225 773	1.9	1 533 748	2.4	25.1
Asia-Oceania	207 757	0.3	571 885	0.9	175.3
Africa	224 909	0.4	166 225	0.3	−26.1
Origin country undetermined	2 578 669	4.0	1 923 581	3.0	−25.4
Total Non-OECD Countries	5 524 351	8.7	5 615 356	8.6	1.6
TOTAL	63 786 457	100.0	65 122 798	100.0	2.1

1. Included in "Other European countries".

ITALY

NIGHTS SPENT BY FOREIGN TOURISTS IN REGISTERED TOURIST ACCOMMODATION
(by month)

	Total number 1986	% Variation over 1985	% of 1985 total	From Germany	% Variation over 1985	From United States	% Variation over 1985
January	2 429 600	2.7	2.4	967 705	1.3	202 138	− 6.4
February	3 055 419	6.6	3.1	1 129 820	6.5	200 761	− 2.6
March	5 547 398	35.2	5.5	3 069 309	59.6	306 138	−13.7
April	4 459 658	−16.7	4.5	1 851 967	−22.2	286 742	−39.6
May	8 269 862	13.9	8.3	4 171 458	34.1	325 617	−56.0
June	11 008 708	−11.9	11.0	4 972 243	−17.1	392 826	−61.3
July	21 003 950	5.3	21.0	8 367 562	12.8	536 674	−55.2
August	20 776 538	4.0	20.8	10 288 613	6.9	474 987	−49.1
September	13 778 252	8.3	13.8	6 807 374	12.3	556 534	−41.1
October	5 892 885	4.6	5.9	2 524 829	13.7	430 203	−41.6
November	1 888 518	− 0.1	1.9	398 211	4.6	213 790	−33.4
December	2 009 863	4.1	2.0	637 559	3.1	195 792	− 7.5
Total	100 120 651	3.7	100.0	45 186 650	8.2	4 122 202	−43.9

(by country of nationality)

	1985	Relative share	1986	Relative share	% Variation over 1985
Austria	6 833 394	7.1	7 150 711	7.1	4.6
Belgium	2 405 796	2.5	2 692 859	2.7	11.9
Denmark	1 040 703	1.1	1 308 428	1.3	25.7
Finland	574 561	0.6	617 925	0.6	7.5
France	7 234 473	7.5	7 694 120	7.7	6.4
Germany (F.R.)	41 754 200	43.4	45 186 650	45.1	8.2
Greece	561 694	0.6	501 995	0.5	−10.6
Iceland [1]					
Ireland	194 880	0.2	235 926	0.2	21.1
Italy					
Luxembourg	225 512	0.2	268 326	0.3	19.0
Netherlands	3 320 613	3.5	3 697 325	3.7	11.3
Norway	506 691	0.5	602 715	0.6	19.0
Portugal	159 890	0.2	173 284	0.2	8.4
Spain	1 292 070	1.3	1 393 696	1.4	7.9
Sweden	1 231 131	1.3	1 440 727	1.4	17.0
Switzerland	6 302 887	6.6	6 594 419	6.6	4.6
Turkey	170 150	0.2	174 999	0.2	2.8
United Kingdom	5 992 420	6.2	7 194 399	7.2	20.1
Other OECD-Europe					
Total Europe	79 801 065	83.0	86 928 504	86.8	8.9
Canada	809 504	0.8	664 847	0.7	−17.9
United States	7 348 677	7.6	4 122 202	4.1	−43.9
Total North America	8 158 181	8.5	4 787 049	4.8	−41.3
Australia	798 993	0.8	639 313	0.6	−20.0
New Zealand					
Japan	628 546	0.7	710 145	0.7	13.0
Total Australasia and Japan	1 427 539	1.5	1 349 458	1.3	−5.5
Total OECD Countries	89 386 785	93.0	93 065 011	93.0	4.1
Yugoslavia (S.F.R.)	462 447	0.5	511 630	0.5	10.6
Other European countries	1 322 329	1.4	1 438 761	1.4	8.8
of which: Bulgaria					
Czechoslovakia					
Hungary					
Poland					
Rumania					
USSR	77 519	0.1	80 764	0.1	4.2
Latin America	1 277 138	1.3	1 750 172	1.7	37.0
Asia-Oceania	236 365	0.2	681 595	0.7	188.4
Africa	286 410	0.3	225 302	0.2	−21.3
Origin country undetermined	3 166 873	3.3	2 448 180	2.4	−22.7
Total Non-OECD Countries	6 751 562	7.0	7 055 640	7.0	4.5
TOTAL	96 138 347	100.0	100 120 651	100.0	4.1

1. Included in "Other European countries".

JAPAN

ARRIVALS OF FOREIGN VISITORS AT FRONTIERS
(by month)

	Total number 1986	% Variation over 1985	% of 1985 total	From United Kingdom	% Variation over 1985	From United States	% Variation over 1985
January	131 951	− 1.1	6.4	10 249	− 2.3	32 352	8.2
February	145 113	− 3.7	7.0	17 176	− 7.2	28 453	8.6
March	164 347	− 7.1	8.0	13 976	7.2	43 826	1.4
April	187 533	−18.4	9.1	11 300	−29.0	51 902	− 0.9
May	188 663	−14.5	9.2	11 101	−12.6	56 281	1.3
June	180 155	−18.4	8.7	9 721	−32.3	53 209	− 1.9
July	188 540	−18.6	9.1	11 493	−44.0	50 178	− 2.4
August	181 319	−21.3	8.8	12 307	−48.0	44 726	− 3.9
September	181 818	−11.4	8.8	10 834	−25.0	50 783	− 4.5
October	205 190	− 4.5	10.0	11 797	−14.3	61 784	− 7.9
November	171 656	2.7	8.3	11 393	− 5.1	46 436	3.9
December	135 241	− 6.9	6.6	10 759	−19.5	32 252	− 4.1
Total	2 061 526	−11.4	100.0	142 106	−22.3	552 182	− 1.0

(by country of nationality)

	1985	Relative share	1986	Relative share	% Variation over 1985
Austria	6 461	0.3	6 220	0.3	−3.7
Belgium	6 165	0.3	5 341	0.3	−13.4
Denmark	7 531	0.3	7 079	0.3	−6.0
Finland	7 979	0.3	8 174	0.4	2.4
France	39 679	1.7	35 322	1.7	−11.0
Germany (F.R.)	48 609	2.1	49 139	2.4	1.1
Greece	2 515	0.1	2 294	0.1	−8.8
Iceland	219	0.0	293	0.0	33.8
Ireland	2 181	0.1	2 234	0.1	2.4
Italy	21 578	0.9	18 820	0.9	−12.8
Luxembourg	257	0.0	246	0.0	−4.3
Netherlands	15 407	0.7	14 484	0.7	−6.0
Norway	8 036	0.3	7 107	0.3	−11.6
Portugal	4 645	0.2	3 508	0.2	−24.5
Spain	7 088	0.3	8 171	0.4	15.3
Sweden	14 648	0.6	14 138	0.7	−3.5
Switzerland	14 399	0.6	14 710	0.7	2.2
Turkey	2 658	0.1	2 228	0.1	−16.2
United Kingdom	182 804	7.9	142 106	6.9	−22.3
Other OECD-Europe					
Total Europe	392 859	16.9	341 614	16.6	−13.0
Canada	61 052	2.6	55 222	2.7	−9.5
United States	558 029	24.0	552 182	26.8	−1.0
Total North America	619 081	26.6	607 404	29.5	−1.9
Australia	57 559	2.5	42 689	2.1	−25.8
New Zealand	17 434	0.7	15 043	0.7	−13.7
Japan					
Total Australasia and Japan	74 993	3.2	57 732	2.8	−23.0
Total OECD Countries	1 086 933	46.7	1 006 750	48.8	−7.4
Yugoslavia (S.F.R.)	1 612	0.1	1 165	0.1	−27.7
Other European countries	23 270	1.0	20 140	1.0	−13.5
of which: Bulgaria	893	0.0	822	0.0	−8.0
Czechoslovakia	1 591	0.1	1 424	0.1	−10.5
Hungary	1 927	0.1	1 671	0.1	−13.3
Poland	1 420	0.1	1 307	0.1	−8.0
Rumania	320	0.0	293	0.0	−8.4
USSR	10 424	0.4	9 326	0.5	−10.5
Latin America	44 083	1.9	41 103	2.0	−6.8
Asia-Oceania	1 151 862	49.5	976 826	47.4	−15.2
Africa	14 198	0.6	11 165	0.5	−21.4
Origin country undetermined	5 089	0.2	4 377	0.2	−14.0
Total Non-OECD Countries	1 240 114	53.3	1 054 776	51.2	−14.9
TOTAL	2 327 047	100.0	2 061 526	100.0	−11.4

NETHERLANDS

ARRIVALS OF FOREIGN TOURISTS IN HOTELS
(by month)

	Total number 1986	% Variation over 1985	% of 1985 total	From Germany	% Variation over 1985	From United States	% Variation over 1985
January	136 800		4.5	25 100		18 200	
February	150 300		4.9	26 100		17 900	
March	228 200		7.5	43 500		26 100	
April	335 500		11.0	64 800		34 700	
May	399 900		13.1	90 700		40 600	
June	292 000		9.6	62 600		42 200	
July	324 000		10.6	72 400		45 500	
August	363 300		11.9	83 200		43 100	
September	305 700		10.0	59 500		43 700	
October							
November							
December							
Total [3]	3 052 533	− 8.3	100.0	634 146	4.2	365 410	−36.6

(by country of residence)

	1985	Relative share	1986	Relative share	% Variation over 1985
Austria					
Belgium	120 729	3.6			
Denmark	60 666	1.8			
Finland	25 615	0.8			
France	233 647	7.0			
Germany (F.R.)	608 585	18.3			
Greece					
Iceland					
Ireland	17 607	0.5			
Italy	108 932	3.3			
Luxembourg	9 632	0.3			
Netherlands					
Norway	48 920	1.5			
Portugal [1]					
Spain [1]	78 507	2.4			
Sweden	105 096	3.2			
Switzerland	70 283	2.1			
Turkey					
United Kingdom	593 347	17.8			
Other OECD-Europe	113 033	3.4			
Total Europe	2 194 599	65.9			
Canada	113 770	3.4			
United States	576 356	17.3			
Total North America	690 126	20.7			
Australia [2]	60 731	1.8			
New Zealand [2]					
Japan	77 019	2.3			
Total Australasia and Japan	137 750	4.1			
Total OECD Countries	3 022 475	90.8			
Yugoslavia (S.F.R.)					
Other European countries					
of which: Bulgaria					
Czechoslovakia					
Hungary					
Poland					
Rumania					
USSR					
Latin America	66 767	2.0			
Asia-Oceania	169 182	5.1			
Africa	70 401	2.1			
Origin country undetermined					
Total Non-OECD Countries	306 350	9.2			
TOTAL	3 328 825	100.0			

1. Spain includes Portugal.
2. Australia includes New Zealand.
3. Estimates.

NETHERLANDS

ARRIVALS OF FOREIGN TOURISTS IN REGISTERED TOURIST ACCOMMODATION

	Total number 1986	% Variation over 1985	% of 1985 total	From Germany	% Variation over 1985	From United States	% Variation over 1985
January							
February							
March							
April							
May							
June							
July							
August							
September							
October							
November							
December							
Total							

(by country of residence)

	1985	Relative share	1986	Relative share	% Variation over 1985
Austria					
Belgium	263 313	5.2			
Denmark	93 058	1.8			
Finland	34 742	0.7			
France	319 329	6.3			
Germany (F.R.)	1 684 426	33.3			
Greece					
Iceland					
Ireland	23 280	0.5			
Italy	145 724	2.9			
Luxembourg	11 528	0.2			
Netherlands					
Norway	60 365	1.2			
Portugal [1]					
Spain [1]	102 700	2.0			
Sweden	130 720	2.6			
Switzerland	86 753	1.7			
Turkey					
United Kingdom	702 597	13.9			
Other OECD-Europe	142 760	2.8			
Total Europe	3 801 295	75.1			
Canada	131 055	2.6			
United States	628 342	12.4			
Total North America	759 397	15.0			
Australia [2]	86 589	1.7			
New Zealand [2]					
Japan	80 345	1.6			
Total Australasia and Japan	166 934	3.3			
Total OECD Countries	4 727 626	93.4			
Yugoslavia (S.F.R.)					
Other European countries					
of which: Bulgaria					
Czechoslovakia					
Hungary					
Poland					
Rumania					
USSR					
Latin America	73 780	1.5			
Asia-Oceania	182 056	3.6			
Africa	78 129	1.5			
Origin country undetermined					
Total Non-OECD Countries	333 965	6.6			
TOTAL	5 061 591	100.0			

1. Spain includes Portugal.
2. Australia includes New Zealand.

NETHERLANDS

	Total number 1986	% Variation over 1985	% of 1985 total	From Germany	% Variation over 1985	From United States	% Variation over 1985
January	284 800		4.3	49 000		39 400	
February	304 000		4.6	49 700		35 700	
March	474 300		7.2	87 700		49 800	
April	712 600		10.8	138 800		69 400	
May	826 200		12.5	193 700		80 200	
June	633 900		9.6	156 800		88 000	
July	751 500		11.4	212 100		98 800	
August	826 500		12.5	253 000		82 600	
September	641 500		9.7	138 100		84 600	
October							
November							
December							
Total [3]	6 591 732	− 2.3	100.0	1 494 724	8.6	749 181	−30.4

(by country of residence)

	1985	Relative share	1986	Relative share	% Variation over 1985
Austria					
Belgium	205 759	3.0			
Denmark	118 980	1.8			
Finland	47 635	0.7			
France	402 055	6.0			
Germany (F.R.)	1 376 357	20.4			
Greece					
Iceland					
Ireland	37 855	0.6			
Italy	222 722	3.3			
Luxembourg	17 377	0.3			
Netherlands					
Norway	90 398	1.3			
Portugal [1]					
Spain [1]	157 929	2.3			
Sweden	187 032	2.8			
Switzerland	140 673	2.1			
Turkey					
United Kingdom	1 292 134	19.2			
Other OECD-Europe	248 826	3.7			
Total Europe	4 545 732	67.4			
Canada	194 286	2.9			
United States	1 076 410	16.0			
Total North America	1 270 696	18.8			
Australia [2]	122 446	1.8			
New Zealand [2]					
Japan	153 138	2.3			
Total Australasia and Japan	275 584	4.1			
Total OECD Countries	6 092 012	90.3			
Yugoslavia (S.F.R.)					
Other European countries					
of which: Bulgaria					
Czechoslovakia					
Hungary					
Poland					
Rumania					
USSR					
Latin America	132 890	2.0			
Asia-Oceania	373 395	5.5			
Africa	148 614	2.2			
Origin country undetermined					
Total Non-OECD Countries	654 899	9.7			
TOTAL	6 746 911	100.0			

1. Spain includes Portugal.
2. Australia includes New Zealand.
3. Estimates.

NETHERLANDS

NIGHTS SPENT BY FOREIGN TOURISTS IN REGISTERED TOURIST ACCOMMODATION

	Total number 1986	% Variation over 1985	% of 1985 total	From Germany	% Variation over 1985	From United States	% Variation over 1985
January							
February							
March							
April							
May							
June							
July							
August							
September							
October							
November							
December							
Total							

(by country of residence)

	1985	Relative share	1986	Relative share	% Variation over 1985
Austria					
Belgium	1 050 204	7.4			
Denmark	194 416	1.4			
Finland	62 715	0.4			
France	566 588	4.0			
Germany (F.R.)	6 925 300	48.5			
Greece					
Iceland					
Ireland	49 719	0.3			
Italy	297 725	2.1			
Luxembourg	22 774	0.2			
Netherlands					
Norway	110 570	0.8			
Portugal [1]					
Spain [1]	209 136	1.5			
Sweden	245 451	1.7			
Switzerland	177 284	1.2			
Turkey					
United Kingdom	1 581 219	11.1			
Other OECD-Europe	368 372	2.6			
Total Europe	11 861 473	83.0			
Canada	222 785	1.6			
United States	1 166 240	8.2			
Total North America	1 389 025	9.7			
Australia [2]	167 939	1.2			
New Zealand [2]					
Japan	158 079	1.1			
Total Australasia and Japan	326 018	2.3			
Total OECD Countries	13 576 516	95.0			
Yugoslavia (S.F.R.)					
Other European countries					
of which: Bulgaria					
Czechoslovakia					
Hungary					
Poland					
Rumania					
USSR					
Latin America	145 096	1.0			
Asia-Oceania	399 287	2.8			
Africa	166 819	1.2			
Origin country undetermined					
Total Non-OECD Countries	711 202	5.0			
TOTAL	14 287 718	100.0			

1. Spain includes Portugal.
2. Australia includes New Zealand.

NEW ZEALAND

ARRIVALS OF FOREIGN TOURISTS AT FRONTIERS
(by month)

	Total number 1986	% Variation over 1985	% of 1985 total	From Australia	% Variation over 1985	From United States	% Variation over 1985
January	54 714	16.4	9.5	19 752	11.9	10 752	51.3
February	55 579	8.7	9.6	16 336	−15.7	12 836	30.1
March	53 650	5.5	9.3	18 905	−15.4	12 624	30.0
April	44 041	8.6	7.6	14 615	−13.5	14 024	25.0
May	29 745	− 0.3	5.1	14 675	−12.0	5 265	12.7
June	27 966	− 2.9	4.8	13 400	−24.2	4 560	20.0
July	31 426	12.0	5.4	12 970	− 9.1	6 420	32.1
August	36 842	− 0.9	6.4	17 221	−17.8	6 876	12.9
September	36 675	14.7	6.3	15 215	−10.0	7 450	30.4
October	46 302	11.2	8.0	11 820	−18.6	15 114	16.8
November	64 537	13.4	11.2	14 521	− 7.7	19 194	22.8
December	96 366	12.5	16.7	37 452	− 5.3	13 284	33.8
Total	577 843	9.1	100.0	206 882	−11.0	128 399	26.5

(by country of residence)

	1985	Relative share	1986	Relative share	% Variation over 1985
Austria	1 052	0.2	1 299	0.2	23.5
Belgium	376	0.1	314	0.1	−16.5
Denmark	1 120	0.2	1 520	0.3	35.7
Finland	208	0.0	347	0.1	66.8
France	1 228	0.3	1 483	0.3	20.8
Germany (F.R.)	8 372	1.7	9 617	1.7	14.9
Greece	188	0.0	121	0.0	−35.6
Iceland	68	0.0	17	0.0	−75.0
Ireland	604	0.1	701	0.1	16.1
Italy	668	0.1	893	0.2	33.7
Luxembourg	32	0.0	37	0.0	15.6
Netherlands	4 477	0.9	4 728	0.8	5.6
Norway	412	0.1	746	0.1	81.1
Portugal	44	0.0	63	0.0	43.2
Spain	280	0.1	355	0.1	26.8
Sweden	2 244	0.5	3 841	0.7	71.2
Switzerland	4 050	0.8	5 558	1.0	37.2
Turkey	24	0.0	29	0.0	20.8
United Kingdom	33 564	7.0	40 103	7.1	19.5
Other OECD-Europe					
Total Europe	59 011	12.3	71 772	12.7	21.6
Canada	25 641	5.3	28 772	5.1	12.2
United States	101 531	21.1	128 399	22.7	26.5
Total North America	127 172	26.4	157 171	27.8	23.6
Australia	232 513	48.3	206 882	36.5	−11.0
New Zealand [1]	1 140	0.2	3 016	0.5	164.6
Japan	42 900	8.9	54 374	9.6	26.7
Total Australasia and Japan	276 553	57.5	264 272	46.7	−4.4
Total OECD Countries	462 736	96.2	493 215	87.1	6.6
Yugoslavia (S.F.R.)	40	0.0	113	0.0	182.5
Other European countries	152	0.0			
of which: Bulgaria					
Czechoslovakia	40	0.0			
Hungary	56	0.0			
Poland	12	0.0			
Rumania	12	0.0			
USSR	32	0.0			
Latin America	1 598	0.3	3 563	0.6	123.0
Asia-Oceania			51 476	9.1	
Africa			2 671	0.5	
Origin country undetermined	16 719	3.5	15 137	2.7	−9.5
Total Non-OECD Countries	18 509	3.8	72 960	12.9	294.2
TOTAL	481 245	100.0	566 175	100.0	17.6

1. New Zealanders who have lived abroad for less than 12 months and who return for a short stay.

NEW ZEALAND

ARRIVALS OF FOREIGN VISITORS AT FRONTIERS
(by month)

	Total number 1986	% Variation over 1985	% of 1985 total	From Australia	% Variation over 1985	From United States	% Variation over 1985
January	67 178	17.0	9.2	25 044	16.0	12 856	45.5
February	69 783	9.4	9.5	21 756	−10.4	15 616	28.2
March	67 044	6.0	9.1	24 217	−12.5	15 020	30.3
April	57 089	9.7	7.8	20 295	− 6.3	16 232	22.6
May	41 080	0.7	5.6	20 065	− 9.1	6 950	16.3
June	39 461	0.3	5.4	19 135	−17.3	6 300	23.6
July	43 041	9.3	5.9	18 410	− 5.7	8 080	25.7
August	50 437	1.1	6.9	23 566	−13.0	8 886	12.5
September	48 836	14.4	6.7	20 730	− 5.8	9 440	31.3
October	60 612	11.7	8.3	17 286	−10.8	17 832	16.8
November	79 483	11.6	10.8	20 365	− 5.4	21 612	20.2
December	109 380	14.6	14.9	42 690	− 2.1	15 150	33.5
Total	733 424	9.5	100.0	273 559	− 6.8	153 974	25.2

(by country of residence)

	1985	Relative share	1986	Relative share	% Variation over 1985
Austria	1 264	0.2	1 616	0.2	27.8
Belgium	632	0.1	579	0.1	−8.4
Denmark	1 672	0.3	2 023	0.3	21.0
Finland	480	0.1	616	0.1	28.3
France	2 429	0.4	2 651	0.4	9.1
Germany (F.R.)	10 656	1.6	12 040	1.7	13.0
Greece	304	0.0	250	0.0	−17.8
Iceland	80	0.0	29	0.0	−63.8
Ireland	844	0.1	848	0.1	0.5
Italy	1 260	0.2	1 712	0.2	35.9
Luxembourg	52	0.0	57	0.0	9.6
Netherlands	5 413	0.8	5 788	0.8	6.9
Norway	772	0.1	1 216	0.2	57.5
Portugal	96	0.0	128	0.0	33.3
Spain	468	0.1	560	0.1	19.7
Sweden	2 964	0.4	4 935	0.7	66.5
Switzerland	4 688	0.7	6 314	0.9	34.7
Turkey	48	0.0	35	0.0	−27.1
United Kingdom	43 612	6.6	49 675	6.8	13.9
Other OECD-Europe					
Total Europe	77 734	11.7	91 072	12.5	17.2
Canada	29 833	4.5	34 326	4.7	15.1
United States	122 960	18.6	153 974	21.1	25.2
Total North America	152 793	23.1	188 300	25.8	23.2
Australia	293 558	44.3	273 559	37.5	−6.8
New Zealand [1]	1 804	0.3	3 862	0.5	114.1
Japan	50 264	7.6	62 656	8.6	24.7
Total Australasia and Japan	345 626	52.1	340 077	46.6	−1.6
Total OECD Countries	576 153	86.9	619 449	84.9	7.5
Yugoslavia (S.F.R.)	84	0.0	137	0.0	63.1
Other European countries	1 396	0.2	2 179	0.3	56.1
of which: Bulgaria	0	0.0			
Czechoslovakia	76	0.0			
Hungary	104	0.0			
Poland	44	0.0			
Rumania	12	0.0			
USSR	1 160	0.2			
Latin America	2 836	0.4	7 070	1.0	149.3
Asia-Oceania	56 773	8.6	76 480	10.5	34.7
Africa	2 933	0.4	3 355	0.5	14.4
Origin country undetermined	22 635	3.4	20 930	2.9	−7.5
Total Non-OECD Countries	86 657	13.1	110 151	15.1	27.1
TOTAL	662 810	100.0	729 600	100.0	10.1

1. New Zealanders who have lived abroad for less than 12 months and who return for a short stay.

NORWAY

NIGHTS SPENT BY FOREIGN TOURISTS IN HOTELS
(by month)

	Total number 1986	% Variation over 1985	% of 1985 total	From Germany	% Variation over 1985	From United States	% Variation over 1985
January	205 880	9.3	6.2	9 818	−2.0	6 909	−4.2
February	290 080	−10.5	8.8	11 202	0.6	10 010	19.5
March	227 998	−13.0	6.9	17 737	−7.6	13 527	12.2
April	158 694	−3.6	4.8	8 965	−28.0	11 086	22.1
May	196 949	−15.1	6.0	22 414	2.3	36 254	−27.6
June	454 461	−18.0	13.8	102 576	−10.6	74 947	−41.0
July	665 965	−12.1	20.2	163 070	5.2	93 740	−43.1
August	514 616	−19.1	15.6	111 493	−5.1	88 496	−44.5
September	231 423	−10.8	7.0	21 164	0.1	50 869	−32.7
October	125 004	1.1	3.8	10 020	22.0	11 999	−16.1
November	101 241	8.4	3.1	7 361	−22.7	6 972	−7.1
December	125 404	7.1	3.8	10 163	8.1	6 374	−16.5
Total	3 297 715	−11.2	100.0	495 983	−2.8	411 183	−36.0

(by country of nationality)

	1985	Relative share	1986	Relative share	% Variation over 1985
Austria [1]					
Belgium [1]					
Denmark	610 972	16.5	575 718	17.5	−5.8
Finland	93 817	2.5	101 942	3.1	8.7
France	101 916	2.7	109 718	3.3	7.7
Germany (F.R.)	510 236	13.7	495 983	15.0	−2.8
Greece [1]					
Iceland [1]					
Ireland [1]					
Italy [1]					
Luxembourg [1]					
Netherlands	132 908	3.6	110 812	3.4	−16.6
Norway					
Portugal [1]					
Spain [1]					
Sweden	559 329	15.1	553 989	16.8	−1.0
Switzerland [1]					
Turkey [1]					
United Kingdom	449 728	12.1	365 138	11.1	−18.8
Other OECD-Europe					
Total Europe	2 458 906	66.2	2 313 300	70.1	−5.9
Canada [1]					
United States	642 959	17.3	411 183	12.5	−36.0
Total North America	642 959	17.3	411 183	12.5	−36.0
Australia [1]					
New Zealand [1]					
Japan	64 365	1.7	46 046	1.4	−28.5
Total Australasia and Japan	64 365	1.7	46 046	1.4	−28.5
Total OECD Countries	3 166 230	85.3	2 770 529	84.0	−12.5
Yugoslavia (S.F.R.) [1]					
Other European countries	243 921	6.6			
of which: Bulgaria					
Czechoslovakia					
Hungary					
Poland					
Rumania					
USSR					
Latin America [1]					
Asia-Oceania [1]					
Africa [1]					
Origin country undetermined	302 482	8.1	527 186	16.0	74.3
Total Non-OECD Countries	546 403	14.7	527 186	16.0	−3.5
TOTAL	3 712 633	100.0	3 297 715	100.0	−11.2

1. Includes in "Origin country undetermined".

PORTUGAL

ARRIVALS OF FOREIGN TOURISTS AT FRONTIERS
(by month)

	Total number 1986	% Variation over 1985	% of 1985 total	From Spain	% Variation over 1985	From United States	% Variation over 1985
January	156 544	7.3	2.9	64 867	− 8.2	6 152	16.7
February	184 025	7.4	3.4	80 283	8.7	6 906	−27.9
March	374 695	22.2	6.9	205 366	30.2	10 087	6.7
April	343 272	−10.0	6.3	174 441	−20.9	8 288	−16.1
May	437 036	23.6	8.1	176 509	30.6	10 029	−54.6
June	477 736	10.6	8.8	181 882	− 3.5	16 199	−13.4
July	899 641	1.1	16.6	414 136	0.1	16 605	−26.2
August	895 279	− 6.4	16.6	473 719	−12.8	9 024	−61.0
September	607 119	13.5	11.2	297 633	8.9	11 952	−28.6
October	427 129	14.7	7.9	179 127	10.8	11 195	−35.2
November	302 356	26.4	5.6	174 137	31.5	7 024	26.4
December	304 369	47.8	5.6	189 828	72.6	958	−80.0
Total	5 409 201	8.4	100.0	2 611 928	5.3	114 419	−30.6

(by country of nationality)

	1985	Relative share	1986	Relative share	% Variation over 1985
Austria	22 812	0.5	27 909	0.5	22.3
Belgium	66 212	1.3	64 818	1.2	−2.1
Denmark	44 020	0.9	55 845	1.0	26.9
Finland	19 650	0.4	25 018	0.5	27.3
France	320 188	6.4	340 608	6.3	6.4
Germany (F.R.)	369 161	7.4	382 562	7.1	3.6
Greece [1]					
Iceland [1]					
Ireland	27 256	0.5	40 977	0.8	50.3
Italy	82 757	1.7	90 635	1.7	9.5
Luxembourg	2 576	0.1	3 546	0.1	37.7
Netherlands	151 350	3.0	163 346	3.0	7.9
Norway	24 641	0.5	30 208	0.6	22.6
Portugal					
Spain	2 480 853	49.7	2 611 928	48.3	5.3
Sweden	48 947	1.0	64 462	1.2	31.7
Switzerland	57 257	1.1	61 243	1.1	7.0
Turkey [1]					
United Kingdom	755 571	15.1	992 697	18.4	31.4
Other OECD-Europe					
Total Europe	4 473 251	89.7	4 955 802	91.6	10.8
Canada	68 894	1.4	72 183	1.3	4.8
United States	164 929	3.3	114 419	2.1	−30.6
Total North America	233 823	4.7	186 602	3.4	−20.2
Australia	16 851	0.3	16 649	0.3	−1.2
New-Zealand [2]					
Japan	18 394	0.4	22 014	0.4	19.7
Total Australasia and Japan	35 245	0.7	38 663	0.7	9.7
Total OECD Countries	4 742 319	95.1	5 181 067	95.8	9.3
Yugoslavia (S.F.R.) [1]					
Other European countries	30 475	0.6	27 123	0.5	−11.0
of which: Bulgaria					
Czechoslovakia					
Hungary					
Poland					
Rumania					
USSR					
Latin America					
Asia-Oceania					
Africa	106 278	2.1	73 978	1.4	−30.4
Origin country undetermined	109 988	2.2	127 033	2.3	15.5
Total Non-OECD Countries	246 741	4.9	228 134	4.2	−7.5
TOTAL	4 989 060	100.0	5 409 201	100.0	8.4

1. Included in "Other European countries".
2. New Zealand included in Australia.

PORTUGAL

ARRIVALS OF FOREIGN VISITORS AT FRONTIERS
(by month)

	Total number 1986	% Variation over 1985	% of 1985 total	From Spain	% Variation over 1985	From United States	% Variation over 1985
January	412 937	8.9	3.2	307 073	7.2	7 144	−3.4
February	466 085	10.9	3.6	352 323	12.2	7 984	−20.8
March	909 012	23.3	7.0	722 676	28.2	12 628	−23.1
April	825 265	−7.3	6.3	629 458	−9.5	10 541	−48.9
May	957 592	39.4	7.3	665 802	53.0	13 576	−47.0
June	894 907	11.1	6.9	582 309	10.2	17 378	−38.9
July	1 834 531	7.1	14.1	1 308 800	12.1	22 810	−33.8
August	2 148 957	−11.0	16.5	1 681 296	−14.1	16 837	−29.4
September	1 491 676	9.2	11.4	1 155 302	8.5	13 003	−36.1
October	1 109 577	17.7	8.5	843 756	19.6	12 058	−42.7
November	887 126	29.0	6.8	732 201	31.2	8 063	−34.2
December	1 119 206	72.5	8.6	979 185	87.6	7 786	−12.7
Total	13 056 871	11.7	100.0	9 960 181	13.2	149 808	−34.7

(by country of nationality)

	1985	Relative share	1986	Relative share	% Variation over 1985
Austria	25 358	0.2	31 103	0.2	22.7
Belgium	67 555	0.6	67 683	0.5	0.2
Denmark	46 934	0.4	59 247	0.5	26.2
Finland	20 105	0.2	25 761	0.2	28.1
France	347 307	3.0	350 134	2.7	0.8
Germany (F.R.)	412 998	3.5	430 282	3.3	4.2
Greece	10 571	0.1	8 924	0.1	−15.6
Iceland	1 684	0.0	1 884	0.0	11.9
Ireland	29 808	0.3	43 266	0.3	45.1
Italy	93 411	0.8	108 545	0.8	16.2
Luxembourg	2 592	0.0	3 613	0.0	39.4
Netherlands	163 794	1.4	171 724	1.3	4.8
Norway	28 574	0.2	31 507	0.2	10.3
Portugal					
Spain	8 798 194	75.3	9 960 181	76.3	13.2
Sweden	54 106	0.5	69 385	0.5	28.2
Switzerland	61 126	0.5	66 425	0.5	8.7
Turkey	2 287	0.0	2 198	0.0	−3.9
United Kingdom	880 388	7.5	1 069 087	8.2	21.4
Other OECD-Europe					
Total Europe	11 046 792	94.5	12 500 949	95.7	13.2
Canada	70 275	0.6	73 825	0.6	5.1
United States	229 496	2.0	149 808	1.1	−34.7
Total North America	299 771	2.6	223 633	1.7	−25.4
Australia	13 809	0.1	14 203	0.1	2.9
New Zealand	3 452	0.0	4 109	0.0	19.0
Japan	19 986	0.2	23 246	0.2	16.3
Total Australasia and Japan	37 247	0.3	41 558	0.3	11.6
Total OECD Countries	11 383 810	97.4	12 766 140	97.8	12.1
Yugoslavia (S.F.R.)	5 009	0.0	4 760	0.0	−5.0
Other European countries	44 571	0.4	42 407	0.3	−4.9
of which: Bulgaria	2 965	0.0			
Czechoslovakia	4 815	0.0			
Hungary	1 683	0.0			
Poland	8 911	0.1			
Rumania	980	0.0			
USSR	21 974	0.2			
Latin America	114 849	1.0	129 247	1.0	12.5
Asia-Oceania	30 625	0.3	34 264	0.3	11.9
Africa	111 602	1.0	78 469	0.6	−29.7
Origin country undetermined	1 248	0.0	1 584	0.0	26.9
Total Non-OECD Countries	307 904	2.6	290 731	2.2	−5.6
TOTAL	11 691 714	100.0	13 056 871	100.0	11.7

1. Other OECD-Europe includes: Iceland, Ireland, Luxembourg and Portugal.
2. Included in "Origin country undetermined".
3. Includes Iraq, Kuwait, Libya, Lebanon, Egypt, Syria, Saudi Arabia, Jordan, Iran and Pakistan.

PORTUGAL

ARRIVALS OF FOREIGN TOURISTS IN HOTELS[1]
(by month)

	Total number 1986	% Variation over 1985	% of 1985 total	From Spain	% Variation over 1985	From United States	% Variation over 1985
January	99 810	− 5.2	3.5	12 442	20.1	8 854	−21.7
February	121 821	− 3.6	4.3	14 572	15.7	10 397	−28.4
March	236 009	20.9	8.3	60 756	108.7	17 197	−15.8
April	213 079	−14.8	7.5	27 075	−47.3	14 881	−45.4
May	288 004	1.7	10.2	40 659	38.4	15 548	−56.3
June	270 896	− 0.8	9.6	28 279	−16.8	15 980	−50.4
July	331 472	2.0	11.7	53 513	9.6	17 295	−48.4
August	406 472	15.6	14.3	102 950	19.4	17 047	−39.7
September	340 171	6.7	12.0	62 024	22.4	18 616	−42.0
October	267 929	6.6	9.5	38 471	8.3	18 698	−42.2
November	135 113	− 6.2	4.8	22 419	−13.0	10 045	−34.8
December	122 405	10.9	4.3	31 889	85.9	7 620	−14.8
Total	2 833 181	3.6	100.0	495 049	14.9	172 178	−41.0

(by country of residence)

	1985	Relative share	1986	Relative share	% Variation over 1985
Austria	21 712	0.8	29 031	1.0	33.7
Belgium	55 028	2.0	60 483	2.1	9.9
Denmark	42 219	1.5	55 120	1.9	30.6
Finland	20 502	0.7	24 423	0.9	19.1
France	220 299	8.1	250 548	8.8	13.7
Germany (F.R.)	288 465	10.5	306 591	10.8	6.3
Greece	4 141	0.2	4 175	0.1	0.8
Iceland	1 964	0.1	1 523	0.1	−22.5
Ireland	21 885	0.8	27 112	1.0	23.9
Italy	81 018	3.0	94 730	3.3	16.9
Luxembourg	3 072	0.1	3 587	0.1	16.8
Netherlands	106 486	3.9	110 053	3.9	3.3
Norway	27 547	1.0	30 887	1.1	12.1
Portugal					
Spain	430 941	15.8	495 049	17.5	14.9
Sweden	57 708	2.1	69 407	2.4	20.3
Switzerland	90 794	3.3	88 078	3.1	−3.0
Turkey	1 075	0.0	1 025	0.0	−4.7
United Kingdom	643 421	23.5	706 871	24.9	9.9
Other OECD-Europe					
Total Europe	2 118 277	77.5	2 358 693	83.3	11.3
Canada	98 383	3.6	92 409	3.3	−6.1
United States	291 874	10.7	172 178	6.1	−41.0
Total North America	390 257	14.3	264 587	9.3	−32.2
Australia	9 641	0.4	8 433	0.3	−12.5
New Zealand	1 655	0.1	1 662	0.1	0.4
Japan	23 102	0.8	24 563	0.9	6.3
Total Australasia and Japan	34 398	1.3	34 658	1.2	0.8
Total OECD Countries	2 542 932	93.0	2 657 938	93.8	4.5
Yugoslavia (S.F.R.)	1 488	0.1	1 468	0.1	−1.3
Other European countries	8 834	0.3	8 848	0.3	0.2
of which: Bulgaria	425	0.0	474	0.0	11.5
Czechoslovakia	1 169	0.0	1 836	0.1	57.1
Hungary	1 243	0.0	1 148	0.0	−7.6
Poland	1 412	0.1	1 024	0.0	−27.5
Rumania	363	0.0	145	0.0	−60.1
USSR	4 222	0.2	4 221	0.1	−0.0
Latin America	97 939	3.6	102 351	3.6	4.5
Asia-Oceania	19 366	0.7	23 424	0.8	21.0
Africa	62 866	2.3	38 175	1.3	−39.3
Origin country undetermined	1 156	0.0	977	0.0	−15.5
Total Non-OECD Countries	191 649	7.0	175 243	6.2	−8.6
TOTAL	2 734 581	100.0	2 833 181	100.0	3.6

1. Includes arrivals at hotels, studio-hotels, holiday-flats, villages, motels, inns and boarding-houses.

PORTUGAL

ARRIVALS OF FOREIGN TOURISTS IN REGISTERED TOURIST ACCOMMODATION[1]
(by month)

	Total number 1986	% Variation over 1985	% of 1985 total	From Spain	% Variation over 1985	From United States	% Variation over 1985
January	102 655	– 4.9	2.9	12 764	21.5	8 973	–21.8
February	125 449	– 3.3	3.5	14 993	15.1	10 545	–28.4
March	249 973	22.6	7.0	65 926	114.8	17 463	–15.5
April	227 346	–14.7	6.4	28 711	–48.9	15 261	–44.8
May	316 320	4.8	8.9	42 879	41.0	16 169	–55.1
June	321 989	2.0	9.1	32 279	–12.7	16 837	–48.8
July	558 492	10.8	15.7	86 658	10.5	18 157	–47.6
August	680 929	20.6	19.2	172 639	26.6	17 801	–39.3
September	418 007	9.3	11.8	74 926	23.0	19 041	–41.6
October	286 948	7.4	8.1	40 777	8.8	19 088	–41.7
November	140 820	– 6.3	4.0	23 042	–13.4	10 316	–34.5
December	126 209	11.1	3.6	32 513	85.6	7 826	–14.3
Total	3 555 137	7.5	100.0	628 107	17.4	177 477	–40.4

(by country of residence)

	1985	Relative share	1986	Relative share	% Variation over 1985
Austria	28 739	0.9	38 482	1.1	33.9
Belgium	71 629	2.2	84 217	2.4	17.6
Denmark	54 276	1.6	71 505	2.0	31.7
Finland	24 473	0.7	25 528	0.7	4.3
France	337 132	10.2	413 473	11.6	22.6
Germany (F.R.)	429 354	13.0	484 006	13.6	12.7
Greece	4 500	0.1	4 610	0.1	2.4
Iceland	1 987	0.1	1 540	0.0	–22.5
Ireland	23 200	0.7	28 606	0.8	23.3
Italy	101 808	3.1	122 175	3.4	20.0
Luxembourg	3 957	0.1	4 360	0.1	10.2
Netherlands	176 387	5.3	198 145	5.6	12.3
Norway	28 689	0.9	31 932	0.9	11.3
Portugal					
Spain	535 079	16.2	628 107	17.7	17.4
Sweden	60 237	1.8	72 028	2.0	19.6
Switzerland	100 930	3.1	98 271	2.8	–2.6
Turkey	1 231	0.0	1 099	0.0	–10.7
United Kingdom	672 342	20.3	739 691	20.8	10.0
Other OECD-Europe					
Total Europe	2 655 950	80.3	3 047 775	85.7	14.8
Canada	102 744	3.1	96 124	2.7	–6.4
United States	297 637	9.0	177 477	5.0	–40.4
Total North America	400 381	12.1	273 601	7.7	–31.7
Australia	19 242	0.6	17 251	0.5	–10.3
New Zealand	5 613	0.2	5 773	0.2	2.9
Japan	23 498	0.7	24 939	0.7	6.1
Total Australasia and Japan	48 353	1.5	47 963	1.3	–0.8
Total OECD Countries	3 104 684	93.9	3 369 339	94.8	8.5
Yugoslavia (S.F.R.)	1 998	0.1	2 047	0.1	2.5
Other European countries	11 861	0.4	11 818	0.3	–0.4
of which: Bulgaria	648	0.0	556	0.0	–14.2
Czechoslovakia	1 649	0.0	2 060	0.1	24.9
Hungary	2 309	0.1	2 481	0.1	7.4
Poland	2 330	0.1	2 019	0.1	–13.3
Rumania	690	0.0	471	0.0	–31.7
USSR	4 235	0.1	4 231	0.1	–0.1
Latin America	100 913	3.1	105 705	3.0	4.7
Asia-Oceania	19 980	0.6	24 206	0.7	21.2
Africa	66 938	2.0	41 000	1.2	–38.7
Origin country undetermined	1 243	0.0	1 022	0.0	–17.8
Total Non-OECD Countries	202 933	6.1	185 798	5.2	–8.4
TOTAL	3 307 617	100.0	3 555 137	100.0	7.5

1. Includes arrivals at hotels, studio-hotels, holiday-flats, villages, motels, inns, boarding-houses, recreation centres for children and camping-sites.

PORTUGAL

NIGHTS SPENT BY FOREIGN TOURISTS IN HOTELS[1]
(by month)

	Total number 1986	% Variation over 1985	% of 1985 total	From Spain	% Variation over 1985	From United States	% Variation over 1985
January	596 023	2.8	4.2	27 780	22.7	32 795	−14.3
February	689 382	1.8	4.8	26 102	− 7.0	42 267	−22.7
March	1 081 170	12.1	7.6	131 417	98.4	57 191	−16.2
April	994 992	− 3.1	7.0	59 074	−48.9	39 477	−47.6
May	1 377 753	15.3	9.6	89 775	37.0	40 272	−54.0
June	1 508 538	14.9	10.6	66 054	−12.7	41 267	−45.0
July	1 770 532	14.8	12.4	132 542	5.2	50 739	−42.8
August	1 965 345	17.5	13.8	251 952	9.2	46 631	−37.5
September	1 677 237	12.2	11.7	133 933	17.6	48 452	−38.4
October	1 363 879	10.4	9.5	77 751	3.7	47 159	−40.1
November	692 243	0.8	4.8	46 071	−11.7	28 282	−32.7
December	566 526	2.6	4.0	59 460	67.6	21 440	−20.4
Total	14 283 620	10.4	100.0	1 101 911	9.5	495 972	−37.1

(by country of residence)

	1985	Relative share	1986	Relative share	% Variation over 1985
Austria	95 689	0.7	125 863	0.9	31.5
Belgium	236 903	1.8	256 756	1.8	8.4
Denmark	237 519	1.8	345 640	2.4	45.5
Finland	134 504	1.0	175 714	1.2	30.6
France	672 954	5.2	748 879	5.2	11.3
Germany (F.R.)	1 699 976	13.1	1 890 917	13.2	11.2
Greece	12 082	0.1	11 420	0.1	−5.5
Iceland	19 026	0.1	19 339	0.1	1.6
Ireland	179 030	1.4	254 885	1.8	42.4
Italy	212 433	1.6	256 329	1.8	20.7
Luxembourg	14 899	0.1	22 088	0.2	48.3
Netherlands	745 545	5.8	815 526	5.7	9.4
Norway	199 496	1.5	221 261	1.5	10.9
Portugal					
Spain	1 006 711	7.8	1 101 911	7.7	9.5
Sweden	374 265	2.9	430 881	3.0	15.1
Switzerland	337 286	2.6	344 485	2.4	2.1
Turkey	2 919	0.0	3 441	0.0	17.9
United Kingdom	4 952 228	38.3	5 821 208	40.8	17.5
Other OECD-Europe					
Total Europe	11 133 465	86.0	12 846 543	89.9	15.4
Canada	388 180	3.0	363 680	2.5	−6.3
United States	788 833	6.1	495 972	3.5	−37.1
Total North America	1 177 013	9.1	859 652	6.0	−27.0
Australia	25 697	0.2	21 355	0.1	−16.9
New Zealand	4 891	0.0	4 704	0.0	−3.8
Japan	49 614	0.4	53 176	0.4	7.2
Total Australasia and Japan	80 202	0.6	79 235	0.6	−1.2
Total OECD Countries	12 390 680	95.8	13 785 430	96.5	11.3
Yugoslavia (S.F.R.)	4 391	0.0	5 446	0.0	24.0
Other European countries	24 874	0.2	27 153	0.2	9.2
of which: Bulgaria	1 138	0.0	2 427	0.0	113.3
Czechoslovakia	3 609	0.0	4 085	0.0	13.2
Hungary	3 502	0.0	5 890	0.0	68.2
Poland	4 402	0.0	4 009	0.0	−8.9
Rumania	1 170	0.0	412	0.0	−64.8
USSR	11 053	0.1	10 330	0.1	−6.5
Latin America	230 850	1.8	245 190	1.7	6.2
Asia-Oceania	55 964	0.4	68 248	0.5	21.9
Africa	229 831	1.8	149 493	1.0	−35.0
Origin country undetermined	3 935	0.0	2 658	0.0	−32.5
Total Non-OECD Countries	549 845	4.2	498 188	3.5	−9.4
TOTAL	12 940 525	100.0	14 283 618	100.0	10.4

1. Includes nights spent at hotels, studio-hotels, holiday-flats, villages, motels, inns and boarding-houses.

PORTUGAL

NIGHTS SPENT BY FOREIGN TOURISTS IN REGISTERED TOURIST ACCOMMODATION [1]
(by month)

	Total number 1986	% Variation over 1985	% of 1985 total	From Spain	% Variation over 1985	From United States	% Variation over 1985
January	622 066	2.1	3.7	28 458	23.1	33 227	−15.0
February	715 826	1.5	4.3	26 983	− 7.4	42 764	−22.6
March	1 131 215	12.5	6.7	143 536	103.1	57 889	−16.3
April	1 042 120	− 3.6	6.2	63 309	−50.7	40 461	−46.8
May	1 458 886	16.5	8.7	95 213	38.5	41 694	−52.9
June	1 670 327	15.4	9.9	77 515	− 7.1	42 887	−44.1
July	2 562 442	21.1	15.3	247 523	12.1	53 169	−42.3
August	2 892 959	19.8	17.2	479 210	21.5	49 188	−37.2
September	1 944 506	13.3	11.6	179 358	22.6	49 887	−38.4
October	1 430 317	10.7	8.5	83 545	4.8	48 076	−39.8
November	722 706	0.8	4.3	47 366	−12.8	29 129	−32.4
December	594 971	3.2	3.5	61 001	68.6	22 181	−19.5
Total	16 788 341	12.4	100.0	1 533 017	14.8	510 552	−36.7

(by country of residence)

	1985	Relative share	1986	Relative share	% Variation over 1985
Austria	117 475	0.8	155 260	0.9	32.2
Belgium	293 910	2.0	339 877	2.0	15.6
Denmark	282 390	1.9	407 316	2.4	44.2
Finland	142 684	1.0	180 347	1.1	26.4
France	1 024 107	6.9	1 202 166	7.2	17.4
Germany (F.R.)	2 242 476	15.0	2 554 325	15.2	13.9
Greece	13 432	0.1	12 558	0.1	−6.5
Iceland	19 096	0.1	19 380	0.1	1.5
Ireland	184 865	1.2	261 246	1.6	41.3
Italy	268 808	1.8	321 978	1.9	19.8
Luxembourg	18 207	0.1	24 808	0.1	36.3
Netherlands	1 012 434	6.8	1 201 345	7.2	18.7
Norway	203 963	1.4	225 066	1.3	10.3
Portugal					
Spain	1 335 280	8.9	1 533 017	9.1	14.8
Sweden	385 463	2.6	441 670	2.6	14.6
Switzerland	370 807	2.5	379 336	2.3	2.3
Turkey	3 756	0.0	3 917	0.0	4.3
United Kingdom	5 087 016	34.1	5 992 905	35.7	17.8
Other OECD-Europe					
Total Europe	13 006 169	87.1	15 256 517	90.9	17.3
Canada	401 156	2.7	374 163	2.2	−6.7
United States	806 857	5.4	510 552	3.0	−36.7
Total North America	1 208 013	8.1	884 715	5.3	−26.8
Australia	53 370	0.4	42 897	0.3	−19.6
New Zealand	16 021	0.1	15 214	0.1	−5.0
Japan	50 620	0.3	54 525	0.3	7.7
Total Australasia and Japan	120 011	0.8	112 636	0.7	−6.1
Total OECD Countries	14 334 193	96.0	16 253 868	96.8	13.4
Yugoslavia (S.F.R.)	6 080	0.0	7 125	0.0	17.2
Other European countries	35 410	0.2	36 759	0.2	3.8
of which: Bulgaria	1 694	0.0	2 856	0.0	68.6
Czechoslovakia	5 166	0.0	5 047	0.0	−2.3
Hungary	7 502	0.1	10 372	0.1	38.3
Poland	6 982	0.0	6 178	0.0	−11.5
Rumania	2 987	0.0	1 943	0.0	−35.0
USSR	11 079	0.1	10 363	0.1	−6.5
Latin America	242 258	1.6	255 028	1.5	5.3
Asia-Oceania	58 664	0.4	69 998	0.4	19.3
Africa	251 979	1.7	162 782	1.0	−35.4
Origin country undetermined	4 356	0.0	2 781	0.0	−36.2
Total Non-OECD Countries	598 747	4.0	534 473	3.2	−10.7
TOTAL	14 932 940	100.0	16 788 341	100.0	12.4

1. Includes nights spent at hotels, studio-hotels, holiday-flats, villages, motels, inns, boarding-houses, recreation centres for children and camping-sites.

SPAIN

ARRIVALS OF FOREIGN VISITORS AT FRONTIERS[1]
(by month)

	Total number 1986	% Variation over 1985	% of 1985 total	From France	% Variation over 1985	From United States	% Variation over 1985
January	1 984 935	9.7	4.2	378 189	8.7	40 301	− 6.2
February	1 760 252	4.8	3.7	361 924	− 9.5	34 573	−29.3
March	2 626 673	22.2	5.5	671 294	29.3	65 232	− 5.7
April	2 645 591	− 9.4	5.6	626 842	−18.9	45 345	−48.6
May	3 501 433	13.7	7.4	878 453	9.3	56 755	−36.3
June	4 248 450	5.7	9.0	954 825	2.1	72 702	−37.3
July	7 403 956	8.3	15.6	1 837 991	6.9	94 808	−28.8
August	9 102 854	13.8	19.2	2 611 582	5.9	100 321	−22.4
September	5 253 947	11.9	11.1	1 062 003	0.4	64 470	−35.4
October	3 279 344	6.0	6.9	826 284	− 6.1	84 286	− 6.5
November	2 398 096	15.7	5.1	492 002	− 0.3	56 913	31.6
December	3 183 262	10.7	6.7	578 352	− 4.5	54 079	13.5
Total	47 388 793	9.6	100.0	11 279 741	2.5	769 785	−22.8

(by country of nationality)

	1985	Relative share	1986	Relative share	% Variation over 1985
Austria	269 377	0.6	258 440	0.5	−4.1
Belgium	1 052 692	2.4	1 120 282	2.4	6.4
Denmark	445 063	1.0	516 207	1.1	16.0
Finland	241 193	0.6	275 781	0.6	14.3
France	11 000 818	25.4	11 279 741	23.8	2.5
Germany (F.R.)	5 644 095	13.1	5 935 429	12.5	5.2
Greece	52 019	0.1	47 957	0.1	−7.8
Iceland	20 465	0.0	13 446	0.0	−34.3
Ireland	206 710	0.5	241 796	0.5	17.0
Italy	1 022 050	2.4	1 089 996	2.3	6.6
Luxembourg	59 887	0.1	67 998	0.1	13.5
Netherlands	1 417 274	3.3	1 556 851	3.3	9.8
Norway	365 688	0.8	423 519	0.9	15.8
Portugal	7 742 427	17.9	9 523 794	20.1	23.0
Spain[2]	1 991 136	4.6	2 006 775	4.2	0.8
Sweden	540 666	1.3	622 679	1.3	15.2
Switzerland	870 447	2.0	920 948	1.9	5.8
Turkey	17 578	0.0	15 854	0.0	−9.8
United Kingdom	5 035 050	11.6	6 429 099	13.6	27.7
Other OECD-Europe[3]	159 086	0.4	176 148	0.4	10.7
Total Europe	38 153 721	88.2	42 522 740	89.7	11.5
Canada	191 087	0.4	176 880	0.4	−7.4
United States	997 774	2.3	769 785	1.6	−22.8
Total North America	1 188 861	2.7	946 665	2.0	−20.4
Australia	53 504	0.1	49 000	0.1	−8.4
New Zealand	18 973	0.0	19 110	0.0	0.7
Japan	126 639	0.3	121 072	0.3	−4.4
Total Australasia and Japan	199 116	0.5	189 182	0.4	−5.0
Total OECD Countries	39 541 698	91.5	43 658 587	92.1	10.4
Yugoslavia (S.F.R.)	29 358	0.1	38 278	0.1	30.4
Other European countries	230 599	0.5	242 304	0.5	5.1
of which: Bulgaria	8 408	0.0			
Czechoslovakia	8 772	0.0			
Hungary	14 244	0.0			
Poland	26 711	0.1			
Rumania	12 522	0.0			
USSR	159 942	0.4			
Latin America	572 934	1.3	579 700	1.2	1.2
Asia-Oceania	189 768	0.4	191 839	0.4	1.1
Africa	2 660 069	6.2	2 667 478	5.6	0.3
Origin country undetermined	10 937	0.0	10 607	0.0	−3.0
Total Non-OECD Countries	3 693 665	8.5	3 730 206	7.9	1.0
TOTAL	43 235 363	100.0	47 388 793	100.0	9.6

1. Includes 47% of arrivals of excursionists.
2. Spanish nationals residing abroad.
3. Includes arrivals from Andorra, Cyprus, Malta, Monaco, and the Vatican States.

SPAIN

ARRIVALS OF FOREIGN TOURISTS IN HOTELS[1]
(by month)

	Total number 1986	% Variation over 1985	% of 1985 total	From United Kingdom	% Variation over 1985	From United States	% Variation over 1985
January	504 093	4.5	3.7	121 074	0.8	37 244	− 4.1
February	503 621	− 3.9	3.7	118 791	−11.0	40 178	− 4.8
March	779 139	9.6	5.7	147 116	− 4.9	76 091	− 7.6
April	995 068	− 1.5	7.3	183 619	− 2.7	71 665	−37.6
May	1 584 900	25.5	11.7	535 570	95.8	65 697	−56.4
June	1 474 457	14.7	10.9	501 397	75.6	71 748	−57.2
July	1 754 192	7.9	12.9	497 539	45.9	85 519	−49.3
August	1 901 966	6.6	14.0	487 193	35.7	57 478	−51.7
September	1 693 038	10.2	12.5	494 076	32.4	74 343	−45.8
October	1 281 682	11.2	9.4	383 715	31.2	68 258	−46.8
November	587 408	7.6	4.3	154 524	6.4	34 811	−33.8
December	527 766	1.4	3.9	130 071	15.9	28 454	−26.8
Total	13 587 330	9.2	100.0	3 754 685	35.1	711 486	−42.7

(by country of nationality)

	1985	Relative share	1986	Relative share	% Variation over 1985
Austria					
Belgium	323 280	2.9			
Denmark	137 860	1.2			
Finland	74 310	0.7			
France	1 347 699	11.9			
Germany (F.R.)	2 499 864	22.1			
Greece					
Iceland					
Ireland					
Italy	1 065 347	9.4			
Luxembourg	18 651	0.2			
Netherlands	435 184	3.8			
Norway	113 188	1.0			
Portugal	283 701	2.5			
Spain					
Sweden	166 763	1.5			
Switzerland	337 627	3.0			
Turkey					
United Kingdom	2 779 377	24.6			
Other OECD-Europe					
Total Europe	9 582 851	84.6			
Canada					
United States	124 087	1.1			
Total North America	124 087	1.1			
Australia					
New Zealand					
Japan	205 381	1.8			
Total Australasia and Japan	205 381	1.8			
Total OECD Countries	9 912 319	87.6			
Yugoslavia (S.F.R.)					
Other European countries	251 954	2.2			
of which: Bulgaria					
Czechoslovakia					
Hungary					
Poland					
Rumania					
USSR					
Latin America	692 137	6.1			
Asia-Oceania					
Africa					
Origin country undetermined	464 750	4.1			
Total Non-OECD Countries	1 408 841	12.4			
TOTAL	11 321 160	100.0			

1. Arrivals recorded in hotels with "estrellas de oro" (golden stars) and "estrellas de plata" (silver stars).

SPAIN

NIGHTS SPENT BY FOREIGN TOURISTS IN HOTELS[1]
(by month)

	Total number 1986	% Variation over 1985	% of 1985 total	From United Kingdom	% Variation over 1985	From United States	% Variation over 1985
January	3 596 452	− 9.5	4.1	1 158 215	− 6.7	106 982	− 1.0
February	3 506 769	− 8.9	4.0	1 098 161	− 9.3	131 959	− 4.0
March	4 185 716	− 1.8	4.8	1 210 327	− 8.6	212 361	−11.3
April	4 776 939	− 7.2	5.4	1 393 753	− 3.2	176 667	−36.8
May	9 224 604	34.6	10.5	4 125 436	87.8	148 408	−57.4
June	10 285 187	22.6	11.7	4 527 613	71.1	159 679	−58.3
July	12 451 430	14.7	14.2	4 861 425	48.7	203 925	−46.2
August	12 976 386	10.0	14.8	4 779 492	37.8	161 057	−44.9
September	11 501 898	13.5	13.1	4 760 049	39.7	184 061	−44.8
October	8 575 688	17.1	9.8	3 589 141	37.0	169 458	−44.6
November	3 468 956	5.2	4.0	1 236 954	0.2	93 625	−24.2
December	3 147 702	3.7	3.6	1 084 089	12.1	78 418	−14.8
Total	87 697 727	11.1	100.0	33 824 655	35.2	1 826 600	−39.6

(by country of nationality)

	1985	Relative share	1986	Relative share	% Variation over 1985
Austria					
Belgium	2 569 998	3.3	2 803 079	3.2	9.1
Denmark	1 053 950	1.3	915 054	1.0	−13.2
Finland	564 616	0.7	490 207	0.6	−13.2
France	5 991 113	7.6	6 202 529	7.1	3.5
Germany (F.R.)	23 613 107	29.9	23 591 705	26.9	−0.1
Greece					
Iceland					
Ireland					
Italy	4 093 160	5.2	3 894 029	4.4	−4.9
Luxembourg	122 381	0.2	171 757	0.2	40.3
Netherlands	3 426 664	4.3	3 895 455	4.4	13.7
Norway	865 745	1.1	754 919	0.9	−12.8
Portugal	565 533	0.7	658 036	0.8	16.4
Spain					
Sweden	1 279 797	1.6	1 107 869	1.3	−13.4
Switzerland	2 067 357	2.6	2 271 681	2.6	9.9
Turkey					
United Kingdom	25 024 453	31.7	33 824 655	38.6	35.2
Other OECD-Europe					
Total Europe	71 237 874	90.3	80 580 975	91.9	13.1
Canada	483 637	0.6	341 574	0.4	−29.4
United States	2 539 092	3.2	1 485 026	1.7	−41.5
Total North America	3 022 729	3.8	1 826 600	2.1	−39.6
Australia					
New Zealand					
Japan	390 805	0.5	421 857	0.5	7.9
Total Australasia and Japan	390 805	0.5	421 857	0.5	7.9
Total OECD Countries	74 651 408	94.6	82 829 432	94.4	11.0
Yugoslavia (S.F.R.)					
Other European countries	1 310 369	1.7	1 831 754	2.1	39.8
of which: Bulgaria					
Czechoslovakia					
Hungary					
Poland					
Rumania					
USSR					
Latin America	1 602 503	2.0	1 719 701	2.0	7.3
Asia-Oceania					
Africa					
Origin country undetermined	1 354 861	1.7	1 316 840	1.5	−2.8
Total Non-OECD Countries	4 267 733	5.4	4 868 295	5.6	14.1
TOTAL	78 919 141	100.0	87 697 727	100.0	11.1

1. Nights recorded in hotels with "estrellas de oro" (golden stars) and "estrellas de plata" (silver stars).

SWEDEN

NIGHTS SPENT BY FOREIGN TOURISTS IN HOTELS
(by month)

	Total number 1986	% Variation over 1985	% of 1985 total	From Norway	% Variation over 1985	From United States	% Variation over 1985
January	131 633	− 2.7	4.0	22 201	3.7	8 427	−18.3
February	161 282	3.1	4.9	31 770	17.5	8 209	−18.1
March	179 390	− 9.5	5.4	39 104	12.0	11 846	− 8.9
April	193 622	− 2.4	5.9	41 615	7.3	14 041	− 0.3
May	267 685	7.7	8.1	49 947	23.4	30 283	−10.8
June	420 645	−14.2	12.7	69 206	− 6.1	58 644	−35.7
July	647 810	− 8.3	19.6	203 161	− 8.3	56 678	−46.7
August	493 278	−11.1	14.9	100 074	− 2.0	56 974	−44.1
September	292 778	− 4.9	8.8	45 415	5.6	40 050	−29.1
October	211 683	−10.5	6.4	45 384	4.7	16 017	−35.1
November	182 377	− 4.0	5.5	45 119	−11.6	14 161	19.9
December	126 861	0.4	3.8	28 008	2.8	10 340	20.4
Total	3 309 044	− 6.7	100.0	721 004	− 0.5	325 670	−32.5

(by country of nationality)

	1985	Relative share	1986	Relative share	% Variation over 1985
Austria [1]					
Belgium [1]					
Denmark	212 045	6.0	213 417	6.4	0.6
Finland	408 134	11.5	404 165	12.2	−1.0
France	84 424	2.4	88 221	2.7	4.5
Germany (F.R.)	420 573	11.9	453 036	13.7	7.7
Greece [1]					
Iceland [1]					
Ireland [1]					
Italy	76 070	2.1	78 925	2.4	3.8
Luxembourg [1]					
Netherlands	77 063	2.2	73 314	2.2	−4.9
Norway	724 581	20.4	722 004	21.8	−0.4
Portugal [1]					
Spain [1]					
Sweden					
Switzerland	58 143	1.6	64 096	1.9	10.2
Turkey [1]					
United Kingdom	259 063	7.3	246 460	7.4	−4.9
Other OECD-Europe					
Total Europe	2 320 096	65.4	2 343 638	70.8	1.0
Canada	28 069	0.8	21 985	0.7	−21.7
United States	482 557	13.6	325 670	9.8	−32.5
Total North America	510 626	14.4	347 655	10.5	−31.9
Australia [2]					
New Zealand [2]					
Japan	57 781	1.6	53 421	1.6	−7.5
Total Australasia and Japan	57 781	1.6	53 421	1.6	−7.5
Total OECD Countries	2 888 503	81.4	2 744 714	82.9	−5.0
Yugoslavia (S.F.R.)					
Other European countries	211 969	6.0	195 510	5.9	−7.8
of which: Bulgaria					
Czechoslovakia					
Hungary					
Poland					
Rumania					
USSR					
Latin America [2]					
Asia-Oceania [2]					
Africa [2]					
Origin country undetermined	448 004	12.6	369 220	11.2	−17.6
Total Non-OECD Countries	659 973	18.6	564 730	17.1	−14.4
TOTAL	3 548 476	100.0	3 309 444	100.0	−6.7

1. Included in "Other European countries".
2. Included in "Origin country undetermined".

SWEDEN

NIGHTS SPENT BY FOREIGN TOURISTS IN REGISTERED TOURIST ACCOMMODATION[1]
(by month)

	Total number 1986	% Variation over 1985	% of 1985 total	From Norway	% Variation over 1985	From United States	% Variation over 1985
January	160 692	3.5	2.2	23 333	− 2.3	8 688	−16.9
February	217 320	11.0	3.0	36 427	27.6	8 659	−15.8
March	258 508	10.9	3.6	48 852	25.0	12 251	− 9.2
April	219 174	− 2.9	3.0	45 502	1.1	14 625	0.3
May	300 573	7.5	4.2	54 468	22.0	31 274	−11.2
June	804 325	− 9.7	11.2	243 302	0.8	61 311	−35.5
July	2 733 663	− 4.7	38.0	1 199 273	− 0.9	59 701	−45.8
August	1 563 638	− 5.5	21.7	585 485	1.1	60 121	−42.6
September	333 417	− 5.3	4.6	50 004	4.1	41 468	−28.7
October	246 786	− 8.1	3.4	48 875	5.6	17 041	−35.0
November	199 585	− 4.9	2.8	51 276	−12.0	14 575	17.6
December	154 186	2.0	2.1	29 335	2.8	11 127	21.7
Total	7 191 867	− 3.9	100.0	2 416 132	1.0	340 841	−31.8

(by country of nationality)

	1985	Relative share	1986	Relative share	% Variation over 1985
Austria [2]					
Belgium [2]					
Denmark	606 808	8.1	627 692	8.8	3.4
Finland	634 169	8.5	652 465	9.1	2.9
France	142 773	1.9	156 808	2.2	9.8
Germany (F.R.)	1 336 901	17.9	1 285 971	17.9	−3.8
Greece [2]					
Iceland [2]					
Ireland [2]					
Italy	82 968	1.1	87 685	1.2	5.7
Luxembourg [2]					
Netherlands	471 118	6.3	378 104	5.3	−19.7
Norway	2 393 071	32.0	2 416 132	33.7	1.0
Portugal [2]					
Spain [2]					
Sweden					
Switzerland	67 169	0.9	74 412	1.0	10.8
Turkey [2]					
United Kingdom	345 991	4.6	333 103	4.6	−3.7
Other OECD-Europe					
Total Europe	6 080 968	81.2	6 012 372	83.8	−1.1
Canada	31 214	0.4	25 168	0.4	−19.4
United States	499 840	6.7	340 841	4.8	−31.8
Total North America	531 054	7.1	366 009	5.1	−31.1
Australia [3]					
New Zealand [3]					
Japan	59 928	0.8	54 689	0.8	−8.7
Total Australasia and Japan	59 928	0.8	54 689	0.8	−8.7
Total OECD Countries	6 671 950	89.1	6 433 070	89.7	−3.6
Yugoslavia (S.F.R.)					
Other European countries	283 415	3.8	278 903	3.9	−1.6
of which: Bulgaria					
Czechoslovakia					
Hungary					
Poland					
Rumania					
USSR					
Latin America [3]					
Asia-Oceania [3]					
Africa [3]					
Origin country undetermined	530 379	7.1	459 894	6.4	−13.3
Total Non-OECD Countries	813 794	10.9	738 797	10.3	−9.2
TOTAL	7 485 744	100.0	7 171 867	100.0	−4.2

1. Change of coverage in 1985. Nights spent in rented rooms, houses and flats are no longer registered.
1. Included in "Other European countries".
2. Included in "Origin country undetermined".

167

SWITZERLAND

ARRIVALS OF FOREIGN TOURISTS IN HOTELS
(by month)

	Total number 1986	% Variation over 1985	% of 1985 total	From Germany	% Variation over 1985	From United States	% Variation over 1985
January	359 180	4.9	5.2	99 764	9.1	41 361	5.8
February	435 367	1.8	6.3	121 839	3.1	44 790	− 2.4
March	616 795	9.9	9.0	212 856	9.9	66 887	− 0.9
April	453 347	− 9.9	6.6	121 302	−17.0	56 142	−28.1
May	600 896	− 4.0	8.7	193 419	21.6	79 799	−47.6
June	681 529	−19.2	9.9	184 546	− 4.8	104 506	−55.2
July	825 224	−15.6	12.0	190 765	4.4	123 800	−53.6
August	956 861	− 4.2	13.9	240 967	7.8	110 787	−46.1
September	789 370	− 8.7	11.5	238 182	5.5	119 081	−45.3
October	541 344	− 3.8	7.9	158 455	11.0	81 428	−39.8
November	292 038	1.2	4.2	67 567	3.2	33 489	−18.1
December	329 381	− 1.3	4.8	89 546	− 1.5	31 586	−15.8
Total	6 881 332	− 6.1	100.0	1 919 208	4.7	893 656	−41.2

(by country of residence)

	1985	Relative share	1986	Relative share	% Variation over 1985
Austria	146 174	2.0	146 641	2.1	0.3
Belgium	201 212	2.7	202 193	2.9	0.5
Denmark	41 352	0.6	44 311	0.6	7.2
Finland	30 513	0.4	31 380	0.5	2.8
France	530 479	7.2	563 879	8.2	6.3
Germany (F.R.)	1 833 430	25.0	1 919 208	27.9	4.7
Greece	56 773	0.8	51 880	0.8	−8.6
Iceland [1]					
Ireland	12 888	0.2	12 532	0.2	−2.8
Italy	453 373	6.2	486 635	7.1	7.3
Luxembourg	20 278	0.3	21 699	0.3	7.0
Netherlands	238 697	3.3	253 410	3.7	6.2
Norway	35 048	0.5	39 912	0.6	13.9
Portugal	31 155	0.4	32 544	0.5	4.5
Spain	157 045	2.1	170 885	2.5	8.8
Sweden	99 852	1.4	106 584	1.5	6.7
Switzerland					
Turkey	34 824	0.5	33 603	0.5	−3.5
United Kingdom	531 506	7.3	539 592	7.8	1.5
Other OECD-Europe					
Total Europe	4 454 599	60.8	4 656 888	67.7	4.5
Canada	142 342	1.9	113 725	1.7	−20.1
United States	1 519 517	20.7	893 656	13.0	−41.2
Total North America	1 661 859	22.7	1 007 381	14.6	−39.4
Australia [2]	121 508	1.7	99 146	1.4	−18.4
New Zealand [2]					
Japan	294 688	4.0	313 295	4.6	6.3
Total Australasia and Japan	416 196	5.7	412 441	6.0	−0.9
Total OECD Countries	6 532 654	89.1	6 076 710	88.3	−7.0
Yugoslavia (S.F.R.)	34 683	0.5	37 303	0.5	7.6
Other European countries	69 480	0.9	71 393	1.0	2.8
of which: Bulgaria					
Czechoslovakia					
Hungary					
Poland					
Rumania					
USSR	7 165	0.1			
Latin America	174 834	2.4	188 995	2.7	8.1
Asia-Oceania	367 660	5.0	373 542	5.4	1.6
Africa	150 381	2.1	133 389	1.9	−11.3
Origin country undetermined					
Total Non-OECD Countries	797 038	10.9	804 622	11.7	1.0
TOTAL	7 329 692	100.0	6 881 332	100.0	−6.1

1. Included in "Other European countries".
2. Australia includes New Zealand.

SWITZERLAND

ARRIVALS OF FOREIGN TOURISTS IN REGISTERED TOURIST ACCOMMODATION
(by month)

	Total number 1986	% Variation over 1985	% of 1985 total	From Germany	% Variation over 1985	From United States	% Variation over 1985
January	558 700	−0.1	6.1	235 200	−3.6	44 700	5.7
February	585 300	1.1	6.4	174 800	3.3	47 100	−1.3
March	896 300	16.4	9.8	399 600	21.3	70 200	−0.7
April	641 600	−11.0	7.0	229 000	−21.3	59 800	−26.4
May	700 300	−0.3	7.6	249 900	26.1	85 100	−46.1
June	820 200	−17.5	9.0	242 500	−7.1	114 600	−53.7
July	1 237 800	−10.1	13.5	311 000	4.6	141 300	−51.6
August	1 463 600	−1.1	16.0	437 600	6.2	123 000	−44.6
September	959 700	−7.5	10.5	334 500	4.1	125 700	−44.5
October	609 000	−2.4	6.7	195 200	11.7	86 000	−38.9
November	313 500	1.3	3.4	77 500	2.6	35 500	−17.1
December	371 500	−1.2	4.1	106 700	−1.1	34 200	−14.5
Total	9 157 500	−3.9	100.0	2 993 500	3.9	967 200	−40.0

(by country of residence)

	1985	Relative share	1986	Relative share	% Variation over 1985
Austria	182 000	1.9	182 800	2.0	0.4
Belgium	313 400	3.3	315 100	3.4	0.5
Denmark	59 500	0.6	64 400	0.7	8.2
Finland	42 000	0.4	41 600	0.5	−1.0
France	697 700	7.3	746 900	8.2	7.1
Germany (F.R.)	2 882 000	30.2	2 993 500	32.7	3.9
Greece	58 700	0.6	54 100	0.6	−7.8
Iceland [1]					
Ireland	20 900	0.2	19 000	0.2	−9.1
Italy	530 100	5.6	569 600	6.2	7.5
Luxembourg	28 400	0.3	30 200	0.3	6.3
Netherlands	475 400	5.0	519 800	5.7	9.3
Norway	41 900	0.4	46 900	0.5	11.9
Portugal	38 100	0.4	39 000	0.4	2.4
Spain	197 200	2.1	216 500	2.4	9.8
Sweden	120 700	1.3	129 900	1.4	7.6
Switzerland					
Turkey	36 100	0.4	34 700	0.4	−3.9
United Kingdom	675 600	7.1	693 800	7.6	2.7
Other OECD-Europe					
Total Europe	6 399 700	67.2	6 697 800	73.1	4.7
Canada	169 400	1.8	137 200	1.5	−19.0
United States	1 611 400	16.9	967 200	10.6	−40.0
Total North America	1 780 800	18.7	1 104 400	12.1	−38.0
Australia [2]	171 400	1.8	151 000	1.6	−11.9
New Zealand [2]					
Japan	306 900	3.2	326 300	3.6	6.3
Total Australasia and Japan	478 300	5.0	477 300	5.2	−0.2
Total OECD Countries	8 658 800	90.9	8 279 500	90.4	−4.4
Yugoslavia (S.F.R.)	37 200	0.4	40 200	0.4	8.1
Other European countries	90 000	0.9	90 900	1.0	1.0
of which: Bulgaria					
Czechoslovakia					
Hungary					
Poland					
Rumania					
USSR					
Latin America	186 200	2.0	201 500	2.2	8.2
Asia-Oceania	391 500	4.1	401 300	4.4	2.5
Africa	164 700	1.7	144 100	1.6	−12.5
Origin country undetermined					
Total Non-OECD Countries	869 600	9.1	878 000	9.6	1.0
TOTAL	9 528 400	100.0	9 157 500	100.0	−3.9

1. Included in "Other European countries".
2. Australia includes New Zealand.

SWITZERLAND

NIGHTS SPENT BY FOREIGN TOURISTS IN HOTELS
(by month)

	Total number 1986	% Variation over 1985	% of 1985 total	From Germany	% Variation over 1985	From United States	% Variation over 1985
January	1 381 922	2.2	7.1	479 735	0.1	129 398	6.8
February	1 637 690	4.3	8.4	491 445	3.2	141 237	−4.6
March	2 277 268	15.7	11.6	998 286	21.0	196 090	−0.8
April	1 247 025	−17.1	6.4	380 230	−31.7	125 241	−24.0
May	1 354 169	−2.4	6.9	459 639	17.6	160 741	−43.9
June	1 708 056	−15.2	8.7	492 386	−4.3	214 262	−51.8
July	2 286 768	−10.9	11.7	588 954	5.8	273 974	−49.8
August	2 704 409	−2.5	13.8	761 949	7.8	254 355	−42.1
September	1 993 731	−6.2	10.2	685 290	4.0	242 635	−43.0
October	1 240 208	−2.2	6.3	374 737	10.7	173 377	−37.5
November	651 332	−2.7	3.3	140 456	1.9	77 426	−25.3
December	1 078 927	−3.8	5.5	342 948	−4.1	90 219	−16.5
Total	19 561 505	−3.7	100.0	6 196 055	3.3	2 078 955	−36.3

(by country of residence)

	1985	Relative share	1986	Relative share	% Variation over 1985
Austria	340 741	1.7	340 129	1.7	−0.2
Belgium	800 075	3.9	825 210	4.2	3.1
Denmark	99 978	0.5	104 967	0.5	5.0
Finland	77 168	0.4	76 517	0.4	−0.8
France	1 612 672	7.9	1 695 151	8.7	5.1
Germany (F.R.)	5 998 347	29.5	6 196 055	31.7	3.3
Greece	147 369	0.7	137 049	0.7	−7.0
Iceland [1]					
Ireland	36 928	0.2	36 021	0.2	−2.5
Italy	912 714	4.5	977 582	5.0	7.1
Luxembourg	76 829	0.4	82 742	0.4	7.7
Netherlands	800 700	3.9	846 833	4.3	5.8
Norway	79 358	0.4	90 265	0.5	13.7
Portugal	72 233	0.4	79 949	0.4	10.7
Spain	298 169	1.5	323 350	1.7	8.4
Sweden	226 108	1.1	250 574	1.3	10.8
Switzerland					
Turkey	131 398	0.6	158 080	0.8	20.3
United Kingdom	1 933 088	9.5	2 016 612	10.3	4.3
Other OECD-Europe					
Total Europe	13 643 875	67.1	14 237 086	72.8	4.3
Canada	317 813	1.6	261 542	1.3	−17.7
United States	3 262 773	16.1	2 078 955	10.6	−36.3
Total North America	3 580 586	17.6	2 340 497	12.0	−34.6
Australia [2]	261 103	1.3	213 080	1.1	−18.4
New Zealand [2]					
Japan	515 961	2.5	536 992	2.7	4.1
Total Australasia and Japan	777 064	3.8	750 072	3.8	−3.5
Total OECD Countries	18 001 525	88.6	17 327 655	88.6	−3.7
Yugoslavia (S.F.R.)	73 000	0.4	80 588	0.4	10.4
Other European countries	213 990	1.1	211 502	1.1	−1.2
of which: Bulgaria					
Czechoslovakia					
Hungary					
Poland					
Rumania					
USSR	45 817	0.2			
Latin America	421 515	2.1	442 626	2.3	5.0
Asia-Oceania	1 101 006	5.4	1 066 649	5.5	−3.1
Africa	508 811	2.5	432 485	2.2	−15.0
Origin country undetermined					
Total Non-OECD Countries	2 318 322	11.4	2 233 850	11.4	−3.6
TOTAL	20 319 847	100.0	19 561 505	100.0	−3.7

1. Included in "Other European countries".
2. Australia includes New Zealand.

SWITZERLAND

NIGHTS SPENT BY FOREIGN TOURISTS IN REGISTERED TOURIST ACCOMMODATION
(by month)

	Total number 1986	% Variation over 1985	% of 1985 total	From Germany	% Variation over 1985	From United States	% Variation over 1985
January	3 288 700	− 2.8	9.4	1 753 500	− 6.1	152 000	5.6
February	2 753 300	1.7	7.9	885 900	2.0	154 000	− 3.0
March	4 768 300	25.7	13.7	2 797 500	32.5	212 400	− 1.4
April	2 942 700	−16.6	8.4	1 519 200	−27.5	135 000	−22.6
May	1 712 800	3.5	4.9	701 600	26.3	173 000	−42.3
June	2 298 600	−14.6	6.6	811 900	−11.1	241 300	−49.5
July	4 469 000	− 5.8	12.8	1 333 200	− 2.6	322 900	−47.2
August	5 947 500	2.7	17.0	2 238 900	6.4	300 200	−39.7
September	3 039 200	− 3.5	8.7	1 422 900	4.1	264 800	−41.3
October	1 587 700	0.5	4.5	612 300	12.0	186 900	−36.3
November	763 500	− 1.7	2.2	210 400	1.9	84 500	−23.3
December	1 357 300	− 2.0	3.9	476 600	− 1.1	100 700	−14.2
Total	34 928 600	− 0.7	100.0	14 763 900	1.9	2 327 700	−34.5

(by country of residence)

	1985	Relative share	1986	Relative share	% Variation over 1985
Austria	498 300	1.4	496 300	1.4	−0.4
Belgium	1 773 900	5.0	1 807 700	5.2	1.9
Denmark	179 400	0.5	198 900	0.6	10.9
Finland	109 200	0.3	102 300	0.3	−6.3
France	2 507 600	7.1	2 664 300	7.6	6.2
Germany (F.R.)	14 486 200	41.2	14 763 900	42.3	1.9
Greece	157 700	0.4	149 500	0.4	−5.2
Iceland [1]					
Ireland	60 800	0.2	54 500	0.2	−10.4
Italy	1 227 500	3.5	1 321 500	3.8	7.7
Luxembourg	154 200	0.4	161 600	0.5	4.8
Netherlands	2 777 400	7.9	3 057 800	8.8	10.1
Norway	98 800	0.3	111 400	0.3	12.8
Portugal	93 400	0.3	99 600	0.3	6.6
Spain	399 700	1.1	444 100	1.3	11.1
Sweden	318 700	0.9	364 000	1.0	14.2
Switzerland					
Turkey	146 500	0.4	167 200	0.5	14.1
United Kingdom	2 734 300	7.8	2 901 600	8.3	6.1
Other OECD-Europe					
Total Europe	27 723 600	78.8	28 866 200	82.6	4.1
Canada	376 000	1.1	314 500	0.9	−16.4
United States	3 552 000	10.1	2 327 700	6.7	−34.5
Total North America	3 928 000	11.2	2 642 200	7.6	−32.7
Australia [2]	359 900	1.0	315 300	0.9	−12.4
New Zealand [2]					
Japan	538 000	1.5	561 800	1.6	4.4
Total Australasia and Japan	897 900	2.6	877 100	2.5	−2.3
Total OECD Countries	32 549 500	92.5	32 385 500	92.7	−0.5
Yugoslavia (S.F.R.)	85 600	0.2	95 200	0.3	11.2
Other European countries	266 000	0.8	260 100	0.7	−2.2
of which: Bulgaria					
Czechoslovakia					
Hungary					
Poland					
Rumania					
USSR					
Latin America	464 400	1.3	490 300	1.4	5.6
Asia-Oceania	1 237 100	3.5	1 209 600	3.5	−2.2
Africa	579 800	1.6	487 900	1.4	−15.9
Origin country undetermined					
Total Non-OECD Countries	2 632 900	7.5	2 543 100	7.3	−3.4
TOTAL	35 182 400	100.0	34 928 600	100.0	−0.7

1. Included in "Other European countries".
2. Australia includes New Zealand.

TURKEY

ARRIVALS OF FOREIGN TRAVELLERS AT FRONTIERS
(by month)

	Total number 1986	% Variation over 1985	% of 1985 total	From Germany	% Variation over 1985	From United States	% Variation over 1985
January	79 502	−22.3	3.3	4 711	8.0	3 960	− 6.1
February	77 964	−27.9	3.3	4 863	23.5	4 519	25.8
March	138 794	−11.4	5.8	21 479	43.8	6 017	−34.2
April	183 026	− 8.5	7.7	26 533	0.6	6 182	−65.1
May	232 468	− 0.9	9.7	56 517	69.2	6 412	−81.1
June	234 671	− 8.0	9.8	40 400	30.3	7 992	−72.5
July	316 749	−14.0	13.2	55 924	36.4	9 707	−56.2
August	338 922	− 8.2	14.2	56 692	18.5	9 142	−46.8
September	277 927	− 7.4	11.6	56 442	21.5	8 143	−66.2
October	231 265	− 4.5	9.7	44 728	24.3	9 207	−62.4
November	151 276	− 1.6	6.3	11 960	44.4	4 988	−26.3
December	128 521	3.2	5.4	7 943	34.1	3 345	−15.3
Total	2 391 085	− 8.6	100.0	388 192	29.6	79 614	−59.4

(by country of nationality)

	1985	Relative share	1986	Relative share	% Variation over 1985
Austria	76 705	2.9	60 365	2.5	−21.3
Belgium	20 138	0.8	20 731	0.9	2.9
Denmark	8 665	0.3	14 349	0.6	65.6
Finland	13 032	0.5	17 013	0.7	30.5
France	149 950	5.7	143 971	6.0	−4.0
Germany (F.R.)	299 509	11.5	388 192	16.2	29.6
Greece	213 222	8.2	211 308	8.8	−0.9
Iceland [1]					
Ireland [1]					
Italy	74 803	2.9	87 622	3.7	17.1
Luxembourg [1]					
Netherlands	31 217	1.2	39 450	1.6	26.4
Norway	6 327	0.2	9 070	0.4	43.4
Portugal [1]					
Spain	18 853	0.7	21 955	0.9	16.5
Sweden	10 938	0.4	15 002	0.6	37.2
Switzerland	36 272	1.4	39 783	1.7	9.7
Turkey					
United Kingdom	124 677	4.8	154 231	6.5	23.7
Other OECD-Europe [1]	6 102	0.2	8 719	0.4	42.9
Total Europe	1 090 410	41.8	1 231 761	51.5	13.0
Canada	21 530	0.8	13 101	0.5	−39.2
United States	196 261	7.5	79 614	3.3	−59.4
Total North America	217 791	8.3	92 715	3.9	−57.4
Australia	22 602	0.9	20 760	0.9	−8.1
New-Zealand [2]			6 107	0.3	
Japan	16 811	0.6	16 740	0.7	−0.4
Total Australasia and Japan	39 413	1.5	43 607	1.8	10.6
Total OECD Countries	1 347 614	51.6	1 368 083	57.2	1.5
Yugoslavia (S.F.R.)	366 473	14.0	366 302	15.3	−0.0
Other European countries	178 457	6.8	146 203	6.1	−18.1
of which: Bulgaria	19 653	0.8	9 135	0.4	−53.5
Czechoslovakia	5 764	0.2	5 798	0.2	0.6
Hungary	37 486	1.4	32 615	1.4	−13.0
Poland	88 339	3.4	63 311	2.6	−28.3
Rumania	12 993	0.5	16 967	0.7	30.6
USSR	11 711	0.4	16 532	0.7	41.2
Latin America	22 434	0.9	15 539	0.6	−30.7
Asia-Oceania [3]	591 734	22.7	424 241	17.7	−28.3
Africa	101 778	3.9	69 107	2.9	−32.1
Origin country undetermined	1 806	0.1	1 610	0.1	−10.9
Total Non-OECD Countries	1 262 682	48.4	1 023 002	42.8	−19.0
TOTAL	2 610 296	100.0	2 391 085	100.0	−8.4

1. Other OECD-Europe includes: Iceland, Ireland, Luxembourg and Portugal.
2. Included in "Origin country undetermined".
3. Includes Iraq, Kuwait, Libya, Lebanon, Egypt, Syria, Saudi Arabia, Jordan, Iran and Pakistan.

TURKEY

ARRIVALS OF FOREIGN TOURISTS IN HOTELS
(by month)

	Total number 1986	% Variation over 1985	% of 1985 total	From Germany	% Variation over 1985	From United States	% Variation over 1985
January	43 085	−16.5	2.3	4 925	7.3	3 672	− 5.2
February	40 810	−18.1	2.1	5 290	28.2	4 005	2.5
March	98 492	− 0.2	5.1	29 323	−20.3	6 253	14.4
April	159 070	12.0	8.3	46 372	28.8	6 568	− 2.2
May	263 844	28.9	13.8	88 917	70.5	7 717	−29.1
June	210 569	7.4	11.0	59 518	34.1	8 424	−22.6
July	225 992	0.1	11.8	51 826	41.2	6 543	−31.6
August	281 158	11.6	14.7	57 505	49.8	7 317	−13.0
September	265 196	28.2	13.9	83 394	75.2	7 546	−28.0
October	194 679	35.7	10.2	70 006	82.6	8 967	− 1.2
November	74 074	22.2	3.9	14 633	43.6	5 318	7.1
December	56 769	19.0	3.0	7 881	68.8	3 833	− 7.4
Total	1 913 738	14.0	100.0	519 590	46.8	76 163	−13.8

(by country of nationality)

	1985	Relative share	1986	Relative share	% Variation over 1985
Austria	72 807	4.3	66 986	3.5	−8.0
Belgium [1]	51 332	3.1	70 056	3.7	36.5
Denmark [2]	23 234	1.4	28 874	1.5	24.3
Finland [2]					
France	297 543	17.7	345 697	18.1	16.2
Germany (F.R.)	353 947	21.1	519 590	27.2	46.8
Greece	53 442	3.2	47 423	2.5	−11.3
Iceland [3]					
Ireland [3]					
Italy	106 117	6.3	114 377	6.0	7.8
Luxembourg [1]					
Netherlands [1]					
Norway [2]					
Portugal [3]					
Spain	25 346	1.5	38 274	2.0	51.0
Sweden [2]					
Switzerland	28 942	1.7	40 648	2.1	40.4
Turkey					
United Kingdom	84 624	5.0	103 239	5.4	22.0
Other OECD-Europe					
Total Europe	1 097 334	65.3	1 375 164	71.9	25.3
Canada	5 553	0.3	7 001	0.4	26.1
United States	88 370	5.3	76 163	4.0	−13.8
Total North America	93 923	5.6	83 164	4.3	−11.5
Australia	4 854	0.3	9 802	0.5	101.9
New Zealand [3]					
Japan	32 956	2.0	43 074	2.3	30.7
Total Australasia and Japan	37 810	2.3	52 876	2.8	39.8
Total OECD Countries	1 229 067	73.2	1 511 204	79.0	23.0
Yugoslavia (S.F.R.)	27 971	1.7	44 699	2.3	59.8
Other European countries	77 687	4.6	67 725	3.5	−12.8
of which: Bulgaria	10 820	0.6	9 120	0.5	−15.7
Czechoslovakia					
Hungary	23 869	1.4	22 069	1.2	−7.5
Poland	38 980	2.3	32 123	1.7	−17.6
Rumania	2 742	0.2	2 340	0.1	−14.7
USSR	1 276	0.1	2 073	0.1	62.5
Latin America					
Asia-Oceania [4]	240 360	14.3	179 653	9.4	−25.3
Africa	23 194	1.4	12 224	0.6	−47.3
Origin country undetermined	81 035	4.8	98 233	5.1	21.2
Total Non-OECD Countries	450 247	26.8	402 534	21.0	−10.6
TOTAL	1 679 314	100.0	1 913 738	100.0	14.0

1. Luxembourg and Netherlands included in Belgium.
2. Finland, Norway and Sweden included in Denmark.
3. Included in "Origin Country undetermined".
4. Includes Iraq, Kuwait, Libya, Lebanon, Egypt, Syria, Saudi Arabia, Jordan, Iran and Pakistan.

TURKEY

ARRIVALS OF FOREIGN TOURISTS IN REGISTERED TOURIST ACCOMMODATION
(by month)

	Total number 1986	% Variation over 1985	% of 1985 total	From Germany	% Variation over 1985	From United States	% Variation over 1985
January	43 092	−16.5	2.1	4 926	7.3	3 672	− 5.4
February	40 846	−18.0	2.0	5 290	28.1	4 005	2.4
March	98 606	− 0.2	4.9	29 323	−20.3	6 253	13.5
April	161 835	12.7	8.0	47 105	30.4	6 584	− 3.3
May	281 358	32.7	14.0	96 076	77.1	7 954	−28.6
June	227 611	11.2	11.3	65 660	40.4	8 556	−22.7
July	240 988	2.4	12.0	57 596	49.7	6 708	−31.2
August	300 437	14.8	14.9	64 912	61.5	7 508	−12.8
September	280 301	28.0	13.9	90 231	78.5	7 656	−28.0
October	202 360	36.3	10.1	74 378	86.7	9 039	− 1.2
November	75 231	24.0	3.7	15 663	53.6	5 321	6.9
December	57 864	21.3	2.9	8 884	90.2	3 856	− 6.9
Total	2 010 529	16.0	100.0	560 044	52.8	77 112	−13.9

(by country of nationality)

	1985	Relative share	1986	Relative share	% Variation over 1985
Austria	82 108	4.7	74 852	3.7	−8.8
Belgium [1]	53 669	3.1	73 694	3.7	37.3
Denmark [2]	23 829	1.4	23 257	1.2	−2.4
Finland [2]					
France	316 448	18.3	372 800	18.6	17.8
Germany (F.R.)	366 597	21.2	560 044	28.0	52.8
Greece	53 604	3.1	47 501	2.4	−11.4
Iceland [3]					
Ireland [3]					
Italy	108 609	6.3	117 039	5.9	7.8
Luxembourg [1]					
Netherlands [1]					
Norway [2]					
Portugal [3]					
Spain	25 586	1.5	38 522	1.9	50.6
Sweden [2]					
Switzerland	30 724	1.8	44 409	2.2	44.5
Turkey					
United Kingdom	86 177	5.0	106 892	5.3	24.0
Other OECD-Europe					
Total Europe	1 147 351	66.2	1 459 010	72.9	27.2
Canada	5 691	0.3	7 085	0.4	24.5
United States	89 572	5.2	77 112	3.9	−13.9
Total North America	95 263	5.5	84 197	4.2	−11.6
Australia	4 859	0.3	9 819	0.5	102.1
New Zealand [3]					
Japan	33 092	1.9	43 244	2.2	30.7
Total Australasia and Japan	37 951	2.2	53 063	2.7	39.8
Total OECD Countries	1 280 565	73.9	1 596 270	79.8	24.7
Yugoslavia (S.F.R.)	27 996	1.6	44 800	2.2	60.0
Other European countries	77 985	4.5	68 084	3.4	−12.7
of which: Bulgaria	10 656	0.6	9 334	0.5	−12.4
Czechoslovakia					
Hungary	24 239	1.4	22 070	1.1	−8.9
Poland	39 040	2.3	32 133	1.6	−17.7
Rumania	2 744	0.2	2 344	0.1	−14.6
USSR	1 306	0.1	2 203	0.1	68.7
Latin America					
Asia-Oceania [4]	240 746	13.9	180 110	9.0	−25.2
Africa	23 247	1.3	12 350	0.6	−46.9
Origin country undetermined	82 711	4.8	98 915	4.9	19.6
Total Non-OECD Countries	452 685	26.1	404 259	20.2	−10.7
TOTAL	1 733 250	100.0	2 000 529	100.0	15.4

1. Luxembourg and Netherlands included in Belgium.
2. Finland, Norway and Sweden included in Denmark.
3. Included in "Origin Country undetermined".
4. Includes Iraq, Kuwait, Libya, Lebanon, Egypt, Syria, Saudi Arabia, Jordan, Iran and Pakistan.

TURKEY

NIGHTS SPENT BY FOREIGN TOURISTS IN HOTELS
(by month)

	Total number 1986	% Variation over 1985	% of 1985 total	From Germany	% Variation over 1985	From United States	% Variation over 1985
January	135 542	− 7.7	2.7	16 614	18.2	12 519	−9.4
February	121 458	−15.4	2.4	17 253	35.3	13 049	−4.7
March	240 597	21.0	4.8	62 229	98.3	18 451	1.1
April	361 622	13.8	7.2	109 540	40.5	17 768	0.6
May	621 597	33.5	12.3	236 874	78.2	20 404	−36.4
June	566 389	7.9	11.2	203 998	29.9	21 141	−30.4
July	634 449	2.5	12.6	188 740	33.9	19 568	−31.1
August	731 285	6.0	14.5	201 290	44.0	20 174	−18.8
September	687 577	17.7	13.7	254 412	58.0	22 412	−21.2
October	549 076	29.3	10.9	228 217	69.3	26 123	−11.5
November	219 000	15.3	4.3	56 884	45.9	16 336	− 1.4
December	167 783	18.9	3.3	32 993	102.2	10 841	−23.9
Total	5 036 375	13.3	100.0	1 609 044	52.1	218 786	−18.3

(by country of nationality)

	1985	Relative share	1986	Relative share	% Variation over 1985
Austria	321 512	7.2	231 817	4.6	−27.9
Belgium [1]	127 593	2.9	156 803	3.1	22.9
Denmark [2]	68 251	1.5	98 125	1.9	43.8
Finland [2]					
France	543 000	12.2	630 525	12.5	16.1
Germany (F.R.)	1 057 967	23.8	1 609 044	31.9	52.1
Greece	115 608	2.6	100 833	2.0	−12.8
Iceland [3]					
Ireland [3]					
Italy	217 034	4.9	239 656	4.8	10.4
Luxembourg [1]					
Netherlands [1]					
Norway [2]					
Portugal [3]					
Spain	53 223	1.2	73 295	1.5	37.7
Sweden [2]					
Switzerland	83 236	1.9	120 601	2.4	44.9
Turkey					
United Kingdom	253 759	5.7	328 187	6.5	29.3
Other OECD-Europe					
Total Europe	2 841 183	63.9	3 588 886	71.3	26.3
Canada	13 978	0.3	16 401	0.3	17.3
United States	267 889	6.0	218 786	4.3	−18.3
Total North America	281 867	6.3	235 187	4.7	−16.6
Australia	10 866	0.2	17 765	0.4	63.5
New Zealand [3]					
Japan	71 683	1.6	89 156	1.8	24.4
Total Australasia and Japan	82 549	1.9	106 921	2.1	29.5
Total OECD Countries	3 205 599	72.1	3 930 994	78.1	22.6
Yugoslavia (S.F.R.)	53 654	1.2	79 022	1.6	47.3
Other European countries	192 795	4.3	195 796	3.9	1.6
of which: Bulgaria	12 863	0.3	11 616	0.2	−9.7
Czechoslovakia					
Hungary	51 471	1.2	56 601	1.1	10.0
Poland	119 417	2.7	117 799	2.3	−1.4
Rumania	6 065	0.1	5 407	0.1	−10.8
USSR	2 979	0.1	4 373	0.1	46.8
Latin America					
Asia-Oceania [4]	681 166	15.3	492 333	9.8	−27.7
Africa	75 288	1.7	41 031	0.8	−45.5
Origin country undetermined	237 547	5.3	297 199	5.9	25.1
Total Non-OECD Countries	1 240 450	27.9	1 105 381	21.9	−10.9
TOTAL	4 446 049	100.0	5 036 375	100.0	13.3

1. Luxembourg and Netherlands included in Belgium.
2. Finland, Norway and Sweden included in Denmark.
3. Included in "Origin Country undetermined".
4. Includes Iraq, Kuwait, Libya, Lebanon, Egypt, Syria, Saudi Arabia, Jordan, Iran and Pakistan.

TURKEY

NIGHTS SPENT BY FOREIGN TOURISTS IN REGISTERED TOURIST ACCOMMODATION
(by month)

	Total number 1986	% Variation over 1985	% of 1985 total	From Germany	% Variation over 1985	From United States	% Variation over 1985
January	135 563	− 7.7	2.3	16 617	18.2	12 519	− 9.4
February	121 520	−15.4	2.0	17 253	35.2	13 049	− 4.8
March	240 870	21.0	4.1	62 229	98.1	18 451	0.8
April	369 806	15.0	6.2	111 141	41.7	17 823	0.2
May	721 564	42.0	12.2	286 413	92.5	20 835	−36.1
June	718 487	19.6	12.1	274 486	51.4	22 112	−28.5
July	812 322	14.4	13.7	268 834	72.0	20 329	−30.2
August	930 280	16.4	15.7	286 081	72.2	21 125	−17.0
September	842 091	26.1	14.2	329 547	77.0	22 977	−20.6
October	622 540	38.1	10.5	277 975	84.1	26 411	−11.0
November	234 273	23.2	3.9	71 201	82.6	16 377	− 1.3
December	182 660	29.4	3.1	47 017	188.0	10 864	−23.7
Total	5 931 976	21.6	100.0	2 048 794	73.4	222 872	−17.8

(by country of nationality)

	1985	Relative share	1986	Relative share	% Variation over 1985
Austria	433 423	8.9	312 552	5.3	−27.9
Belgium [1]	152 897	3.1	186 247	3.1	21.8
Denmark [2]	71 776	1.5	137 284	2.3	91.3
Finland [2]					
France	654 137	13.4	826 635	13.9	26.4
Germany (F.R.)	1 181 708	24.2	2 048 794	34.5	73.4
Greece	116 020	2.4	101 091	1.7	−12.9
Iceland [3]					
Ireland [3]					
Italy	236 156	4.8	264 298	4.4	11.9
Luxembourg [1]					
Netherlands [1]					
Norway [2]					
Portugal [3]					
Spain	54 109	1.1	80 353	1.4	48.5
Sweden [2]					
Switzerland	94 997	1.9	162 530	2.7	71.1
Turkey					
United Kingdom	265 663	5.4	353 020	5.9	32.9
Other OECD-Europe					
Total Europe	3 260 886	66.8	4 472 804	75.3	37.2
Canada	14 308	0.3	16 802	0.3	17.4
United States	271 143	5.6	222 872	3.8	−17.8
Total North America	285 451	5.9	239 674	4.0	−16.0
Australia	10 871	0.2	17 806	0.3	63.8
New Zealand [3]					
Japan	71 970	1.5	99 494	1.7	38.2
Total Australasia and Japan	82 841	1.7	117 300	2.0	41.6
Total OECD Countries	3 629 178	74.4	4 829 778	81.3	33.1
Yugoslavia (S.F.R.)	53 689	1.1	79 141	1.3	47.4
Other European countries	194 128	4.0	196 486	3.3	1.2
of which: Bulgaria	12 887	0.3	12 013	0.2	−6.8
Czechoslovakia					
Hungary	52 625	1.1	56 605	1.0	7.6
Poland	119 534	2.5	117 837	2.0	−1.4
Rumania	6 073	0.1	5 427	0.1	−10.6
USSR	3 009	0.1	4 604	0.1	53.0
Latin America					
Asia-Oceania [4]	682 379	14.0	494 800	8.3	−27.5
Africa	75 545	1.5	41 637	0.7	−44.9
Origin country undetermined	243 898	5.0	300 134	5.1	23.1
Total Non-OECD Countries	1 249 639	25.6	1 112 198	18.7	−11.0
TOTAL	4 878 817	100.0	5 941 976	100.0	21.8

1. Luxembourg and Netherlands included in Belgium.
2. Finland, Norway and Sweden included in Denmark.
3. Included in "Origin Country undetermined".
4. Includes Iraq, Kuwait, Libya, Lebanon, Egypt, Syria, Saudi Arabia, Jordan, Iran and Pakistan.

UNITED KINGDOM

ARRIVALS OF FOREIGN VISITORS AT FRONTIERS

	Total number 1986	% Variation over 1985	% of 1985 total	From Germany	% Variation over 1985	From United States	% Variation over 1985
January	920 000	11.7	6.7				
February	726 000	10.7	5.3	284 000	22.4	437 000	6.1
March	914 000	4.8	6.6				
April	1 025 000	−15.1	7.4				
May	1 123 000	−12.4	8.2	396 000	−11.0	523 000	−43.6
June	1 164 000	−20.7	8.5				
July	1 677 000	−8.0	12.2				
August	2 043 000	−4.8	14.8	585 000	8.3	863 000	−34.0
September	1 334 000	−8.1	9.7				
October	1 159 000	1.6	8.4				
November	883 000	9.8	6.4	324 000	21.3	462 000	−11.0
December	804 000	−0.9	5.8				
Total	13 772 000	−4.9	100.0	1 589 000	7.1	2 285 000	−27.8

(by country of residence)

	1985	Relative share	1986	Relative share	% Variation over 1985
Austria	108 100	0.7	115 800	0.8	7.1
Belgium	475 700	3.3	473 900	3.4	−0.4
Denmark	200 900	1.4	243 200	1.8	21.1
Finland	70 200	0.5	67 400	0.5	−4.0
France	1 620 300	11.2	1 750 000	12.7	8.0
Germany (F.R.)	1 484 000	10.2	1 588 600	11.5	7.0
Greece	118 300	0.8	94 100	0.7	−20.5
Iceland	21 700	0.1	28 100	0.2	29.5
Ireland	1 001 500	6.9	983 900	7.1	−1.8
Italy	494 300	3.4	487 800	3.5	−1.3
Luxembourg	27 700	0.2	19 700	0.1	−28.9
Netherlands	762 200	5.3	760 200	5.5	−0.3
Norway	237 100	1.6	279 400	2.0	17.8
Portugal	64 000	0.4	80 900	0.6	26.4
Spain	341 900	2.4	363 500	2.6	6.3
Sweden	379 700	2.6	405 800	2.9	6.9
Switzerland	338 700	2.3	342 700	2.5	1.2
Turkey	44 600	0.3	34 600	0.3	−22.4
United Kingdom					
Other OECD-Europe					
Total Europe	7 790 900	53.8	8 119 600	59.0	4.2
Canada	631 200	4.4	546 300	4.0	−13.5
United States	3 166 100	21.9	2 284 900	16.6	−27.8
Total North America	3 797 300	26.2	2 831 200	20.6	−25.4
Australia	472 700	3.3	467 400	3.4	−1.1
New Zealand	83 300	0.6	91 700	0.7	10.1
Japan	210 700	1.5	205 400	1.5	−2.5
Total Australasia and Japan	766 700	5.3	764 500	5.6	−0.3
Total OECD Countries	12 354 900	85.3	11 715 300	85.1	−5.2
Yugoslavia (S.F.R.)	26 100	0.2	35 600	0.3	36.4
Other European countries	154 800	1.1	156 900	1.1	1.4
of which: Bulgaria					
Czechoslovakia					
Hungary [1]	67 700	0.5			
Poland					
Rumania					
USSR					
Latin America	166 000	1.1	180 800	1.3	8.9
Asia-Oceania	1 077 400	7.4	1 011 600	7.3	−6.1
Africa	632 800	4.4	611 900	4.4	−3.3
Origin country undetermined	70 800	0.5	60 200	0.4	−15.0
Total Non-OECD Countries	2 127 900	14.7	2 057 000	14.9	−3.3
TOTAL	14 482 800	100.0	13 772 300	100.0	−4.9

1. Includes Bulgaria, Czechoslovakia, Hungary, Rumania, USSR, Albania, and German Democratic Republic.

177

UNITED KINGDOM

NIGHTS SPENT BY FOREIGN TOURISTS IN TOURIST ACCOMMODATION[1]

	Total number 1986	% Variation over 1985	% of 1985 total	From Germany	% Variation over 1985	From United States	% Variation over 1985
January							
February	25 377 000	− 2.3	16.3	2 733 000	36.7	3 661 000	− 8.3
March							
April							
May	32 921 000	−13.9	21.1	3 490 000	−12.2	5 241 000	−30.8
June							
July							
August	66 951 000	− 6.9	43.0	7 188 000	5.3	10 243 000	−22.4
September							
October							
November	30 440 000	− 3.3	19.6	2 795 000	56.8	5 448 000	−15.4
December							
Total	155 689 000	− 7.1	100.0	16 206 000	11.1	24 593 000	−21.2

(by country of residence)

	1985	Relative share	1986	Relative share	% Variation over 1985
Austria	1 213 000	0.7	1 395 000	0.9	15.0
Belgium	1 960 000	1.2	1 996 000	1.3	1.8
Denmark	1 983 000	1.2	2 416 000	1.6	21.8
Finland	884 000	0.5	633 000	0.4	−28.4
France	12 793 000	7.6	12 112 000	7.8	−5.3
Germany (F.R.)	14 586 000	8.7	16 206 000	10.4	11.1
Greece	1 621 000	1.0	1 344 000	0.9	−17.1
Iceland	188 000	0.1	314 000	0.2	67.0
Ireland	8 385 000	5.0	7 843 000	5.0	−6.5
Italy	6 963 000	4.2	6 042 000	3.9	−13.2
Luxembourg	184 000	0.1	94 000	0.1	−48.9
Netherlands	5 374 000	3.2	4 333 000	2.8	−19.4
Norway	2 068 000	1.2	2 361 000	1.5	14.2
Portugal	785 000	0.5	883 000	0.6	12.5
Spain [2]	5 269 000	3.1	6 089 000	3.9	15.6
Sweden	4 049 000	2.4	3 649 000	2.3	−9.9
Switzerland	4 320 000	2.6	3 391 000	2.2	−21.5
Turkey	521 000	0.3	478 000	0.3	−8.3
United Kingdom					
Other OECD-Europe					
Total Europe	73 146 000	43.6	71 579 000	46.0	−2.1
Canada	9 113 000	5.4	8 172 000	5.2	−10.3
United States	31 204 000	18.6	24 592 000	15.8	−21.2
Total North America	40 317 000	24.0	32 764 000	21.0	−18.7
Australia	11 934 000	7.1	10 861 000	7.0	−9.0
New Zealand	2 480 000	1.5	2 735 000	1.8	10.3
Japan	2 398 000	1.4	1 754 000	1.1	−26.9
Total Australasia and Japan	16 812 000	10.0	15 350 000	9.9	−8.7
Total OECD Countries	130 275 000	77.7	119 693 000	76.9	−8.1
Yugoslavia (S.F.R.)	365 000	0.2	447 000	0.3	22.5
Other European countries	2 838 000	1.7	2 824 000	1.8	−0.5
of which: Bulgaria					
Czechoslovakia					
Hungary [3]	1 487 000	0.9			
Poland					
Rumania					
USSR					
Latin America	1 783 000	1.1	1 790 000	1.1	0.4
Asia-Oceania	19 677 000	11.7	19 006 000	12.2	−3.4
Africa	11 343 000	6.8	10 617 000	6.8	−6.4
Origin country undetermined	1 378 000	0.8	1 317 000	0.8	−4.4
Total Non-OECD Countries	37 384 000	22.3	36 001 000	23.1	−3.7
TOTAL	167 659 000	100.0	155 694 000	100.0	−7.1

1. Estimates of total number of nights spent in all forms of accommodation, including stays with friends and relatives. Excluding: visitors in transit, visits of merchant seamen, airline personnel and military on duty.
2. Including Canary Islands.
3. Includes Bulgaria, Czechoslovakia, Hungary, Rumania, USSR, Albania and German Democratic Republic.

UNITED STATES

ARRIVALS OF FOREIGN TOURISTS AT FRONTIERS

	Total number 1986	% Variation over 1985	% of 1985 total	From Canada	% Variation over 1985	
January						
February						
March						
April						
May						
June						
July						
August						
September						
October						
November						
December						
Total	22 003 501	5.0	100.0	10 942 753	0.6	

(by country of residence)

	1985	Relative share	1986	Relative share	% Variation over 1985
Austria	44 581	0.2	55 938	0.3	25.5
Belgium			79 764	0.4	
Denmark			68 519	0.3	
Finland			41 609	0.2	
France	335 564	1.6	439 611	2.0	31.0
Germany (F.R.)	509 131	2.4	669 845	3.0	31.6
Greece	44 121	0.2	49 017	0.2	11.1
Iceland			9 484	0.0	
Ireland			93 925	0.4	
Italy	220 346	1.0	268 270	1.2	21.7
Luxembourg			5 362	0.0	
Netherlands	131 398	0.6	162 740	0.7	23.9
Norway			77 729	0.4	
Portugal			24 730	0.1	
Spain	90 321	0.4	108 614	0.5	20.3
Sweden			140 322	0.6	
Switzerland	149 073	0.7	182 836	0.8	22.6
Turkey			15 142	0.1	
United Kingdom	860 837	4.1	1 133 683	5.2	31.7
Other OECD-Europe	452 378	2.2			
Total Europe	2 837 750	13.5	3 627 140	16.5	27.8
Canada	10 880 131	51.8	10 942 753	49.7	0.6
United States					
Total North America	10 880 131	51.8	10 942 753	49.7	0.6
Australia	239 553	1.1	247 493	1.1	3.3
New Zealand			106 621	0.5	
Japan	1 496 202	7.1	1 681 071	7.6	12.4
Total Australasia and Japan	1 735 755	8.3	2 035 185	9.2	17.3
Total OECD Countries	15 453 636	73.5	16 605 078	75.5	7.5
Yugoslavia (S.F.R.)			22 623	0.1	
Other European countries	72 513	0.3	81 060	0.4	11.8
of which: Bulgaria					
Czechoslovakia					
Hungary					
Poland					
Rumania					
USSR	66 861	0.3			
Latin America [1]	2 600 000	12.4	3 456 216	15.7	32.9
Asia-Oceania	569 757	2.7	599 377	2.7	5.2
Africa	131 456	0.6	146 082	0.7	11.1
Origin country undetermined [2]	2 190 261	10.4	1 092 965	5.0	−50.1
Total Non-OECD Countries	5 563 987	26.5	5 398 323	24.5	−3.0
TOTAL	21 017 623	100.0	22 003 401	100.0	4.7

1. Mexico only.
2. Of which for 1985: Argentina (87 759 arrivals), Brazil (191 783 arrivals), Venezuela (161 644 arrivals), Other South America (340 926 arrivals), Central America (286 188 arrivals), Caribbean (727 422 arrivals), and Middle East (313 406 arrivals).

YUGOSLAVIA

ARRIVALS OF FOREIGN VISITORS AT FRONTIERS
(by month)

	Total number 1986	% Variation over 1985	% of 1985 total		
January	872 011	17.8	3.5		
February	605 155	− 5.9	2.4		
March	1 056 891	19.1	4.3		
April	1 200 564	0.2	4.9		
May	1 691 900	6.7	6.8		
June	2 183 291	− 9.3	8.8		
July	4 828 381	7.0	19.5		
August	5 894 837	10.9	23.8		
September	2 791 617	8.2	11.3		
October	1 478 532	3.2	6.0		
November	1 042 554	5.4	4.2		
December	1 101 311	3.8	4.5		
Total	24 747 044	5.9	100.0		

ARRIVALS OF FOREIGN TOURISTS IN HOTELS
(by month)

	Total number 1986	% Variation over 1985	% of 1985 total	From Germany	% Variation over 1985	From United States	% Variation over 1985
January	63 074	− 4.2	1.2	10 423	− 1.5	2 620	−26.8
February	72 493	− 3.6	1.4	10 489	4.5	2 729	−41.4
March	191 057	25.8	3.8	54 447	26.1	4 737	−41.9
April	270 109	−19.0	5.3	67 992	−13.5	7 335	−48.2
May	605 888	5.5	12.0	189 606	11.6	12 891	−53.7
June	660 900	− 8.2	13.1	163 686	−15.5	19 892	−35.1
July	813 224	− 0.8	16.1	202 345	1.8	21 091	−40.0
August	993 127	− 0.4	19.6	269 050	− 0.2	16 363	−38.1
September	765 008	4.2	15.1	217 634	6.5	21 089	−38.3
October	379 504	1.6	7.5	124 651	14.7	13 906	−46.2
November	119 864	1.7	2.4	29 488	19.3	5 363	− 7.8
December	121 289	18.5	2.4	21 396	43.3	3 263	− 7.5
Total	5 055 537	− 0.2	100.0	1 361 207	2.6	131 279	−40.3

NIGHTS SPENT BY FOREIGN TOURISTS IN HOTELS
(by month)

	Total number 1986	% Variation over 1985	% of 1985 total	From Germany	% Variation over 1985	From United States	% Variation over 1985
January	220 990	− 9.7	0.8	50 706	− 6.3	7 461	−41.2
February	273 094	− 1.8	1.0	47 523	16.6	8 349	−44.9
March	617 301	18.5	2.2	228 146	38.0	12 179	−55.0
April	920 913	−20.1	3.3	267 724	−25.2	18 833	−52.9
May	2 983 573	8.4	10.8	1 137 485	14.7	30 163	−51.3
June	4 141 345	− 6.6	15.0	1 362 415	−18.5	40 970	−34.2
July	5 341 550	2.0	19.4	1 696 225	1.6	46 641	−35.2
August	5 804 263	1.2	21.1	2 016 820	2.8	37 105	−37.1
September	4 690 130	5.2	17.0	1 711 058	3.1	48 563	−36.4
October	1 826 707	2.5	6.6	707 585	14.9	34 605	−38.8
November	312 574	−14.6	1.1	90 086	− 6.2	13 929	−20.3
December	392 283	27.1	1.4	114 209	77.4	8 107	−18.5
Total	27 524 723	0.9	100.0	9 429 982	0.9	306 905	−39.9

YUGOSLAVIA

ARRIVALS OF FOREIGN TOURISTS IN REGISTERED TOURIST ACCOMMODATION
(by month)

	Total number 1986	% Variation over 1985	% of 1985 total	From Germany	% Variation over 1985	From United States	% Variation over 1985
January	79 400	− 6.4	0.9	15 300	−13.7	2 724	−26.6
February	86 598	− 3.4	1.0	13 789	−11.6	2 837	−40.6
March	211 178	25.0	2.5	61 254	23.5	4 988	−39.9
April	302 928	−17.1	3.6	79 423	−10.7	7 629	−47.2
May	761 098	7.0	9.0	268 808	11.1	13 811	−52.6
June	1 038 110	− 8.1	12.3	308 929	−18.5	22 018	−33.9
July	1 925 773	0.3	22.8	577 149	3.3	25 572	−37.1
August	2 237 933	0.2	26.4	731 542	1.6	20 672	−34.4
September	1 103 111	4.0	13.0	374 429	3.3	23 181	−36.5
October	431 362	2.7	5.1	142 186	13.9	14 573	−44.9
November	140 809	6.3	1.7	36 756	28.1	5 586	− 6.2
December	145 727	20.7	1.7	28 651	34.5	3 528	− 2.7
Total	**8 464 027**	**0.3**	**100.0**	**2 638 216**	**1.1**	**147 119**	**−38.3**

(by country of residence)

	1985	Relative share	1986	Relative share	% Variation over 1985
Austria	765 155	9.1	781 443	9.2	2.1
Belgium	133 982	1.6	120 203	1.4	−10.3
Denmark	153 551	1.8	176 456	2.1	14.9
Finland	28 042	0.3	23 492	0.3	−16.2
France	456 240	5.4	412 352	4.9	−9.6
Germany (F.R.)	2 608 629	30.9	2 638 216	31.2	1.1
Greece	129 782	1.5	119 338	1.4	−8.0
Iceland [1]	6 168	0.1	3 343	0.0	−45.8
Ireland [1]	13 159	0.2	13 465	0.2	2.3
Italy	1 108 838	13.1	1 073 387	12.7	−3.2
Luxembourg [1]					
Netherlands	418 771	5.0	426 934	5.0	1.9
Norway	44 030	0.5	42 722	0.5	−3.0
Portugal [1]	7 647	0.1	6 608	0.1	−13.6
Spain [1]	47 926	0.6	55 738	0.7	16.3
Sweden	97 321	1.2	118 357	1.4	21.6
Switzerland	127 528	1.5	122 328	1.4	−4.1
Turkey	98 566	1.2	89 173	1.1	−9.5
United Kingdom	595 119	7.1	625 005	7.4	5.0
Other OECD-Europe					
Total Europe	**6 840 454**	**81.1**	**6 848 560**	**80.9**	**0.1**
Canada	39 501	0.5	34 434	0.4	−12.8
United States	238 405	2.8	147 119	1.7	−38.3
Total North America	**277 906**	**3.3**	**181 553**	**2.1**	**−34.7**
Australia [2]	25 690	0.3	27 632	0.3	7.6
New Zealand [2]	4 699	0.1	6 292	0.1	33.9
Japan	10 042	0.1	11 624	0.1	15.8
Total Australasia and Japan	**40 431**	**0.5**	**45 548**	**0.5**	**12.7**
Total OECD Countries	**7 158 791**	**84.9**	**7 075 661**	**83.6**	**−1.2**
Yugoslavia (S.F.R.)					
Other European countries	1 125 730	13.3	1 182 068	14.0	5.0
of which: Bulgaria	30 407	0.4	23 856	0.3	−21.5
Czechoslovakia	430 907	5.1	420 328	5.0	−2.5
Hungary	200 301	2.4	225 964	2.7	12.8
Poland	99 579	1.2	162 065	1.9	62.8
Rumania	16 765	0.2	15 301	0.2	−8.7
USSR	225 074	2.7	264 037	3.1	17.3
Latin America [2]					
Asia-Oceania [2]					
Africa [2]					
Origin country undetermined	151 206	1.8	206 298	2.4	36.4
Total Non-OECD Countries	**1 276 936**	**15.1**	**1 388 366**	**16.4**	**8.7**
TOTAL	**8 435 727**	**100.0**	**8 464 027**	**100.0**	**0.3**

1. Included in "Other European countries".
2. Included in "Origin country undetermined".

YUGOSLAVIA

NIGHTS SPENT BY FOREIGN TOURISTS IN REGISTERED TOURIST ACCOMMODATION
(by month)

	Total number 1986	% Variation over 1985	% of 1985 total	From Germany	% Variation over 1985	From United States	% Variation over 1985
January	258 084	– 9.6	0.5	58 376	– 7.2	7 685	–41.6
February	314 917	0.3	0.6	55 272	14.7	8 608	–44.4
March	687 330	20.0	1.3	245 478	39.5	13 131	–52.7
April	1 024 523	–18.4	2.0	293 552	–23.3	19 741	–52.1
May	3 735 204	12.3	7.3	1 567 834	19.4	32 978	–49.7
June	6 461 590	– 9.4	12.6	2 437 413	–22.8	50 259	–30.9
July	13 796 913	0.7	26.8	4 988 945	2.8	68 832	–32.3
August	15 096 243	1.7	29.4	6 092 019	6.3	59 183	–30.8
September	7 111 366	6.8	13.8	2 956 646	4.1	56 595	–33.2
October	2 071 478	6.0	4.0	789 714	19.0	37 013	–36.7
November	380 148	– 9.0	0.7	106 511	2.6	14 875	–17.8
December	461 745	33.8	0.9	135 764	78.8	8 908	–13.5
Total	51 399 541	1.1	100.0	19 727 524	1.6	377 808	–36.5

(by country of residence)

	1985	Relative share	1986	Relative share	% Variation over 1985
Austria	5 280 291	10.4	5 200 003	10.1	–1.5
Belgium	845 404	1.7	721 020	1.4	–14.7
Denmark	993 238	2.0	1 142 789	2.2	15.1
Finland	176 092	0.3	137 600	0.3	–21.9
France	1 543 527	3.0	1 440 503	2.8	–6.7
Germany (F.R.)	19 410 269	38.2	19 727 524	38.4	1.6
Greece	173 833	0.3	166 890	0.3	–4.0
Iceland [1]	39 697	0.1	11 250	0.0	–71.7
Ireland [1]	61 819	0.1	83 525	0.2	35.1
Italy	4 965 718	9.8	4 645 276	9.0	–6.5
Luxembourg [1]					
Netherlands	2 898 402	5.7	3 025 524	5.9	4.4
Norway	330 752	0.7	328 364	0.6	–0.7
Portugal [1]	25 991	0.1	17 056	0.0	–34.4
Spain [1]	92 107	0.2	99 299	0.2	7.8
Sweden	571 341	1.1	706 890	1.4	23.7
Switzerland	621 753	1.2	587 851	1.1	–5.5
Turkey	118 567	0.2	108 898	0.2	–8.2
United Kingdom	4 963 210	9.8	5 324 833	10.4	7.3
Other OECD-Europe					
Total Europe	43 112 011	84.8	43 475 095	84.6	0.8
Canada	112 269	0.2	97 435	0.2	–13.2
United States	594 562	1.2	377 808	0.7	–36.5
Total North America	706 831	1.4	475 243	0.9	–32.8
Australia [2]	56 450	0.1	58 084	0.1	2.9
New Zealand [2]	10 060	0.0	12 467	0.0	23.9
Japan	20 082	0.0	24 594	0.0	22.5
Total Australasia and Japan	86 592	0.2	95 145	0.2	9.9
Total OECD Countries	43 905 434	86.4	44 045 483	85.7	0.3
Yugoslavia (S.F.R.)					
Other European countries	6 371 257	12.5	6 665 422	13.0	4.6
of which: Bulgaria	84 399	0.2	56 546	0.1	–33.0
Czechoslovakia	3 680 828	7.2	3 603 921	7.0	–2.1
Hungary	842 835	1.7	1 034 873	2.0	22.8
Poland	463 443	0.9	773 755	1.5	67.0
Rumania	121 508	0.2	83 410	0.2	–31.4
USSR	618 222	1.2	737 834	1.4	19.3
Latin America [2]					
Asia-Oceania [2]					
Africa [2]					
Origin country undetermined	539 142	1.1	688 636	1.3	27.7
Total Non-OECD Countries	6 910 399	13.6	7 354 058	14.3	6.4
TOTAL	50 815 833	100.0	51 399 541	100.0	1.1

1. Included in "Other European countries".
2. Included in "Origin country undetermined".

9. Average length of stay of foreign tourists

	Tourists from all foreign countries			Tourists from Europe (OECD)			Tourists from North America (OECD)			Tourists from Pacific (OECD)		
	1984	1985	1986	1984	1985	1986	1984	1985	1986	1984	1985	1986
	Average length of stay in tourist accommodation[1]											
Austria	5.7	5.6	5.7	6.2	6.1	6.0	2.4	2.4	2.8	2.1	2.1	2.1
France	9.0	9.0	9.2	8.4	8.3	8.5	11.2	11.5	14.2	7.0	6.9	7.1
Germany	2.2	2.2	2.3	2.2	2.2	2.3	1.9	1.9	2.0	1.8	1.8	1.8
Italy	4.9	4.9	5.2	5.9	5.8	5.8	2.5	2.6	2.9	2.4	2.4	2.3
Luxembourg												
Netherlands	2.8	2.8		3.1	3.1		1.8	1.8		1.8	2.0	
Portugal	4.4	4.5	4.7	4.9	4.9	5.0	2.8	3.0	3.2	2.5	2.5	2.3
Switzerland	3.7	3.7	3.8	4.3	4.3	4.3	2.2	2.2	2.4	1.9	1.9	1.8
Turkey	2.7	2.8	3.0	2.7	2.8	3.1	3.2	3.0	2.8	2.0	2.2	2.2
Yugoslavia	5.9	6.0	6.1	6.1	6.3	6.3	2.7	2.5	2.6	2.8	2.1	2.1

1. Average length of stay in tourist accommodation is obtained by dividing the number of nights recorded in particular means of accommodation by the number of arrivals of tourists at the same means of accommodation (see country tables).

	Tourists from all foreign countries			Tourists from Europe (OECD)			Tourists from North America (OECD)			Tourists from Pacific (OECD)		
	1984	1985	1986	1984	1985	1986	1984	1985	1986	1984	1985	1986
	Average length of stay in the country visited[1]											
Greece[2]	14.0	14.0	14.0									
Ireland[3]	10.0	10.0	9.8	9.0	11.0	9.6	10.0	10.0	11.2	13.0	12.0	12.0
Portugal[2]	8.9	8.4		8.8	8.5		12.5	10.0		4.8	6.1	
Spain	6.8	6.3	6.5				2.5	2.4	2.6	2.6	2.5	2.4
United Kingdom	11.0	12.0	11.0	9.0	9.0	9.0	11.0	11.0	12.0	21.0	22.0	20.0
Canada	5.9	5.9	5.9	14.4	14.2	13.8	4.7	4.7	4.7	9.5	8.8	9.8
Australia	30.0			38.0			27.0			18.0		
Japan	11.1	11.4	13.0									

1. Average length of stay in the country visited expressed in number of nights spent.
2. Greece and Portugal : number of days.
3. Ireland : excluding visitors from Northern Ireland.

10. Nights spent by foreign and domestic tourists in all means of accommodation[1]

In thousands

	Nights spent by foreign tourists			Nights spent by domestic tourists			Total nights			Proportion spent by foreign tourists (%)	
	1985	1986	% 86/85	1985	1986	% 86/85	1985	1986	% 86/85	1985	1986
Austria	85 075.9	85 393.3	0.4	27 510.4	28 228.0	2.6	112 586.2	113 621.3	0.9	75.6	75.2
Belgium	9 843.5	9 815.8	−0.3	21 296.9	21 824.6	2.5	31 140.4	31 640.3	1.6	31.6	31.0
Denmark	8 971.5	8 511.0	−5.1	11 444.3	11 756.1	2.7	20 415.8	20 267.2	−0.7	43.9	42.0
Finland[2]	2 487.1	2 294.2	−7.8	8 431.9	8 572.2	1.7	10 919.0	10 866.4	−0.5	22.8	21.1
France[3]	329 595.0	332 208.0	0.8								
Germany	32 005.2	31 735.6	−0.8	198 682.4	203 420.5	2.4	230 687.5	235 156.2	1.9	13.9	13.5
Italy	96 524.5	99 694.3	3.3	239 768.6			336 293.0			28.7	
Norway[4]	5 254.5	5 039.1	−4.1	11 115.2	11 542.3	3.8	16 369.7	16 581.4	1.3	32.1	30.4
Portugal[3]	14 932.9	16 788.3	12.4	12 345.1	11 517.2	−6.7	27 278.0	28 305.6	3.8	54.7	59.3
Sweden	7 485.7	7 171.9	−4.2	24 688.7	26 097.6	5.7	32 174.5	33 269.5	3.4	23.3	21.6
Switzerland	35 182.4	34 928.6	−0.7	38 541.0	38 947.8	1.1	73 723.4	73 876.4	0.2	47.7	47.3
Turkey[5]	5 014.9	6 126.8	22.2	4 648.2	4 950.5	6.5	9 663.1	11 077.3	14.6	51.9	55.3
Canada[6]	77 125.7	91 470.5	18.6	258 212.0			349 682.5				26.2
Yugoslavia	50 815.8	51 459.5	1.3	58 321.6	59 734.1	2.4	109 137.5	111 193.7	1.9	46.6	46.3

1. For "Types of accommodation covered by the statistics", see Table A of the annex.
2. Finland: see notes to tables 11 and 12.
3. France and Portugal: see notes to table 11.
4. Norway: see notes to table 12.
5. Turkey: figures based on a monthly sample survey carried out amoung establishments licenced by the Ministry of Tourism and Culture.
6. Canada: person-nights: covers all forms of accommodation, including homes of friends or relatives and rented chalets; domestic figures based on a biennial survey.

11. Nights spent by foreign and domestic tourists in hotels and similar establishments[1]

In thousands

	Nights spent by foreign tourists			Nights spent by domestic tourists			Total nights			Proportion spent by foreign tourists (%)	
	1985	1986	% 86/85	1985	1986	% 86/85	1985	1986	% 86/85	1985	1986
Austria	54 587.9	54 532.4	−0.1	13 948.2	14 282.2	2.4	68 536.1	68 814.6	0.4	79.6	79.2
Belgium	5 536.2	5 292.4	−4.4	2 371.7	2 419.6	2.0	7 907.9	7 712.0	−2.5	70.0	68.6
Denmark	4 590.7	4 338.3	−5.5	4 153.1	4 442.7	7.0	8 743.8	8 781.0	0.4	52.5	49.4
Finland[2]	2 097.1	2 021.7	−3.6	6 691.9	6 872.3	2.7	8 789.0	8 894.0	1.2	23.9	22.7
France[3]	18 166.4	15 046.3	−17.2	9 986.7	10 693.3	7.1	28 153.1	25 739.7	−8.6	64.5	58.5
Germany	23 895.3	23 472.5	−1.8	104 614.4	107 826.3	3.1	128 509.7	131 298.8	2.2	18.6	17.9
Italy	63 786.5	65 122.8	2.1	106 998.3			170 784.8			37.3	
Norway	3 712.6	3 297.7	−11.2	8 192.6	8 356.1	2.0	11 905.2	11 653.9	−2.1	31.2	28.3
Portugal[4]	12 940.5	14 283.6	10.4	5 716.2	5 416.8	−5.2	18 656.7	19 700.5	5.6	69.4	72.5
Spain[5]	78 919.1	87 697.7	11.1	42 096.7	41 816.4	−0.7	121 015.8	129 514.1	7.0	65.2	67.7
Sweden	3 548.5	3 309.0	−6.7	11 984.2	12 444.8	3.8	15 532.7	15 753.8	1.4	22.8	21.0
Switzerland	20 319.9	19 561.5	−3.7	13 013.1	13 226.4	1.6	33 333.0	32 787.9	−1.6	61.0	59.7
Turkey[6]	4 446.0	5 036.4	13.3	4 262.8	4 509.0	5.8	8 708.9	9 545.4	9.6	51.1	52.8
Canada[7]				47 502.0							
Yugoslavia	27 270.1	27 584.7	1.2	22 501.4	23 125.2	2.8	49 771.5	50 709.9	1.9	54.8	54.4

1. For "Types of accommodation covered by the statistics", see Table A of the annex.
2. Finland: change of coverage; from 1986 no longer includes "holiday villages".
3. France: data concerns Ile-de-France region only.
4. Portugal: hotels includes "studio-hotels", "holiday flats", and "holiday villages".
5. Spain: hotels includes "paradors" and boarding houses.
6. Turkey: hotels includes thermal resorts in 1985.
7. Canada: includes nights spent by canadians in the United States with final destination in Canada.

12. Nights spent by foreign and domestic tourists in supplementary means of accommodation[1]

In thousands

	Nights spent by foreign tourists			Nights spent by domestic tourists			Total nights			Proportion spent by foreign tourists (%)	
	1985	1986	% 86/85	1985	1986	% 86/85	1985	1986	% 86/85	1985	1986
Austria	30 488.0	30 861.0	1.2	13 562.2	13 945.8	2.8	44 050.1	44 806.8	1.7	69.2	68.9
Belgium	4 307.3	4 523.4	5.0	18 925.2	19 405.0	2.5	23 232.5	23 928.3	3.0	18.5	18.9
Denmark	4 380.8	4 172.7	−4.8	7 291.2	7 313.4	0.3	11 672.0	11 486.2	−1.6	37.5	36.3
Finland[2]	390.0	272.5	−30.1	1 740.0	1 699.8	−2.3	2 130.0	1 972.4	−7.4	18.3	13.8
France											
Germany	8 109.9	8 263.1	1.9	94 067.9	95 594.2	1.6	102 177.8	103 857.3	1.6	7.9	8.0
Italy	32 738.0	34 571.5	5.6	132 770.2			165 508.3			19.8	
Netherlands											
Norway[3]	1 541.8	1 741.4	12.9	2 922.6	3 186.1	9.0	4 464.5	4 927.5	10.4	34.5	35.3
Portugal	1 992.4	2 504.7	25.7	6 628.8	6 100.4	−8.0	8 621.2	8 605.1	−0.2	23.1	29.1
Sweden[4]	3 937.3	3 862.8	−1.9	12 704.6	13 652.8	7.5	16 641.8	17 515.6	5.3	23.7	22.1
Switzerland	14 862.5	15 367.1	3.4	25 527.9	25 721.4	0.8	40 390.4	41 088.5	1.7	36.8	37.4
Turkey	568.9	1 090.4	91.7	385.4	441.5	14.6	954.3	1 531.9	60.5	59.6	71.2
Canada[5]				210 710.0							
Australia											
Yugoslavia	23 545.8	23 874.8	1.4	35 820.2	36 608.9	2.2	59 366.0	60 483.8	1.9	39.7	39.5

Of which: **on camping sites**

	1985	1986	% 86/85	1985	1986	% 86/85	1985	1986	% 86/85	1985	1986
Austria	5 067.9	4 961.0	−2.1	1 179.2	1 215.7	3.1	6 247.1	6 176.7	−1.1	81.1	80.3
Belgium	1 839.0	2 024.0	10.1	7 423.2	7 726.4	4.1	9 262.3	9 750.4	5.3	19.9	20.8
Denmark	3 986.4	3 779.5	−5.2	6 849.7	6 846.8	0.0	10 836.1	10 626.3	−1.9	36.8	35.6
Finland[2]	390.0	272.5	−30.1	1 740.0	1 699.8	−2.3	2 130.0	1 972.4	−7.4	18.3	13.8
France											
Germany	3 926.0	3 923.5	−0.1	13 679.7	12 627.7	−7.7	17 605.6	16 551.2	−6.0	22.3	23.7
Italy											
Netherlands											
Norway	1 326.0	1 535.0	15.8	2 746.0	3 016.0	9.8	4 072.0	4 551.0	11.8	32.6	33.7
Portugal	1 911.4	2 420.6	26.6	5 788.8	5 320.3	−8.1	7 700.2	7 740.9	0.5	24.8	31.3
Spain											
Sweden	3 159.5	3 017.5	−4.5	9 424.1	10 134.9	7.5	12 583.6	13 152.4	4.5	25.1	22.9
Switzerland	2 044.6	2 201.3	7.7	4 912.5	4 982.6	1.4	6 957.1	7 183.9	3.3	29.4	30.6
Turkey	136.1	194.8	43.1	90.7	67.0	−26.1	226.8	261.8	15.5	60.0	74.4
Canada[5]				24 484.0							
Australia											
Yugoslavia	13 346.7	13 190.5	−1.2	7 100.9	7 554.2	6.4	20 447.6	20 744.7	1.5	65.3	63.6

Of which: **in youth hostels**

	1985	1986	% 86/85	1985	1986	% 86/85	1985	1986	% 86/85	1985	1986
Austria	502.5	520.7	3.6	547.1	537.7	−1.7	1 049.5	1 058.4	0.8	47.9	49.2
Denmark	394.4	393.2	−0.3	441.5	466.6	5.7	835.9	859.9	2.9	47.2	45.7
Germany	889.1	902.3	1.5	10 060.0	9 858.2	−2.0	10 949.1	10 760.6	−1.7	8.1	8.4
Italy											
Netherlands											
Norway	215.8	206.4	−4.4	176.6	170.1	−3.7	392.5	376.5	−4.1	55.0	54.8
Sweden	210.9	203.3	−3.6	701.2	740.4	5.6	912.1	943.7	3.5	23.1	21.5
Switzerland	475.4	467.6	−1.6	333.9	334.2	0.1	809.3	801.8	−0.9	58.7	58.3
Australia											
Yugoslavia	359.9	376.3	4.6	4 306.7	4 646.2	7.9	4 666.6	5 022.5	7.6	7.7	7.5

Of which: **in private rooms, rented apartments and houses**

	1985	1986	% 86/85	1985	1986	% 86/85	1985	1986	% 86/85	1985	1986
Austria	16 957.1	16 567.2	−2.3	4 440.6	4 569.9	2.9	21 397.7	21 137.0	−1.2	79.2	78.4
Belgium	973.0	883.0	−9.2	6 926.1	6 752.2	−2.5	7 899.1	7 635.3	−3.3	12.3	11.6
Germany	1 496.1	1 630.0	8.9	14 195.7	15 315.7	7.9	15 691.9	16 945.7	8.0	9.5	9.6
Italy											
Sweden											
Switzerland	10 065.0	10 400.0	3.3	13 935.0	14 050.0	0.8	24 000.0	24 450.0	1.9	41.9	42.5
Australia											
Yugoslavia	8 764.5	9 274.7	5.8	10 811.2	10 650.2	−1.5	19 575.7	19 924.9	1.8	44.8	46.5

1. For "Types of accommodatiom covered by the statistics", see Table A of the annex.
2. Finland: change in coverage; since 1986 also includes holiday villages.
3. Norway: nights spent on camping sites are not included for 1985.
4. Sweden: change in coverage in 1985. Nights spent in rented rooms, houses, and flats are no longer registered.
5. Canada: person-nights: includes nights spent by Canadians in the United States with final destination in Canada.

13. Capacity in hotels and similar establishments

In thousands

	Hotels			Motels			Boarding houses			Inns			Others			Total		
	1985	1986	% 86/85	1985	1986	% 86/85	1985	1986	% 86/85	1985	1986	% 86/85	1985	1986	% 86/85	1985	1986	% 86/85
Austria[1]																653.8	655.2	0.2
Belgium[2]	86.9	86.8	-0.1													86.9	86.8	-0.1
Denmark[3]																71.0	73.6	3.7
Finland[4]	61.9	63.0	1.8							7.9	7.2	-8.7	7.4	7.4	0.5	77.1	77.6	0.6
France[5]	993.4															993.4		
Germany[6]	679.1	689.8	1.6				147.7	144.1	-2.4	249.8	247.9	-0.8				1 076.6	1 081.7	0.5
Greece[7]	308.6	315.8	2.3	2.6	3.2	22.6	13.3	14.3	7.7	4.9	5.0	3.5	4.8	5.3	9.4	334.2	343.6	2.8
Ireland[8]	39.4	39.6	0.6				4.0	4.0	-0.6							43.4	43.6	0.5
Italy																		
Netherlands																		
Norway[9]													97.2	101.9	4.8	97.2	101.9	4.8
Portugal[10]	64.9			0.8			39.5			3.6			22.1			131.0	142.3	8.7
Spain[11]	622.4	637.1	2.4				170.7	155.2	-9.1				220.9	227.8	3.1	1 014.0	1 020.0	0.6
Sweden[12]	84.0	103.9	23.6	20.4			46.6	44.5	-4.4							151.1	148.5	-1.7
Switzerland[13]	236.6	237.6	0.5	7.1	7.2	1.7	2.4	2.4	-0.7	31.7	32.2	1.6				275.4	277.1	0.6
Turkey[14]	51.0	60.5	18.7	8.5	5.4	-36.3	2.7	3.0	8.6					0.1		64.0	71.3	11.5
Australia[15]	90.2			223.8												314.0		
Yugoslavia[16]	298.6	314.1	5.2	10.5	10.9	3.6	4.4	4.3	-2.1	1.6	2.1	34.8	6.2	6.5	5.2	321.3	338.0	5.2

Notice : this table contains data on available bed capacity unless otherwise stated in the following notes by country.

1. Austria : position at 31st August.
2. Belgium : hotels includes motels, inns and boarding houses. Others includes non-licenced establishments.
3. Denmark : position at 31st July.
4. Finland : position at 31st December. Hotels includes motels. Boarding houses includes inns. Others includes some youth hostels and holiday villages.
5. France : position at April.
6. Germany : position at April.
7. Greece : motels includes bungalows.
8. Ireland : hotels includes motels. Boarding houses includes inns.
9. Norway : position at 31st December.
10. Portugal : position at 31st July. Hotels includes studio-hotels. Inns includes private and State-owned inns. Others includes holiday flats and villages.
11. Spain : position at 31st December. Boarding houses = «fondas» and «casas de huespedes».
12. Sweden : hotels include motels (since 1986) and boarding houses includes resort hotels.
13. Switzerland : position at 31st December. Hotels includes boarding houses.
14. Turkey : position at 31st December. Hotels includes boarding houses.
15. Australia : position at December. Number of rooms.
16. Yugoslavia : position at 31st August.

14. Capacity in supplementary means of accommodation

In thousands

	Youth hostels			Camping sites — Places			Holiday villages			Rented rooms, houses and flats			Sanatoria and health establishments			Recreational camps			Others			Total		
	1985	1986	% 86/85	1985	1986	% 86/85	1985	1986	% 86/85	1985	1986	% 86/85	1985	1986	% 86/85	1985	1986	% 86/85	1985	1986	% 86/85	1985	1986	% 86/85
Austria [1]	9.2	10.5	14.8				86.9	98.2	13.1	368.2	351.5	-4.5	16.9	17.6	4.5	30.4	30.1	-1.2	28.0	26.7	-4.7	539.6	534.7	-0.9
Belgium [2]				339.5	356.7	5.1							2.6	3.7	41.7	27.2	27.2	0.2	48.1	53.0	10.3	417.4	440.7	5.6
Denmark	9.7	9.9	2.2																			9.7	9.9	2.2
France [3]	20.2			2498.0			201.0												262.1			2981.3		
Germany [4]	93.1	93.0	-0.1				30.7	31.2	1.5	143.2	152.3	6.3	115.4	115.9	0.5				121.2	123.9	2.3	503.6	516.3	2.5
Greece [5]				62.4	65.8	5.5				5.0	5.0	0.0							8.9	8.9	0.0	188.0	95.4	-49.3
Italy																								
Netherlands	6.8	6.4	-7.0																			6.8	6.4	-7.0
Norway																9.0								
Portugal [6]				215.2			8.3	8.3	0.0													224.1		
Spain	14.4	14.7	1.8	385.4	406.5	5.5	41.2	40.5	-1.5	298.0	290.0	-2.7	6.8	6.7	-1.8				8311.5	9235.0	11.1	9003.2	9939.8	10.4
Sweden	7.9	8.0	1.3	320.0	350.0	9.4							0.3	0.3	0.0				1.6	2.0	22.3	305.6	405.2	32.6
Switzerland [7]				270.0	274.0	1.5	8.9	10.6	20.0	360.0	360.0	0.0							214.0	236.0	10.3	858.7	884.7	3.0
Turkey [8]				10.6	7.9	-25.4																11.0	20.8	88.8
Canada	3.4																					3.4		
Australia [9]				209.8																		209.8		
Yugoslavia [10]	58.1	62.6	7.8	346.4	353.9	2.2	114.1	109.2	-4.3	383.7	419.2	9.2	15.5	17.1	10.6				21.7	21.9	0.8	939.6	983.9	4.7

Notice: this table contains data on available bed capacity, unless otherwise stated in the following notes by country.
1. Austria: others includes mountain huts and shelters, 8.3 thousand beds in 1985.
2. Belgium: others includes youth hostels, holiday villages and social tourism establishments.
3. France: others includes shelters, rooms in families' homes, and guesthouses.
4. Germany: youth hostels includes mountain huts and shelters. Others includes holiday centers, holiday houses and educational centers.
5. Greece: others includes holiday centers. In addition to these supplementary means of accomodation, there were 46 251 rooms to be rented in 1985.
6. Portugal: recreation homes for children includes youth hostels.
7. Switzerland: others includes dormitories in: recreational camps ,tourist camps, mountain huts and shelters.
8. Turkey: others includes establishments with special licences.
9. Australia: number of rooms. Camping sites includes all sites (with and without facilities), cabins and flats.
10. Yugoslavia: others includes mountain huts and shelters, i.e. 7.1 thousands beds in 1985

15. Monthly hotel occupancy rates

	Austria [1] (B)	Denmark (R)	Finland [2] (R)	Germany [3] (B)	Italy (B)	Norway [4] (B)	Spain	Sweden [5] (B)	Switzerland (B)	Turkey [6] (B)	United Kingdom [7] (B)	Australia [8] (B)	Japan [9] (B)	Yugoslavia [10] (B)
1984 January	31.6	34.1	45.7	24.1	25.2	29.6	41.3	26.1	30.4	33.1	26.0		60.6	28.5
February	38.7	39.5	54.7	27.9	28.7	42.5	45.4	35.8	35.8	37.2	32.0	34.8	72.1	28.4
March	32.0	44.5	57.5	28.8	28.3	45.3	47.7	36.8	37.6	37.2	36.0		75.2	28.3
April	18.5	42.8	50.9	33.7	34.3	35.5	52.7	34.0	30.4	46.1	41.0		74.0	42.2
May	12.4	51.6	54.2	39.4	29.9	28.6	55.8	34.2	26.6	46.4	45.0	33.6	73.3	56.2
June	25.6	57.3	54.0	46.7	40.8	41.9	59.7	38.7	37.9	47.4	53.0		67.5	70.4
July	46.1	67.8	57.0	52.6	55.3	54.1	68.7	55.0	48.3	65.8	57.0		68.7	76.0
August	51.3	67.3	56.8	52.6	68.6	48.3	77.6	42.0	50.2	72.7	60.0	35.3	77.8	84.8
September	27.4	57.0	58.6	48.2	45.0	38.9	68.1	35.1	43.3	60.6	57.0		71.1	72.1
October	10.2	51.7	55.9	38.1	30.4	35.7	56.9	33.0	27.9	49.1	48.0		79.8	43.4
November	6.0	49.9	54.6	25.9	21.9	34.6	43.9	30.8	16.0	42.7	38.0	32.7	76.1	26.7
December	20.2	31.8	38.3	23.7	23.0	30.1	38.4	24.4	22.9	36.6	31.0		56.9	24.1
1985 January	31.8	38.5	44.5	25.0		31.9	41.6	25.6	28.0	32.2	26.0		59.2	24.9
February	43.2	42.9	53.0	29.5		48.0	45.6	34.8	39.0	35.2	32.0		71.4	27.9
March	32.9	45.9	58.9	29.8		47.1	47.7	36.9	38.3	37.1	36.0		75.5	30.1
April	19.0	44.6	53.2	32.7		42.1	48.6	33.0	30.6	41.0	41.0		75.7	39.4
May	13.7	52.0	54.1	40.1		31.9	48.0	30.1	27.0	49.1	48.0		76.0	61.2
June	25.1	60.0	55.3	46.5		49.2	52.7	39.7	37.7	54.9	53.0		72.2	77.7
July	44.1	67.0	58.7	51.3		59.4	62.7	54.2	48.6	66.4	59.0		70.5	84.0
August	48.7	68.6	55.6	52.5		53.3	74.7	40.7	50.2	73.1	59.0		78.8	88.7
September	27.0	58.0	57.4	48.2		42.8	62.6	30.9	44.1	63.3	57.0		71.2	79.3
October	10.9	52.0	56.8	40.0		40.3	52.8	30.2	30.3	48.8	49.0		77.3	48.3
November	6.1	50.4	55.0	26.6		40.3	43.8	28.6	15.5	39.5	37.0		75.4	26.5
December	19.5	31.3	38.6	24.0		33.1	37.8	22.4	21.5	36.4	30.0		54.3	23.5
1986 January	31.7		44.5	25.7		36.1	40.4	41.6	28.8	32.2	26.0		56.5	26.9
February	46.1		54.0	31.0		49.8	43.9	33.7	39.9	32.7	31.0		69.8	29.3
March	41.6		52.8	31.8		49.1	48.8	33.9	43.0	37.3	36.0		72.7	30.2
April	15.4		54.2	31.6		38.1	44.7	33.8	26.3	40.5	36.0		68.4	35.9
May	14.5		50.6	41.5		32.6	55.4	30.1	26.5	49.7	43.0		71.1	60.6
June	21.4		52.6	44.7		45.3	58.8	35.6	33.8	52.3	48.0		63.7	70.4
July	44.1		54.7	51.4		56.6	68.8	50.9	46.1	58.6	55.0		64.9	79.8
August	49.9		54.0	53.7		49.6	77.7	38.5	49.8	65.7	57.0		72.3	85.9
September	27.7		59.4	49.5		40.1	67.9	31.6	43.0	60.9	55.0		66.3	77.7
October	11.3		55.0	40.9		38.5	56.7	28.4	30.3	50.7	48.0		76.5	47.7
November	6.3		53.7	27.5		37.4	44.9	27.4	15.5	36.9	36.0		74.6	25.3
December	21.0		39.7	25.0		30.4	40.4	23.1	21.1	32.2	33.0		53.4	23.2

B = Beds.
R = Rooms.
Occupancy rates registered in hotels only, unless otherwise stated.
1. Austria: bed occupancy rates based on all forms of accommodation.
2. Finland: room occupancy rates in hotels and motels.
3. Germany: change of series from 1984; occupancy rates do not cover the same establishments.
4. Norway: Change of coverage from 1984; bed occupancy rates covers registered accommodation with 20 beds or more during summer season (May to September) and with 50 beds or more during the rest of the year.
5. Sweden: occupancy rates in hotels, motels, resort hotels, holiday villages and youth hostels.
6. Turkey: bed occupancy rates in hotels, motels, boarding houses, inns, holiday villages and thermal resorts.
7. United Kingdom: figures apply to England only.
8. Australia: quarterly figures in bed-places in hotels and motels with facilities in most rooms.
9. Japan: rates concerning hotels which are members of the "Japan Hotel Association".
10. Yugoslavia: bed occupancy rates in hotels.

16. International fare payments
Rail, air, sea and road transport
In million dollars

	Receipts			Expenditure		
	1984	1985	1986	1984	1985	1986
Austria[1]	270.7	274.7	347.9	98.9	96.4	104.5
Finland	217.6	224.8		181.2	161.4	
France[2]						
Germany[3]	2 031.7	2 030.4	2 254.7	1 870.4	1 936.3	2 427.4
Greece	4.9	7.9	11.9	74.8	93.9	97.0
Ireland	161.5	176.6	210.3	110.5	116.3	139.3
Italy[4]	962.0	979.4		313.1	340.4	
Spain	574.0	605.1	706.6	56.0	105.3	220.8
Sweden[5]	407.2	428.3	517.9	402.9	403.3	336.3
Switzerland	915.0	974.6	1 162.1	517.1	569.7	789.6
Turkey[6]	168.8	200.8	214.2	1.1	1.5	1.5
United Kingdom[7]						
Canada	529.7	544.7	676.5	1 057.1	1 058.7	1 078.2
New Zealand	277.3					
Japan						

1. Austria: rail, air, inland waterways and road transport.
2. France: air transport.
3. Germany: air, sea and rail transport.
4. Italy: air and sea transport.
5. Sweden: sea and rail transport.
6. Turkey: air, sea and rail transport for receipts; rail transport only for expenditure.
7. United Kingdom: air and sea transport.

17. Nominal exchange rates of national currencies against the dollar

	Exchange rates (units per dollar)			Per cent changes[1]	
	1984	1985	1986	85/84	86/85
Austria	20.01	20.69	15.27	3.4	−26.2
Belgium-Luxembourg	57.76	59.43	44.69	2.9	−24.8
Denmark	10.36	10.59	8.09	2.3	−23.6
Finland	6.00	6.20	5.07	3.2	−18.2
France	8.74	8.98	6.93	2.8	−22.9
Germany	2.85	2.94	2.17	3.4	−26.2
Greece	112.66	138.05	139.48	22.5	1.0
Iceland	31.73	41.54	42.11	30.9	1.4
Ireland	0.92	0.95	0.75	2.5	−21.1
Italy	1 756.73	1 909.42	1 491.05	8.7	−21.9
Netherlands	3.21	3.32	2.45	3.5	−26.3
Norway	8.16	8.59	7.39	5.3	−14.0
Portugal	146.38	169.93	148.17	16.1	−12.8
Spain	160.80	170.06	139.97	5.8	−17.7
Sweden	8.27	8.60	7.12	4.0	−17.2
Switzwerland	2.35	2.46	1.80	4.6	−26.8
Turkey	363.46	519.57	669.03	42.9	28.8
United Kingdom	0.75	0.78	0.68	3.7	−12.5
Canada	1.30	1.37	1.39	5.5	1.7
United States	1.00	1.00	1.00	0.0	0.0
Australia	1.14	1.43	1.50	25.5	4.5
New Zealand	1.77	2.03	1.92	14.6	−5.4
Japan	237.55	238.62	168.52	0.5	−29.4
Yugoslavia	124.80	185.70	264.50	48.8	42.4

Source: OECD Balance of Payments Division, except for Yugoslavia.
1. Minus signs indicate an appreciation of national currencies against the dollar.

18. International tourist receipts (R) and expenditure (E) in dollars

Regional breakdown

In million

	R/E	Europe			North America			Australasia-Japan		
		1985	1986	% 86/85	1985	1986	% 86/85	1985	1986	% 86/85
Austria[1]	R	4 444.8	6 274.6	41.2	531.9	506.5	−4.8	15.6	24.3	56.1
	E	2 210.6	3 451.9	56.2	286.7	410.5	43.2	10.9	16.0	47.5
Belgium-Luxembourg	R									
	E									
Denmark	R	1 038.4	1 423.3	37.1	204.4	215.2	5.3	6.3	9.5	50.5
	E	1 118.9	1 731.1	54.7	174.4	220.8	26.6	4.0	5.7	43.4
Finland	R	412.2	518.3	25.7	59.7	50.5	−15.4	3.2	5.3	65.0
	E	611.2	822.6	34.6	111.4	173.2	55.5	4.5	7.9	74.6
France	R	4 225.6			2 817.2					
	E	2 412.5			1 283.0					
Germany	R	4 315.7	6 304.6	46.1	827.9	655.2	−20.9	209.9	268.4	27.9
	E	12 198.9	17 046.4	39.7	543.5	863.3	58.8	90.7	145.0	59.9
Greece	R	879.3	1 211.0	37.7	499.9	499.9	0.0	24.4	24.8	1.6
	E	203.6	282.5	38.7	143.2	167.0	16.6	1.9	3.7	93.2
Iceland	R	18.9			23.0					
	E	38.0			38.7					
Ireland[2]	R	340.5	442.0	29.8	179.8	182.2	1.3			
	E	387.0	610.8	57.8	32.8	64.3	96.1			
Italy	R	5 938.6	7 693.8	29.6	2 729.0	2 066.0	−24.3	17.5	50.3	188.2
	E	1 353.8	1 785.7	31.9	890.0	924.1	3.8	6.2	12.8	105.7
Netherlands	R	1 080.6	1 480.2	37.0	352.5	339.2	−3.8	13.8	21.6	56.3
	E	2 673.1	3 791.9	41.9	282.3	388.6	37.6	12.9	20.4	57.7
Norway	R	569.4	774.8	36.1	178.4	207.0	16.0	3.5	5.5	58.9
	E	1 411.7	1 961.1	38.9	262.9	423.2	61.0	7.0	9.9	41.5
Portugal	R	724.5	1 108.1	53.0	382.2	449.4	17.6	1.5	3.0	100.1
	E	151.5	244.3	61.2	76.9	80.1	4.2	1.0	1.0	−5.0
Spain	R	4 926.6	9 748.1	97.9	481.1	534.3	11.1		59.7	
	E		946.7			75.0				
Sweden	R	883.5	1 131.5	28.1	168.4	180.5	7.2	4.8	6.3	32.5
	E	1 479.2	2 141.5	44.8	277.4	398.4	43.6	12.4	16.6	33.2
Switzerland	R									
	E									
Turkey	R									
	E									
United Kingdom[3]	R	2 285.4	2 953.9	29.3	2 193.0	2 135.9	−2.6	510.7	609.8	19.4
	E	4 352.6	6 083.7	39.8	563.3	913.3	62.1	187.3	227.2	21.3
Canada[4]	R	306.0	411.7	34.5	2 482.8	3 004.2	21.0	95.2	140.3	47.5
	E	900.6	865.1	−3.9	2 551.6	2 672.4	4.7	87.9	103.6	18.0
United States	R									
	E									
Australia	R	279.4			236.8			256.3		
	E									
New Zealand[5]	R									
	E									
Japan	R									
	E									
Yugoslavia	R									
	E									

Important notice: the amounts, excluding those concerning Canada, United States, Ireland, Italy, United Kingdom and Switzerland, refer to receipts and expenditure registered in foreign currency grouped regionally according to the denomination of the currency.
1. Austria: including international fare payments.

18. International tourist receipts (R) and expenditure (E) in dollars (Continued)

Regional breakdown

In million

Total OECD countries			Non-Member countries			All countries			
1985	1986	% 86/85	1985	1986	% 86/85	1985	1986	% 86/85	
4 992.3	6 805.3	36.3	92.8	123.0	32.5	5 085.1	6 928.3	36.2	Austria[1]
2 508.2	3 878.4	54.6	215.1	328.3	52.6	2 723.4	4 206.7	54.5	
						1 660.8	2 269.2	36.6	Belgium-Luxembourg
						2 047.9	2 886.9	41.0	
1 249.1	1 648.0	31.9	76.9	111.1	44.5	1 326.0	1 759.2	32.7	Denmark
1 297.3	1 957.6	50.9	105.7	155.8	47.3	1 403.0	2 113.3	50.6	
476.4	574.1	20.5	25.0	22.7	−9.3	501.4	596.8	19.0	Finland
727.2	1 004.3	38.1	50.7	65.7	29.6	777.9	1 069.9	37.5	
7 042.8			885.8			7 928.6	9 580.2	20.8	France
3 695.5			855.7			4 551.3	6 383.4	40.3	
5 353.5	7 228.2	35.0	535.7	597.6	11.6	5 889.2	7 825.9	32.9	Germany
12 833.2	18 054.7	40.7	1 800.5	2 608.8	44.9	14 633.6	20 663.5	41.2	
1 403.6	1 735.8	23.7	21.8	99.3	354.8	1 425.5	1 835.1	28.7	Greece
348.8	453.2	29.9	20.3	44.3	118.0	369.1	497.5	34.8	
41.9			0.0			41.9			Iceland
76.8			0.0			76.8			
520.2	624.2	20.0	28.6	34.8	22.0	548.8	659.0	20.1	Ireland[2]
419.8	675.1	60.8	5.3	8.0	52.0	425.1	683.1	60.7	
8 685.1	9 810.1	13.0	72.6	42.7	−41.2	8 757.6	9 852.8	12.5	Italy
2 250.1	2 722.7	21.0	33.5	35.3	5.4	2 283.6	2 758.0	20.8	
1 439.7	1 834.5	27.4	57.8	71.0	22.9	1 497.5	1 905.6	27.3	Netherlands
3 008.8	4 283.0	42.4	107.5	147.0	36.8	3 116.2	4 430.0	42.2	
751.2	987.3	31.4	4.3	4.7	10.0	755.5	992.0	31.3	Norway
1 681.6	2 394.2	42.4	42.0	34.8	−17.2	1 723.6	2 428.9	40.9	
1 108.8	1 561.0	40.8	19.7	21.5	9.0	1 128.5	1 582.5	40.2	Portugal
229.6	325.5	41.8	6.1	7.5	23.8	235.6	333.0	41.3	
5 407.7	10 342.1	91.2	2 676.0	1 603.0	−40.1	8 083.7	11 945.2	47.8	Spain
	1 021.7		999.7	481.5	−51.8	999.7	1 503.2	50.4	
1 056.8	1 318.4	24.8	127.4	224.7	76.4	1 184.2	1 543.2	30.3	Sweden
1 770.2	2 557.9	44.5	194.6	252.7	29.8	1 964.8	2 810.5	43.0	
						3 163.9	4 239.9	34.0	Switzerland
						2 413.1	3 378.0	40.0	
						1 478.6	1 227.9	−17.0	Turkey
						327.0	311.9	−4.6	
4 995.5	5 704.0	14.2	1 999.2	2 216.5	10.9	6 994.7	7 920.5	13.2	United Kingdom[3]
5 107.1	7 231.5	41.6	1 149.7	1 454.2	26.5	6 256.9	8 685.8	38.8	
2 884.0	3 556.2	23.3	217.5	296.5	36.4	3 101.5	3 852.7	24.2	Canada[4]
3 540.0	3 641.1	2.9	585.0	654.2	11.8	4 125.1	4 295.4	4.1	
						11 675.0	12 913.0	10.6	United States
						16 482.0	17 627.0	6.9	
772.5			312.9			1 085.4	1 366.3	25.9	Australia
						1 904.7	1 925.2	1.1	
						277.1			New Zealand[5]
						415.8			
						1 130.9	1 442.8	27.6	Japan
						4 770.9	7 138.3	49.6	
						1 050.2	1 105.1	5.2	Yugoslavia

2. Ireland: receipts from and expenditure to Northern Ireland excluded. The receipts exclude all passenger fares; the expenditure exclude passenger fares to Irish carriers only.
3. United Kingdom: including estimates for the Channel Islands receipts and expenditure, and cruise expenditure.
4. Canada: excluding international fare payments and crew spending.
5. New Zealand: new series from 1986; estimate based on survey data.

19. Foreign tourism by purpose of visit

	1985						1986					
	Business journeys (%)[1]	Private journeys (%)				Total volume in thousands	Business journeys (%)[1]	Private journeys (%)				Total volume in thousands
		Holidays	VFR[2]	Others	Total			Holidays	VFR[2]	Others	Total	
Greece[3]	7.0	83.0	1.0	9.0	93.0	6 574.0	7.0	83.0	1.0	9.0	93.0	7 024.8
Ireland[4]	15.2	41.4	37.3	6.1	84.8	1 911.0	17.4	35.4	38.6	8.6	82.6	1 812.0
Portugal[5]	3.9	92.3	1.2	2.6	96.1	4 989.1						
Spain[6]	5.0	90.0		5.0	95.0	27 497.7	4.7	90.3		5.0	95.3	29 910.0
United Kingdom[7]	20.8	46.0	20.0	13.2	79.2	14 483.0						
Canada[8]	17.2	57.1	22.0	3.7	82.8	13 170.7	13.7	62.1	21.4	2.8	86.3	15 621.3
Australia[9]	15.6	43.8	25.1	15.5	84.4	1 142.6	13.7	48.6	22.8	14.9	86.3	1 429.4
New zealand[10]	11.6	61.4	21.6	5.4	88.4	637.6	13.0	73.3		13.7	87.0	581.9
Japan[11]	23.9	57.1		19.0	76.1	2 327.0	27.0	51.2		21.8	73.0	2 061.5

1. Includes : business, congresses, seminars, on missions, etc.
2. VFR : visits to friends and relatives.
3. Greece : number of tourists. "Others" includes journeys combining visiting relatives and holiday or business and holiday.
4. Ireland : number of journeys. Excluding visitors from Northern Ireland.
5. Portugal : number of tourists. "Others" includes visits for cultural purposes and journeys for educational reasons.
6. Spain : number of tourists. "Others" includes journeys for educational reasons (1% in 1985).
7. United Kingdom : "Others" includes journeys for educational reasons (3.1% in 1985).
8. Canada : number of tourists.
9. Australia : short-term visitors (less than one year). "Others" includes journeys for educational reasons.
10. New Zealand : number of visitors. "Others" includes journeys for educational reasons (0.6% in 1985).
11. Japan : number of visitors. "Others" includes journeys for educational reasons (1.7 % in 1985).

20. Foreign tourism by mode of transport

	1985					1986				
	Breakdown of arrivals (%)				Total volume in thousands	Breakdown of arrivals (%)				Total volume in thousands
	Air	Sea	Rail	Road		Air	Sea	Rail	Road	
Belgium[1]	28.9	21.1		50.0	20 860.1	30.9	19.1		50.0	19 800.9
Greece[2]	74.1	10.1	2.5	13.3	6 547.0					
Iceland	96.0	3.9			97.4					
Ireland[3]	9.2	10.0	1.0	79.7	9 940.0	46.5	44.5	4.1	5.0	1 993.0
Italy[3]	9.0	2.1	9.6	79.3	53 634.4					
Portugal[3]	15.4	1.8	1.0	81.8	11 691.7					
Spain[4]	29.3	3.3	5.9	61.5	43 235.4	29.8	3.0	5.5	61.8	47 388.8
Turkey[5]	33.2	20.0	2.0	44.8	2 614.9	40.4	18.5	2.2	38.9	2 391.1
United Kingdom[3]	64.9	35.1			14 482.0					
Canada[6]	23.8	2.1	0.5	73.6	13 170.7	23.7	2.1	0.4	73.8	15 621.3
Australia[7]	99.1	0.9			1 142.6	99.1	0.9			1 429.4
New Zealand[3]	99.1	0.9			669.6	98.9	1.1			733.4
Japan[8]	97.8	2.2			2 488.9	97.7	2.3			2 244.3
Yugoslavia[3]	5.6	2.7	4.7	87.1	23 357.3	4.9	2.0	4.0	89.2	27 748.7

1. Belgium: air and sea include both arrivals and departures of foreign and domestic visitors. Rail refers to international traffic only.
2. Greece: visitor arrivals including departures of foreign and domestic visitors. Rail refers to international traffic only.
3. Ireland, Italy, Portugal, United Kingdom, New Zealand and Yugoslavia : visitor arrivals.
4. Spain: visitor arrivals, including Spaniards living abroad.
5. Turkey: traveller arrivals.
6. Canada: tourist arrivals.
7. Australia: arrivals of short-term visitors (less than one year).
8. Japan: visitor arrivals, including those of returning residents and excluding crew members.

21. Staff employed in tourism

		1984			1985			1986		
		Total	Men %	Women %	Total	Men %	Women %	Total	Men %	Women %
Austria [1]	HR	115 981	35.7	64.3	117 028	36.2	63.8	114 489	37.1	62.9
Belgium										
Finland [2]	HR	65 000	20.0	80.0	63 000	20.6	79.4	67 000	22.4	77.6
France [3]	H	127 694	49.2	50.8	127 656	49.7	50.3			
	R	156 782	59.7	40.3	162 134	60.2	39.8			
	HR	284 476	55.0	45.0	289 790	55.6	44.4			
	V	19 119	37.6	62.4	19 539	36.7	63.3			
	A	400	62.5	37.5	400	62.5	37.5			
	O	125 433	45.9	54.1	123 098	45.9	54.1			
Germany [4]	HR	724 000	32.0	68.0	736 000	32.6	67.3			
Greece [5]	H	36 000			39 600			42 028		
	HR	36 000			39 600			42 028		
Netherlands [6]	H	17 700	54.2	45.8	17 900	55.3	45.3	20 000	51.0	49.0
	R	31 800	58.5	41.5	35 100	59.8	39.9	37 500	57.9	42.1
	HR	49 500	57.0	43.0	53 000	58.3	41.7	57 500	55.5	44.5
	V	5 800	41.4	58.6	5 200	42.3	57.7	5 700	40.4	59.6
Norway [7]	HR	45 000	28.9	71.1	48 000	25.0	75.0	50 000	26.0	74.0
Portugal [8]	H	32 899	52.7	47.3						
	HR	32 899	52.7	47.3						
Sweden [9]	HR	80 000	36.2	63.8	82 250	36.4	63.6	87 375	36.1	63.9
Switzerland [10]	HR	174 600			178 200			181 100		
Turkey [11]	HR	76 082			95 563			100 580		
	V	1 275			1 426			1 470		
	A	1 290	56.4	43.6	9 257	66.2	33.8	9 532	65.9	34.1
	O	1 150			1 262			1 239		
United Kingdom [12]	H	239 500	37.2	62.8	254 900	37.1	62.9	264 500	36.9	63.1
	R	209 700	37.8	62.2	217 100	38.2	61.8	220 000	37.4	62.6
	HR	449 200	37.5	62.5	472 000	37.6	62.4	484 200	37.2	62.8
	O	712 800	39.6	60.4	757 600	40.2	59.8	773 800	41.0	59.0
Australia [13]	H	73 900	39.9	60.1	78 500	36.6	63.4			
	A	95	52.6	47.4	95	52.6	47.4			
	O				311 410	65.5	34.5			

H: staff employed in hotels.
R: staff employed in restaurants.
HR: staff employed in hotels and restaurants.
V: staff employed in travel agencies.
A: staff employed in national tourism administrations.
O: staff employed in other sectors of tourist industry.
 1. Austria: weighted average of peak season (August) and low season (November).
 2. Finland: weighted average of peak season (July) and low season (January).
 3. France: concerns only employees. A = representations abroad and regional tourist offices.
 4. Germany: of which 159 000 foreigners in 1984.
 5. Greece: statistics covering only hotel employees insured by Hotel Employees Insurance Fund (36 000 out of 50 000 in 1984).
 6. Netherlands: from 1984 includes staff employed less than 15 hours a week.
 7. Norway: average of 1st and 4th quarters.
 8. Portugal: data registered at 31 July of each year.
 9. Sweden: of which 15 000 foreigners in 1984, and 14 500 in 1985.
10. Switzerland: of which 68 000 foreigners in 1984.
11. Turkey: data registered at 31 December of each year, except for O registered at 31 March and V registered at 31 October in 1985. V = minimum number of persons
    which travel agencies (central and local offices) have to employ. A includes regional tourism administrations (of which 30 persons are employed abroad in 1985)
    and staff working at the Culture section of the Ministry of Culture and Tourism. O = tourist guides whose licences have been renewed.
12. United Kingdom: weighted average of peak season (September) and low season (March). O = "pubs", bars, night clubs, clubs, librairies, museums, art galleries,
    sports and other recreational services.
13. Australia: data registered at December of each year.

22. Trends in tourism prices

		%81/80	%82/81	%83/82	%84/83	%85/84	%86/85
Austria	H	7.0	7.7	6.3	3.7	4.5	3.9
	R	5.8	5.8	4.3	6.1	3.3	4.3
	T	7.9	6.1	4.2	5.1	3.5	1.8
	C	7.6	5.9	3.0	5.8	3.4	1.5
Finland [1]	H	15.0	16.0	15.0	7.0	11.0	7.0
	R	14.0	11.0	12.0	7.0	7.0	5.0
	T	9.0	7.0	10.0	7.0	4.0	
	C	11.9	9.2	8.5	6.8	6.0	3.6
France	H	18.1	14.5	12.0	6.5	7.1	5.4
	R	14.6	13.1	10.5	6.8	6.1	5.1
	T						
	C	12.8	11.2	9.6	7.2	5.5	2.2
Germany	H	8.4	7.5	4.7	2.7	3.8	4.2
	R	6.0	5.2	3.3	2.5	1.5	2.0
	T	9.0	6.1	4.8	2.9	4.8	4.8
	C	6.2	4.8	3.2	2.5	2.1	−0.4
Greece	H	19.0	20.0	20.0	12.0	21.0	18.0
	R						
	T						
	C	23.3	21.2	18.2	17.7	18.6	22.1
Italy [2]	H	26.3	18.3	19.3	15.8	9.8	
	R	20.2	18.2	16.0	11.8	11.6	
	T	21.7	18.8	16.5	10.8	11.5	
	C	19.2	17.1	15.2	11.1	9.4	6.1
Netherlands [3]	H	8.0	6.0	3.0	1.0	3.0	0.0
	R	5.0	6.0	4.0	4.0	2.0	2.0
	T						
	C	6.4	5.3	2.8	2.5	2.6	0.0
Norway [4]	H	15.0	19.5	15.6	9.4	9.1	10.8
	R	22.2	20.5	10.7	5.1	4.9	8.2
	T						
	C	13.5	11.0	8.4	6.6	5.8	7.4
Portugal [5]	H	29.0	15.0	22.0	25.0	28.0	
	R	27.0	27.0	57.0	13.0	24.0	
	T						
	C	21.3	19.4	25.5	29.3	19.3	11.7
Spain [6]	H	16.7	18.6	16.8	17.2	16.5	11.6
	R				13.5	10.7	12.5
	T	15.6	17.7	15.6	12.3	9.7	11.1
	C	14.3	14.5	12.3	10.7	8.3	8.9
Sweden [7]	H	18.2	11.3	16.8	12.4	11.6	11.0
	R	11.6	12.9	13.2	11.8	10.3	10.4
	T						
	C	11.3	10.3	10.6	8.2	7.3	4.7
Switzerland [8]	H	7.3	8.3	5.1	6.2	6.3	6.3
	R	6.0	6.6	3.8	2.8	5.0	3.4
	T						
	C	6.6	5.5	2.8	3.4	3.6	0.4
Turkey [9]	H	70.0	61.0	50.0	50.0	50.0	
	R	25.0		50.0	55.0	45.0	50.0
	T						
	C	45.8	27.2	30.3	53.0	43.7	34.0
United Kingdom [10]	H	26.0	15.0	8.9	13.4	10.7	9.6
	R	8.0	8.0	7.4	6.5	5.6	6.3
	T	13.0	9.0	6.4	6.6	7.4	7.1
	C	11.4	8.7	5.0	4.7	5.4	3.7
Canada [11]	H	16.3	16.3	5.7	4.2	5.7	9.0
	R	9.6	10.2	5.7	4.1	4.2	4.7
	T	15.9	14.0	5.5	5.1	4.9	5.6
	C	11.2	10.3	6.2	4.4	4.1	4.1
Australia [12]	H	12.0	10.3	5.9	8.4	14.8	
	R	9.6	10.8	8.4	0.1	9.4	
	T			9.1	3.5	13.2	
	C	9.1	10.8	9.7	6.8	7.4	9.5
Yugoslavia [13]	H	29.8	44.4	27.3	48.6	60.0	14.1
	R						
	T						
	C	40.7	31.7	40.9	53.2	73.5	88.6

194

NOTES TO TABLE 22.

H: average increase in hotel prices.
R: average increase in restaurant prices.
T: average increase in travel prices.
C: average increase in consumer prices (CPI). Source: OECD Balance of Payments Division.
 1. Finland: H = hotels, R = food, T = transports et communications.
 2. Italy: T = hotels, restaurants and public establishments (bars, night club, sea-side resorts....).
 3. Netherlands: H = price of a night spent in an hotel, R = price of a certain number of typical expenses made in bars and restaurants (cup of coffee, fruit drinks, beer, jenever, croquette, fried potatoes, several hot meals, ham roll, ice cream).
 4. Norway: H = approved hotels and boarding houses, R = restaurants and cafés.
 5. Portugal: H = hotels of from 1 to 5 stars, R concerns Lisbon only.
 6. Spain: H takes into account the types of accommodation presented in the official guide.
 7. Sweden: position at December of each year H = hotel room, R = meals not taken at home (lunch, dinner, coffee with bread, hot sausage with bread).
 8. Switzerland: H = hotels and similar establishments. R is estimated.
 9. Turkey: H = hotels, motels, inns, boarding houses, holiday villages, health resorts. R = 1st and 2nd class restaurants. In 1983 H and R = freely determined prices approved by the Ministry of Culture and Tourism. C concerns the city of Ankara only.
10. United Kingdom: H = all holiday accommodation. R = meals and snacks including take-away. T = accommodation, meals, food, alcohol, tobacco, durable household goods, clothes, footwear, motoring and cycling fares, entertainment and other services.
11. Canada: H = hotels and motels. R = food purchases for restaurants, T is calculated from domestic tourist spending patterns only.
12. Australia: position every fourth quarter of each year. H = change in the price of a room in hotels, motels, and similar establishments. R = change in the price of meals taken outside home and take-away food (one component of the CPI). C = weighted average of eight State capital cities. T = air, bus and rail fares, hotel, motel and caravan park charges, package tours.
13. Yugoslavia: H = all categories of hotel charges on a full board basis.

EXTRACT FROM THE TOURISM COMMITTEE'S RESOLUTION ADOPTED IN 1981 FOR THE IMPROVEMENT OF INTERNATIONAL COMPARABILITY OF TOURISM STATISTICS PUBLISHED BY OECD MEMBER COUNTRIES

Upon reviewing the statistics of OECD Member countries on movements of visitors at frontiers and nights spent in the country by tourists from abroad, the TOURISM COMMITTEE AGREED:

That definitions of Visitors, Tourists and Excursionnists by the World Tourism Organisation (WTO) are a coherent means for assessing international tourism and should be adopted in principle by all Member countries and in practice to the maximum extent possible, especially when reviewing their systems of collecting and publishing tourism statistics and whenever surveys are undertaken in the future.

That the selection criterion of residence is the best one for measuring tourist flows at frontiers and tourists' stay at all types of accommodation in economic terms and should therefore be generally used by all Member countries.

That, by extension of the selection criterion of residence, it is relevant:

- that nationals of the tourist receiving country who reside abroad be recorded as visitors from abroad in statistics of tourist movements at frontiers and in statistics of tourist arrivals and nights in all types of accommodation of this country and, when possible, that visitors of this group be recorded separately;
- that crew members of all modes of transport who do not reside in the country they enter be recorded as visitors from abroad, without necessarily implying that they should specifically be identified among all visitors as crew members.

That the most important data breakdown for market analysis are: *i)* country of residence; *ii)* purpose of visit (according to WTO recommendations, with particular emphasis on the distinction between business and private travel) and *iii)* modes of transport (giving separately travel by private car, coach and bus, air, sea and train).

That one of the best economic indicators for international tourism is the number of nights spent by tourists from abroad in all means of accommodation and, for practical purpose, that this figure should be broken down to distinguish nights spent in commercial establishments from private accommodation and other types of accommodation (such as those run by non-profit organisations).

OECD SALES AGENTS
DÉPOSITAIRES DES PUBLICATIONS DE L'OCDE

ARGENTINA - ARGENTINE
Carlos Hirsch S.R.L.,
Florida 165, 4º Piso,
(Galeria Guemes) 1333 Buenos Aires
Tel. 33.1787.2391 y 30.7122

AUSTRALIA-AUSTRALIE
D.A. Book (Aust.) Pty. Ltd.
11-13 Station Street (P.O. Box 163)
Mitcham, Vic. 3132   Tel. (03) 873 4411

AUSTRIA - AUTRICHE
OECD Publications and Information Centre,
4 Simrockstrasse,
5300 Bonn (Germany)   Tel. (0228) 21.60.45
Local Agent:
Gerold & Co., Graben 31, Wien 1   Tel. 52.22.35

BELGIUM - BELGIQUE
Jean de Lannoy, Service Publications OCDE,
avenue du Roi 202
B-1060 Bruxelles   Tel. (02) 538.51.69

CANADA
Renouf Publishing Company Ltd/
Éditions Renouf Ltée,
1294 Algoma Road, Ottawa, Ont. K1B 3W8
Tel: (613) 741-4333

Toll Free/Sans Frais:
Ontario, Quebec, Maritimes:
1-800-267-1805
Western Canada, Newfoundland:
1-800-267-1826
Stores/Magasins:
61 rue Sparks St., Ottawa, Ont. K1P 5A6
Tel: (613) 238-8985
211 rue Yonge St., Toronto, Ont. M5B 1M4
Tel: (416) 363-3171
Sales Office/Bureau des Ventes:
7575 Trans Canada Hwy, Suite 305,
St. Laurent, Quebec H4T 1V6
Tel: (514) 335-9274

DENMARK - DANEMARK
Munksgaard Export and Subscription Service
35, Nørre Søgade, DK-1370 København K
Tel. +45.1.12.85.70

FINLAND - FINLANDE
Akateeminen Kirjakauppa,
Keskuskatu 1, 00100 Helsinki 10   Tel. 0.12141

FRANCE
OCDE/OECD
Mail Orders/Commandes par correspondance :
2, rue André-Pascal,
75775 Paris Cedex 16
Tel. (1) 45.24.82.00
Bookshop/Librairie : 33, rue Octave-Feuillet
75016 Paris
Tel. (1) 45.24.81.67 or/ou (1) 45.24.81.81
Principal correspondant :
Librairie de l'Université,
12a, rue Nazareth,
13602 Aix-en-Provence   Tel. 42.26.18.08

GERMANY - ALLEMAGNE
OECD Publications and Information Centre,
4 Simrockstrasse,
5300 Bonn   Tel. (0228) 21.60.45

GREECE - GRÈCE
Librairie Kauffmann,
28, rue du Stade, 105 64 Athens   Tel. 322.21.60

HONG KONG
Government Information Services,
Publications (Sales) Office,
Beaconsfield House, 4/F.,
Queen's Road Central

ICELAND - ISLANDE
Snæbjörn Jónsson & Co., h.f.,
Hafnarstræti 4 & 9,
P.O.B. 1131 – Reykjavik
Tel. 13133/14281/11936

INDIA - INDE
Oxford Book and Stationery Co.,
Scindia House, New Delhi 1 Tel. 331.5896/5308
17 Park St., Calcutta 700016   Tel. 240832

INDONESIA - INDONÉSIE
Pdii-Lipi, P.O. Box 3065/JKT.Jakarta
Tel. 583467

IRELAND - IRLANDE
TDC Publishers - Library Suppliers,
12 North Frederick Street, Dublin 1.
Tel. 744835-749677

ITALY - ITALIE
Libreria Commissionaria Sansoni,
Via Lamarmora 45, 50121 Firenze
Tel. 579751/584468
Via Bartolini 29, 20155 Milano   Tel. 365083
Sub-depositari :
Editrice e Libreria Herder,
Piazza Montecitorio 120, 00186 Roma
Tel. 6794628
Libreria Hœpli,
Via Hœpli 5, 20121 Milano   Tel. 865446
Libreria Scientifica
Dott. Lucio de Biasio "Aeiou"
Via Meravigli 16, 20123 Milano   Tel. 807679
Libreria Lattes,
Via Garibaldi 3, 10122 Torino   Tel. 519274
La diffusione delle edizioni OCSE è inoltre
assicurata dalle migliori librerie nelle città più
importanti.

JAPAN - JAPON
OECD Publications and Information Centre,
Landic Akasaka Bldg., 2-3-4 Akasaka,
Minato-ku, Tokyo 107   Tel. 586.2016

KOREA - CORÉE
Kyobo Book Centre Co. Ltd.
P.O.Box: Kwang Hwa Moon 1658,
Seoul   Tel. (REP) 730.78.91

LEBANON - LIBAN
Documenta Scientifica/Redico,
Edison Building, Bliss St.,
P.O.B. 5641, Beirut   Tel. 354429-344425

MALAYSIA - MALAISIE
University of Malaya Co-operative Bookshop
Ltd.,
P.O.Box 1127, Jalan Pantai Baru,
Kuala Lumpur   Tel. 577701/577072

NETHERLANDS - PAYS-BAS
Staatsuitgeverij
Chr. Plantijnstraat, 2 Postbus 20014
2500 EA S-Gravenhage   Tel. 070-789911
Voor bestellingen: Tel. 070-789880

NEW ZEALAND - NOUVELLE-ZÉLANDE
Government Printing Office Bookshops:
Auckland: Retail Bookshop, 25 Rutland Street,
Mail Orders, 85 Beach Road
Private Bag C.P.O.
Hamilton: Retail: Ward Street,
Mail Orders, P.O. Box 857
Wellington: Retail, Mulgrave Street, (Head
Office)
Cubacade World Trade Centre,
Mail Orders, Private Bag
Christchurch: Retail, 159 Hereford Street,
Mail Orders, Private Bag
Dunedin: Retail, Princes Street,
Mail Orders, P.O. Box 1104

NORWAY - NORVÈGE
Tanum-Karl Johan
Karl Johans gate 43, Oslo 1
PB 1177 Sentrum, 0107 Oslo 1Tel. (02) 42.93.10

PAKISTAN
Mirza Book Agency
65 Shahrah Quaid-E-Azam, Lahore 3 Tel. 66839

PORTUGAL
Livraria Portugal,
Rua do Carmo 70-74, 1117 Lisboa Codex.
Tel. 360582/3

SINGAPORE - SINGAPOUR
Information Publications Pte Ltd
Pei-Fu Industrial Building,
24 New Industrial Road No. 02-06
Singapore 1953   Tel. 2831786, 2831798

SPAIN - ESPAGNE
Mundi-Prensa Libros, S.A.,
Castelló 37, Apartado 1223, Madrid-28001
Tel. 431.33.99
Libreria Bosch, Ronda Universidad 11,
Barcelona 7   Tel. 317.53.08/317.53.58

SWEDEN - SUÈDE
AB CE Fritzes Kungl. Hovbokhandel,
Box 16356, S 103 27 STH,
Regeringsgatan 12,
DS Stockholm   Tel. (08) 23.89.00
Subscription Agency/Abonnements:
Wennergren-Williams AB,
Box 30004, S104 25 Stockholm.
Tel. (08)54.12.00

SWITZERLAND - SUISSE
OECD Publications and Information Centre,
4 Simrockstrasse,
5300 Bonn (Germany)   Tel. (0228) 21.60.45
Local Agent:
Librairie Payot,
6 rue Grenus, 1211 Genève 11
Tel. (022) 31.89.50

TAIWAN - FORMOSE
Good Faith Worldwide Int'l Co., Ltd.
9th floor, No. 118, Sec.2
Chung Hsiao E. Road
Taipei   Tel. 391.7396/391.7397

THAILAND - THAILANDE
Suksit Siam Co., Ltd.,
1715 Rama IV Rd.,
Samyam Bangkok 5   Tel. 2511630

TURKEY - TURQUIE
Kültur Yayinlari Is-Türk Ltd. Sti.
Atatürk Bulvari No: 191/Kat. 21
Kavaklidere/Ankara   Tel. 25.07.60
Dolmabahce Cad. No: 29
Besiktas/Istanbul   Tel. 160.71.88

UNITED KINGDOM - ROYAUME-UNI
H.M. Stationery Office,
Postal orders only: (01)211-5656
P.O.B. 276, London SW8 5DT
Telephone orders: (01) 622.3316, or
Personal callers:
49 High Holborn, London WC1V 6HB
Branches at: Belfast, Birmingham,
Bristol, Edinburgh, Manchester

UNITED STATES - ÉTATS-UNIS
OECD Publications and Information Centre,
2001 L Street, N.W., Suite 700,
Washington, D.C. 20036 - 4095
Tel. (202) 785.6323

VENEZUELA
Libreria del Este,
Avda F. Miranda 52, Aptdo. 60337,
Edificio Galipan, Caracas 106
Tel. 32.23.01/33.26.04/31.58.38

YUGOSLAVIA - YOUGOSLAVIE
Jugoslovenska Knjiga, Knez Mihajlova 2,
P.O.B. 36, Beograd   Tel. 621.992

Orders and inquiries from countries where Sales
Agents have not yet been appointed should be sent
to:
OECD, Publications Service, Sales and
Distribution Division, 2, rue André-Pascal, 75775
PARIS CEDEX 16.

Les commandes provenant de pays où l'OCDE n'a
pas encore désigné de dépositaire peuvent être
adressées à :
OCDE, Service des Publications. Division des
Ventes et Distribution. 2, rue André-Pascal. 75775
PARIS CEDEX 16.

70712-04-1987

OECD PUBLICATIONS, 2, rue André-Pascal, 75775 PARIS CEDEX 16 - No. 44089 1987
PRINTED IN FRANCE
(78 87 01 1) ISBN 92-64-13004-7